STUDENT'S SOLUTIONS MANUAL

GAIL ILLICH
McLennan Community College

PAUL ILLICH
Southeast Community College

BASIC BUSINESS STATISTICS: CONCEPTS AND APPLICATIONS

FOURTEENTH EDITION

Mark L. Berenson
Montclair State University

David M. Levine
Baruch College, City University of New York

Kathryn A. Szabat
La Salle University

David F. Stephan
Two Bridges Instructional Technology

ISBN-13: 978-0-13-468504-5
ISBN-10: 0-13-468504-0

Table of Contents

FIRST THINGS FIRST

OBJECTIVES
- Statistics is a way of thinking that can lead to better decision making
- Statistics requires analytics skills and is an important part of your business education
- Recent developments such as the use of business analytics and "big data" have made knowing statistics even more critical
- The DCOVA framework guides your application of statistics
- The opportunity business analytics represents for business students

OVERVIEW AND KEY CONCEPTS
Think Differently About Statistics
Case illustrates some of the newer applications of statistics and business analytics are affecting business. **Statistics** are the methods that allow you to work with data effectively. Business statistics provides you with a formal basis to summarize and visualize business data, reach conclusions about that data, make reliable predictions about business activities, and improve business processes. The **D**efine **C**ollect **O**rganize **V**isualize **A**nalyze framework helps minimize possible errors of thinking and analysis.
- **D**efine the data that you want to study in order to solve a problem or meet an objective.
- **C**ollect the data from appropriate sources.
- **O**rganize the data collected by developing tables.
- **V**isualize the data collected by developing charts.
- **A**nalyze the data collected to reach conclusions and present those results.

Understand that analytical skills are more important than arithmetic skills.
Distinguish between statistic and Statistics.

Key Definitions
- **Data** are the facts about the world that one seeks to study and explore. Data can be **unsummarized** or **summarized**.
- **Big data** are collections of data that cannot be easily browsed or analyzed using traditional methods.
- **Variable** defines a characteristic, or property, of an item or individual that can vary among the occurrences of those items or individuals.
- The methods that primarily help summarize and present data comprise **descriptive statistics**.
- Methods that use data collected from a small group to reach conclusions about a larger group comprise **inferential statistics**.
- **Business analytics** combine traditional statistical methods with methods from management science and information systems to form an interdisciplinary tool that supports fact-based decision making.
- **Logical causality** means that you can plausibly claim something directly causes something else.

Starting Point for Using Software
Understand basic computer operations. Understand how software represents and stores data. Understand conventions used for software instructions in this book. Review Principles of Using Software Properly (Exhibit FTF.1).

CHAPTER 1

1.2   Three sizes of U.S. businesses are classified into distinct categories—small, medium, and large—in which order is implied.

1.4   (a)   The number of cellphones is a numerical variable that is discrete because the outcome is a count. It is ratio scaled because it has a true zero point.

   (b)   Monthly data usage is a numerical variable that is continuous because any value within a range of values can occur. It is ratio scaled because it has a true zero point.

   (c)   Number of text messages exchanged per month is a numerical variable that is discrete because the outcome is a count. It is ratio scaled because it has a true zero point.

   (d)   Voice usage per month is a numerical variable that is continuous because any value within a range of values can occur. It is ratio scaled because it has a true zero point.

   (e)   Whether a cellphone is used for email is a categorical variable because the answer can be only yes or no. This also makes it a nominal-scaled variable.

1.6   (a)   Categorical, nominal scale.
   (b)   Numerical, continuous, ratio scale.
   (c)   Categorical, nominal scale.
   (d)   Numerical, discrete, ratio scale.
   (e)   Categorical, nominal scale.

1.8   (a)   numerical, continuous, ratio scale *
   (b)   numerical, discrete, ratio scale
   (c)   numerical, continuous, ratio scale *
   (d)   categorical, nominal
   *Some researchers consider money as a discrete numerical variable because it can be "counted."

1.10   The underlying variable, ability of the students, may be continuous, but the measuring device, the test, does not have enough precision to distinguish between the two students.

1.12   The answer depends on the chosen data set.

1.14   The answer depends on the specific story.

1.16   The information presented there is based mainly on a mixture of data distributed by an organization and data collected by ongoing business activities.

1.18   Sample without replacement: Read from left to right in 3-digit sequences and continue unfinished sequences from end of row to beginning of next row.
   Row 05: 338 505 855 551 438 855 077 186 579 488 767 833 170
   Rows 05–06: 897
   Row 06: 340 033 648 847 204 334 639 193 639 411 095 924
   Rows 06–07: 707
   Row 07: 054 329 776 100 871 007 255 980 646 886 823 920 461
   Row 08: 893 829 380 900 796 959 453 410 181 277 660 908 887
   Rows 08–09: 237
   Row 09: 818 721 426 714 050 785 223 801 670 353 362 449
   Rows 09–10: 406
   Note: All sequences above 902 and duplicates are discarded.

1.20 A simple random sample would be less practical for personal interviews because of travel costs (unless interviewees are paid to attend a central interviewing location).

1.22 Here all members of the population are equally likely to be selected and the sample selection mechanism is based on chance. But not every sample of size 2 has the same chance of being selected. For example the sample "B and C" is impossible.

1.24 (a) Row 16: 2323 6737 5131 8888 1718 0654 6832 4647 6510 4877
Row 17: 4579 4269 2615 1308 2455 7830 5550 5852 5514 7182
Row 18: 0989 3205 0514 2256 8514 4642 7567 8896 2977 8822
Row 19: 5438 2745 9891 4991 4523 6847 9276 8646 1628 3554
Row 20: 9475 0899 2337 0892 0048 8033 6945 9826 9403 6858
Row 21: 7029 7341 3553 1403 3340 4205 0823 4144 1048 2949
Row 22: 8515 7479 5432 9792 6575 5760 0408 8112 2507 3742
Row 23: 1110 0023 4012 8607 4697 9664 4894 3928 7072 5815
Row 24: 3687 1507 7530 5925 7143 1738 1688 5625 8533 5041
Row 25: 2391 3483 5763 3081 6090 5169 0546
Note: All sequences above 5000 are discarded. There were no repeating sequences.

(b)   089   189   289   389   489   589   689   789   889   989
1089 1189 1289 1389 1489 1589 1689 1789 1889 1989
2089 2189 2289 2389 2489 2589 2689 2789 2889 2989
3089 3189 3289 3389 3489 3589 3689 3789 3889 3989
4089 4189 4289 4389 4489 4589 4689 4789 4889 4989

(c) With the single exception of invoice #0989, the invoices selected in the simple random sample are not the same as those selected in the systematic sample. It would be highly unlikely that a random process would select the same units as a systematic process.

1.26 Before accepting the results of a survey of college students, you might want to know, for example:

Who funded the survey? Why was it conducted? What was the population from which the sample was selected? What sampling design was used? What mode of response was used: a personal interview, a telephone interview, or a mail survey? Were interviewers trained? Were survey questions field-tested? What questions were asked? Were they clear, accurate, unbiased, valid? What operational definition of "vast majority" was used? What was the response rate? What was the sample size?

1.28 The results are based on an online survey. If the frame is supposed to be smart phone and tablet users, how is the population defined? This is a self-selecting sample of people who responded online, so there is an undefined nonresponse error. Sampling error cannot be determined since this is not a random sample.

1.30 Before accepting the results of the survey, you might want to know, for example: Who funded the study? Why was it conducted? What was the population from which the sample was selected? What sampling design was used? What mode of response was used: a personal interview, a telephone interview, or a mail survey? Were interviewers trained? Were survey questions field-tested? What other questions were asked? Were the questions clear, accurate, unbiased, and valid? What was the response rate? What was the margin of error? What was the sample size? What frame was used?

1.32   A statistic is a summary measure describing a sample whereas a parameter is a summary measure describing an entire population.

1.34   Discrete random variables produce numerical responses that arise from a counting process. Continuous random variables produce numerical responses that arise from a measuring process.

1.36   Both interval scaled and ratio scaled variables are numerical variables in which the difference between measurements is meaningful but an interval scaled variable does not involve a true zero such as standardized exam scores while a ratio scaled variable involves a true zero such as height.

1.38   Microsoft Excel or Minitab could be used to perform various statistical computations that were possible only with a slide-rule or hand-held calculator in the old days.

1.40   The answers to this question depend on which article and its corresponding data set is being selected.

1.42   The answers to this question depend on which data set is being selected.

1.44   (a)   The population of interest was the collection of all the 10,000 benefitted employees at the University of Utah when the study was conducted.
        (b)   The sample consisted of the 3,095 benefitted employees participated in the study.
        (c)   gender: categorical; age: numerical; education level: numerical; marital status: categorical; household income: numerical; employment category: categorical

1.46   Microsoft Excel:
        This product features a spreadsheet-based interface that allows users to organize, calculate, and organize data. Excel also contains many statistical functions to assist in the description of a dataset. Excel can be used to develop worksheets and workbooks to calculate a variety of statistics including introductory and advanced statistics. Excel also includes interactive tools to create graphs, charts, and pivot tables. Excel can be used to summarize data to better understand a population of interest, compare across groups, predict outcomes, and to develop forecasting models. These capabilities represent those that are generally relevant to the current course. Excel also includes many other statistical capabilities that can be further explored on the Microsoft Office Excel official website.

        Minitab 18:
        Minitab 18 has a comprehensive set of statistical methods including introductory and advanced statistical procedures. Minitab 18 features include basic descriptive statistical procedures, graph and chart creation, diagnostic tests, analysis of variance, regression, time series and forecasting analyses, nonparametric analyses, cross-tabulation, chi-square and related tests, and other statistical procedures. Minitab 18 utilizes a user friendly interface that allows one to quickly identify the appropriate procedure. The interface also allows one to easily export results including charts and graphs to facilitate the creation of presentations and reports. These Minitab 18 features would allow one to summarize data to better understand a population of interest, compare across groups, predict outcomes, and to develop forecasting models. These capabilities represent those that are generally relevant to the current course. Minitab 18 also includes many other statistical capabilities that can be further explored on the Minitab official website.

1.46   JMP:
cont.   JMP has a comprehensive set of statistical methods including introductory and advanced statistical procedures. JMP features include basic descriptive statistical procedures, graph and chart creation, diagnostic tests, analysis of variance, regression, time series and forecasting analyses, nonparametric analyses, cross-tabulation, chi-square and related tests, and other statistical procedures. JMP utilizes a user friendly interface that allows one to quickly identify the appropriate procedure. JMP also contains predictive analytic tools such as classification trees to classify data into groups. These JMP features would allow one to summarize data to better understand a population of interest, compare across groups, predict outcomes, and to develop forecasting models. These capabilities represent those that are generally relevant to the current course. JMP also includes many other statistical capabilities that can be further explored on the JMP official website.

1.48   The answers are based on an article titled "U.S. Satisfaction Still Running at Improved Level" and written by Lydia Saad (August 15, 2018). The article is located on the following site: https://news.gallup.com/poll/240911/satisfaction-running-improved-level.aspx?g_source=link_NEWSV9&g_medium=NEWSFEED&g_campaign=item_&g_content=U.S.%2520Satisfaction%2520Still%2520Running%2520at%2520Improved%2520Level

The population of interest includes all individuals aged 18 and older who live within the 50 U.S. states and the District of Columbia.
The collected sample includes a random sample of 1,024 individuals aged 18 and older who live within the 50 U.S. states and the District of Columbia.
A parameter of interest is the percentage of the population of individuals aged 18 and older and live within the 50 U.S. states and the District of Columbia who are satisfied with the direction of the U.S.
A statistic used to the estimate the parameter in (c) is the percentage of the 1,024 individuals included in the sample. In this case, the statistic is 36%.

1.50   (a)   One variable collected with the American Community Survey is marital status with the following possible responses: now married, widowed, divorced, separated, and never married.
        (b)   The variable in (a) represents a categorical variable.
        (c)   Because the variable in (a) is a categorical, this question is not applicable. If one had chosen age in years from the American Community Survey as the variable, the answer to (c) would be discrete.

1.52   (a)   The population of interest consisted of 10,000 benefited employees of the University of Utah.
        (b)   The sample consisted of 3,095 employees of the University of Utah.
        (c)   Gender, marital status, and employment category represent categorical variables. Age in years, education level in years completed, and household income represent numerical variables.

CHAPTER 2

2.2   (a)   Table frequencies for all student responses

Gender	Student Major Categories			
	A	C	M	Totals
Male	14	9	2	25
Female	6	6	3	15
Totals	20	15	5	40

  (b)   Table percentages based on overall student responses

Gender	Student Major Categories			
	A	C	M	Totals
Male	35.0%	22.5%	5.0%	62.5%
Female	15.0%	15.0%	7.5%	37.5%
Totals	50.0%	37.5%	12.5%	100.0%

Table based on row percentages

Gender	Student Major Categories			
	A	C	M	Totals
Male	56.0%	36.0%	8.0%	100.0%
Female	40.0%	40.0%	20.0%	100.0%
Totals	50.0%	37.5%	12.5%	100.0%

Table based on column percentages

Gender	Student Major Categories			
	A	C	M	Totals
Male	70.0%	60.0%	40.0%	62.5%
Female	30.0%	40.0%	60.0%	37.5%
Totals	100.0%	100.0%	100.0%	100.0%

2.4   (a)

Category	Total	Percentages
Bank Account or Service	202	9.330%
Consumer Loan	132	6.097%
Credit Card	175	8.083%
Credit Reporting	581	26.836%
Debt Collection	486	22.448%
Mortgage	442	20.416%
Student Loan	75	3.464%
Other	72	3.326%
Grand Total	2165	

  (b)   There are more complaints for credit reporting, debt collection, and mortgage than the other categories. These categories account for about 70% of all the complaints.

2.4   (c)
cont.

Company	Total	Percentage
Bank of America	42	3.64%
Capital One	93	8.07%
Citibank	59	5.12%
Ditech Financial	31	2.69%
Equifax	217	18.82%
Experian	177	15.35%
JPMorgan	128	11.10%
Nationstar Mortgage	39	3.38%
Navient	38	3.30%
Ocwen	41	3.56%
Synchrony	43	3.73%
Trans-Union	168	14.57%
Wells Fargo	77	6.68%
Grand Total	1153	

(d)   Equifax, Trans-Union, and Experion, all of which are credit score companies, have the most complaints.

2.6   The largest sources of summer power-generating capacity in the United States are natural gas followed by coal. Nuclear, hydro, wind and other generate about the same, and solar generates very little.

2.8   (a)   Table of row percentages:

	GENDER		
OVERLOADED	Male	Female	Total
Yes	44.08%	55.92%	100.00%
No	53.54%	46.46%	100.00%
Total	51.64%	48.36%	100.00%

Table of column percentages:

	GENDER		
OVERLOADED	Male	Female	Total
Yes	17.07%	23.13%	20.00%
No	82.93%	76.87%	80.00%
Total	100.00%	100.00%	100.00%

2.8   (a)   Table of total percentages:

cont.

	GENDER		
OVERLOADED	Male	Female	Total
Yes	8.82%	11.18%	20.00%
No	42.83%	37.17%	80.00%
Total	51.64%	48.36%	100.00%

(b)   Approximately the same percentages of males and females as a percentage of the total number of people surveyed feel overloaded with too much information. As percentages of those who do and do not feel overloaded, the genders differ mildly. However, four times as many people do not feel overloaded at work than those that do.

2.10   Social recommendations had very little impact on correct recall. Those who arrived at the link from a recommendation had a correct recall of 73.07% as compared to those who arrived at the link from browsing who had a correct recall of 67.96%.

2.12   Ordered array: 73 78 78 78 85 88 91

2.14 $\dfrac{216,000 - 61,000}{6} = 33,333.33$ so choose 40,000 as interval width

(a) $60,000 – under $100,000; $100,000 – under $140,000; $140,000 – under $180,000; $180,000 – under $220,000; $220,000 – under $260,000; $260,000 – under $300,000

(b) $40,000

(c) $\dfrac{60,000 + 100000}{2} = 80000$ similarly, the remaining class midpoints are $120,000; $160,000; $200,000; $240,000; $280,000

2.16   (a)

Electricity Costs

Electricity Costs	Frequency	Percentage
$80 but less than $100	4	8%
$100 but less than $120	7	14%
$120 but less than $140	9	18%
$140 but less than $160	13	26%
$160 but less than $180	9	18%
$180 but less than $200	5	10%
$200 but less than $220	3	6%

2.16   (b)
cont.

Electricity Costs	Frequency	Percentage	Cumulative %
$ 99	4	8.00%	8.00%
$119	7	14.00%	22.00%
$139	9	18.00%	40.00%
$159	13	26.00%	66.00%
$179	9	18.00%	84.00%
$199	5	10.00%	94.00%
$219	3	6.00%	100.00%

(c)   The majority of utility charges are clustered between $120 and $180.

2.18   (a), (b)

Credit Score	Frequency	Percent (%)	Cumulative Percent (%)
560 – under 580	4	0.16	0.16
580 – under 600	24	0.93	1.09
600 – under 620	68	2.65	3.74
620 – under 640	290	11.28	15.02
640 – under 660	548	21.32	36.34
660 – under 680	560	21.79	58.13
680 – under 700	507	19.73	77.86
700 – under 720	378	14.71	92.57
720 – under 740	168	6.54	99.11
740 – under 760	22	0.86	99.96
760 – under 780	1	0.04	100.00

(c)   The average credit scores are concentrated between 620 and 720.

2.20   (a), (b)

Time in Seconds	Frequency	Percent (%)
5 – under 10	8	16%
10 – under 15	8	30%
15 – under 20	8	36%
20 – under 25	8	12%
25 – under 30	8	6%

2.20   (b)
cont.

Time in Seconds	Percentage Less Than
5	0
10	16
15	46
20	82
25	94
30	100

(c)   The target is being met since 82% of the calls are being answered in less than 20 seconds

2.22   (a), (b) Manufacturer A:

Bin Cell	Frequency	Percentage	Cumulative Pctage.
6,500 but less than 7,500	3	7.50%	7.50%
7,500 but less than 8,500	5	12.50%	20.00%
8,500 but less than 9,500	20	50.00%	70.00%
9,500 but less than 10,500	9	22.50%	92.50%
10,500 but less than 11,500	3	7.50%	100.00%

(a)   Manufacturer B:

Bin Cell	Frequency	Percentage	Cumulative Pctage.
7,500 but less than 8,500	2	5.00%	5.00%
9,500 but less than 9,500	8	20.00%	25.00%
9,500 but less than 10,500	16	40.00%	65.00%
10,500 but less than 11,500	9	22.50%	87.50%
11,500 but less than 12,500	5	12.50%	100.00%

(c)   Manufacturer B produces bulbs with longer lives than Manufacturer A. The cumulative percentage for Manufacturer B shows 65% of its bulbs lasted less than 10,500 hours, contrasted with 70% of Manufacturer A's bulbs, which lasted less than 9,500 hours. None of Manufacturer A's bulbs lasted more than 11,499 hours, but 12.5% of Manufacturer B's bulbs lasted between 11,500 and 12,499 hours. At the same time, 7.5% of Manufacturer A's bulbs lasted less than 7,500 hours, whereas all of Manufacturer B's bulbs lasted at least 7,500 hours

2.24   (a)

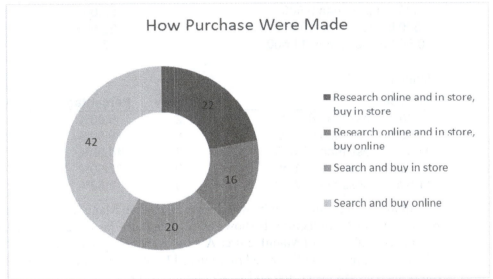

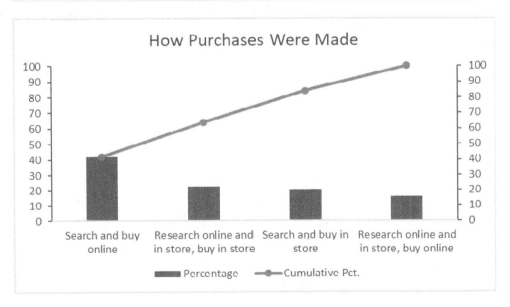

2.24   (b)   The Pareto chart is best for portraying these data because it not only sorts the frequencies
cont.   in descending order but also provides the cumulative line on the same chart.
       (c)   You can conclude that searching and buying online was the highest category and the
             other three were equally likely.

2.26   (a)

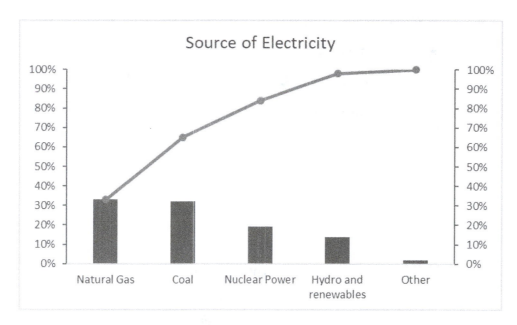

       (b)   32% + 19% + 33% = 84%
       (c)

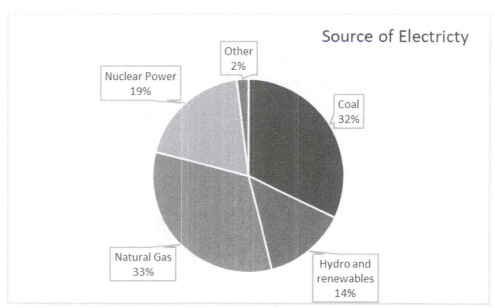

       (d)   The Pareto diagram is better than the pie chart because it not only sorts the frequencies in
             descending order, it also provides the cumulative polygon on the same scale.

2.28   (a)

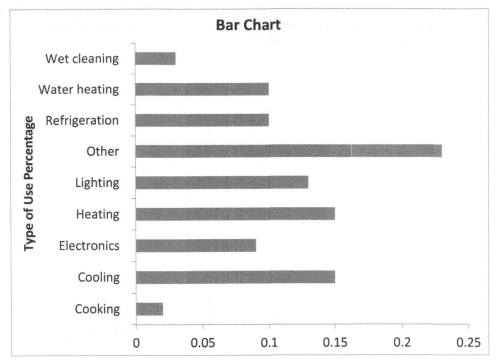

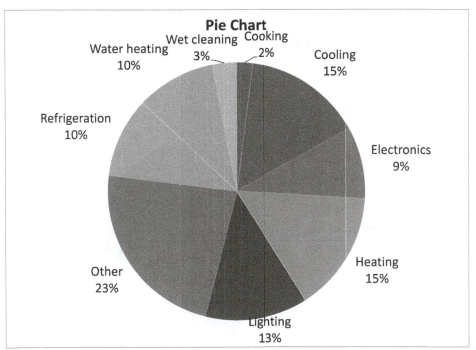

2.28   (a)
cont.

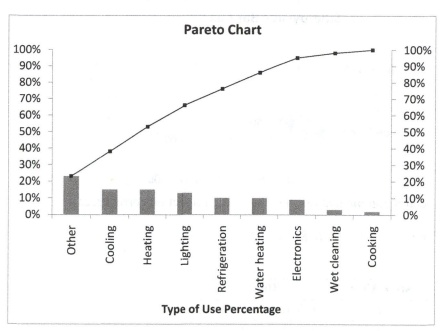

(b)   The Pareto diagram is better than the pie chart and bar chart because it not only sorts the frequencies in descending order; it also provides the cumulative polygon on the same scale.

(c)   Other, cooling, heating and lighting accounted for 66% of the residential electricity consumption in the United States.

2.30   (a)

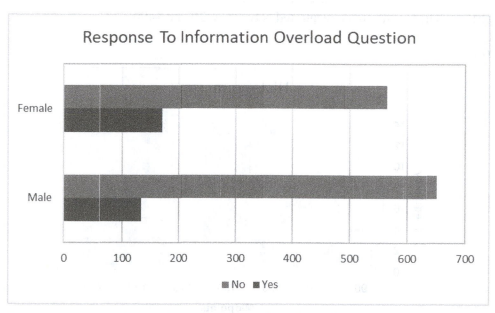

(b)   Females are more likely to be overloaded with information.

2.32   (a)

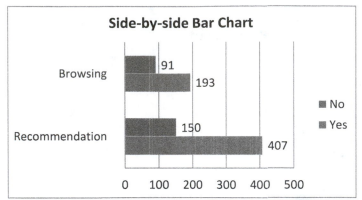

(b)   Social recommendations had very little impact on correct recall.

2.34   Ordered array: 50 74 74 76 81 89 92

2.36   (a)

Stem Unit	100
2	2 6 6 8 8 9
3	0 2 2 3 5 5 8
4	0 2 2 2 3 4 9
5	1 4 7 9
6	
7	0 2 3 9
8	8

(b)   The results are concentrated between $220 and $490.

2.38   (a)

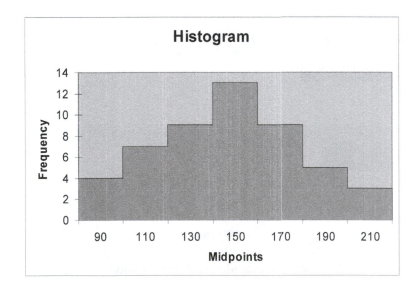

2.38   (a)
cont.

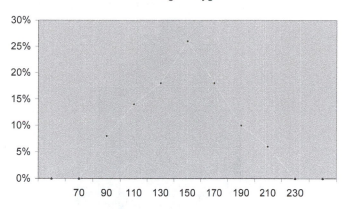

Percentage Polygon

(b)

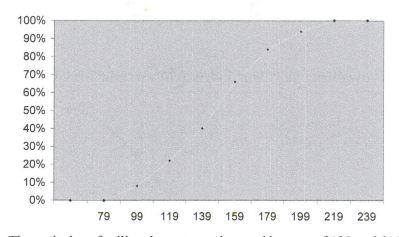

Cumulative Percentage Polygon

(c)   The majority of utility charges are clustered between $120 and $180.

2.40   Property taxes on a $176K home seem concentrated between $700 and $2,200 and also between $3,200 and $3,700.

2.42   (a)

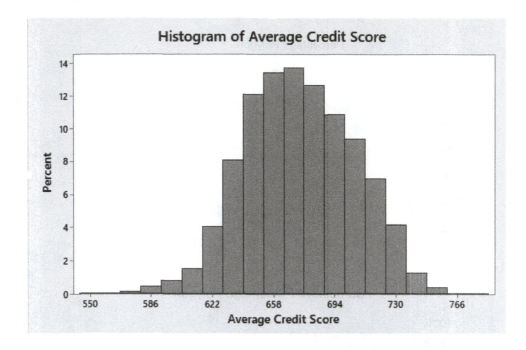

(b)

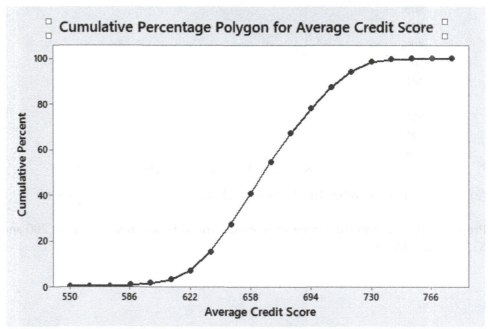

(c)   The average credit scores are concentrated between 622 and 730.

2.44   (a)

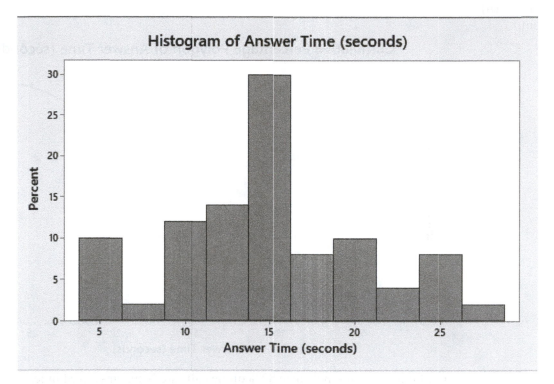

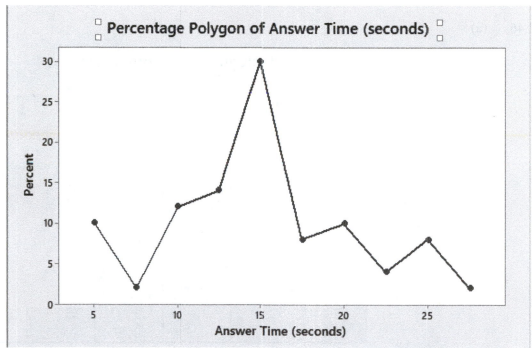

2.44   (b)
cont.

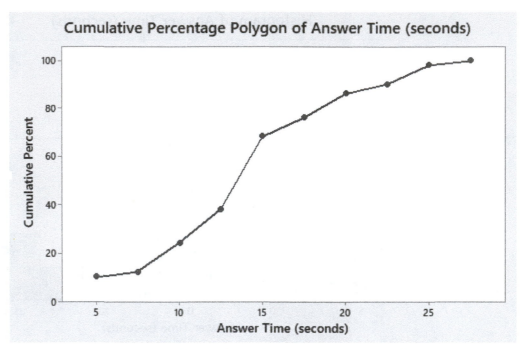

(c)   The target is being met since 82% of the calls are being answered in less than 20 seconds.

2.46   (a)

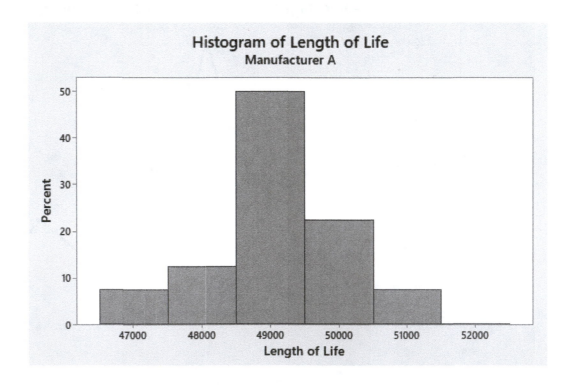

2.46   (a)
cont.

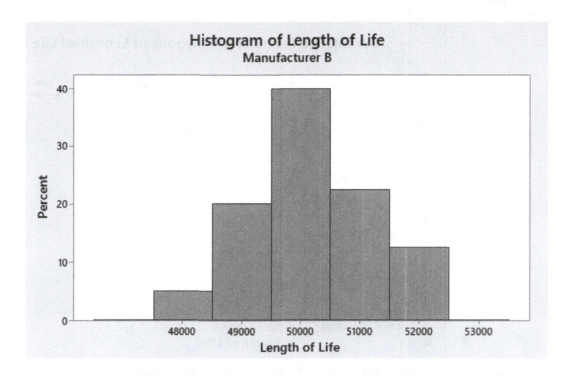

(b)

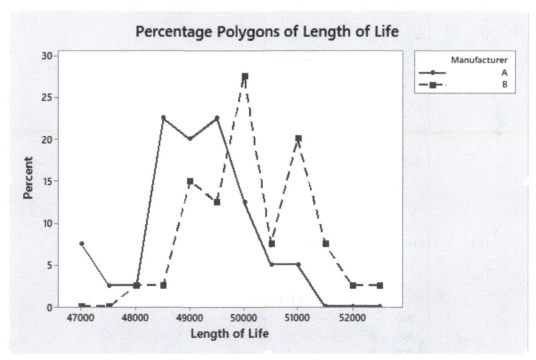

2.46   (b)
cont.

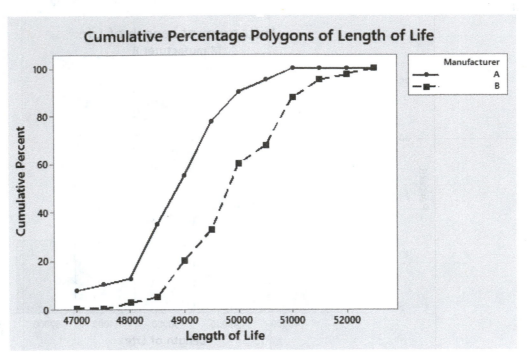

(c)   Manufacturer B produces bulbs with longer lives than Manufacturer A

2.48   (a)

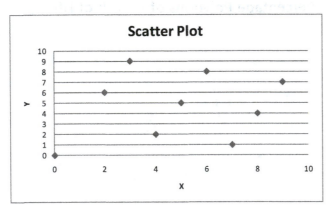

(b)   There is no relationship between X and Y.

2.50   (a)

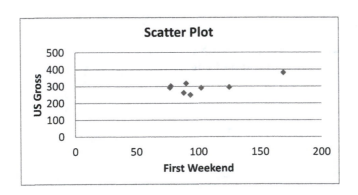

2.50   (b)
cont.

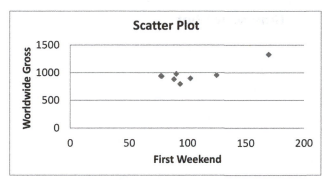

(c)   There appears to be a linear relationship between the first weekend gross and either the U.S. gross or the worldwide gross of Harry Potter movies. However, this relationship is greatly affected by the results of the last movie, *Deathly Hallows, Part II*.

2.52   (a)   There appears to be a positive relationship between the download speed and the upload speed.

(b)

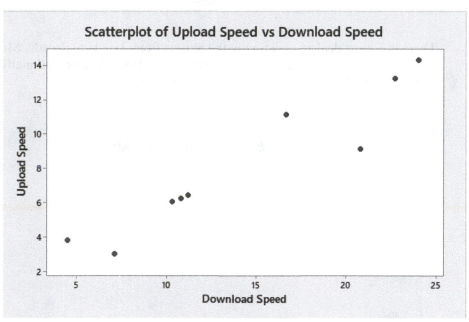

(c)   Yes, this is borne out by the data

2.54　(a)　Excel output:

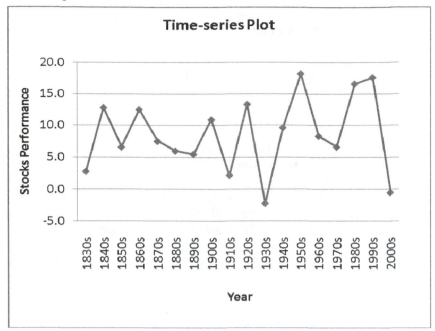

(b)　There is a great deal of variation in the returns from decade to decade. Most of the returns are between 5% and 15%. The 1950s, 1980s, and 1990s had exceptionally high returns, and only the 1930s and 2000s had negative returns.

2.56　(a)

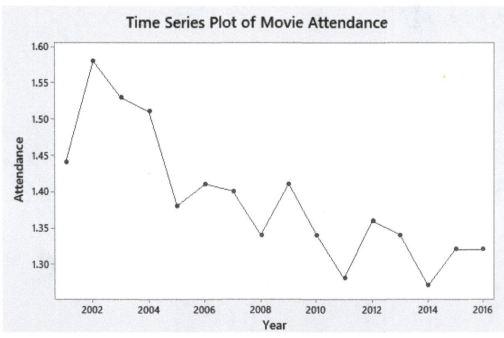

(b)　There was a decline in movie attendance from 2001 to 2016. During that time, movie attendance increased from 2001 to 2002 but then by 2016 decreased to a level below 2001.

2.58 (a)   Pivot Table in terms of %

Count of Type	Star Rating					
Type	One	Two	Three	Four	Five	Grand Total
Growth	**5.43%**	**17.12%**	**27.35%**	**11.27%**	**2.71%**	**63.88%**
Large	3.76%	7.72%	13.57%	5.43%	1.67%	32.15%
Mid-Cap	1.25%	5.43%	7.52%	3.13%	0.63%	17.96%
Small	0.42%	3.97%	6.26%	2.71%	0.42%	13.78%
Value	**2.92%**	**10.65%**	**13.99%**	**7.31%**	**1.25%**	**36.12%**
Large	2.09%	6.68%	9.19%	3.97%	1.25%	23.18%
Mid-Cap	0.63%	2.09%	2.71%	1.04%	0.00%	6.47%
Small	0.21%	1.88%	2.09%	2.30%	0.00%	6.48%
Grand Total	**8.35%**	**27.77%**	**41.34%**	**18.58%**	**3.97%**	**100.00%**

(b)   The growth and value funds have similar patterns in terms of star rating and type. Both growth and value funds have more funds with a rating of three. Very few funds have ratings of five.

(c)   Pivot Table in terms of Average Three-Year Return

Count of Type	Star Rating					
Type	One	Two	Three	Four	Five	Grand Total
Growth	**5.41**	**7.04**	**8.94**	**10.14**	**12.83**	**8.51**
Large	6.97	9.43	10.62	11.83	14.25	10.30
Mid-Cap	2.27	5.07	7.93	8.77	11.22	6.93
Small	0.78	5.09	6.52	8.35	9.53	6.39
Value	**4.43**	**5.49**	**7.29**	**8.34**	**10.23**	**6.84**
Large	5.23	6.05	7.58	8.85	10.23	7.29
Mid-Cap	2.79	5.77	7.32	9.26	–	6.69
Small	1.33	3.20	5.93	7.04	–	5.39
Grand Total	**5.07**	**6.45**	**8.38**	**9.43**	**12.01**	**7.91**

(d)   There are 65 large cap growth funds with a rating of three. Their average three year return is 10.62.

2.60

Count of Type	Star Rating					
Type	One	Two	Three	Four	Five	Grand Total
Growth	**5.43%**	**17.12%**	**27.35%**	**11.27%**	**2.71%**	**63.88%**
Large	1.25%	2.09%	4.80%	3.55%	1.46%	13.15%
Mid-Cap	1.67%	7.72%	15.87%	6.05%	0.42%	31.73%
Small	2.51%	7.31%	6.68%	1.67%	0.84%	19.00%
Value	**2.92%**	**10.65%**	**13.99%**	**7.31%**	**1.25%**	**36.12%**
Large	0.84%	4.38%	7.10%	4.38%	0.84%	17.54%
Mid-Cap	1.25%	4.80%	5.85%	2.71%	0.42%	15.03%
Small	0.84%	1.46%	1.04%	0.21%	0.00%	3.55%
Grand Total	**8.35%**	**27.77%**	**41.34%**	**18.58%**	**3.96%**	**100.00%**

(b)   Patterns of star rating conditioned on risk:
For the growth funds as a group, most are rated as three-star, followed by two-star, four-star, one-star, and five-star. The pattern of star rating is different among the various risk growth funds.

2.60
cont.

(b)   For the value funds as a group, most are rated as three-star, followed by two-star, four-star, one-star and five-star. Among the high-risk value funds, more are two-star than three-star.

Most of the growth funds are rated as average-risk, followed by high-risk and then low-risk. The pattern is not the same among all the rating categories.

Most of the value funds are rated as low-risk, followed by average-risk and then high-risk. The pattern is the same among the three-star, four-star, and five-star value funds. Among the one-star and two-star funds, there are more average risk funds than low risk funds.

(c)

| Count of Type | Star Rating | | | | | |
Type	One	Two	Three	Four	Five	Grand Total
Growth	**5.41**	**7.04**	**8.94**	**10.14**	**12.83**	**8.51**
Large	7.53	8.60	9.89	10.29	12.64	9.87
Mid-Cap	6.17	7.99	9.28	10.43	11.96	9.06
Small	3.83	5.59	7.45	8.76	13.59	6.64
Value	**4.43**	**5.49**	**7.29**	**8.34**	**10.23**	**6.84**
Large	5.29	7.00	7.66	8.57	10.74	7.76
Mid-Cap	5.01	4.98	6.97	7.96	9.23	6.41
Small	2.71	2.63	6.53	8.39	–	4.13
Grand Total	**5.07**	**6.45**	**8.38**	**9.43**	**12.01**	**7.91**

The three-year returns for growth funds is higher than for value funds. The return is higher for funds with higher ratings than lower ratings. This pattern holds for the growth funds for each risk level. For the low risk and average risk value funds, the return is lowest for the funds with a two-star rating.

(d)   There are 32 growth funds with high risk with a rating of three. These funds have an average three-year return of 7.45.

2.62   The fund with the highest five-year return of 15.72 is a large cap growth fund that has a four-star rating and low risk.

2.64   Funds 479, 471, 347, 443, and 477 have the lowest five-year return.

2.66   The five funds with the lowest five-year return have (1) midcap growth, average risk, one-star rating, (2) midcap growth, high risk, two-star rating, (3) large value, average risk, two-star rating, (4) midcap growth, high risk, one-star rating, and (5) small value, average risk, two-star rating.

2.68   There has been a decline in the price of natural gas over time. However, there is no pattern within the years. For some years, the price is higher in the beginning of the year. For other years, the price is higher in the latter part of the year. Sometimes, there is little variation within the year.

2.70   Student project answers will vary

2.72   (a)   There is a title.
        (b)   The simplest possible visualization is not used.
        (c)

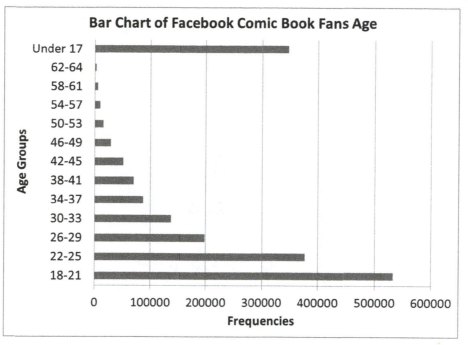

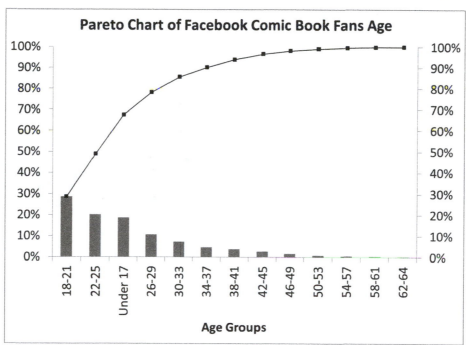

2.74   Answers will vary depending on selection of source.

2.76   (a)

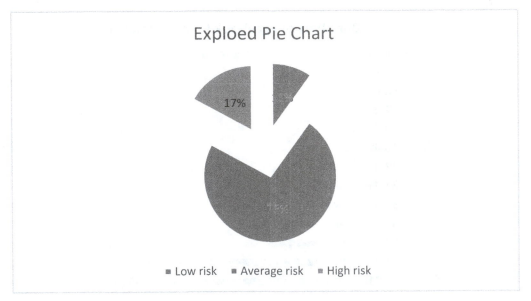

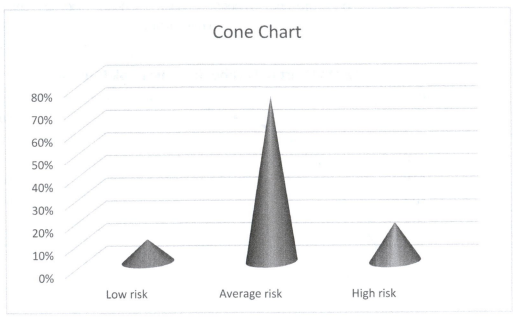

2.76   (a)
cont.

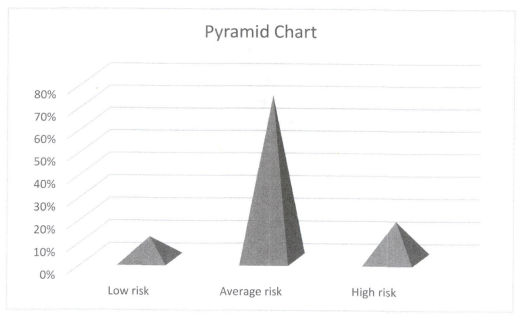

(b)   The bar chart and the pie chart should be preferred over the exploded pie chart, doughnut chart, the cone chart and the pyramid chart since the former set is simpler and easier to interpret.

2.78   A summary table allows one to determine the frequency or percentage of occurrences in each category.

2.80   The bar chart for categorical data is plotted with the categories on the vertical axis and the frequencies or percentages on the horizontal axis. In addition, there is a separation between categories. The histogram is plotted with the class grouping on the horizontal axis and the frequencies or percentages on the vertical axis. This allows one to more easily determine the distribution of the data. In addition, there are no gaps between classes in the histogram.

2.82   Because the categories are arranged according to frequency or importance, it allows the user to focus attention on the categories that have the greatest frequency or importance.

2.84   A contingency table contains information on two categorical variables whereas a multidimensional table can display information on more than two categorical variables.

2.86   In a PivotTable in Excel, double-clicking a cell drills down and causes Excel to display the underlying data in a new worksheet to enable you to then observe the data for patterns. In Excel, a slicer is a panel of clickable buttons that appears superimposed over a worksheet to enable you to work with many variables at once in a way that avoids creating an overly complex multidimensional contingency table that would be hard to comprehend and interpret.

2.88   (a)

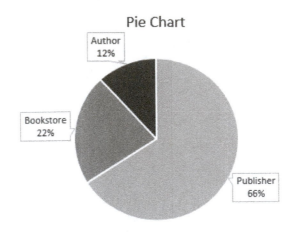

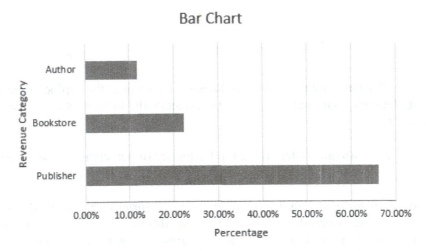

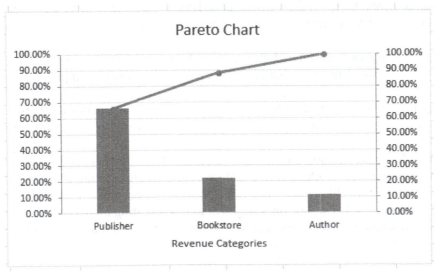

2.88   (b)
cont.

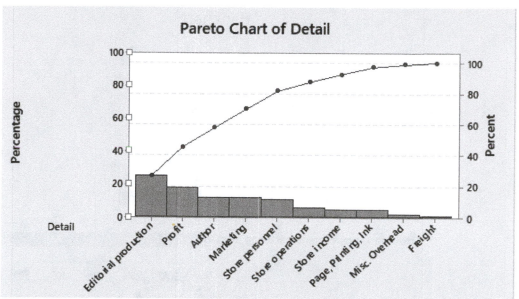

(c)   The publisher gets the largest portion (66.06%) of the revenue. 24.93% is editorial production manufacturing costs. The publisher's marketing accounts for the next largest share of the revenue, at 11.6%. Author and bookstore personnel each account for around 11 to 12% of the revenue, whereas the publisher and bookstore profit and income account for more than 26% of the revenue. Yes, the bookstore gets almost twice the revenue of the authors.

2.90   (a)

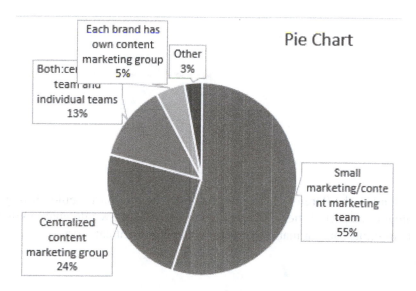

2.90   (a)
cont.

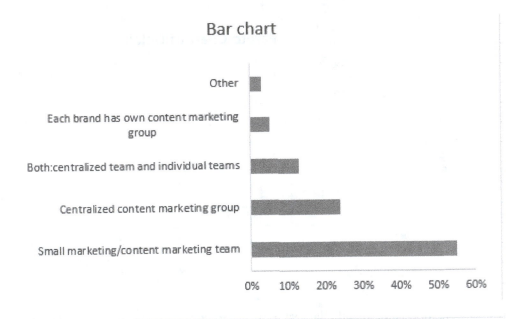

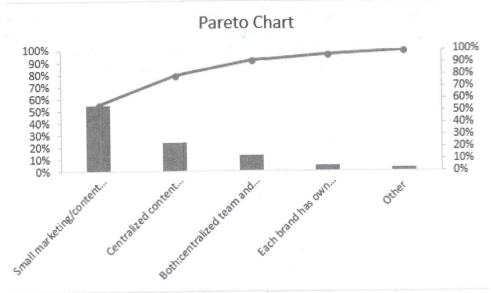

(b)   The pie chart or the Pareto chart would be best. The pie chart would allow you to see each category as part of the whole, while the Pareto chart would enable you to see that Small marketing/content marketing team is the dominant category.

2.90   (c)
cont.

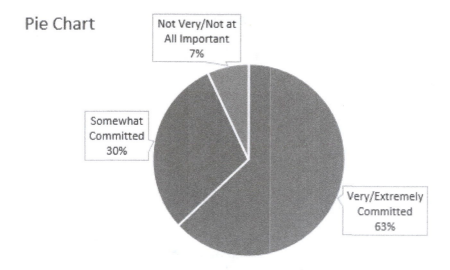

Pie Chart

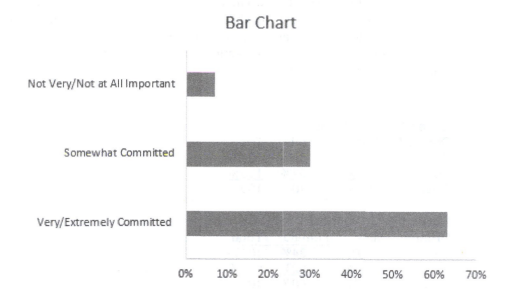

Bar Chart

2.90   (c)
cont.

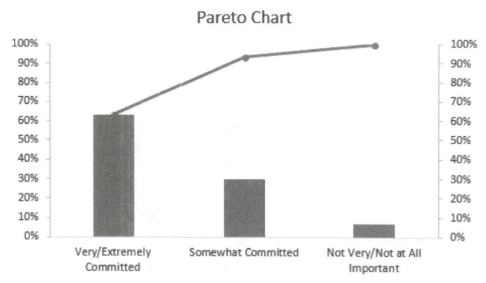

(d)   The pie chart or the Pareto chart would be best. The pie chart would allow you to see each category as part of the whole while the Pareto chart would enable you to see that very committed to content marketing is the dominant category.

(e)   Most organizations have a small marketing/content marketing team and are very committed to content marketing.

2.92   (a)

Dessert Ordered	Gender Male	Female	Total
Yes	66%	34%	100%
No	48%	52%	100%
Total	52%	48%	100%

Dessert Ordered	Gender Male	Female	Total
Yes	29%	34%	100%
No	71%	52%	100%
Total	100%	48%	100%

Dessert Ordered	Gender Male	Female	Total
Yes	15%	8%	23%
No	37%	40%	77%
Total	52%	48%	100%

Dessert Ordered	Gender Male	Female	Total
Yes	52%	48%	100%
No	25%	75%	100%
Total	31%	69%	100%

2.92   (a)
cont.

Dessert	Gender		
Ordered	Male	Female	Total
Yes	38%	16%	23%
No	62%	84%	77%
Total	100%	100%	100%

Dessert	Gender		
Ordered	Male	Female	Total
Yes	11.75%	10.79%	22.54%
No	19.52%	57.94%	77.46%
Total	31.27%	68.73%	100%

(b)   If the owner is interested in finding out the percentage of males and females who order dessert or the percentage of those who order a beef entrée and a dessert among all patrons, the table of total percentages is most informative. If the owner is interested in the effect of gender on ordering of dessert or the effect of ordering a beef entrée on the ordering of dessert, the table of column percentages will be most informative. Because dessert is usually ordered after the main entrée, and the owner has no direct control over the gender of patrons, the table of row percentages is not very useful here.

(c)   29% of the men ordered desserts, compared to 17 of the women; men are almost twice as likely to order dessert as women. Almost 38% of the patrons ordering a beef entrée ordered dessert, compared to 16% of patrons ordering all other entrées. Patrons ordering beef are more than 2.3 times as likely to order dessert as patrons ordering any other entrée.

2.94   (a)

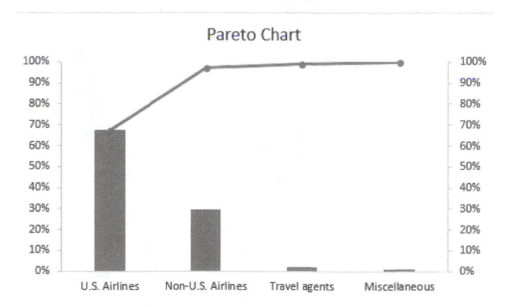

Most of the complaints were against U.S. airlines.

2.94   (b)
cont.

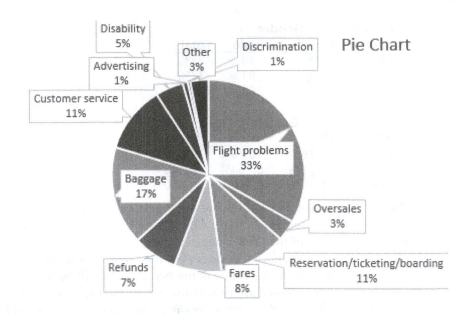

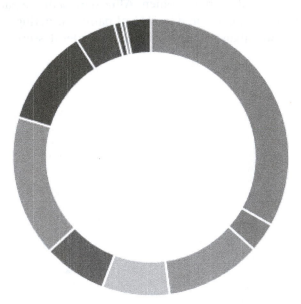

- Flight problems
- Oversales
- Reservation/ticketing/boarding
- Fares
- Refunds
- Baggage
- Customer service
- Disability
- Advertising
- Discrimination
- Other

More of the complaints were due to flight problems.

2.96   (a)

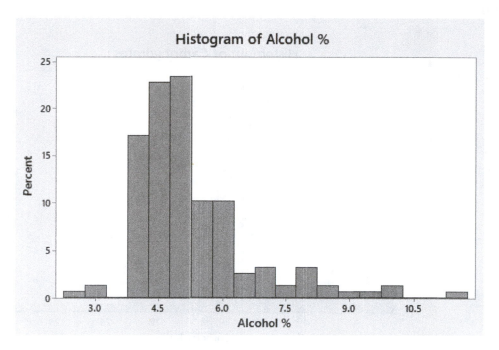

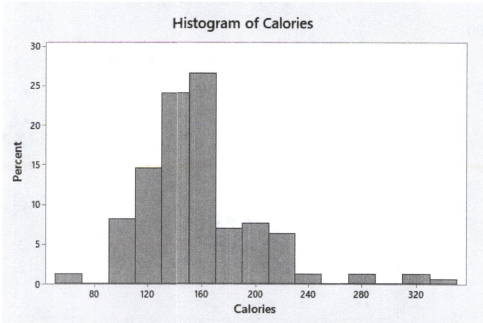

2.96   (a)
cont.

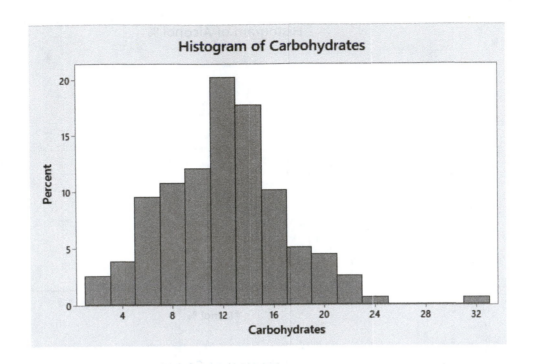

(b)

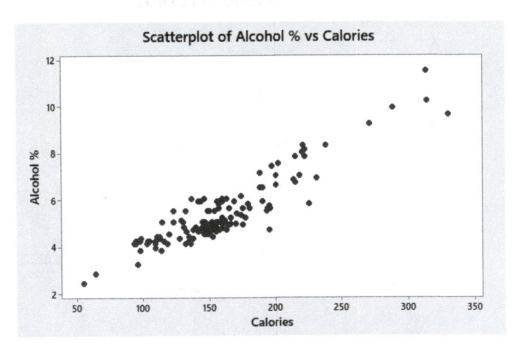

2.96   (b)
cont.

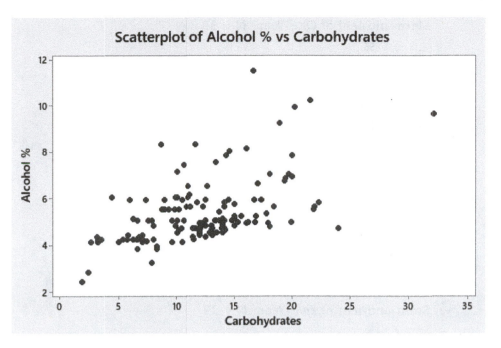

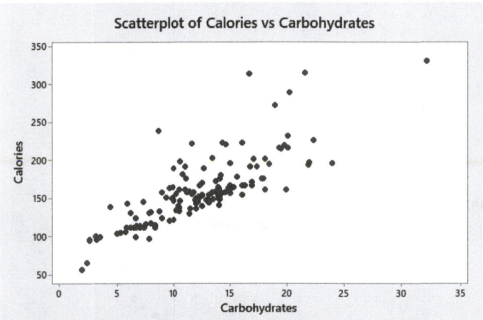

(c)   The alcohol percentage is concentrated between 4% and 6%, with more between 4% and 5%. The calories are concentrated between 140 and 160. The carbohydrates are concentrated between 12 and 15. There are outliers in the percentage of alcohol in both tails. There are a few beers with alcohol content as high as around 11.5%. There are a few beers with calorie content as high as around 313 and carbohydrates as high as 32.1. There is a strong positive relationship between percentage of alcohol and calories and between calories and carbohydrates, and there is a moderately positive relationship between percentage alcohol and carbohydrates.

2.98   (a)

Stem-and-leaf of One-Year   N = 39

```
 2    0   55
 6    1   0055
11    2   05558
13    3   05
16    4   055
19    5   000
19    6
(1)   7   5
19    8   0
18    9   55
16   10   00567
11   11   55
 9   12   015688
 3   13   015
```

Leaf Unit = 0.01

Stem-and-leaf of Five-Year   N = 39

```
 2    0   11
 3    0   3
 5    0   55
10    0   66777
11    0   9
15    1   0011
18    1   223
(2)   1   55
19    1   666677777
10    1   888889
 4    2   00
 2    2   22
```

Leaf Unit = 0.1

(b)

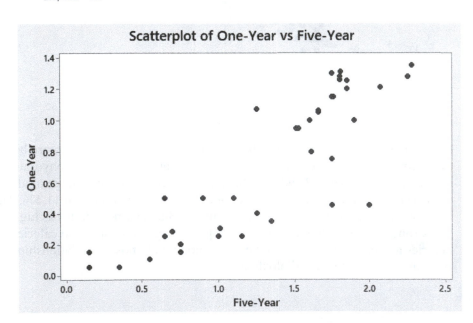

2.98   (c)   There appears to be a strong positive relationship between the yield of the one-year CD
cont.   and the five-year CD.

2.100   (a)

Frequencies (Boston)

Weight (Boston)	Frequency	Percentage
3015 but less than 3050	2	0.54%
3050 but less than 3085	44	11.96%
3085 but less than 3120	122	33.15%
3120 but less than 3155	131	35.60%
3155 but less than 3190	58	15.76%
3190 but less than 3225	7	1.90%
3225 but less than 3260	3	0.82%
3260 but less than 3295	1	0.27%

(b)

Frequencies (Vermont)

Weight (Vermont)	Frequency	Percentage
3550 but less than 3600	4	1.21%
3600 but less than 3650	31	9.39%
3650 but less than 3700	115	34.85%
3700 but less than 3750	131	39.70%
3750 but less than 3800	36	10.91%
3800 but less than 3850	12	3.64%
3850 but less than 3900	1	0.30%

(c)

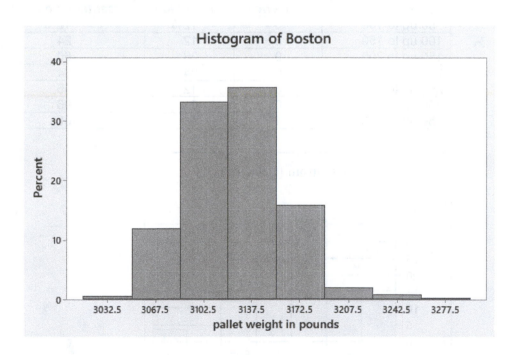

2.100   (c)
cont.

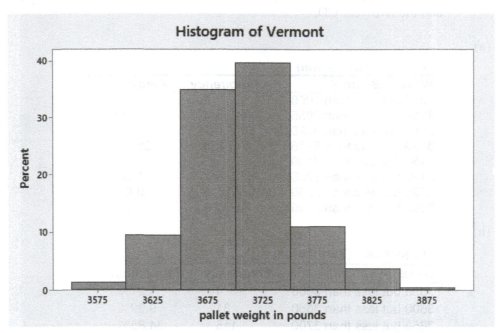

Histogram of Vermont

(d)   0.54% of the "Boston" shingles pallets are underweight while 0.27% are overweight.
1.21% of the "Vermont" shingles pallets are underweight while 3.94% are overweight.

2.102   (a)

Calories	Frequency	Percentage	Percentage Less Than
50 up to 100	3	12%	12%
100 up to 150	3	12	24
150 up to 200	9	36	60
200 up to 250	6	24	84
250 up to 300	3	12	96
300 up to 350	0	0	96
350 up to 400	1	4	100

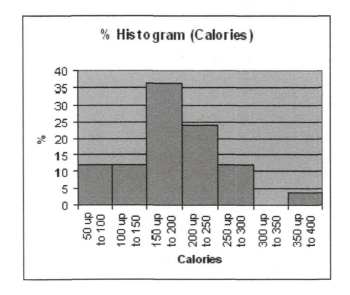

% Histogram (Calories)

2.102   (b)
cont.

Cholesterol	Frequency	Percentage	Percentage Less Than
0 up to 50	2	8	8%
50 up to 100	17	68	76
100 up to 150	4	16	92
150 up to 200	1	4	96
200 up to 250	0	0	96
250 up to 300	0	0	96
300 up to 350	0	0	96
350 up to 400	0	0	96
400 up to 450	0	0	96
450 up to 500	1	4	100

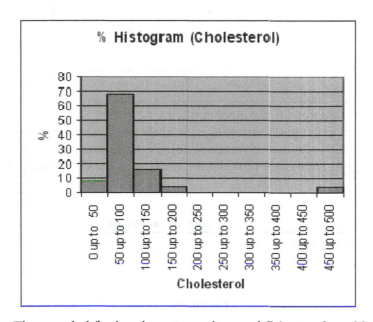

(c)   The sampled fresh red meats, poultry, and fish vary from 98 to 397 calories per serving, with the highest concentration between 150 to 200 calories. One protein source, spareribs, with 397 calories, is more than 100 calories above the next highest caloric food. The protein content of the sampled foods varies from 16 to 33 grams, with 68% of the data values falling between 24 and 32 grams. Spareribs and fried liver are both very different from other foods sampled—the former on calories and the latter on cholesterol content.

2.104   (a)

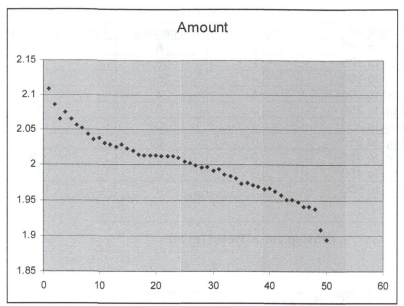

(b)   There is a downward trend in the amount filled.

(c)   The amount filled in the next bottle will most likely be below 1.894 liter.

(d)   The scatter plot of the amount of soft drink filled against time reveals the trend of the data, whereas a histogram only provides information on the distribution of the data.

2.106   (a)

Variations	Percentage of Download
Original Call to Action Button	9.64%
New Call to Action Button	13.64%

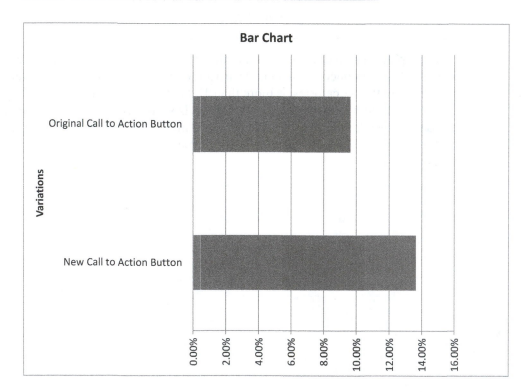

2.106   (c)   The New Call to Action Button has a higher percentage of downloads at 13.64% when
cont.   compared to the Original Call to Action Button with a 9.64% of downloads.

(d)

Variations	Percentage of Downloads
Original web design	8.90%
New web design	9.41%

(e)

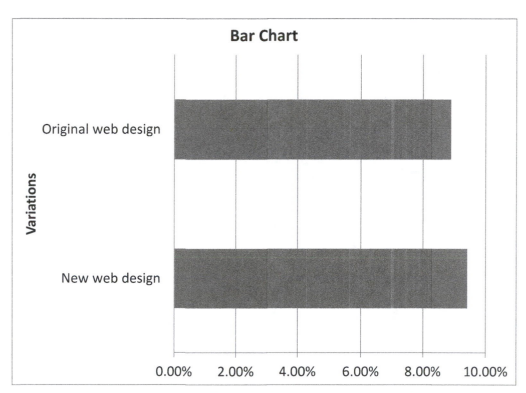

(f)   The New web design has only a slightly higher percentage of downloads at 9.41% when
       compared to the Original web design with an 8.90% of downloads.

(g)   The New web design is only slightly more successful than the Original web design while
       the New Call to Action Button is much more successful than the Original Call to Action
       Button with about 41% higher percentage of downloads.

(h)

Call to Action Button	Web Design	Percentage of Downloads
Old	Old	8.30%
New	Old	13.70%
Old	New	9.50%
New	New	17.00%

(i)   The combination of the New Call to Action Button and the New web design results in
       slightly more than twice as high a percentage of downloads than the combination of the
       Old Call to Action Button and Old web design.

2.106   (j)   The New web design is only slightly more successful than the Original web design while
cont.   the New Call to Action Button is much more successful than the Original Call to Action
                 Button with about 41% higher percentage of downloads. However, the combination of
                 the New Call to Action Button and New web design results in more than twice as high a
                 percentage of downloads than the combination of the Old Call to Action Button and Old
                 web design.

2.108   Class project – answers will vary depending on student responses.

CHAPTER 3

3.2   (a)   Excel output:

X	
Mean	7
Median	7
Mode	7
Standard Deviation	3.286335
Sample Variance	10.8
Range	9
Minimum	3
Maximum	12
Sum	42
Count	6
First Quartile	4
Third Quartile	9
Interquartile Range	5
Coefficient of Variation	46.9476%

(b)   Mean = 7   Median = 7   Mode = 7
        Range = 9   Variance = 10.8
        Standard deviation = 3.286
        Coefficient of variation = (3.286/7) • 100% = 46.948%

(c)   Z scores: 0, –0.913, 0.609, 0, –1.217, 1.522
        None of the Z scores is larger than 3.0 or smaller than –3.0. There is no outlier.

(d)   Since the mean equals the median, the distribution is symmetrical.

3.4   Excel output:

X	
Mean	2
Median	7
Mode	7
Standard Deviation	7.874007874
Sample Variance	62
Range	17
Minimum	–8
Maximum	9
Sum	10
Count	5
First Quartile	–6.5
Third Quartile	8
Interquartile Range	14.5
Coefficient of Variation	393.7004%

(a)   Mean = 2   Median = 7   Mode = 7
(b)   Range = 17   Variance = 62
        Standard deviation = 7.874   Coefficient of variation = (7.874/2) • 100% = 393.7%

3.4   (c)   Z scores: 0.635, –0.889, –1.270, 0.635, 0.889. No outliers.
cont.   (d)   Since the mean is less than the median, the distribution is left-skewed.

3.6 $\bar{R}_G = \left[(1+0.2)(1-0.3) \right]^{1/2} - 1 = -8.348\%$

3.8   (a)

	Grade X	Grade Y
Mean	575	575.4
Median	575	575
Standard deviation	6.4	2.1

(b)   If quality is measured by central tendency, Grade X tires provide slightly better quality because X's mean and median are both equal to the expected value, 575 mm. If, however, quality is measured by consistency, Grade Y provides better quality because, even though Y's mean is only slightly larger than the mean for Grade X, Y's standard deviation is much smaller. The range in values for Grade Y is 5 mm compared to the range in values for Grade X, which is 16 mm.

(c)   Excel output:

Grade X	
Mean	575
Median	575
Mode	#N/A
Standard Deviation	6.403124
Sample Variance	41
Range	16
Minimum	568
Maximum	584
Sum	2875
Count	5

Grade Y	
Mean	577.4
Median	575
Mode	#N/A
Standard Deviation	6.107373
Sample Variance	37.3
Range	15
Minimum	573
Maximum	588
Sum	2887
Count	5

	Grade X	Grade Y, Altered
Mean	575	577.4
Median	575	575
Standard deviation	6.4	6.1

When the fifth Y tire measures 588 mm rather than 578 mm, Y's mean inner diameter becomes 577.4 mm, which is larger than X's mean inner diameter, and Y's standard deviation increases from 2.1 mm to 6.1 mm. In this case, X's tires are providing better quality in terms of the mean inner diameter, with only slightly more variation among the tires than Y's.

3.10   (a), (b)

	Download Speed (Mbps)	Upload Speed (Mbps)
Mean	14.2333	8.1222
Median	11.2	6.4
Minimum	4.5	3
Maximum	24	14.3
Range	19.5	11.3
Variance	49.7950	16.2319
Standard Deviation	7.0566	4.0289
Coefficient of variance	49.58%	49.60%
Skewness	0.1932	0.3862
Kurtosis	−1.5292	−1.2358
Sample size	9	9

(c)   The mean is greater than the median for both the download speed and the upload speed indicating a right or positive skewed distribution (the skewness statistic is also positive). The kurtosis statistic is negative for both the download speed and the upload speed indicating distributions that are less peaked than a normal (bell-shaped) distribution.

(d)   The mean download speed is much higher than the mean upload speed. The median download speed indicates that half the carriers have a download speed of at least 11.2 mbps as compared to a median upload speed of 6.4 mbps that indicates that half the carriers have an upload speed of at least 6.4 mbps. There is much more variation in the download speed than the upload speed because the standard deviation is 7.0566 as compared to 4.0289

3.12   (a), (b)

	60-Second Ads	30-Second Ads
Mean	5.10	4.90
Median	5.30	4.81
Minimum	3.22	3.55
Maximum	6.91	6.64
Range	3.69	3.09
Variance	1.1088	0.6745
Standard Deviation	1.0530	0.8213
Coefficient of variance	20.63%	16.76%
Skewness	−0.5268	0.4382
Kurtosis	−0.3289	−0.2371
Sample size	17	40

(c)   The mean score is less than the median for the 60-second ads indicating a left- or negative-skewed distribution (the skewness statistic is also negative). The mean score is slightly greater than the median for the 30-second ads indicating a right- or positive-skewed distribution (the skewness statistic is also positive). The kurtosis statistic is slightly negative for both the 60- and 30-second ads indicating distributions that are less peaked than a normal (bell-shaped) distribution.

3.12   (d)   The mean ad score is higher for the 60-second ads than for the 30-second ads.
cont.   The median ad score for the 60-second ads indicates that half the scores are at least 5.30
                as compared to a median ad score for the 30-second ads that indicates that half scores are
                at least 4.81. There is much more variation in the scores of the 60-second ads than the 30-
                second ads because the standard deviation is 1.0530 as compared to 0.8213.

3.14   (a), (b)

Mobile Commerce Penetration (%)	
Mean	29.6786
Median	27.5
Mode	23
Minimum	11
Maximum	55
Range	44
Variance	94.8188
Standard Deviation	9.7375
Coefficient of variance	32.81%
Skewness	0.5506
Kurtosis	0.5024
Count	28
Standard Error	1.8402

Country	Mobile Commerce Penetration (%)	Z score
Argentina	23	0.68586
Australia	27	−0.27508
Brazil	26	−0.3777
Canada	25	−0.48047
China	40	1.059968
France	19	−1.09664
Germany	26	−0.37777
Hong Kong	36	0.649184
India	23	−0.68586
Indonesia	33	−0.341097
Italy	23	−0.68586
Japan	11	−1.91821
Malaysia	38	0.854576
Mexico	21	−0.89125
Philippines	26	−0.37777
Poland	23	−0.68586
Russia	21	−0.89125
Saudi Arabia	33	−0.341097
Singapore	40	1.059968

3.14   (a), (b)
cont.

South Africa	15	−1.50743
South Korea	55	2.600405
Spain	30	0.033009
Thailand	41	−1.162664
Turkey	31	0.135705
Unite Arab Republic	47	1.778838
United Kingdom	37	0.75188
United States	33	0.341097
Vietnam	28	−0.17238

Because there are no Z values below -3.0 or above 3.0, there are no outliers.

(c)   The mean is greater than the median, so Mobile Commerce Penetration is right-skewed.

(d)   The mean Mobile Commerce Penetration is 29.6786% and half the countries have values greater than or equal to 27.5%. The average scatter around the mean is 9.375%. The lowest value is 11% (Japan) and the highest value is 55% (South Korea).

3.16   (a), (b)

Price (USD)	
Mean	117.4615
Median	116
Mode	138
Range	53
Variance	263.6025
Standard Deviation	16.2358

(c)   The mean room price is $117.4615 and half the room prices are greater than or equal to $116, so room price is slightly right-skewed. The average scatter around the mean is 16.2358. The lowest room price is $85 in Mexico and the highest room price is $138 in Japan.

(d)   The mean increases to 120.7692, while the median and the mode remain the same. The data is now slightly more right-skewed. The average scatter around the mean increases to 22.5876. The range is now 90.

3.18   (a)   Mean = 7.11   Median = 6.68

(b)   Variance = 4.336   Standard Deviation = 2.082   Range = 6.67
Coefficient of variation = 29.27%

Waiting Time	Z Score		Waiting Time	Z Score
9.66	1.222431		10.49	1.62105
5.90	−0.58336		6.68	−0.20875
8.02	0.434799		5.64	−0.70823
5.79	−0.63619		4.08	−1.45744
8.73	0.775786		6.17	−0.45369
3.82	−1.58231		9.91	1.342497
8.01	0.429996		5.47	−0.78987
8.35	0.593286			

Since there are no Z values below −3.0 or above 3.0, there are no outliers.

3.18   (c)   Because the mean is greater than the median, the distribution is right-skewed.

cont.   (d)   The mean and median are both greater than five minutes. The distribution is right-skewed, meaning that there are some unusually high values. Further, 13 of the 15 bank customers sampled (or 86.7%) had waiting times greater than five minutes. So the customer is likely to experience a waiting time in excess of five minutes. The manager overstated the bank's service record in responding that the customer would "almost certainly" not wait longer than five minutes for service.

3.20   (a) $[(1+0.3415)\times(1+(0.0993))]^{1/2}-1=0.2144$ or 21.44%.

         (b) $=(\$1,000)\times(1+0.2144)\times(1+0.2144)=\$1,474.77$

         (c)   The result for Facebook was better than the result for GE, which was worth $1,250.37.

3.22   (a)   Platinum = –10.09% gold = –9.33% silver = –10.48%.

         (b)   All the metals had about the same negative return of approximately 10%.

         (c)   All the metals had negative returns, whereas the three stock indices all had positive returns.

3.24   (a)

Mean of 3YrReturn%	Rating					
Type	One	Two	Three	Four	Five	Grand Total
Growth	**5.41**	**7.04**	**8.94**	**10.14**	**12.83**	**8.51**
Large	6.97	9.43	10.62	11.83	14.25	10.30
Mid-Cap	2.27	5.07	7.93	8.77	11.22	6.93
Small	0.78	5.09	6.52	8.35	9.53	6.39
Value	**4.43**	**5.49**	**7.29**	**8.34**	**10.23**	**6.84**
Large	5.23	6.05	7.58	8.85	10.23	7.29
Mid-Cap	2.79	5.77	7.32	9.26	–	6.69
Small	1.33	3.20	5.93	7.04	–	5.39

         (b)

StdDev of 3Yr Return%	Rating					
Type	One	Two	Three	Four	Five	Grand Total
Growth	**3.72**	**2.85**	**2.71**	**2.23**	**2.12**	**3.19**
Large	2.86	1.34	2.23	1.43	0.89	2.56
Mid-Cap	3.49	2.04	2.08	1.03	1.02	2.86
Small	0.84	2.40	2.08	2.11	0.62	2.52
Value	**2.07**	**2.40**	**1.20**	**2.09**	**1.32**	**2.33**
Large	1.81	1.68	0.98	1.63	1.32	1.93
Mid-Cap	1.00	2.90	1.13	0.99	–	2.51
Small	–	2.88	1.36	2.62	–	2.35
Grand Total	**3.24**	**2.78**	**2.44**	**2.34**	**2.24**	**3.02**

         (c)   The mean three-year return of small-cap funds is much lower than mid-cap and large funds. Five-star funds for all market cap categories show the highest mean three-year returns. The mean three-year returns for all combinations of type and market cap rises as the star rating rises, consistent to the mean three-year returns for all growth and value funds. The standard deviations of the three-year return for large-cap and mid-cap value funds vary greatly among star rating categories.

3.26   (a)

Mean of 3Yr Return%	Rating					
Type	One	Two	Three	Four	Five	Grand Total
Growth	**5.41**	**7.04**	**8.94**	**10.14**	**12.83**	**8.51**
Low	7.53	8.60	9.89	10.29	12.64	9.87
Average	6.17	7.99	9.28	10.43	11.96	9.06
High	3.83	5.59	7.45	8.76	13.59	6.64
Value	**4.43**	**5.49**	**7.29**	**8.34**	**10.23**	**6.84**
Low	5.29	7.00	7.66	8.57	10.74	7.76
Average	5.01	4.98	6.97	7.96	9.23	6.41
High	2.71	2.63	6.53	8.39	–	4.13
Grand Total	**5.07**	**6.45**	**8.38**	**9.43**	**12.01**	**7.91**

(b)

StdDev of 3Yr Return%	Rating					
	One	Two	Three	Four	Five	Grand Total
Growth	3.72	2.85	2.71	2.23	2.12	3.19
Low	3.27	1.57	2.02	2.05	2.04	2.42
Average	4.37	2.43	2.67	2.42	2.51	2.86
High	2.98	2.92	2.73	1.43	2.47	3.39
Value	**2.07**	**2.40**	**1.20**	**2.09**	**1.32**	**2.33**
Low	1.46	1.12	1.00	2.15	0.85	1.72
Average	2.11	2.43	1.25	2.09	1.87	2.27
High	–	2.88	1.36	2.62	–	2.35
Grand Total	**3.24**	**2.78**	**2.44**	**2.34**	**2.24**	**3.02**

(c)   The mean three-year return of high-risk funds is much lower than the other risk categories except for five-star funds. In all risk categories, five-star funds have the highest mean three-year return. The mean three-year returns for high-risk growth and value funds for one-, two-, and three-star rating funds are lower than the means for the other risk categories.

The standard deviations of the three-year return for low-risk funds show the most consistency across star rating categories and the standard deviations of the three-year return for low-risk funds are the lowest across categories. They also vary greatly among star rating categories.

3.28   (a) $Q_1 = 4$, $Q_3 = 9$, interquartile range = 5
        (b)   Five-number summary: 3 4 7 9 12
        (c)

The distances between the median and the extremes are close, 4 and 5, but the differences in the tails are different (1 on the left and 3 on the right), so this distribution is slightly right-skewed.
        (d)   In 3.2 (d), because the mean and median are equal , the distribution is symmetric. The box part of the graph is symmetric, but the tails show right-skewness.

3.30   (a) $Q_1 = -6.5$, $Q_3 = 8$, interquartile range = 14.5
        (b)   Five-number summary: -8 -6.5 7 8 9

3.30   (c)
cont.

Box-and-whisker Plot

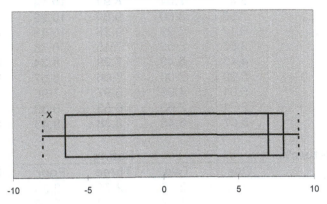

The distribution is left-skewed.

(d)   This is consistent with the answer in 3.4 (d).

3.32   Excel Output:

Statistic	Mobile Commerce Penetration (%)
Minimum	11.000
Maximum	55.000
1st Quartile	23.000
Median	27.500
3rd Quartile	36.250

Box plots:

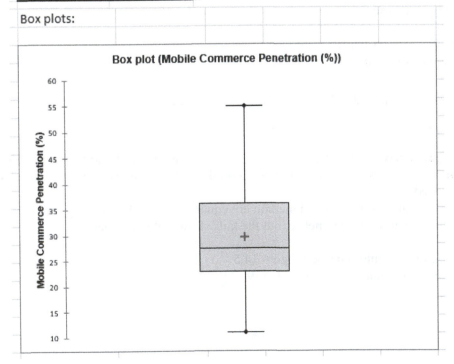

3.32   (a), (b)   Minimum = 11 Q_1 = 23, Median = 27.5 Q_3 = 37, Maximum = 55 Interquartile range = 14
cont.   (c)   the boxplot is right skewed.

3.34   (a)   Minitab Output:

Variable	Minimum	Q1	Median	Q3	Maximum	IQR
60 Second Ads	3.220	4.460	5.300	5.880	6.910	1.420
30 Second Ads	3.550	4.370	4.805	5.303	6.640	0.933

       (b)   five number summaries see Min, Q1, Median, Q3, Max
                *Note Minitab and Excel compute Q1 and Q3 differently then the method described in
                the text.
       (c)   Minitab Boxplots

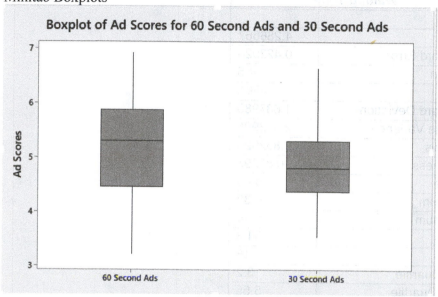

                The boxplot plot for 60 seconds ads is approximately symmetrical while the boxplot for
                the 30 seconds ads is right-skewed.

3.36   Excel output for Residential Area:

Waiting Time	
Mean	7.114667
Median	6.68
Mode	#N/A
Standard Deviation	2.082189
Sample Variance	4.335512
Range	6.67
Minimum	3.82
Maximum	10.49
Sum	106.72
Count	15
First Quartile	5.64
Third Quartile	8.73
Interquartile Range	3.09
Coefficient of Variation	29.2662%

3.36
cont.
Excel output for Residential Area:

Box-and-whisker Plot	
Five-number Summary	
Minimum	3.82
First Quartile	5.64
Median	6.68
Third Quartile	8.73
Maximum	10.49

Excel output for Commercial District:

Waiting Time	
Mean	4.286667
Standard Error	0.422926
Median	4.5
Mode	#N/A
Standard Deviation	1.637985
Sample Variance	2.682995
Kurtosis	0.832925
Skewness	−0.83295
Range	6.08
Minimum	0.38
Maximum	6.46
Sum	64.3
Count	15
First Quartile	3.2
Third Quartile	5.55
Interquartile Range	2.35
Coefficient of Variation	38.2112%

Box-and-whisker Plot	
Five-number Summary	
Minimum	0.38
First Quartile	3.2
Median	4.5
Third Quartile	5.55
Maximum	6.46

(a)   **Commercial district**: Five-number summary: 0.38 3.2 4.5 5.55 6.46
        Residential area: Five-number summary: 3.82 5.64 6.68 8.73 10.49

3.36   (b)   **Commercial district:**
cont.

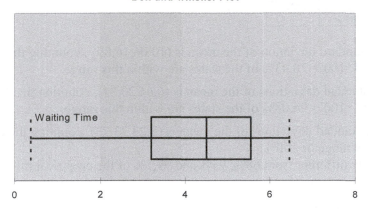

The distribution is skewed to the left.
Residential area:

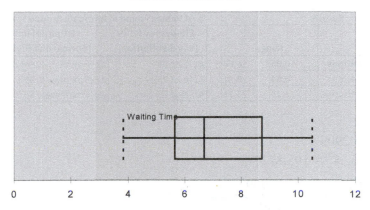

The distribution is skewed slightly to the right.

(c)   The central tendency of the waiting times for the bank branch located in the commercial district of a city is lower than that of the branch located in the residential area. There are a few longer than normal waiting times for the branch located in the residential area whereas there are a few exceptionally short waiting times for the branch located in the commercial area.

3.38   (a)   Population Mean = 6
        (b) $\sigma^2 = 2.8$ $\sigma = 1.67$

3.40   (a)   68%
        (b)   95%
        (c)   not calculable   75%   88.89%
        (d) $\mu - 4\sigma$ to $\mu + 4\sigma$ or −2.8 to 19.2

3.42   (a)

mean	13.477
variance	11.679
standard deviation	3.417

(b)   Within one standard deviation of the mean is $(10.06, 16.89)$, counting the data reveals 40 states or $40/51*100 = 78.43\%$ of the states are within this range.

Within two standad deviations of the mean is $(6.64, 20.31)$, counting the data reveals 49 states or $49/51*100 = 96.08\%$ of the states are within this range.

Within three standad deviations of the mean is $(3.23, 23.73)$, counting the data reveals all are within this range or 100%.

(c)   This is slightly different from 68%, 95% and 99.7% of the empirical rule.

Excel Output:

Variability in a Distribution				
Data				
Mean	13.477			
Standard Deviation	3.417			
Results			**% of Values Found in Intervals Around the Mean**	
			Chebyshev Rule	**Empirical Rule**
	Range		**(any distribution)**	**(normal distribution)**
±1 standard deviations	10.06	16.89	At least 0%	Approximately 68%
±2 standard deviations	6.64	20.31	At least 75%	Approximately 95%
±3 standard deviations	3.23	23.73	At least 88.89%	Approximately 99.7%

3.44   (a) $cov(X, Y) = 65.2909$

(b) $S_X^2 = 21.7636$, $S_Y^2 = 195.8727$

$$r = \frac{cov(X,Y)}{\sqrt{S_X^2}\sqrt{S_Y^2}} = \frac{65.2909}{\sqrt{21.7636}\sqrt{195.8727}} = +1.0$$

(c)   There is a perfect positive linear relationship between X and Y; all the points lie exactly on a straight line with a positive slope.

3.46   (a) $cov(X, Y) = 133.3333$

(b) $S_X^2 = 2200$, $S_Y^2 = 11.4762$

$$r = \frac{cov(X,Y)}{S_X S_Y} = 0.8391$$

(c)   The correlation coefficient is more valuable for expressing the relationship between calories and sugar because it does not depend on the units used to measure calories and sugar.

(d)   There is a strong positive linear relationship between calories and sugar.

3.48   Excel Output:

	A	B	C	D	E
1	Carrier	Download Speed	Upload Speed		
2	Verizon	24.0	14.3		
3	T-Mobile	22.7	13.2		
4	AT&T	20.8	9.1		
5	Metro PCS	16.7	11.1		
6	Sprint	11.2	6.4		
7	Virgin Mobile	10.8	6.2		
8	Boost	10.3	6.0		
9	Straight Talk	7.1	3.0		
10	Cricket	4.5	3.8		
11					
12	Covariance	26.9842	=COVARIANCE.S(B2:B10,C2:C10)		
13	r	0.94914	=CORREL(B2:B10,C2:C10)		
14					

(a) $cov(X,Y) = 26.9842$
(b)   Correlation = r = 0.9491
(c)   The is a strong positive linear relationship between download speed and upload speed.

3.50   We should look for ways to describe the typical value, the variation, and the distribution of the data within a range.

3.52   The arithmetic mean is a simple average of all the values, but is subject to the effect of extreme values. The median is the middle ranked value, but varies more from sample to sample than the arithmetic mean, although it is less susceptible to extreme values. The mode is the most common value, but is extremely variable from sample to sample.

3.54   Variation is the amount of dispersion, or "spread," in the data.

3.56   The range is a simple measure, but only measures the difference between the extremes. The interquartile range measures the range of the center fifty percent of the data. The standard deviation measures variation around the mean while the variance measures the squared variation around the mean, and these are the only measures that take into account each observation. The coefficient of variation measures the variation around the mean relative to the mean. The range, standard deviation, variance and coefficient of variation are all sensitive to outliers while the interquartile range is not.

3.58   The Chebyshev rule applies to any type of distribution while the empirical rule applies only to data sets that are approximately bell-shaped. The empirical rule is more accurate than the Chebyshev rule in approximating the concentration of data around the mean.

3.60   The arithmetic mean is appropriate if you want to obtain a typical value and serves as a "balance point" in a set of data, similar to the fulcrum on a seesaw. The geometric mean is appropriate when you want to measure the rate of change of a variable over time.

3.62   The covariance measures the strength of the linear relationship between two numerical variables while the coefficient of correlation measures the relative strength of the linear relationship. The value of the covariance depends very much on the units used to measure the two numerical variables while the value of the coefficient of correlation is totally free from the units used.

3.64   Excel output:

Time	
Mean	43.88889
Standard Error	4.865816
Median	45
Mode	17
Standard Deviation	25.28352
Sample Variance	639.2564
Range	76
Minimum	16
Maximum	92
First Quartile	18
Third Quartile	63
interquartile range	45
C.V	57.61%

(a)   Mean = 43.89   Median = 45   1st quartile = 18   3rd quartile = 63

(b)   Range = 76   Interquartile range = 45   Variance = 639.2564
       Standard Deviation = 25.28   Coefficient of variation = 57.61%

(c)

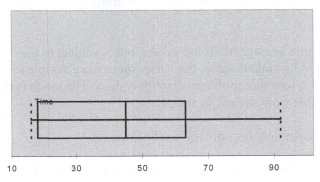

Box-and-whisker Plot

The distribution is skewed to the right because there are a few policies that require an exceptionally long period to be approved even though the mean is smaller than the median.

(d)   The mean approval process takes 43.89 days with 50% of the policies being approved in less than 45 days. 50% of the applications are approved between 18 and 63 days. About 67% of the applications are approved between 18.6 to 69.2 days.

3.66   (a)   Excel output:

Statistic	r Time (seconds)
Nbr. of observations	50
Minimum	5.000
Maximum	28.000
1st Quartile	12.000
Median	15.000
3rd Quartile	18.000
Mean	14.980
Standard deviation (n-1)	5.557

Box plots:

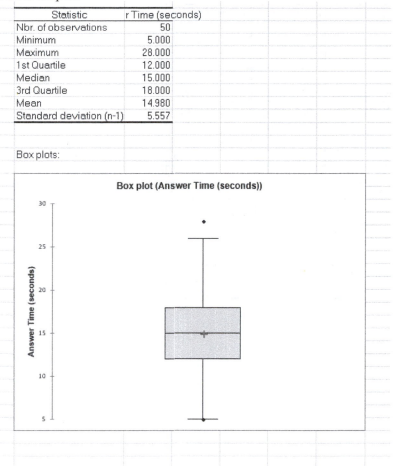

Minitab Output:

Variable	Mean	StDev	Median	Range
Answer Time (seconds)	14.980	5.557	15.000	23.000

(b)   Using the formulas in the text with n= 50, Q1 = (50+1)/4 ranked value = 12.75 ranked value so choose 13th ranked value which is 12. Q3 = 3(50+1)/4 ranked value = 38.25 ranked value so choose 38th ranked value which is 18
Therefore 5 number summary is min, Q1, median, Q3, max = 5, 12, 15, 18, 28

* Note Minitab uses a slightly different formula to calculate the quartiles

Variable	Minimum	Q1	Median	Q3	Maximum
Answer Time (seconds)	5.000	11.750	15.000	18.250	28.000

(c)   The distribution is symmetric.
(d)   The service level is met because 75% of the class are answered in less than 18 seconds.

3.68   (a), (b)

	Bundle Score	Typical Cost ($)
Mean	54.775	24.175
Standard Error	4.367344951	2.866224064
Median	62	20
Mode	75	8
Standard Deviation	27.62151475	18.12759265
Sample Variance	762.9480769	328.6096154
Kurtosis	-0.845357193	2.766393511
Skewness	-0.48041728	1.541239625
Range	98	83
Minimum	2	5
Maximum	100	88
Sum	2191	967
Count	40	40
First Quartile	34	9
Third Quartile	75	31
Interquartile Range	41	22
CV	50.43%	74.98%

(c)

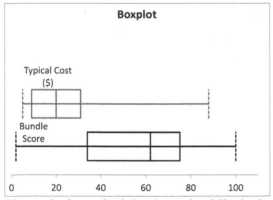

The typical cost is right-skewed, while the bundle score is left-skewed.

(d) $r = \dfrac{\text{cov}(X, Y)}{S_X S_Y} = 0.3465$

(e)   The mean typical cost is $24.18, with an average spread around the mean equaling $18.13. The spread between the lowest and highest costs is $83. The middle 50% of the typical cost fall over a range of $22 from $9 to $31, while half of the typical cost is below $20. The mean bundle score is 54.775, with an average spread around the mean equaling 27.6215. The spread between the lowest and highest scores is 98. The middle 50% of the scores fall over a range of 41 from 34 to 75, while half of the scores are below 62. The typical cost is right-skewed, while the bundle score is left-skewed. There is a weak positive linear relationship between typical cost and bundle score.

3.70   (a)   Excel output:

Five-number Summary

	Boston	Vermont
Minimum	0.04	0.02
First Quartile	0.17	0.13
Median	0.23	0.2
Third Quartile	0.32	0.28
Maximum	0.98	0.83

(b)

Box-and-whisker Plot

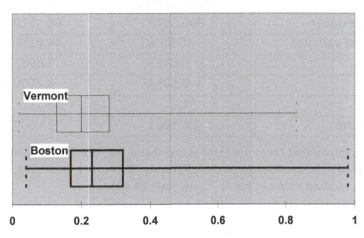

Both distributions are right skewed.

(c)   Both sets of shingles did quite well in achieving a granule loss of 0.8 gram or less. The Boston shingles had only two data points greater than 0.8 gram. The next highest to these was 0.6 gram. These two data points can be considered outliers. Only 1.176% of the shingles failed the specification. In the Vermont shingles, only one data point was greater than 0.8 gram. The next highest was 0.58 gram. Thus, only 0.714% of the shingles failed to meet the specification.

3.72   (a), (b), (c)

	Calories	*Protein*	*Cholesterol*
Calories	1		
Protein	0.464411	1	
Cholesterol	0.177665	0.141673	1

(d)   There is a rather weak positive linear relationship between calories and protein with a correlation coefficient of 0.46. The positive linear relationship between calories and cholesterol is quite weak at .178.

3.74   (a), (b)

	Annual Taxes on $176 Home	Median Home Value ($000)
Mean	1,979.490196	195.6509804
Median	1,763	165.9
Mode	#NA	#NA
Minimum	489	100.2
Maximum	4,029	504.5
Range	3,540	404.3
Variance	11,065.8549	7,418.7265
Standard Deviation	900.5919	86.1320
Coefficient of variance	45.50%	44.02%
Skewness	0.6423	1.6988
Kurtosis	−0.5014	3.3069
Count	51	51
Standard Error	126.1081	12.0609

(c)   The box plot shows that taxes are right skewed and the median value of homes is highly right skewed.(d) The coefficient of correlation is -0.041. (e) There is a large variation in taxes and the median value of homes from state to state.

3.76   (a), (b)

	Abandonment rate in % (7:00AM-3:00PM)
Mean	13.86363636
Standard Error	1.625414306
Median	10
Mode	9
Standard Deviation	7.623868875
Sample Variance	58.12337662
Kurtosis	0.723568739
Skewness	1.180708144
Range	29
Minimum	5
Maximum	34
Sum	305
Count	22
First Quartile	9
Third Quartile	20
Interquartile Range	11
CV	54.99%

3.76   (c)
cont.

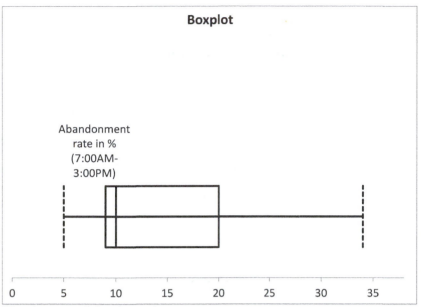

The data are right-skewed.

(d) $r = 0.7575$

(e)   The average abandonment rate is 13.86%. Half of the abandonment rates are less than 10%. One-quarter of the abandonment rates are less than 9% while another one-quarter are more than 20%. The overall spread of the abandonment rates is 29%. The middle 50% of the abandonment rates are spread over 11%. The average spread of abandonment rates around the mean is 7.62%. The abandonment rates are right-skewed.

3.78   (a)–(c) Excel output:

Statistic	/erage Credit Score
Range	214.510
1st Quartile	649.835
Median	672.015
3rd Quartile	697.195
Mean	673.244
Variance (n-1)	1005.878
Standard deviation (n-1)	31.716
IQR	47.360
Variation coefficient	0.047

3.78   (a)–(c)
cont.

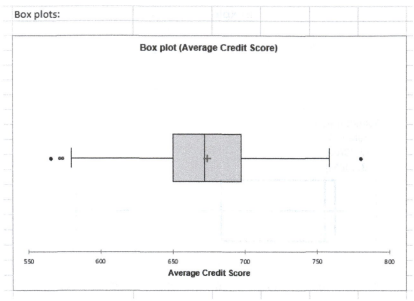

Box plots:

Box plot (Average Credit Score)

Average Credit Score

The data are symmetrical.

(d)   The mean of the average credit scores is 673.24. Half of the average credit scores are less than 672.02. One-quarter of the average credit scores are less than 649.84 while another one-quarter is more than 697.2. The range of the average credit score is 214.51. The middle 50% of the average credit scores is spread over 47.36. The typical spread of the average credit scores around the mean is 31.716.

3.80   Excel Output:

Statistic	Alcohol %	Carbohydrates	Calories
Nbr. of observations	158	158	158
Minimum	2.400	1.900	55.000
Maximum	11.500	32.100	330.000
Range	9.100	30.200	275.000
1st Quartile	4.425	8.750	131.250
Median	4.910	12.000	150.500
3rd Quartile	5.675	14.450	169.750
Mean	5.276	11.970	155.449
Variance (n-1)	1.845	23.617	1897.931
Standard deviation (n-1)	1.358	4.860	43.565
IQR	1.250	5.700	38.500
Variation coefficient	0.257	0.405	0.279
Skewness (Pearson)	1.797	0.451	1.213
Kurtosis (Pearson)	4.256	1.101	2.928
Standard error of the mean	0.108	0.387	3.466

3.80
cont.

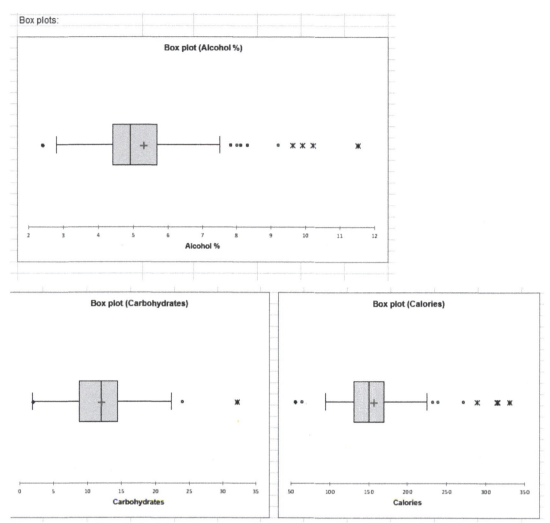

The amount of % alcohol is right skewed with an average at 5.27%. Half of the beers have % alcohol below 4.91%. The middle 50% of the beers have alcohol content spread over a range of 1.25%. The highest alcohol content is at 11.5% while the lowest is at 2.4%. The typical spread of alcohol content around the mean is 1.358%.

The number of calories is symmetric with two high outliers with an average at 155.449. Half of the beers have calories below 150.5. The middle 50% of the beers have calories spread over a range of 39. The highest number of calories is 330 while the lowest is 55. The typical spread of calories around the mean is 43.565.

The number of carbohydrates is right-skewed from the boxplot with an average at 11.970, which is almost identical to the median at 12.000. Half of the beers have carbohydrates below 12.000. The middle 50% of the beers have carbohydrates spread over a range of 5.7. The highest number of carbohydrates is 32.1 while the lowest is 1.9. The typical spread of carbohydrates around the mean is 4.860.

CHAPTER 4

4.2   (a)   Simple events include selecting a red ball.
      (b)   Selecting a white ball
      (c)   The sample space is the collection of "a red ball being selected" and "a white ball being selected."

4.4   (a) $\dfrac{60}{100} = \dfrac{3}{5} = 0.6$

      (b) $\dfrac{10}{100} = \dfrac{1}{10} = 0.1$

      (c) $\dfrac{35}{100} = \dfrac{7}{20} = 0.35$

      (d) $\dfrac{60}{100} + \dfrac{65}{100} - \dfrac{35}{100} = \dfrac{90}{100} = \dfrac{9}{10} = 0.9$

4.6   (a)   Mutually exclusive, not collectively exhaustive.
      (b)   Not mutually exclusive, not collectively exhaustive.
      (c)   Mutually exclusive, not collectively exhaustive.
      (d)   Mutually exclusive, collectively exhaustive

4.8   (a)   "Is a millennial."
      (b)   "Is a millennial and feels tense or stressed out at work."
      (c)   "Does not feel tense or stressed out at work."
      (d)   Is a millennial and feels tense or stressed out at work is a joint event because it consists of two characteristics.

4.10   Answers will vary.
      (a)   A marketer who plans to increase use of LinkedIn.
      (b)   A B2B marketer who plans to increase use of LinkedIn.
      (c)   A marketer who does not plan to increase use of LinkedIn.
      (d)   A marketer who plans to increase use of LinkedIn and is a B2C marketer is a joint event because it consists of two characteristics, plans to increase use of LinkedIn and is a B2C marketer.

4.12   (a) P(indicates gains in students learning justifies colleges spending) $= \dfrac{1,010}{1,740} = 0.5805$

      (b) P(is a technology leader) $= \dfrac{69}{1,740} = 0.0397$

      (c) P(indicates student gains have justified colleges spending in this area *or* is a technology leader) $= \dfrac{1,010}{1,740} + \dfrac{69}{1,740} - \dfrac{58}{1,740} = \dfrac{1,021}{1,740} = 0.5868$

      (d)   The probability in (c) includes the probability of selecting a professor who perceives that gains in students' learning attributable to education technology have justified colleges' spending, and therefore goes beyond the probability of selecting a technology leader.

4.14

Feels Overloaded	Male	Female	Total
Yes	134	170	304
No	651	565	1,216
Total	785	735	1,520

(a) $P(\text{feels overloaded}) = \dfrac{304}{1,520} = 0.20$

(b) $P(\text{female and feels overloaded}) = \dfrac{170}{1,520} = 0.1118$

(c) $P(\text{female or feels overloaded}) = \dfrac{735 + 304 - 170}{1,520} = \dfrac{869}{1,520} = 0.5717$

(d) $P(\text{male or female}) = \dfrac{1,520}{1,520} = 1.00$

4.16   (a) $P(A \mid B) = \dfrac{10}{30} = \dfrac{1}{3} = 0.33$

(b) $P(A \mid B') = \dfrac{20}{60} = \dfrac{1}{3} = 0.33$

(c) $P(A' \mid B') = \dfrac{40}{60} = \dfrac{2}{3} = 0.67$

(d)   Since $P(A \mid B) = P(A) = \dfrac{1}{3}$, events A and B are statistically independent.

4.18 $P(A \mid B) = \dfrac{P(A \text{ and } B)}{P(B)} = \dfrac{0.4}{0.8} = \dfrac{1}{2} = 0.5$

4.20   Since $P(A \text{ and } B) = 0.20$ and $P(A)\,P(B) = 0.12$, events A and B are not statistically independent.

4.22   (a) $P(\text{Increased use of LinkedIn} \mid \text{B2B marketer}) = \dfrac{1,353}{1,780} = 0.7601$

(b) $P(\text{Increased use of LinkedIn} \mid \text{B2C marketer}) = \dfrac{1,719}{3,306} = 0.5200$

(c) $P(\text{Increased use of LinkedIn}) = 0.6040$ and
$P(\text{Increased use of LinkedIn} \mid \text{B2B marketer}) = 0.7601$ are not equal.
Therefore, increased use of LinkedIn and business focus are not independent.

4.24   (a) $P(\text{gains in learning justifiy spending} \mid \text{professor}) = \dfrac{952}{1,671} = 0.5697$

(b) $P(\text{gains in learning do not justifiy spending} \mid \text{professor}) = \dfrac{719}{1,671} = 0.4303$

(c) $P(\text{gains in learning justifiy spending} \mid \text{technology leader}) = \dfrac{58}{69} = 0.8406$

4.24   (d) P(gains in learning do not justifiy spending | technology leader) = $\dfrac{11}{69} = 0.1594$

cont.

4.26

Needs Warranty-Related Repair	U.S.	Non-U.S.	Total
Yes	0.025	0.015	0.04
No	0.575	0.385	0.96
Total	0.600	0.400	1.00

(a) P(needs warranty repair | manufacturer based in U.S.) = $\dfrac{0.025}{0.6} = 0.0417$

(b) P(needs warranty repair | manufacturer not based in U.S.) = $\dfrac{0.015}{0.4} = 0.0375$

(c)   Since P(needs warranty repair | manufacturer based in U.S.) = $\dfrac{0.025}{0.6} = 0.0417$ is not

equal to P(needs warranty repair) = 0.04, the two events are not independent.

4.28   (a) P(both queens) = $\dfrac{4}{52} \cdot \dfrac{3}{51} = \dfrac{12}{2,652} = \dfrac{1}{221} = 0.0045$

(b) P(10 followed by 5 or 6) = $\dfrac{4}{52} \cdot \dfrac{8}{51} = \dfrac{32}{2,652} = \dfrac{8}{663} = 0.012$

(c) P(both queens) = $\dfrac{4}{52} \cdot \dfrac{4}{52} = \dfrac{16}{2,704} = \dfrac{1}{169} = 0.0059$

(d) P(blackjack) = $\dfrac{16}{52} \cdot \dfrac{4}{51} + \dfrac{4}{52} \cdot \dfrac{16}{51} = \dfrac{128}{2,652} = \dfrac{32}{663} = 0.0483$

4.30 $P(B \mid A) = \dfrac{P(A \mid B) \cdot P(B)}{P(A \mid B) \cdot P(B) + P(A \mid B') \cdot P(B')} = \dfrac{0.8 \cdot 0.05}{0.8 \cdot 0.05 + 0.4 \cdot 0.95} = \dfrac{0.04}{0.42} = 0.095$

4.32   (a) D = has disease T = tests positive

$P(D \mid T) = \dfrac{P(T \mid D) \cdot P(D)}{P(T \mid D) \cdot P(D) + P(T \mid D') \cdot P(D')} = \dfrac{0.9 \cdot 0.03}{0.9 \cdot 0.03 + 0.01 \cdot 0.97} = \dfrac{0.027}{0.0367} = 0.736$

(b) $P(D' \mid T') = \dfrac{P(T' \mid D') \cdot P(D')}{P(T' \mid D') \cdot P(D') + P(T' \mid D) \cdot P(D)}$

$= \dfrac{0.99 \cdot 0.97}{0.99 \cdot 0.97 + 0.10 \cdot 0.03} = \dfrac{0.9603}{0.9633} = 0.997$

4.34   (a) B = Base Construction Co. enters a bid O = Olive Construction Co. wins the contract

$P(B' \mid O) = \dfrac{P(O \mid B') \cdot P(B')}{P(O \mid B') \cdot P(B') + P(O \mid B) \cdot P(B)} = \dfrac{0.5 \cdot 0.3}{0.5 \cdot 0.3 + 0.25 \cdot 0.7} = \dfrac{0.15}{0.325} = 0.4615$

(b) $P(O) = 0.175 + 0.15 = 0.325$

4.36   (a) $P(\text{huge success} \mid \text{favorable review}) = \dfrac{0.099}{0.459} = 0.2157$

$P(\text{moderate success} \mid \text{favorable review}) = \dfrac{0.14}{0.459} = 0.3050$

$P(\text{break even} \mid \text{favorable review}) = \dfrac{0.16}{0.459} = 0.3486$

$P(\text{loser} \mid \text{favorable review}) = \dfrac{0.06}{0.459} = 0.1307$

   (b) $P(\text{favorable review}) = 0.99(0.1) + 0.7(0.2) + 0.4(0.4) + 0.2(0.3) = 0.459$

4.38 $3^{10} = 59049$

4.40   (a) $2^7 = 128$
        (b) $6^7 = 279936$
        (c)   There are two mutually exclusive and collectively exhaustive outcomes in (a) and six in (b).

4.42 $(5)(7)(4)(5) = 700$

4.44 $5! = (5)(4)(3)(2)(1) = 120;$ not all the orders are equally likely because the teams have a different probability of finishing first through fifth.

4.46 $n! = 6! = 720$

4.48 $_{10}C_4 = \dfrac{10!}{4!(6!)} = 210$

4.50 $_{100}C_2 = \dfrac{100!}{2!(98!)} = \dfrac{(100)(99)}{2} = 4950$

4.52   With a priori probability, the probability of success is based on prior knowledge of the process involved. With empirical probability, outcomes are based on observed data. Subjective probability refers to the chance of occurrence assigned to an event by a particular individual.

4.54   The general addition rule is used by adding the probability of A and the probability of B and then subtracting the joint probability of A and B.

4.56   If events A and B are statistically independent, the conditional probability of event A given B is equal to the probability of A.

4.58   Bayes' theorem uses conditional probabilities to revise the probability of an event in the light of new information.

4.60   For Counting Rule 1, the number of possible events is the same for each trial. Counting Rule 2 allows for the number of possible events to differ for each trial.

4.62   (a)

	Generation		
Prefer Hybrid Advice	**Boomers**	**Millennials**	**Total**
Yes	140	320	460
No	360	180	540
Total	500	500	1,000

(b)   A simple event is "prefers hybrid investment advice." A joint event is "being a baby boomer and preferring hybrid investment advice."

(c) $P(\text{prefers hybrid advice}) = \dfrac{460}{1,000} = 0.46$

(d) $P(\text{prefers hybrid advice } and \text{ is a baby boomer}) = \dfrac{140}{1,000} = 0.14$

(e)   They are not independent because baby boomers and millennials have different probabilities of preferring hybrid investment advice.

4.64   (a) $P(\text{creative display}) = \dfrac{82}{276} = 0.2971$

(b) $P(\text{creative display } or \text{ informational resources}) = \dfrac{82 + 33}{276} = \dfrac{115}{276} = 0.4167$

(c) $P(\text{business website } or \text{ online sales}) = \dfrac{129 + 45 - 32}{276} = \dfrac{142}{276} = 0.5145$

(d) $P(\text{business website } and \text{ online sales}) = \dfrac{32}{276} = 0.1159$

(e) $P(\text{online business presence} \mid \text{personal website}) = \dfrac{4}{147} = 0.0272$

4.66   (a) $P(\text{lack of process tools is a factor}) = \dfrac{125}{386} = 0.3238$

(b) $P(\text{lack of process tools is a factor} \mid \text{B2B firm}) = \dfrac{90}{272} = 0.3309$

(c) $P(\text{lack of process tools is a factor} \mid \text{B2C firm}) = \dfrac{35}{114} = 0.3070$

(d) $P(\text{lack of people who can link to practice}) = \dfrac{111}{386} = 0.2876$

(e) $P(\text{lack of people who can link to practice} \mid \text{B2B firm}) = \dfrac{75}{272} = 0.2757$

(f) $P(\text{lack of people who can link to practice} \mid \text{B2C firm}) = \dfrac{36}{114} = 0.3158$

(g)   There is very little difference between B2B and B2C firms.

CHAPTER 5

5.2 PHStat output:

Probabilities & Outcomes:	P	X
	0.1	0
	0.2	1
	0.45	2
	0.15	3
	0.05	4
	0.05	5
Statistics		
E(X)	2	
E(Y)	0	
Variance(X)	1.4	
Standard Deviation(X)	1.183216	
Variance(Y)	0	
Standard Deviation(Y)	0	
Covariance(XY)	0	
Variance(X+Y)	1.4	
Standard Deviation(X+Y)	1.183216	

(a)–(b)

X	$P(x)$	$X*P(X)$	$(X-\mu_X)^2$	$(X-\mu_X)^2*P(X)$
0	0.10	0.00	4	0.40
1	0.20	0.20	1	0.20
2	0.45	0.90	0	0.00
3	0.15	0.45	1	0.15
4	0.05	0.20	4	0.20
5	0.05	0.25	9	0.45

(a) Mean = 2.00 Variance = 1.40

(b) Stdev = 1.18321596

(c) $P(X \geq 2) = 0.45 + 0.15 + 0.05 + 0.05 = 0.70$

5.4 (a)

X	$P(X)$
$\$-1$	21/36
$\$+1$	15/36

(b)

X	$P(X)$
$\$-1$	21/36
$\$+1$	15/36

(c)

X	$P(X)$
$\$-1$	30/36
$\$+4$	6/36

5.4   (d) $ – 0.167 for each method of play
cont.

5.6   Excel Output:

	A	B	C	D	E	F
1	Arrivals = X	Frequency	Probability = Frequency/n	[X-E(X)]^2		
2	0	13	0.125	4.434	=(A2-B12)^2	
3	1	25	0.240384615	1.223	=(A3-B12)^2	
4	2	32	0.307692308	0.011	=(A4-B12)^2	
5	3	17	0.163461538	0.800	=(A5-B12)^2	
6	4	9	0.086538462	3.588	=(A6-B12)^2	
7	5	6	0.057692308	8.377	=(A7-B12)^2	
8	6	1	0.009615385	15.165	=(A8-B12)^2	
9	7	1	0.009615385	23.953	=(A9-B12)^2	
10			Statistics			
11	n		104 =SUM(B2:B9)			
12	E(x)		2.105769231 =SUMPRODUCT(A2:A9,C2:C9)			
13	Variance (X)		2.152274408 =SUMPRODUCT(C2:C9,D2:D9)			
14	Standard Deviation (X)		1.467063192 =SQRT(B13)			
15	P(X>1)		0.634615385 =SUM(C4:C9)			

(a) $\mu = E(X) = 2.1058$
(b) $\sigma = 1.4671$
(c)   P(X>1) = P(X=2)+ P(X=3)+ P(X=4)+ P(X=5)+ P(X=6)+ P(X=7) = 0.6346

5.8   Excel Output:

	A	B	C	D	E
1	Corporate Bond Fund X	Probability	[X-E(X)]^2		
2	-300	0.01	128307.24	=(A2-B12)^2	
3	-70	0.09	16435.24	=(A3-B12)^2	
4	30	0.15	795.24	=(A4-B12)^2	
5	60	0.35	3.24	=(A5-B12)^2	
6	100	0.3	1747.24	=(A6-B12)^2	
7	120	0.1	3819.24	=(A7-B12)^2	
8					
9					
10					
11			Statistics		
12	E(X)		58.2 =SUMPRODUCT(A2:A7,B2:B7)		
13	Variance(X)		3788.76 =SUMPRODUCT(B2:B7,C2:C7)		
14	Standard Deviation (X)		61.55290407 =SQRT(B13)		
15					
16					

5.8
cont.

	A	B	C	D	E
1	**Common Stock Fund** **X**	**Probability**	**[X−E(X)]^2**		
2	-999	0.01	1127865.24	=(A2-B12)^2	
3	-300	0.09	131776.2601	=(A3-B12)^2	
4	-100	0.15	26572.2601	=(A4-B12)^2	
5	100	0.35	1368.2601	=(A5-B12)^2	
6	150	0.3	7567.2601	=(A6-B12)^2	
7	350	0.1	82363.2601	=(A7-B12)^2	
8					
9					
10					
11		**Statistics**			
12	**E(X)**		63.01	=SUMPRODUCT(A2:A7,B2:B7)	
13	**Variance(X)**		38109.7499	=SUMPRODUCT(B2:B7,C2:C7)	
14	**Standard Deviation (X)**		195.2171865	=SQRT(B13)	
15					

(a)   E(Bond Fund) = \$58.20; E(Common Stock Fund) = \$63.01

(b) $\sigma_{\text{bond fund}}$ = \$61.55; $\sigma_{\text{common stock fund}}$ = \$195.22

(c)   Based on the expected value criteria, you would choose the common stock fund.
      However, the common stock fund also has a standard deviation more than three times
      higher than that for the corporate bond fund. An investor should carefully weigh the
      increased risk.

(d)   If you chose the common stock fund, you would need to assess your reaction to the small
      possibility that you could lose virtually all of your entire investment.

5.10   (a) $E(\text{total time}) = E(\text{time waiting}) + E(\text{time served}) = 4 + 5.5 = 9.5$ minutes

       (b) $\sigma(\text{total time}) = \sqrt{1.2^2 + 1.5^2} = 1.9209$ minutes

5.12   Excel Output:

	A	B	C	D
1	Binomial Probabilities			
2				
3	Data			
4	Sample size	6		
5	Probability of an event of interest	0.51		
6				
7	Parameters			
8	Mean	3.06		
9	Variance	1.4994		
10	Standard deviation	1.2245		
11				
12	Binomial Probabilities Table			
13	X	P(X)		
14	0	0.0138		
15	1	0.0864		
16	2	0.2249		
17	3	0.3121		
18	4	0.2436		
19	5	0.1014		
20	6	0.0176		
21				
22	Prob(at least 4) = P(X>= 4)	0.3627	=SUM(B18:B20)	
23				

(a) $P(X = 4) = 0.2436$

(b) $P(X = 6) = 0.0176$

(c) $P(X \geq 4) = 0.2436 + 0.1014 + 0.0176 = 0.3627$

(d) $\mu = 3.06$, $\sigma = 1.2245$

(e)   That each American adult owns a tablet or does not own a tablet and that next six adults selected are independent.

5.14   Excel Output:

	A	B	C	D
1	**Binomial Probabilities**			
2				
3	**Data**			
4	**Sample size**	10		
5	**Probability of an event of interest**	0.03		
6				
7	**Parameters**			
8	**Mean**	0.3		
9	**Variance**	0.291		
10	**Standard deviation**	0.53944		
11				
12	**Binomial Probabilities Table**			
13		**X**	**P(X)**	
14		0	0.7374	
15		1	0.2281	
16		2	0.0317	
17		3	0.0026	
18		4	0.0001	
19		5	0.0000	
20		6	0.0000	
21		7	0.0000	
22		8	0.0000	
23		9	0.0000	
24		10	0.0000	
25				
26	Prob(two or fewer) = P(X<=2)		0.9972	=SUM(B14:B16)
27	Prob(Three or more) = P(X>=3)		0.0028	=SUM(B17:B24)
28				

(a) $P(X = 0) = 0.7374$
(b) $P(X = 1) = 0.2281$
(c) $P(X \leq 2) = 0.9972$
(d) $P(X \geq 3) = 0.0028$

5.16   Excel Output:

▲	A	B	C	D
1	Binomial Probabilities			
2				
3	Data			
4	Sample size	3		
5	Probability of an event of interest	0.905		
6				
7	Parameters			
8	Mean	2.715		
9	Variance	0.25793		
10	Standard deviation	0.50786		
11				
12	Binomial Probabilities Table			
13	X	P(X)		
14	0	0.0009		
15	1	0.0245		
16	2	0.2334		
17	3	0.7412		
18				
19	Prob(at least 2) = P(X>=2)	0.9746	=SUM(B16:B17)	
20				

(a) $P(X = 3) = 0.7412$
(b) $P(X = 0) = 0.0009$
(c) $P(X \geq 2) = 0.9746$
(d) $E(X) = 2.715$ $\sigma_X = .5079$

On the average, over the long run, you theoretically expect 2.715 orders to be filled correctly in a sample of 3 orders with a standard deviation of 0.5079

(e)   McDonald's has a slightly higher probability of filling orders correctly.

5.18   (a)   Partial PHStat output:

Poisson Probabilities						
Data						
Average/Expected number of successes:			2.5			
Poisson Probabilities Table						
	X	P(X)	P(<=X)	P(<X)	P(>X)	P(>=X)
	2	0.256516	0.543813	0.287297	0.456187	0.712703

Using the equation, if $\lambda = 2.5$, $P(X = 2) = \dfrac{e^{-2.5} \cdot (2.5)^2}{2!} = 0.2565$

5.18   (b)   Partial PHStat output:
cont.

Poisson Probabilities						
Data						
Average/Expected number of successes:			8			
Poisson Probabilities Table						
	X	P(X)	P(<=X)	P(<X)	P(>X)	P(>=X)
	8	0.139587	0.592547	0.452961	0.407453	0.547039

If $\lambda = 8.0$, $P(X = 8) = 0.1396$

(c)   Partial PHStat output:

Poisson Probabilities						
Data						
Average/Expected number of successes:			0.5			
Poisson Probabilities Table						
	X	P(X)	P(<=X)	P(<X)	P(>X)	P(>=X)
	0	0.606531	0.606531	0.000000	0.393469	1.000000
	1	0.303265	0.909796	0.606531	0.090204	0.393469

If $\lambda = 0.5$, $P(X = 1) = 0.3033$

(d)   Partial PHStat output:

Poisson Probabilities						
Data						
Average/Expected number of successes:			3.7			
Poisson Probabilities Table						
	X	P(X)	P(<=X)	P(<X)	P(>X)	P(>=X)
	0	0.024724	0.024724	0.000000	0.975276	1.000000

If $\lambda = 3.7$, $P(X = 0) = 0.0247$

5.20   PHStat output for (a) – (d)

Poisson Probabilities Table	X	P(X)	P(<=X)	P(<X)	P(>X)	P(>=X)
	0	0.006738	0.006738	0.000000	0.993262	1.000000
	1	0.033690	0.040428	0.006738	0.959572	0.993262
	2	0.084224	0.124652	0.040428	0.875348	0.959572
	3	0.140374	0.265026	0.124652	0.734974	0.875348
	4	0.175467	0.440493	0.265026	0.559507	0.734974
	5	0.175467	0.615961	0.440493	0.384039	0.559507
	6	0.146223	0.762183	0.615961	0.237817	0.384039
	7	0.104445	0.866628	0.762183	0.133372	0.237817
	8	0.065278	0.931906	0.866628	0.068094	0.133372
	9	0.036266	0.968172	0.931906	0.031828	0.068094
	10	0.018133	0.986305	0.968172	0.013695	0.031828
	11	0.008242	0.994547	0.986305	0.005453	0.013695
	12	0.003434	0.997981	0.994547	0.002019	0.005453
	13	0.001321	0.999302	0.997981	0.000698	0.002019
	14	0.000472	0.999774	0.999302	0.000226	0.000698
	15	0.000157	0.999931	0.999774	0.000069	0.000226
	16	0.000049	0.999980	0.999931	0.000020	0.000069
	17	0.000014	0.999995	0.999980	0.000005	0.000020
	18	0.000004	0.999999	0.999995	0.000001	0.000005
	19	0.000001	1.000000	0.999999	0.000000	0.000001
	20	0.000000	1.000000	1.000000	0.000000	0.000000

Given $\lambda = 5.0$,
(a) $P(X = 1) = 0.0337$
(b) $P(X < 1) = 0.0067$
(c) $P(X > 1) = 0.9596$
(d) $P(X \leq 1) = 0.0404$

5.22   (a)–(c)   Portion of PHStat output

	Data					
	Average/Expected number of successes:			6		
	Poisson Probabilities Table					
	X	P(X)	P(<=X)	P(<X)	P(>X)	P(>=X)
	0	0.002479	0.002479	0.000000	0.997521	1.000000
	1	0.014873	0.017351	0.002479	0.982649	0.997521
	2	0.044618	0.061969	0.017351	0.938031	0.982649
	3	0.089235	0.151204	0.061969	0.848796	0.938031
	4	0.133853	0.285057	0.151204	0.714943	0.848796
	5	(b)	0.445680	(a)	0.554320	(c)
		0.160623		0.285057		0.714943
	6	0.160623	0.606303	0.445680	0.393697	0.554320
	7	0.137677	0.743980	0.606303	0.256020	0.393697
	8	0.103258	0.847237	0.743980	0.152763	0.256020
	9	0.068838	0.916076	0.847237	0.083924	0.152763
	10	0.041303	0.957379	0.916076	0.042621	0.083924
	11	0.022529	0.979908	0.957379	0.020092	0.042621
	12	0.011264	0.991173	0.979908	0.008827	0.020092
	13	0.005199	0.996372	0.991173	0.003628	0.008827
	14	0.002228	0.998600	0.996372	0.001400	0.003628
	15	0.000891	0.999491	0.998600	0.000509	0.001400
	16	0.000334	0.999825	0.999491	0.000175	0.000509
	17	0.000118	0.999943	0.999825	0.000057	0.000175

(a) $P(X < 5) = P(X = 0) + P(X = 1) + P(X = 2) + P(X = 3) + P(X = 4)$

$$= \frac{e^{-6}(6)^0}{0!} + + \frac{e^{-6}(6)^2}{2!} + \frac{e^{-6}(6)^3}{3!} + \frac{e^{-6}(6)^4}{4!}$$

$$= 0.002479 + 0.014873 + 0.044618 + 0.089235 + 0.133853 = 0.2851$$

(b) $P(X = 5) = \dfrac{e^{-6}(6)^5}{5!} = 0.1606$

(c) $P(X \geq 5) = 1 - P(X < 5) = 1 - 0.2851 = 0.7149$

(d) $P(X = 4 \text{ or } X = 5) = P(X = 4) + P(X = 5) = \dfrac{e^{-6}(6)^4}{4!} + \dfrac{e^{-6}(6)^5}{5!} = 0.2945$

$$= \frac{e^{-6}(6)^1}{1!}$$

5.24   Excel Output:

	A	B	C	D	E	F
1	Poisson Probabilities					
2						
3				Data		
4	Mean/Expected number of events of interest:				1.35	
5						
6	Poisson Probabilities Table					
7	X	P(X)		(b) P(At least 1) = 1- P(X = 0)		0.7408
8	0	0.2592		c) P(At least 2) = 1 - P(X <=1)		0.3908
9	1	0.3500				
10	2	0.2362				
11	3	0.1063				
12	4	0.0359				
13	5	0.0097				
14	6	0.0022				
15	7	0.0004				
16	8	0.0001				
17	9	0.0000				
18	10	0.0000				

(a) $P(X = 0) = 0.2592$
(b) $P(X \geq 1) = 1 - P(X = 0) = 1-0.2592 = 0.7408$
(c) $P(X \geq 2) = 1 - P(X \leq 1) = 1 - [0.2592 + 0.35] = 0.3908$

5.26   Excel Output:

	A	B	C	D	E	F	G
1	Poisson Probabilities						
2							
3				Data			
4	Mean/Expected number of events of interest:				3.5		
5							
6	Poisson Probabilities Table						
7	X	P(X)		(c) P(more than 1) = 1- P(X < =1)		0.8641	
8	0	0.0302		(d) P(fewer than 2) = P(X <=1)		0.1359	
9	1	0.1057					
10	2	0.1850					
11	3	0.2158					
12	4	0.1888					
13	5	0.1322					
14	6	0.0771					
15	7	0.0385					
16	8	0.0169					
17	9	0.0066					
18	10	0.0023					
19	11	0.0007					
20	12	0.0002					
21	13	0.0001					

(a) $P(X = 0) = 0.0302$
(b) $P(X = 1) = 0.1057$

5.26   (c) $P(X > 1) = 1 - P(X \le 1) = 1 - [0.0302 + 0.1057] = 0.8641$
cont. (d) $P(X < 2) = P(X \le 1) = 0.0302 + 0.1057 = 0.1359$

5.28   Excel Output:

	A	B	C	D	E	F
1	Poisson Probabilities					
2						
3				Data		
4	Mean/Expected number of events of interest:				0.93	
5						
6	Poisson Probabilities Table					
7	X	P(X)		(c) P(x<=2)		0.9321
8	0	0.3946				
9	1	0.3669				
10	2	0.1706				
11	3	0.0529				
12	4	0.0123				
13	5	0.0023				
14	6	0.0004				
15	7	0.0000				

(a) $P(X = 0) = 0.3946$
(b) $P(X \le 2) = P(X = 0) + P(X = 1) + P(X = 2) = 0.9321$
(c)   Because Ford had a higher mean rate of problems per car than Toyota, the probability of a randomly selected Ford having zero problems and the probability of no more than two problems are both lower than for Toyota.

5.30   The expected value is the average of a probability distribution. It is the value that can be expected to occur on the average, in the long run.

5.32   The four properties of a situation that must be present in order to use the Poisson distribution are (i) you are interested in counting the number of times a particular event occurs in a given area of opportunity (defined by time, length, surface area, and so forth), (ii) the probability that an event occurs in a given area of opportunity is the same for all of the areas of opportunity, (iii) the number of events that occur in one area of opportunity is independent of the number of events that occur in other areas of opportunity and (iv) the probability that two or more events will occur in an area of opportunity approaches zero as the area of opportunity becomes smaller.

5.34   (a)   0.67

5.34   (b)   0.67
cont.   Partial PHstat output:
                Binomial Probabilities

Data	
Sample size	5
Probability of an event of interest	0.67

Statistics	
Mean	3.35
Variance	1.1055
Standard deviation	1.0514

Binomial Probabilities Table

X	P(X)	P(<=X)	P(<X)	P(>X)	P(>=X)
0	0.0039	0.0039	0.0000	0.9961	1.0000
1	0.0397	0.0436	0.0039	0.9564	0.9961
2	0.1613	0.2050	0.0436	0.7950	0.9564
3	0.3275	0.5325	0.2050	0.4675	0.7950
4	0.3325	0.8650	0.5325	0.1350	0.4675
5	0.1350	1.0000	0.8650	0.0000	0.1350

$\pi = 0.67$, $n = 5$

(c) $P(X = 4) = 0.3325$

(d) $P(X = 0) = 0.0039$

(e)   Stock prices tend to rise in the years when the economy is expanding and fall in the years of recession or contraction. Hence, the probability that the price will rise in one year is not independent from year to year.

5.36   Excel Output

Binomial Probabilities		
Data		
Sample size	14	
Probability of an event of interest	0.5	
Parameters		
Mean	7	
Variance	3.5	
Standard deviation	1.87083	
Binomial Probabilities Table		
	X	**P(X)**
	0	0.0001
	1	0.0009
	2	0.0056
	3	0.0222
	4	0.0611
	5	0.1222
	6	0.1833
	7	0.2095
	8	0.1833
	9	0.1222
	10	0.0611
	11	0.0222
	12	0.0056
	13	0.0009
	14	0.0001
P(X>=11)	0.0287	=SUM(B25:B28)

(a) $P(X \geq 11) = 0.0287$

5.36
cont.
(b)   Excel Output

	A	B	C	D
1	Binomial Probabilities			
2				
3	Data			
4	Sample size	14		
5	Probability of an event of interest	0.75		
6				
7	Parameters			
8	Mean	10.5		
9	Variance	2.625		
10	Standard deviation	1.62019		
11				
12	Binomial Probabilities Table			
13	X	P(X)		
14	0	0.0000		
15	1	0.0000		
16	2	0.0000		
17	3	0.0000		
18	4	0.0003		
19	5	0.0018		
20	6	0.0082		
21	7	0.0280		
22	8	0.0734		
23	9	0.1468		
24	10	0.2202		
25	11	0.2402		
26	12	0.1802		
27	13	0.0832		
28	14	0.0178		
29				
30	P(X>=11)	0.5213	=SUM(B25:B28)	
31				

$P(X \geq 11) = 0.5213$

5.38   Excel Output:

	A	B	C	D
1	Binomial Probabilities			
2				
3	Data			
4	Sample size	10		
5	Probability of an event of interest	0.4		
6				
7	Parameters			
8	Mean	4		
9	Variance	2.4		
10	Standard deviation	1.54919		
11				
12	Binomial Probabilities Table			
13	X	P(X)		
14	0	0.0060		
15	1	0.0403		
16	2	0.1209		
17	3	0.2150		
18	4	0.2508		
19	5	0.2007		
20	6	0.1115		
21	7	0.0425		
22	8	0.0106		
23	9	0.0016		
24	10	0.0001		
25				
26	P(x >5)	0.1662	=SUM(B20:B24)	

(a) $P(X=0) = 0.0060$

(b) $P(X=5) = .2007$

(c) $P(X > 5) = 0.1662$

(d) $\mu = 4$, $\sigma = 2.4$

(e)   Since the percentage of bills containing an error is lower in this problem, the probability is higher in (a) and (b) of this problem and lower in (c).

5.40   Excel Output:

	A	B	C	D
1	Binomial Probabilities			
2				
3	Data			
4	Sample size	20		
5	Probability of an event of interest	0.46		
6				
7	Parameters			
8	Mean	9.2		
9	Variance	4.968		
10	Standard deviation	2.2289		
11				
12	Binomial Probabilities Table			
13	X	P(X)		
14	0	0.0000		
15	1	0.0001		
16	2	0.0006		
17	3	0.0031		
18	4	0.0113		
19	5	0.0309		
20	6	0.0658		
21	7	0.1122		
22	8	0.1553		
23	9	0.1763		
24	10	0.1652		
25	11	0.1280		
26	12	0.0818		
27	13	0.0429		
28	14	0.0183		
29	15	0.0062		
30	16	0.0017		
31	17	0.0003		
32	18	0.0000		
33	19	0.0000		
34	20	0.0000		
35				
36	P(No more than 5) = P(X<=5)	0.0461	=SUM(B14:B19)	
37	P(5 or more) = P(X>=5)	0.9848	=SUM(B19:B34)	

(a) $E(X) = \mu = 9.2$

(b) $\sigma = 2.2289$

(c) $P(X = 10) = 0.1652$

(d) $P(X \leq 5) = 0.0461$

(e) $P(X \geq 5) = 0.9848$

5.42   (a) $\pi = 0.5$, $P(X \geq 7) = 2.2169 \times 10^{-7}$

       (b) $\pi = 0.7$, $P(X \geq 7) = 0.0054$

       (c) $\pi = 0.9$, $P(X \geq 37) = 0.7604$

       (d)   Based on the results in (a)–(c), the probability that the Standard & Poor's 500 index will increase if there is an early gain in the first five trading days of the year is very likely to be close to 0.90 because that yields a probability of 76.04% that at least 37 of the 42 years the Standard & Poor's 500 index will increase the entire year.

5.44   Excel Output

◢	A	B	C	D	E
1	Poisson Probabilities				
2					
3			Data		
4	Mean/Expected number of events of interest:				7
5					
6	Poisson Probabilities Table				
7	X	P(X)			
8	0	0.0009			
9	1	0.0064			
10	2	0.0223			
11	3	0.0521			
12	4	0.0912			
13	5	0.1277			
14	6	0.1490			
15	7	0.1490			
16	8	0.1304			
17	9	0.1014			
18	10	0.0710			
19	11	0.0452			
20	12	0.0263			
21	13	0.0142			
22	14	0.0071			
23	15	0.0033			
24	16	0.0014			
25	17	0.0006			
26	18	0.0002			
27	19	0.0001			
28	20	0.0000			
29					
30	P(10 or fewer)	0.9015	=SUM(B8:B18)		
31	P(11 or more))	0.0985	=SUM(B19:B28)		
32					

       (a)   The assumptions needed are (i) the probability that a questionable claim is referred by an investigator is constant, (ii) the probability that a questionable claim is referred by an investigator approaches 0 as the interval gets smaller, and (iii) the probability that a questionable claim is referred by an investigator is independent from interval to interval.

       (b) $P(X=5) = 0.1277$

       (c) $P(X \leq 10) = 0.9015$

       (d) $P(X \geq 11) = 0.0985$

CHAPTER 6

6.2   PHStat output:

Normal Probabilities				
Common Data				
Mean	0			
Standard Deviation	1			
			Probability for a Range	
Probability for X <=			From X Value	1.57
X Value	−1.57		To X Value	1.84
Z Value	−1.57		Z Value for 1.57	1.57
P(X<=−1.57)	0.0582076		Z Value for 1.84	1.84
			P(X<=1.57)	0.9418
Probability for X >			P(X<=1.84)	0.9671
X Value	1.84		P(1.57<=X<=1.84)	0.0253
Z Value	1.84			
P(X>1.84)	0.0329		**Find X and Z Given Cum. Pctage.**	
			Cumulative Percentage	84.13%
Probability for X<−1.57 or X >1.84			Z Value	0.999815
P(X<−1.57 or X >1.84)	0.0911		X Value	0.999815

(a) $P(-1.57 < Z < 1.84) = 0.9671 - 0.0582 = 0.9089$
(b) $P(Z < -1.57) + P(Z > 1.84) = 0.0582 + 0.0329 = 0.0911$
(c)   If $P(Z > A) = 0.025$, $P(Z < A) = 0.975$. $A = +1.96$.
(d)   If $P(-A < Z < A) = 0.6826$, $P(Z < A) = 0.8413$. So 68.26% of the area is captured between $-A = -1.00$ and $A = +1.00$.

6.4   PHStat output:

Normal Probabilities				
Common Data				
Mean	0			
Standard Deviation	1			
			Probability for a Range	
Probability for X <=			From X Value	−1.96
X Value	−0.21		To X Value	−0.21
Z Value	−0.21		Z Value for −1.96	−1.96
P(X<=−0.21)	0.4168338		Z Value for −0.21	−0.21
			P(X<=−1.96)	0.0250
Probability for X >			P(X<=−0.21)	0.4168
X Value	1.08		P(−1.96<=X<=−0.21)	0.3918
Z Value	1.08			
P(X>1.08)	0.1401		**Find X and Z Given Cum. Pctage.**	
			Cumulative Percentage	84.13%
Probability for X<−0.21 or X >1.08			Z Value	0.999815
P(X<−0.21 or X >1.08)	0.5569		X Value	0.999815

(a) $P(Z > 1.08) = 1 - 0.8599 = 0.1401$

6.4	(b)	$P(Z < -0.21) = 0.4168$
cont.	(c)	$P(-1.96 < Z < -0.21) = 0.4168 - 0.0250 = 0.3918$
	(d)	$P(Z > A) = 0.1587$, $P(Z < A) = 0.8413$. $A = +1.00$.

6.6   (a)   Partial PHStat output:

Common Data					
Mean	50				
Standard Deviation	4				
				Probability for a Range	
Probability for X <=				From X Value	42
X Value	42			To X Value	43
Z Value	−2			Z Value for 42	−2
P(X<=42)	0.0227501			Z Value for 43	−1.75
				P(X<=42)	0.0228
Probability for X >				P(X<=43)	0.0401
X Value	43			P(42<=X<=43)	0.0173
Z Value	−1.75				
P(X>43)	0.9599			**Find X and Z Given Cum. Pctage.**	
				Cumulative Percentage	5.00%
Probability for X<42 or X >43				Z Value	−1.644854
P(X<42 or X >43)	0.9827			X Value	43.42059

$$P(X > 43) = P(Z > -1.75) = 1 - 0.0401 = 0.9599$$

(b) $P(X < 42) = P(Z < -2.00) = 0.0228$

(c) $P(X < A) = 0.05$,

$$Z = -1.645 = \frac{A - 50}{4} \qquad A = 50 - 1.645(4) = 43.42$$

(d)   Partial PHStat output:

Find X and Z Given Cum. Pctage.	
Cumulative Percentage	80.00%
Z Value	0.841621
X Value	53.36648

$P(X_{lower} < X < X_{upper}) = 0.60$

$P(Z < -0.84) = 0.20$ and $P(Z < 0.84) = 0.80$

$$Z = -0.84 = \frac{X_{lower} - 50}{4} \qquad Z = +0.84 = \frac{X_{upper} - 50}{4}$$

$X_{lower} = 50 - 0.84(4) = 46.64$ and $X_{upper} = 50 + 0.84(4) = 53.36$

6.8   Partial PHStat output:

Common Data	
Mean	50
Standard Deviation	12

Probability for X <=	
X Value	30
Z Value	−1.666667
P(X<=30)	0.0477904

Probability for X >	
X Value	60
Z Value	0.8333333
P(X>60)	0.2023

Probability for X<30 or X >60	
P(X<30 or X >60)	0.2501

Probability for a Range	
From X Value	34
To X Value	50
Z Value for 34	−1.333333
Z Value for 50	0
P(X<=34)	0.0912
P(X<=50)	0.5000
P(34<=X<=50)	0.4088

Find X and Z Given Cum. Pctage.	
Cumulative Percentage	20.00%
Z Value	−0.841621
X Value	39.90055

(a) $P(34 < X < 50) = P(-1.33 < Z < 0) = 0.4088$

(b) $P(X < 30) + P(X > 60) = P(Z < -1.67) + P(Z > 0.83)$
$$= 0.0475 + (1.0 - 0.7967) = 0.2508$$

(c) $P(X > A) = 0.80$ $P(Z < -0.84) \cong 0.20$ $Z = -0.84 = \dfrac{A - 50}{12}$

$A = 50 - 0.84(12) = 39.92$ thousand miles or 39,920 miles

(d)   Partial PHStat output:

Common Data	
Mean	50
Standard Deviation	10

Probability for X <=	
X Value	30
Z Value	−2
P(X<=30)	0.0227501

Probability for X >	
X Value	60
Z Value	1
P(X>60)	0.1587

Probability for X<30 or X >60	
P(X<30 or X >60)	0.1814

Probability for a Range	
From X Value	34
To X Value	50
Z Value for 34	−1.6
Z Value for 50	0
P(X<=34)	0.0548
P(X<=50)	0.5000
P(34<=X<=50)	0.4452

Find X and Z Given Cum. Pctage.	
Cumulative Percentage	20.00%
Z Value	−0.841621
X Value	41.58379

The smaller standard deviation makes the Z-values larger.

(a) $P(34 < X < 50) = P(-1.60 < Z < 0) = 0.4452$

(b) $P(X < 30) + P(X > 60) = P(Z < -2.00) + P(Z > 1.00)$
$$= 0.0228 + (1.0 - 0.8413) = 0.1815$$

(c) $A = 50 - 0.84(10) = 41.6$ thousand miles or 41,600 miles

6.10   PHStat output:

Common Data	
Mean	73
Standard Deviation	8

Probability for X <=	
X Value	91
Z Value	2.25
P(X<=91)	0.9877755

Probability for X >	
X Value	81
Z Value	1
P(X>81)	0.1587

Probability for X<91 or X >81	
P(X<91 or X >81)	1.1464

Probability for a Range	
From X Value	65
To X Value	89
Z Value for 65	−1
Z Value for 89	2
P(X<=65)	0.1587
P(X<=89)	0.9772
P(65<=X<=89)	0.8186

Find X and Z Given Cum. Pctage.	
Cumulative Percentage	95.00%
Z Value	1.644854
X Value	86.15883

(a) $P(X < 91) = P(Z < 2.25) = 0.9878$

(b) $P(65 < X < 89) = P(-1.00 < Z < 2.00) = 0.9772 - 0.1587 = 0.8185$

(c) $P(X > A) = 0.05$ $P(Z < 1.645) = 0.9500$

$$Z = 1.645 = \frac{A - 73}{8}$$ $A = 73 + 1.645(8) = 86.16\%$

(d)   Option 1: $P(X > A) = 0.10$ $P(Z < 1.28) \cong 0.9000$

$$Z = \frac{81 - 73}{8} = 1.00$$

Since your score of 81% on this exam represents a Z-score of 1.00, which is below the minimum Z-score of 1.28, you will not earn an "A" grade on the exam under this grading option.

Option 2: $Z = \frac{68 - 62}{3} = 2.00$

Since your score of 68% on this exam represents a Z-score of 2.00, which is well above the minimum Z-score of 1.28, you will earn an "A" grade on the exam under this grading option. You should prefer Option 2.

6.12   (a) $P(X > 750) = P(Z > 1) = 0.1587$

Probability for X >	
X Value	750
Z Value	1
P(X>750)	0.1587

6.12   (b) $P(450 < X < 500) = P(-2 < Z < -1.5) = 0.0441$
cont.

Probability for a Range	
From X Value	450
To X Value	500
Z Value for 450	-2
Z Value for 500	-1.5
P(X<=450)	0.0228
P(X<=500)	0.0668
P(450<=X<=500)	0.0441

(c) $P(X < 450) = P(Z < -2) = 0.0228$

Probability for X <=	
X Value	450
Z Value	-2
P(X<=450)	0.0228

(d) $P(X < A) = 0.99$ $Z = 2.33$ $A = 882.6348$

Find X and Z Given a Cum. Pctage.	
Cumulative Percentage	99.00%
Z Value	2.33
X Value	882.63

6.14   With 39 values, the smallest of the standard normal quantile values covers an area under the normal curve of 0.025. The corresponding Z value is −1.96. The middle (20th) value has a cumulative area of 0.50 and a corresponding Z value of 0.0. The largest of the standard normal quantile values covers an area under the normal curve of 0.975, and its corresponding Z value is +1.96.

6.16   (a)   Excel output

Statistic	Score
Nbr. of observations	57
Minimum	3.220
Maximum	6.910
Range	3.690
1st Quartile	4.370
Median	4.940
3rd Quartile	5.560
Mean	4.960
Variance (n-1)	0.796
Standard deviation (n-1)	0.892
Variation coefficient	0.178
Skewness (Fisher)	0.083
Kurtosis (Fisher)	-0.458
IQR	1.190
1.33S	1.186
6S	5.352
Standard error of the mean	0.118

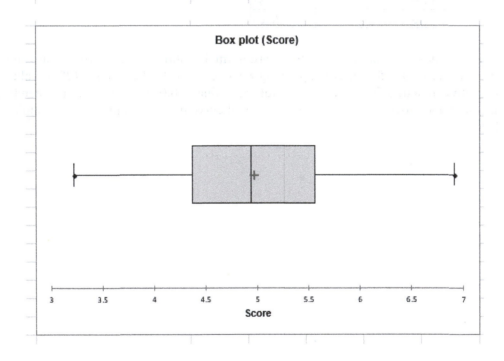

6.16   (a)   The mean is approximately the same as the median. The range is much less than 6S, and
cont.   the interquartile range is approximately the same as 1.33S. The boxplot appears
                symmetrical.

        (b)   The normal probability plot appears to be a straight line indicating a normal distribution.

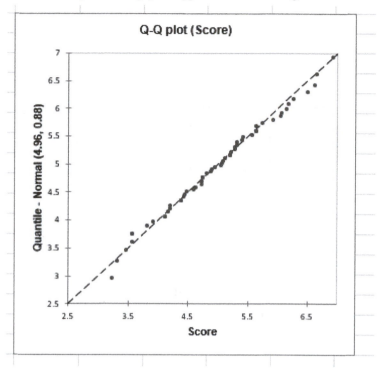

6.18   (a)(b)   Excel Output:

Descriptive statistics (Quantitative data):			
Statistic	Taxes on $176K House		
Nbr. of observations	51		
Minimum	489.000		
Maximum	4029.000		
Range	3540.000	6S	5405.362
1st Quartile	1334.000		
Median	1763.000		
3rd Quartile	2614.500		
Mean	1979.941		
IQR	1280.500	1.33S	1198.189
Variance (n-1)	811609.376		
Standard deviation (n-1)	900.894		
Variation coefficient	0.451		
Skewness (Fisher)	0.641		
Skewness (Bowley)	0.330		
Kurtosis (Fisher)	-0.506		

6.18   (a)(b)
cont.

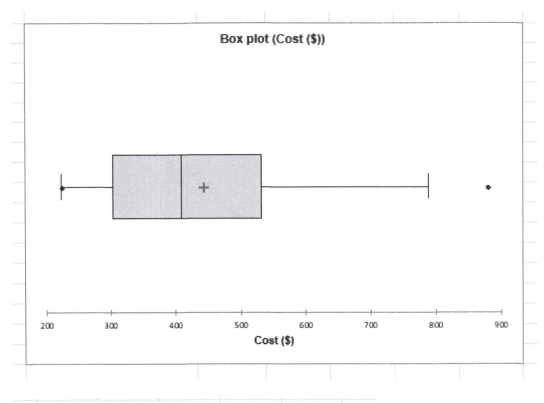

Normal Q-Q plots:

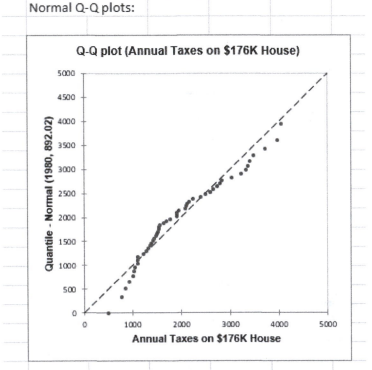

(a)(b)   The mean is greater than the median. The range is much less than 6S, and the IQR is more than 1.33S. The box plot is right skewed. The normal probability plot along with the skewness and kurtosis statistics indicate a departure from the normal distribution.

6.20   Excel output:

Error	
Mean	−0.00023
Median	0
Mode	0
Standard Deviation	0.001696
Sample Variance	2.88E-06
Range	0.008
Minimum	−0.003
Maximum	0.005
First Quartile	−0.0015
Third Quartile	0.001
1.33 Std Dev	0.002255
Interquartile Range	0.0025
6 Std Dev	0.010175

(a)   Because the interquartile range is close to 1.33S and the range is also close to 6S, the data appear to be approximately normally distributed.

(b)

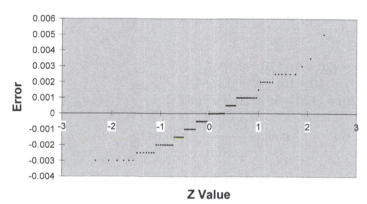

Normal Probability Plot

The normal probability plot suggests that the data appear to be approximately normally distributed.

6.22   (a)   Five-number summary: 82   127   148.5   168   213   mean = 147.06
range = 131   interquartile range = 41   standard deviation = 31.69

The mean is very close to the median. The five-number summary suggests that the distribution is quite symmetrical around the median. The interquartile range is very close to 1.33 times the standard deviation. The range is about $50 below 6 times the standard deviation. In general, the distribution of the data appears to closely resemble a normal distribution.
Note: The quartiles are obtained using PHStat without any interpolation.

6.22   (b)
cont.

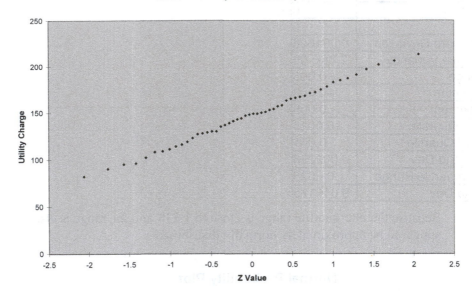

The normal probability plot confirms that the data appear to be approximately normally distributed.

6.24   (a) $P(0 < X < 20) = (20 - 0) / 120 = 0.1667$
       (b) $P(10 < X < 30) = (30 - 10)/120 = 0.1667$
       (c) $P(35 < X < 120) = (120 - 35)/120 = 0.7083$

       (d) $\mu = \dfrac{0 + 120}{2} = 60$ $\sigma = \sqrt{\dfrac{(120 - 0)^2}{12}} = 34.6410$

6.26   (a) $P(X < 30) = (30 - 29)/(43 - 29) = 0.0714$
       (b) $P(X > 36) = (43 - 36)/(43 - 29) = 0.5$
       (c) $P(30 < X < 40) = (40 - 30)/(43 - 29) = 0.7143$

       (d) $\mu = \dfrac{(29 + 43)}{2} = 36$ $\sigma = \sqrt{\dfrac{(43 - 29)^2}{12}} = 4.0415$

6.28   Using Table E.2, first find the cumulative area up to the larger value, and then subtract the cumulative area up to the smaller value.

6.30   The normal distribution is bell-shaped; its measures of central tendency are all equal; its middle 50% is within 1.33 standard deviations of its mean; and 99.7% of its values are contained within three standard deviations of its mean.

6.32   If the distribution is normal, the plot of the Z values on the horizontal axis and the original values on the vertical axis will be a straight line.

6.34   (a)   Partial PHStat output:

Probability for a Range	
From X Value	1.9
To X Value	2
Z Value for 1.9	–2
Z Value for 2	0
P(X<=1.9)	0.0228
P(X<=2)	0.5000
P(1.9<=X<=2)	0.4772

$P(1.90 < X < 2.00) = P(-2.00 < Z < 0) = 0.4772$

(b)   Partial PHStat output:

Probability for a Range	
From X Value	1.9
To X Value	2.1
Z Value for 1.9	–2
Z Value for 2.1	2
P(X<=1.9)	0.0228
P(X<=2.1)	0.9772
P(1.9<=X<=2.1)	0.9545

$P(1.90 < X < 2.10) = P(-2.00 < Z < 2.00) = 0.9772 - 0.0228 = 0.9544$

(c)   Partial PHStat output:

Probability for X<1.9 or X >2.1	
P(X<1.9 or X >2.1)	0.0455

$P(X < 1.90) + P(X > 2.10) = 1 - P(1.90 < X < 2.10) = 0.0456$

(d)   Partial PHStat output:

Find X and Z Given Cum. Pctage.	
Cumulative Percentage	1.00%
Z Value	–2.326348
X Value	1.883683

$P(X > A) = P(Z > -2.33) = 0.99 A = 2.00 - 2.33(0.05) = 1.8835$

(e)   Partial PHStat output:

Find X and Z Given Cum. Pctage.	
Cumulative Percentage	99.50%
Z Value	2.575829
X Value	2.128791

$P(A < X < B) = P(-2.58 < Z < 2.58) = 0.99$
$A = 2.00 - 2.58(0.05) = 1.8710$ $B = 2.00 + 2.58(0.05) = 2.1290$

6.36   (a)   Partial PHStat output:

Probability for X <=	
X Value	210
Z Value	-2
P(X<=210)	0.0228

$P(X < 210) = P(Z < -2) = 0.0228$

6.36 (b)
cont.

Probability for a Range	
From X Value	270
To X Value	300
Z Value for 270	1
Z Value for 300	2.5
P(X<=270)	0.8413
P(X<=300)	0.9938
P(270<=X<=300)	0.1524

$P(270 < X < 300) = P(1.0 < Z < 2.5) = 0.1524$

(c)

Find X and Z Given Cum. Pctage.	
Cumulative Percentage	90.00%
Z Value	1.2816
X Value	275.6310

$P(X < A) = P(Z < 1.2816) = 0.90 A = 250 + 20(1.2816) = \$275.63$

(d)

Find X Values Given a Percentage	
Percentage	80.00%
Z Value	-1.28
Lower X Value	224.37
Upper X Value	275.63

$P(A < X < B) = P(-1.2816 < Z < 1.2816) = 0.80$
$A = 250 - 1.28(500) = \$224.37$
$B = 250 + 1.28(500) = \$275.63$

6.38 (a) Waiting time will more closely resemble an exponential distribution.
(b) Seating time will more closely resemble a normal distribution.
(c)

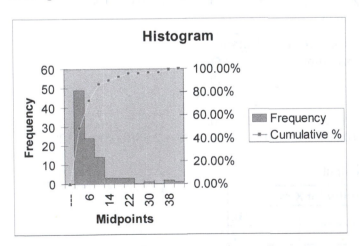

6.38   (c)
cont.

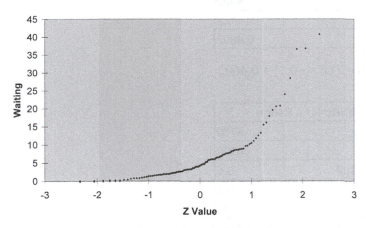

Both the histogram and normal probability plot suggest that waiting time more closely resembles an exponential distribution.

(d)

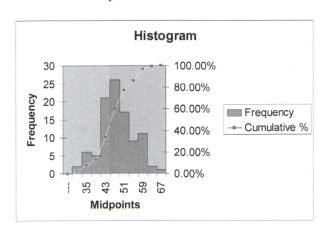

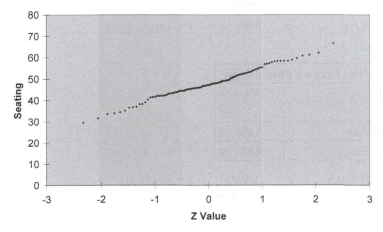

Both the histogram and normal probability plot suggest that seating time more closely resembles a normal distribution.

6.40   (a)   Excel Output:

Probability for X <=	
X Value	5900
Z Value	-0.1
P(X<=5900)	0.4602

$P(X < \$5900) = P(Z < -0.1) = 0.4602$

(b)   Excel Output:

Probability for a Range	
From X Value	5700
To X Value	6100
Z Value for 5700	-0.6
Z Value for 6100	0.4
P(X<=5700)	0.2743
P(X<=6100)	0.6554
P(5700<=X<=6100)	0.3812

$P(\$5700 < X < \$6100) = P(-0.6 < Z < 0.4) = 0.3812$

(c)   Excel Output:

Probability for X >	
X Value	6500
Z Value	1.4
P(X>6500)	0.0808

$P(X > \$6500) = P(Z > 1.4) = 0.0808$

(d)   Excel Output:

Find X and Z Given a Cum. Pctage.	
Cumulative Percentage	1.00%
Z Value	-2.33
X Value	5009.46

$P(A < X) = 0.01$ $Z = -2.33$ $A = \$5009.46$

(e)   Excel Output:

Find X Values Given a Percentage	
Percentage	95.00%
Z Value	-1.96
Lower X Value	5156.01
Upper X Value	6723.99

$P(A < X < B) = 0.95$ $Z = -1.9600$ $A = \$5156.01$
$Z = 1.96$ $B = \$6723.99$

6.42   *Class project solutions may vary.*

CHAPTER 7

7.2   PHStat output:

Common Data	
Mean	50
Standard Deviation	0.5

Probability for X <=	
X Value	47
Z Value	−6
P(X<=47)	9.866E-10

Probability for X >	
X Value	51.5
Z Value	3
P(X>51.5)	0.0013

Probability for X<47 or X >51.5	
P(X<47 or X >51.5)	0.0013

Probability for X >	
X Value	51.1
Z Value	2.2
P(X>51.1)	0.0139

Probability for a Range	
From X Value	47
To X Value	49.5
Z Value for 47	−6
Z Value for 49.5	−1
P(X<=47)	0.0000
P(X<=49.5)	0.1587
P(47<=X<=49.5)	0.1587

Find X and Z Given Cum. Pctage.	
Cumulative Percentage	65.00%
Z Value	0.38532
X Value	50.19266

(a) $P(\overline{X} < 47) = P(Z < -6.00) =$ virtually zero

(b) $P(47 < \overline{X} < 49.5) = P(-6.00 < Z < -1.00) = 0.1587 - 0.00 = 0.1587$

(c) $P(\overline{X} > 51.1) = P(Z > 2.20) = 1.0 - 0.9861 = 0.0139$

(d) $P(\overline{X} > A) = P(Z > 0.39) = 0.35$ $\overline{X} = 50 + 0.39(0.5) = 50.195$

7.4   (a)   Sampling Distribution of the Mean for $n = 2$ (without replacement)

Sample Number	Outcomes	Sample Means $\overline{X}_i$
1	1, 3	$\overline{X}_1 = 2$
2	1, 6	$\overline{X}_2 = 3.5$
3	1, 7	$\overline{X}_3 = 4$
4	1, 9	$\overline{X}_4 = 5$
5	1, 10	$\overline{X}_5 = 5.5$
6	3, 6	$\overline{X}_6 = 4.5$
7	3, 7	$\overline{X}_7 = 5$
8	3, 9	$\overline{X}_8 = 6$
9	3, 10	$\overline{X}_9 = 6.5$
10	6, 7	$\overline{X}_{10} = 6.5$
11	6, 9	$\overline{X}_{11} = 7.5$
12	6, 10	$\overline{X}_{12} = 8$
13	7, 9	$\overline{X}_{13} = 8$
14	7, 10	$\overline{X}_{14} = 8.5$
15	9, 10	$\overline{X}_{15} = 9.5$

Mean of All Possible Sample Means: Mean of All Population Elements:

$$\mu_{\overline{X}} = \frac{90}{15} = 6 \qquad\qquad \mu = \frac{1+3+6+7+9+10}{6} = 6$$

Both means are equal to 6. This property is called unbiasedness.

7.4 (b)   Sampling Distribution of the Mean for $n = 3$ (without replacement)
cont.

Sample Number	Outcomes	Sample Means $\overline{X}_i$
1	1, 3, 6	$\overline{X}_1 = 3\ 1/3$
2	1, 3, 7	$\overline{X}_2 = 3\ 2/3$
3	1, 3, 9	$\overline{X}_3 = 4\ 1/3$
4	1, 3, 10	$\overline{X}_4 = 4\ 2/3$
5	1, 6, 7	$\overline{X}_5 = 4\ 2/3$
6	1, 6, 9	$\overline{X}_6 = 5\ 1/3$
7	1, 6, 10	$\overline{X}_7 = 5\ 2/3$
8	3, 6, 7	$\overline{X}_8 = 5\ 1/3$
9	3, 6, 9	$\overline{X}_9 = 6$
10	3, 6, 10	$\overline{X}_{10} = 6\ 1/3$
11	6, 7, 9	$\overline{X}_{11} = 7\ 1/3$
12	6, 7, 10	$\overline{X}_{12} = 7\ 2/3$
13	6, 9, 10	$\overline{X}_{13} = 8\ 1/3$
14	7, 9, 10	$\overline{X}_{14} = 8\ 2/3$
15	1, 7, 9	$\overline{X}_{15} = 5\ 2/3$
16	1, 7, 10	$\overline{X}_{16} = 6$
17	1, 9, 10	$\overline{X}_{17} = 6\ 2/3$
18	3, 7, 9	$\overline{X}_{18} = 6\ 1/3$
19	3, 7, 10	$\overline{X}_{19} = 6\ 2/3$
20	3, 9, 10	$\overline{X}_{20} = 7\ 1/3$

$\mu_{\overline{X}} = \dfrac{120}{20} = 6$ This is equal to μ, the population mean.

  (c)   The distribution for $n = 3$ has less variability. The larger sample size has resulted in sample means being closer to μ.

  (d)   (a) Sampling Distribution of the Mean for $n = 2$ (with replacement)

Sample Number	Outcomes	Sample Means $\overline{X}_i$
1	1, 1	$\overline{X}_1 = 1$
2	1, 3	$\overline{X}_2 = 2$
3	1, 6	$\overline{X}_3 = 3.5$
4	1, 7	$\overline{X}_4 = 4.5$
5	1, 9	$\overline{X}_5 = 5$
6	1, 10	$\overline{X}_6 = 5.5$
7	3, 1	$\overline{X}_7 = 2$
8	3, 3	$\overline{X}_8 = 3$
9	3, 6	$\overline{X}_9 = 4.5$

(table continues on next page)

7.4   (d)   (a)
cont.

Sample Number	Outcomes	Sample Means $\overline{X}_i$
10	3, 7	$\overline{X}_{10} = 5$
11	3, 9	$\overline{X}_{11} = 6$
12	3, 10	$\overline{X}_{12} = 6.5$
13	6, 1	$\overline{X}_{13} = 3.5$
14	6, 3	$\overline{X}_{14} = 4.5$
15	6, 6	$\overline{X}_{15} = 6$
16	6, 7	$\overline{X}_{16} = 6.5$
17	6, 9	$\overline{X}_{17} = 7.5$
18	6, 10	$\overline{X}_{18} = 8$
19	7, 1	$\overline{X}_{19} = 4$
20	7,3	$\overline{X}_{20} = 5$
21	7, 6	$\overline{X}_{21} = 6.5$
22	7, 7	$\overline{X}_{22} = 7$
23	7, 9	$\overline{X}_{23} = 8$
24	7, 10	$\overline{X}_{24} = 8.5$
25	9, 1	$\overline{X}_{25} = 5$
26	9, 3	$\overline{X}_{26} = 6$
27	9, 6	$\overline{X}_{27} = 7.5$
28	9, 7	$\overline{X}_{28} = 8$
29	9, 9	$\overline{X}_{29} = 9$
30	9, 10	$\overline{X}_{30} = 9.5$
31	10, 1	$\overline{X}_{31} = 5.5$
32	10, 3	$\overline{X}_{32} = 6.5$
33	10, 6	$\overline{X}_{33} = 8$
34	10, 7	$\overline{X}_{34} = 8.5$
35	10, 9	$\overline{X}_{35} = 9.5$
36	10, 10	$\overline{X}_{36} = 10$

Mean of All Possible Sample Means:

$$\mu_{\overline{X}} = \frac{216}{36} = 6$$

Mean of All Population Elements:

$$\mu = \frac{1+3+6+7+7+12}{6} = 6$$

Both means are equal to 6. This property is called unbiasedness.

(b) Repeat the same process for the sampling distribution of the mean for $n = 3$ (with replacement). There will be $6^3 = 216$ different samples.

$\mu_{\overline{X}} = 6$ This is equal to μ, the population mean.

(c) The distribution for $n = 3$ has less variability. The larger sample size has resulted in more sample means being close to μ.

7.6   (a) $P(X < 42.035) = P(Z < -0.6) = 0.2743$
Excel Output:

▲	A	B
4	Mean	42.05
5	Standard Deviation	0.025
6		
7	Probability for X <=	
8	X Value	42.035
9	Z Value	-0.6
10	P(X<=42.035)	0.2743

(b)   Because the weight of an energy bar is approximately normally distributed, the sampling distribution of samples of 4 will also be approximately normal with a mean of

$$\mu_{\bar{X}} = \mu = 42.05 \text{ and } \sigma_{\bar{X}} = \frac{\sigma}{\sqrt{n}} = 0.0125.$$

$P(\bar{X} < 42.035) = P(Z < -1.2) = 0.1151$
Excel Output:

▲	A	B
4	Mean	42.05
5	Standard Deviation	0.0125
6		
7	Probability for X <=	
8	X Value	42.035
9	Z Value	-1.2
10	P(X<=42.035)	0.1151

(c)   Because the weight of an energy bar is approximately normally distributed, the sampling distribution of samples of 25 will also be approximately normal with a mean of

$$\mu_{\bar{X}} = \mu = 42.05 \text{ and } \sigma_{\bar{X}} = \frac{\sigma}{\sqrt{n}} = 0.005.$$

$P(\bar{X} < 42.035) = P(Z < -3) = 0.0013$
Excel Output:

▲	A	B
4	Mean	42.05
5	Standard Deviation	0.005
6		
7	Probability for X <=	
8	X Value	42.035
9	Z Value	-3
10	P(X<=42.035)	0.0013
11		

(d)   (a) refers to an individual energy bar while (c) refers to the mean of a sample of 25 energy bars. There is a 27.43% chance that an individual energy bar will have a weight below 42.05 grams but only a chance of 0.135% that a mean of 25 energy bars will have a weight below 42.05 grams.

(e)   Increasing the sample size from four to 25 reduced the probability the mean will have a weight below 42.05 grams from 11.51% to 0.135%.

7.8   (a)   When $n = 4$, the shape of the sampling distribution of $\overline{X}$ should closely resemble the shape of the distribution of the population from which the sample is selected. Because the mean is larger than the median, the distribution of the sales price of new houses is skewed to the right, and so is the sampling distribution of $\overline{X}$ although it will be less skewed than the population.

(b)   If you select samples of $n = 100$, the shape of the sampling distribution of the sample mean will be very close to a normal distribution with a mean of $370,800 and a standard deviation of $\sigma_{\overline{X}} = \dfrac{\sigma}{\sqrt{n}} = \$9,000$.

(c) $P(\overline{X} < 370000) = P(Z < -0.0889) = 0.4646$
Excel Output:

1	Normal Probabilities	
2		
3	Common Data	
4	Mean	370800
5	Standard Deviation	9000
6		
7	Probability for X <=	
8	X Value	370000
9	Z Value	-0.088889
10	P(X<=370000)	0.4646

(d) $P(350000 < \overline{X} < 365000) = P(-2.31 < Z < -0.644) = 0.2492$
Excel Output:

20	Probability for a Range	
21	From X Value	350000
22	To X Value	365000
23	Z Value for 350000	-2.311111
24	Z Value for 365000	-0.644444
25	P(X<=350000)	0.0104
26	P(X<=365000)	0.2596
27	P(350000<=X<=365000)	0.2492

7.10   (a) $\mu_{\overline{X}} = \mu = 15$ and $\sigma_{\overline{X}} = \dfrac{\sigma}{\sqrt{n}} = 1$

$P(\overline{X} > 14) = P(Z > -1) = 0.8413$
Excel Output:

12	Probability for X >	
13	X Value	14
14	Z Value	-1
15	P(X>14)	0.8413

7.10   (b) $P(\overline{X} < A) = P(Z < 1.04) = 0.85$ $\overline{X} = 15 + 1.04\ (1) = 16.04$
cont.   Excel Output:

29	Find X and Z Given a Cum. Pctage.	
30	Cumulative Percentage	85.00%
31	Z Value	1.04
32	X Value	16.04

         (c)   To be able to use the standardized normal distribution as an approximation for the area
                 under the curve, you must assume that the population is approximately symmetrical.

         (d) $P(\overline{X} < A) = P(Z < 1.04) = 0.85$ $\overline{X} = 15 + 1.04\ (.5) = 15.52$
                 Excel Output:

29	Find X and Z Given a Cum. Pctage.	
30	Cumulative Percentage	85.00%
31	Z Value	1.04
32	X Value	15.52

7.12   (a) $p = \dfrac{20}{50} = 0.40$

         (b) $\sigma_p = \sqrt{\dfrac{(0.45)(0.55)}{50}} = 0.0704$

7.14   (a) $\mu_p = \pi = 0.80,\ \sigma_p = \sqrt{\dfrac{\pi(1-\pi)}{n}} = \sqrt{\dfrac{0.80(1-0.80)}{100}} = 0.04$
                 Partial PHStat output:

Probability for X<=	
X Value	0.85
Z Value	1.2500
P(X<=0.85)	0.8944

                 $P(p < 0.85) = P\ (Z < 1.2500) = 0.8944$
         (b)   Partial PHStat output:

Probability for a Range	
From X Value	0.75
To X Value	0.85
Z Value for 0.75	-1.2500
Z Value for 0.85	1.2500
P(X<=0.75)	0.1056
P(X<=0.85)	0.8944
P(0.75<=X<=0.85)	0.7887

                 $P(0.75 < p < 0.85) = P\ (-1.2500 < Z < 1.2500) = 0.7887$

7.14   (c)   Partial PHStat output:
cont.

Probability for X >	
X Value	0.82
Z Value	0.5000
P(X>0.82)	0.3085

$P(p > 0.82) = P(Z > 0.5000) = 0.3085$

(d) $\mu_p = \pi = 0.80, \ \sigma_p = \sqrt{\dfrac{\pi(1-\pi)}{n}} = \sqrt{\dfrac{0.80(1-0.80)}{400}} = 0.02$

(a)   Partial PHStat output:

Probability for X <=	
X Value	0.85
Z Value	2.5000
P(X<=0.85)	0.9938

$P(p < 0.85) = P(Z < 2.5000) = 0.9938$

(b)   Partial PHStat output:

Probability for a Range	
From X Value	0.75
To X Value	0.85
Z Value for 0.75	-2.5000
Z Value for 0.85	2.5000
P(X<=0.75)	0.0062
P(X<=0.85)	0.9938
P(0.75<=X<=0.85)	0.9876

$P(0.75 < p < 0.85) = P(-2.5000 < Z < 2.5000) = 0.9876$

(c)   Partial PHStat output:

Probability for X >	
X Value	0.82
Z Value	1.0000
P(X>0.82)	0.1587

$P(p > 0.82) = P(Z > 1.0000) = 0.1587$

7.16 $\mu_p = \pi = 0.65, \ \sigma_p = \sqrt{\dfrac{\pi(1-\pi)}{n}} = \sqrt{\dfrac{0.65(1-0.65)}{100}} = 0.0477$

(a) $P(p < .7) = P(Z < 1.0483) = 0.8527$
Excel Output:

7	Probability for X <=	
8	X Value	0.7
9	Z Value	1.0482848
10	P(X<=0.7)	0.8527

7.16   (b) $P(.6 < p < .7) = P(-1.05 < Z < 1.05) = 0.7055$
cont.   Excel Output:

20	Probability for a Range	
21	From X Value	0.6
22	To X Value	0.7
23	Z Value for 0.6	-1.048285
24	Z Value for 0.7	1.0482848
25	P(X<=0.6)	0.1473
26	P(X<=0.7)	0.8527
27	P(0.6<=X<=0.7)	0.7055
28		

(c) $P(p > 0.7) = P(Z > 1.048) = 0.1473$
Excel Output:

2	Probability for X >	
3	X Value	0.7
4	Z Value	1.0482848
5	P(X>0.7)	0.1473
6		

(d) $\mu_p = \pi = 0.65, \ \sigma_p = \sqrt{\dfrac{\pi(1-\pi)}{n}} = \sqrt{\dfrac{0.65(1-0.65)}{400}} = 0.0238$

$P(p < .7) = P(Z < 2.0966) = 0.982$
$P(.6 < p < .7) = P(-2.0966 < Z < 2.0966) = 0.9640$
$P(p > 0.7) = P(Z > 2.0966) = 0.0180$
Excel Output:

1	Normal Probabilities	
2		
3	Common Data	
4	Mean	0.65
5	Standard Deviation	0.0238485
6		
7	Probability for X <=	
8	X Value	0.7
9	Z Value	2.0965697
10	P(X<=0.7)	0.9820
11		
12	Probability for X >	
13	X Value	0.7
14	Z Value	2.0965697
15	P(X>0.7)	0.0180
16		

7.16 (d)
cont.

Probability for a Range	
From X Value	0.6
To X Value	0.7
Z Value for 0.6	-2.09657
Z Value for 0.7	2.0965697
P(X<=0.6)	0.0180
P(X<=0.7)	0.9820
P(0.6<=X<=0.7)	0.9640

7.18 (a) $\mu_p = \pi = 0.34$, $\sigma_p = \sqrt{\dfrac{\pi(1-\pi)}{n}} = \sqrt{\dfrac{0.34(1-0.34)}{200}} = 0.033496$

$P(0.30 < p < 0.38) = P(-1.194 < Z < 1.194) = 0.7676$

Excel Output:

Probability for a Range	
From X Value	0.3
To X Value	0.38
Z Value for 0.3	-1.194163
Z Value for 0.38	1.1941629
P(X<=0.3)	0.1162
P(X<=0.38)	0.8838
P(0.3<=X<=0.38)	0.7676

(b) The probability is 90% that the sample percentage will be contained between 0.2849 and 0.3951.

Excel Output:

Find X Values Given a Percentage	
Percentage	90.00%
Z Value	-1.6449
Lower X Value	0.2849
Upper X Value	0.3951

(c) The probability is 95% that the sample percentage will be contained between 0.2743 and 0.4057.

Excel Output:

Find X Values Given a Percentage	
Percentage	95.00%
Z Value	-1.9600
Lower X Value	0.2743
Upper X Value	0.4057

7.20 $\mu_p = \pi = 0.26$, $\sigma_p = \sqrt{\dfrac{\pi(1-\pi)}{n}} = \sqrt{\dfrac{0.26(1-0.26)}{100}} = 0.0439$

(a) $P(p < 0.21) = P(Z < -1.1399) = 0.1272$
Excel Output:

7	Probability for X <=	
8	X Value	0.21
9	Z Value	-1.139902
10	P(X<=0.21)	0.1272

(b) $\mu_p = \pi = 0.26$, $\sigma_p = \sqrt{\dfrac{\pi(1-\pi)}{n}} = \sqrt{\dfrac{0.26(1-0.26)}{500}} = 0.0196$

$P(p < 0.21) = P(Z < -2.5489) = 0.0054$
Excel Output:

2		
3	Common Data	
4	Mean	0.26
5	Standard Deviation	0.0196163
6		
7	Probability for X <=	
8	X Value	0.21
9	Z Value	-2.548898
10	P(X<=0.21)	0.0054
11		

(c)   Increasing the sample size by a factor of 5 decreases the standard error by a factor of more than 2. The sampling distribution of the proportion becomes more concentrated around the true proportion of 0.26 and, hence, the probability in (b) becomes smaller than that in (a).

7.22   The variation of the sample means becomes smaller as larger sample sizes are taken. This is due to the fact that an extreme observation will have a smaller effect on the mean in a larger sample than in a small sample. Thus, the sample means will tend to be closer to the population mean as the sample size increases.

7.24   The population distribution is the distribution of a particular variable of interest, while the sampling distribution represents the distribution of a statistic.

7.26 $\mu_{\bar{X}} = 0.753$ $\sigma_{\bar{X}} = \dfrac{\sigma}{\sqrt{n}} = \dfrac{0.004}{5} = 0.0008$

PHStat output:

Common Data	
Mean	0.753
Standard Deviation	0.0008

Probability for X <=	
X Value	0.74
Z Value	−16.25
P(X<=0.74)	1.117E-59

Probability for X >	
X Value	0.76
Z Value	8.75
P(X>0.76)	0.0000

Probability for X<0.74 or X >0.76	
P(X<0.74 or X >0.76)	0.0000

Probability for a Range	
From X Value	0.74
To X Value	0.75
Z Value for 0.74	−16.25
Z Value for 0.75	−3.75
P(X<=0.74)	0.0000
P(X<=0.75)	0.0001
P(0.74<=X<=0.75)	0.00009

Probability for a Range	
From X Value	0.75
To X Value	0.753
Z Value for 0.75	−3.75
Z Value for 0.753	0
P(X<=0.75)	0.0001
P(X<=0.753)	0.5000
P(0.75<=X<=0.753)	0.4999

Find X and Z Given Cum. Pctage.	
Cumulative Percentage	7.00%
Z Value	−1.475791
X Value	0.751819

(a) $P(0.75 < \bar{X} < 0.753) = P(-3.75 < Z < 0) = 0.5 - 0.00009 = 0.4999$

(b) $P(0.74 < \bar{X} < 0.75) = P(-16.25 < Z < -3.75) = 0.00009$

(c) $P(\bar{X} > 0.76) = P(Z > 8.75) =$ virtually zero

(d) $P(\bar{X} < 0.74) = P(Z < -16.25) =$ virtually zero

(e) $P(\bar{X} < A) = P(Z < -1.48) = 0.07$ $X = 0.753 - 1.48(0.0008) = 0.7518$

7.28 $\mu_{\overline{X}} = 4.7$ $\sigma_{\overline{X}} = \dfrac{\sigma_X}{\sqrt{n}} = \dfrac{0.40}{5} = 0.08$

PHstat output:

Common Data	
Mean	4.7
Standard Deviation	0.08
Probability for X >	
X Value	4.6
Z Value	−1.25
P(X>4.6)	0.8944

Find X and Z Given Cum. Pctage.	
Cumulative Percentage	23.00%
Z Value	−0.738847
X Value	4.640892

Find X and Z Given Cum. Pctage.	
Cumulative Percentage	15.00%
Z Value	−1.036433
X Value	4.6170853

Find X and Z Given Cum. Pctage.	
Cumulative Percentage	85.00%
Z Value	1.036433
X Value	4.782915

(a) $P(4.60 < \overline{X}) = P(-1.25 < Z) = 1 - 0.1056 = 0.8944$

(b) $P(A < \overline{X} < B) = P(-1.04 < Z < 1.04) = 0.70$
        $A = 4.70 - 1.04(0.08) = 4.6168$ ounces $X = 4.70 + 1.04(0.08) = 4.7832$ ounces

(c) $P(\overline{X} > A) = P(Z > -0.74) = 0.77$ $A = 4.70 - 0.74(0.08) = 4.6408$

7.30 $\mu_{\overline{X}} = 17.5$ $\sigma_{\overline{X}} = \dfrac{\sigma}{\sqrt{n}} = \dfrac{20}{4} = 5$

Excel Output:

Common Data	
Mean	17.5
Standard Deviation	5

Probability for X <=	
X Value	0
Z Value	-3.5
P(X<=0)	0.0002

Probability for X >	
X Value	10
Z Value	-1.5
P(X>10)	0.9332

Probability for a Range	
From X Value	0
To X Value	10
Z Value for 0	-3.5
Z Value for 10	-1.5
P(X<=0)	0.0002
P(X<=10)	0.0668
P(0<=X<=10)	0.0666

7.30   (a) $P(p < 0) = P\ (Z < -3.5) = 0.0002$
cont.   (b) $P(0 < p < 10) = P(.0002 < Z < 0.0668) = 0.0666$
        (c) $P(p > 10) = P\ (Z > -1.5) = 0.9332$

7.32   Class Project answers will vary. The mean of the uniform distribution is $\dfrac{a+b}{2}$, since the random
        numbers in the table range from 0 to 9 the mean is 4.5. When $n = 2$, the frequency distribution of
        the sample means for the class should be centered around 4.5 and have a shape similar to column
        B with $n = 2$ in Figure 7.4 page 260 of text. As the sample size increases the frequency
        distribution of the sample means should have the shape similar to a normal distribution centered
        around 4.5.

7.34   Class Project answers will vary. Population mean is 1.310 and population standard deviation is
        1.13

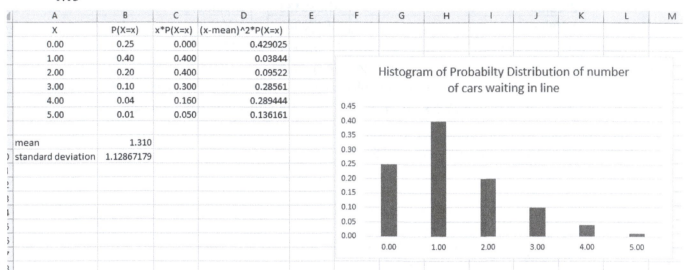

	A	B	C	D
	X	P(X=x)	x*P(X=x)	(x-mean)^2*P(X=x)
	0.00	0.25	0.000	0.429025
	1.00	0.40	0.400	0.03844
	2.00	0.20	0.400	0.09522
	3.00	0.10	0.300	0.28561
	4.00	0.04	0.160	0.289444
	5.00	0.01	0.050	0.136161
mean		1.310		
standard deviation		1.12867179		

Histogram of Probabilty Distribution of number of cars waiting in line

        Depending on class results, one should expect similar results to example 7.5 on page 261 of text.
        The frequency distributions of the sample means for each sample size should progress from a
        skewed population toward a bell-shaped distribution as the sample size increases.

8.2 $\quad \overline{X} \pm Z \cdot \dfrac{\sigma}{\sqrt{n}} = 125 \pm 2.58 \cdot \dfrac{24}{\sqrt{36}}$ $\qquad 114.68 \le \mu \le 135.32$

8.4 $\quad$ Yes, it is true since 5% of intervals will not include the population mean.

8.6 $\quad$ (a) $\quad$ You would compute the mean first because you need the mean to compute the standard deviation. If you had a sample, you would compute the sample mean. If you had the population mean, you would compute the population standard deviation.

$\qquad$ (b) $\quad$ If you have a sample, you are computing the sample standard deviation not the population standard deviation needed in Equation 8.1. If you have a population, and have computed the population mean and population standard deviation, you don't need a confidence interval estimate of the population mean since you already have computed it.

8.8 $\quad$ Equation (8.1) assumes that you know the population standard deviation. Because you are selecting a sample of 100 from the population, you are computing a sample standard deviation, not the population standard deviation.

8.10 $\quad$ (a) $\qquad \overline{X} \pm Z \cdot \dfrac{\sigma}{\sqrt{n}} = 49875 \pm 1.96 \cdot \dfrac{1500}{\sqrt{64}}$ $\qquad 49507.51 \le \mu \le 50242.49$

$\qquad$ Excel Output:

	A	B
1	Confidence Estimate for the Mean	
2		
3	Data	
4	Population Standard Deviation	1500
5	Sample Mean	49875
6	Sample Size	64
7	Confidence Level	95%
8		
9	Intermediate Calculations	
10	Standard Error of the Mean	187.5
11	Z Value	-1.9600
12	Interval Half Width	367.4932
13		
14	Confidence Interval	
15	Interval Lower Limit	49507.5068
16	Interval Upper Limit	50242.4932
17		

$\qquad$ (b) $\quad$ Yes, because the confidence interval includes 50,000 hours the manufacturer can support a claim that the bulbs have a mean of 50,000 hours.

$\qquad$ (c) $\quad$ No. Because σ is known and $n = 64$, from the Central Limit Theorem, you know that the sampling distribution of $\overline{X}$ is approximately normal.

8.10 (d) $\bar{X} \pm Z \cdot \dfrac{\sigma}{\sqrt{n}} = 49875 \pm 1.96 \cdot \dfrac{500}{\sqrt{64}}$ $49752.50 \le \mu \le 49997.50$

cont.   The confidence interval is narrower, based on the population standard deviation of 500 hours and the confidence interval no longer includes 50,000 so the manufacturer could not state that the LED bulbs have a mean life of 50,000 hours.

Excel Output:

	A	B
1	Confidence Estimate for the Mean	
2		
3	Data	
4	Population Standard Deviation	500
5	Sample Mean	49875
6	Sample Size	64
7	Confidence Level	95%
8		
9	Intermediate Calculations	
10	Standard Error of the Mean	62.5
11	Z Value	-1.9600
12	Interval Half Width	122.4977
13		
14	Confidence Interval	
15	Interval Lower Limit	49752.5023
16	Interval Upper Limit	49997.4977
17		

8.12 (a) $df = 9,\ \alpha = 0.05,\ t_{\alpha/2} = 2.2622$

     (b) $df = 9,\ \alpha = 0.01,\ t_{\alpha/2} = 3.2498$

     (c) $df = 31,\ \alpha = 0.05,\ t_{\alpha/2} = 2.0395$

     (d) $df = 64,\ \alpha = 0.05,\ t_{\alpha/2} = 1.9977$

     (e) $df = 15,\ \alpha = 0.1,\ t_{\alpha/2} = 1.7531$

8.14 Original data: $5.8571 \pm 2.4469 \cdot \dfrac{6.4660}{\sqrt{7}}$ $-0.1229 \le \mu \le 11.8371$

Altered data: $4.00 \pm 2.4469 \cdot \dfrac{2.1602}{\sqrt{7}}$ $2.0022 \le \mu \le 5.9978$

The presence of an outlier in the original data increases the value of the sample mean and greatly inflates the sample standard deviation.

8.16   (a) $\bar{X} \pm t \cdot \dfrac{S}{\sqrt{n}} = 87 \pm 1.9781 \cdot \dfrac{9}{\sqrt{133}}$ $85.46 \le \mu \le 88.54$

3	Data	
4	Sample Standard Deviation	9
5	Sample Mean	87
6	Sample Size	133
7	Confidence Level	95%
8		
9	Intermediate Calculations	
10	Standard Error of the Mean	0.7804
11	Degrees of Freedom	132
12	t Value	1.9781
13	Interval Half Width	1.5437
14		
15	Confidence Interval	
16	Interval Lower Limit	85.46
17	Interval Upper Limit	88.54

(b)   You can be 95% confident that the population mean one-time gift donations is somewhere between $85.46 and $88.54.

8.18   (a) $6.32 \le \mu \le 7.87$
Minitab Output:

One-Sample T: Cost ($)

Descriptive Statistics

N	Mean	StDev	SE Mean	95% CI for μ
15	7.093	1.406	0.363	(6.315, 7.872)

μ: mean of Cost ($)

(b)   You can be 95% confident that the population mean amount spent for lunch at a fast-food restaurant is between $6.31 and $7.87.
(c)   That the population distribution is normally distributed.
(d)   The assumption of normality is not seriously violated and with a sample of 15, the validity of the confidence interval is not seriously impacted.

8.20   (a)   For 30-second ads: $4.64 \le \mu \le 5.16$
For 60-second ads: $4.56 \le \mu \le 5.65$
Minitab Output:

One-Sample T: 60 Second Ads, 30 Second Ads

Descriptive Statistics

Sample	N	Mean	StDev	SE Mean	95% CI for μ
60 Second Ads	17	5.105	1.053	0.255	(4.563, 5.646)
30 Second Ads	40	4.899	0.821	0.130	(4.636, 5.161)

μ: mean of 60 Second Ads, 30 Second Ads

8.20   (b)   You are 95% confident that the mean rating for 30-second ads is between 4.56 and 5.16.
cont.   You are 95% confident that the mean rating for 60-second ads is between 4.64 and 5.65.
         (c)   The confidence intervals for 30-second ads and 60-second ads are very similar
         (d)   You need to assume that the distributions of the rating for 30-second ads and 60-second
                 ads are normally distributed.
         (e)   The distribution of the 30-second ads is slightly right-skewed. With a sample of 40, the
                 validity of the confidence interval is not in question. The distribution of the 60-second
                 ads is slightly left-skewed. With a sample of 17, the validity of the confidence interval is
                 not seriously in question.

         Minitab Output:

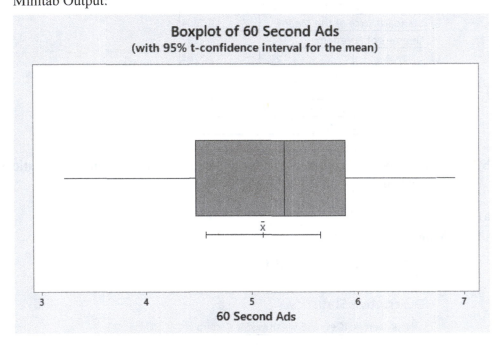

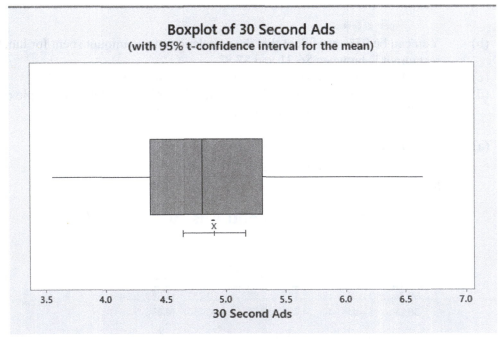

8.22   (a) $\bar{X} \pm t \cdot \dfrac{S}{\sqrt{n}} = 43.04 \pm 2.0096 \cdot \dfrac{41.9261}{\sqrt{50}}$ $31.12 \le \mu \le 54.96$

(b)   The population distribution needs to be normally distribution.

(c)

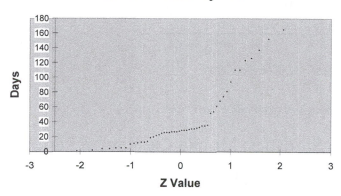

Normal Probability Plot

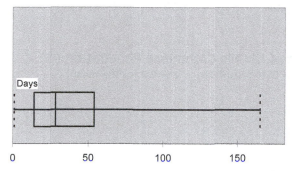

Box-and-whisker Plot

Both the normal probability plot and the boxplot suggest that the distribution is skewed to the right.

(d)   Even though the population distribution is not normally distributed, with a sample of 50, the t distribution can still be used due to the Central Limit Theorem.

8.24   (a) $31.12 \le \mu \le 54.96$

(b)   The number of days is approximately normally distributed.

(c)   No, the outliers skew the data.

(d)   Because the sample size is fairly large, at $n = 50$, the use of the t distribution is appropriate.

8.24   (d)   Minitab Output:
cont.

One-Sample T: Mobile Commerce Penetration (%)

Descriptive Statistics

N	Mean	StDev	SE Mean	95% CI for μ
28	29.68	9.74	1.84	(25.90, 33.45)

μ: mean of Mobile Commerce Penetration (%)

Boxplot of Mobile Commerce Penetration (%)

Descriptive Statistics: Mobile Commerce Penetration (%)

Statistics

Variable	Skewness	Kurtosis
Mobile Commerce Penetration (%)	0.55	0.50

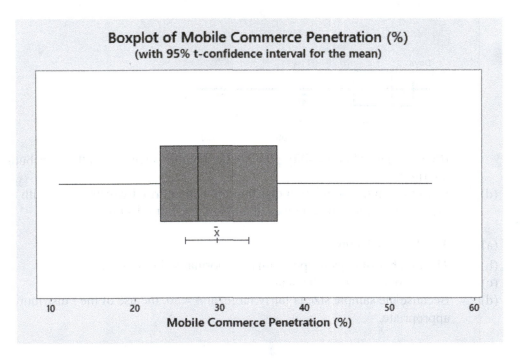

8.26 $p = \dfrac{X}{n} = \dfrac{50}{200} = 0.25$ $p \pm Z \cdot \sqrt{\dfrac{p(1-p)}{n}} = 0.25 \pm 1.96 \sqrt{\dfrac{0.25(0.75)}{200}}$

$0.19 \leq \pi \leq 0.31$

8.28   (a)

	A	B
1	Purchase Additional Telephone Line	
2		
3	Sample Size	500
4	Number of Successes	135
5	Confidence Level	99%
6	Sample Proportion	0.27
7	Z Value	-2.57583451
8	Standard Error of the Proportion	0.019854471
9	Interval Half Width	0.05114183
10	Interval Lower Limit	0.21885817
11	Interval Upper Limit	0.32114183

$$p = \frac{X}{n} = \frac{135}{500} = 0.27 \quad p \pm Z \cdot \sqrt{\frac{p(1-p)}{n}} = 0.27 \pm 2.5758 \sqrt{\frac{0.27(1-0.27)}{500}}$$

$0.22 \le \pi \le 0.32$

(b)   The manager in charge of promotional programs concerning residential customers can infer that the proportion of households that would purchase a new cellphone if it were made available at a substantially reduced installation cost is between 0.22 and 0.32 with a 99% level of confidence.

8.30   (a)   Excel Output:

3	Data	
4	Sample Size	1000
5	Number of Successes	260
6	Confidence Level	95%
7		
8	Intermediate Calculations	
9	Sample Proportion	0.26
10	Z Value	-1.9600
11	Standard Error of the Proportion	0.013871
12	Interval Half Width	0.0272
13		
14	Confidence Interval	
15	Interval Lower Limit	0.2328
16	Interval Upper Limit	0.2872
17		

$$p = 0.26 \quad p \pm Z \sqrt{\frac{p(1-p)}{n}} = 0.26 \pm 1.96 \sqrt{\frac{0.26(1-0.26)}{1000}}$$

$0.2328 \le \pi \le 0.2872$

(b)   No, you cannot because the interval estimate includes 0.25 (25%).

8.30   (c)   Excel Output:

cont.

	Data	
Sample Size		10000
Number of Successes		2600
Confidence Level		95%
	Intermediate Calculations	
Sample Proportion		0.26
Z Value		-1.9600
Standard Error of the Proportion		0.004386
Interval Half Width		0.0086
	Confidence Interval	
Interval Lower Limit		0.2514
Interval Upper Limit		0.2686

$$p = 0.26 \quad p \pm Z\sqrt{\frac{p(1-p)}{n}} = 0.26 \pm 1.96\sqrt{\frac{0.26(1-0.26)}{10000}}$$

$$0.2514 \leq \pi \leq 0.2686$$

Yes, you can claim more than a quarter of all consumers value personalized experience most when shopping in retail store because the interval is above 0.25 (25%)

(d)   The larger the sample size, the narrower the confidence interval, holding everything else constant.

8.32   (a)   Excel Output:

	Data	
Sample Size		4787
Number of Successes		4178
Confidence Level		95%
	Intermediate Calculations	
Sample Proportion		0.87278
Z Value		-1.9600
Standard Error of the Proportion		0.004816
Interval Half Width		0.0094
	Confidence Interval	
Interval Lower Limit		0.8633
Interval Upper Limit		0.8822

$$p = 0.87 \quad p \pm Z\sqrt{\frac{p(1-p)}{n}} = 0.87 \pm 1.96\sqrt{\frac{0.87(1-0.87)}{4787}}$$

$$0.8633 \leq \pi \leq 0.8822$$

8.32   (b)   Excel Output:
cont.

3	Data	
4	Sample Size	4178
5	Number of Successes	789
6	Confidence Level	95%
7		
8	Intermediate Calculations	
9	Sample Proportion	0.188846
10	Z Value	-1.9600
11	Standard Error of the Proportion	0.006055
12	Interval Half Width	0.0119
13		
14	Confidence Interval	
15	Interval Lower Limit	0.1770
16	Interval Upper Limit	0.2007
17		

$$p = 0.19 \quad p \pm Z\sqrt{\frac{p(1-p)}{n}} = 0.19 \pm 1.96\sqrt{\frac{0.19(1-0.19)}{4178}}$$

$0.1770 \leq \pi \leq 0.2007$

(c)   Because almost 90% of adults have purchased something online, but only about 20% are weekly online shoppers, the director of e-commerce sales may want to focus on those adults who are weekly online shoppers.

8.34 $n = \dfrac{Z^2\sigma^2}{e^2} = \dfrac{1.96^2 \cdot 15^2}{5^2} = 34.57$ Use $n = 35$

8.36 $n = \dfrac{Z^2\pi(1-\pi)}{e^2} = \dfrac{2.58^2(0.5)(0.5)}{(0.04)^2} = 1,040.06$ Use $n = 1,041$

8.38   (a) $n = \dfrac{Z^2\sigma^2}{e^2} = \dfrac{1.96^2 \cdot 400^2}{50^2} = 245.86$ Use $n = 246$

       (b) $n = \dfrac{Z^2\sigma^2}{e^2} = \dfrac{1.96^2 \cdot 400^2}{25^2} = 983.41$ Use $n = 984$

8.40   Excel Output:

3	Data	
4	**Population Standard Deviation**	**1500**
5	**Sampling Error**	**400**
6	**Confidence Level**	**95%**
7		
8	Intemediate Calculations	
9	Z Value	-1.9600
10	Calculated Sample Size	54.0205
11		
12	Result	
13	**Sample Size Needed**	**55**
14		

$$n = \frac{Z^2\sigma^2}{e^2} = \frac{1.96^2 \cdot 1500^2}{400^2} = 54.0225 \qquad\qquad \text{Use } n = 55$$

8.42   (a) $n = \dfrac{Z^2\sigma^2}{e^2} = \dfrac{2.5758^2 \cdot 20^2}{5^2} = 106.1583 \qquad\qquad \text{Use } n = 107$

(b) $n = \dfrac{Z^2\sigma^2}{e^2} = \dfrac{1.96^2 \cdot 20^2}{5^2} = 61.4633 \qquad\qquad \text{Use } n = 62$

8.44   Note: All the answers are computed using PHStat. Answers computed otherwise may be slightly different due to rounding.

(a) $n = \dfrac{Z^2\sigma^2}{e^2} = \dfrac{1.96^2 \cdot 2^2}{0.25^2} = 245.85 \qquad\qquad \text{Use } n = 246$

(b) $n = \dfrac{Z^2\sigma^2}{e^2} = \dfrac{1.96^2 \cdot 2.5^2}{0.25^2} = 384.15 \qquad\qquad \text{Use } n = 385$

(c) $n = \dfrac{Z^2\sigma^2}{e^2} = \dfrac{1.96^2 \cdot 3.0^2}{0.25^2} = 553.17 \qquad\qquad \text{Use } n = 554$

(d)   When there is more variability in the population, a larger sample is needed to accurately estimate the mean.

8.46   (a)   Excel Output:

Data	
Sample Size	115
Number of Successes	81
Confidence Level	95%

Intermediate Calculations	
Sample Proportion	0.704348
Z Value	-1.9600
Standard Error of the Proportion	0.042553
Interval Half Width	0.0834

Confidence Interval	
Interval Lower Limit	0.6209
Interval Upper Limit	0.7878

$$p = 0.70 \quad p \pm Z\sqrt{\frac{p(1-p)}{n}} = 0.70 \pm 1.96\sqrt{\frac{0.70(1-0.70)}{115}}$$

$0.6209 \leq \pi \leq 0.7878$

(b)   Excel Output

Data	
Sample Size	115
Number of Successes	68
Confidence Level	95%

Intermediate Calculations	
Sample Proportion	0.591304
Z Value	-1.9600
Standard Error of the Proportion	0.045841
Interval Half Width	0.0898

Confidence Interval	
Interval Lower Limit	0.5015
Interval Upper Limit	0.6812

$$p = 0.59 \quad p \pm Z\sqrt{\frac{p(1-p)}{n}} = 0.59 \pm 1.96\sqrt{\frac{0.59(1-0.59)}{115}}$$

$0.5015 \leq \pi \leq 0.6812$

8.46 (c) Excel Output:
cont.

Data	
Sample Size	115
Number of Successes	16
Confidence Level	95%

Intermediate Calculations	
Sample Proportion	0.13913
Z Value	-1.9600
Standard Error of the Proportion	0.032272
Interval Half Width	0.0633

Confidence Interval	
Interval Lower Limit	0.0759
Interval Upper Limit	0.2024

$$p = 0.14 \quad p \pm Z\sqrt{\frac{p(1-p)}{n}} = 0.14 \pm 1.96\sqrt{\frac{0.14(1-0.14)}{115}}$$

$$0.0759 \leq \pi \leq 0.2024$$

(d) (a) Excel Output:

Data	
Estimate of True Proportion	0.7
Sampling Error	0.02
Confidence Level	95%

Intermediate Calculations	
Z Value	-1.9600
Calculated Sample Size	2016.7659

Result	
Sample Size Needed	2017

$$n = \frac{Z^2\pi(1-\pi)}{e^2} = \frac{1.96^2 \cdot (0.7)(1-0.7)}{.02^2} = 2016.84 \qquad \text{Use } n = 2017$$

8.46   (c)   (b) Excel Output:

cont.

3	Data	
4	**Estimate of True Proportion**	0.59
5	**Sampling Error**	0.02
6	Confidence Level	95%
7		
8	Intermediate Calculations	
9	Z Value	-1.9600
10	Calculated Sample Size	2323.1222
11		
12	Result	
13	Sample Size Needed	2324

$$n = \frac{Z^2 \pi(1-\pi)}{e^2} = \frac{1.96^2 \cdot (0.59)(1-0.59)}{.02^2} = 2323.208 \text{ Use } n = 2324$$

(c) Excel Output:

3	Data	
4	**Estimate of True Proportion**	0.14
5	**Sampling Error**	0.02
6	Confidence Level	95%
7		
8	Intermediate Calculations	
9	Z Value	-1.9600
10	Calculated Sample Size	1156.2791
11		
12	Result	
13	Sample Size Needed	1157

$$n = \frac{Z^2 \pi(1-\pi)}{e^2} = \frac{1.96^2 \cdot (0.14)(1-0.14)}{.02^2} = 1156.322 \text{ Use } n = 1157$$

8.48   (a)   If you conducted a follow-up study, you would use $\pi = 0.38$ in the sample size formula because it is based on past information on the proportion.

8.48   (b)   Excel Output:
cont.

	Data	
3	Data	
4	Estimate of True Proportion	0.38
5	Sampling Error	0.03
6	Confidence Level	95%
7		
8	Intermediate Calculations	
9	Z Value	-1.9600
10	Calculated Sample Size	1005.6086
11		
12	Result	
13	Sample Size Needed	1006
14		

$$n = \frac{Z^2 \pi(1-\pi)}{e^2} = \frac{1.96^2 \cdot (0.38)(1-0.38)}{.03^2} = 1005.646 \qquad \text{Use } n = 1006$$

8.50   The only way to have 100% confidence is to obtain the parameter of interest, rather than a sample statistic. From another perspective, the range of the normal and t distribution is infinite, so a Z or t value that contains 100% of the area cannot be obtained.

8.52   If the confidence level is increased, a greater area under the normal or t distribution needs to be included. This leads to an increased value of Z or t, and thus a wider interval.

8.54   (a)   PC/laptop Excel Output:

	Data	
3	Data	
4	Sample Size	1000
5	Number of Successes	840
6	Confidence Level	95%
7		
8	Intermediate Calculations	
9	Sample Proportion	0.84
10	Z Value	-1.9600
11	Standard Error of the Proportion	0.011593
12	Interval Half Width	0.0227
13		
14	Confidence Interval	
15	Interval Lower Limit	0.8173
16	Interval Upper Limit	0.8627
17		

$$p = 0.84 \quad p \pm Z\sqrt{\frac{p(1-p)}{n}} = 0.84 \pm 1.96\sqrt{\frac{0.84(1-0.84)}{1000}}$$

$$0.8173 \leq \pi \leq 0.8627$$

8.54   (a)   Smartphone Excel Output:
cont.

	Data	
3		
4	Sample Size	1000
5	Number of Successes	910
6	Confidence Level	95%
7		
8	Intermediate Calculations	
9	Sample Proportion	0.91
10	Z Value	-1.9600
11	Standard Error of the Proportion	0.00905
12	Interval Half Width	0.0177
13		
14	Confidence Interval	
15	Interval Lower Limit	0.8923
16	Interval Upper Limit	0.9277

$$p = 0.91 \quad p \pm Z\sqrt{\frac{p(1-p)}{n}} = 0.91 \pm 1.96\sqrt{\frac{0.91(1-0.91)}{1000}}$$

$$0.8923 \leq \pi \leq 0.9277$$

Tablet Excel Output:

	Data	
	Sample Size	1000
	Number of Successes	500
	Confidence Level	95%
	Intermediate Calculations	
	Sample Proportion	0.5
	Z Value	-1.9600
	Standard Error of the Proportion	0.015811
	Interval Half Width	0.0310
	Confidence Interval	
	Interval Lower Limit	0.4690
	Interval Upper Limit	0.5310

$$p = 0.5 \quad p \pm Z\sqrt{\frac{p(1-p)}{n}} = 0.5 \pm 1.96\sqrt{\frac{0.5(1-0.5)}{1000}}$$

$$0.469 \leq \pi \leq 0.5310$$

8.54   (a)   Smart Watch Excel Output:
cont.

Data	
Sample Size	1000
Number of Successes	100
Confidence Level	95%

Intermediate Calculations	
Sample Proportion	0.1
Z Value	-1.9600
Standard Error of the Proportion	0.009487
Interval Half Width	0.0186

Confidence Interval	
Interval Lower Limit	0.0814
Interval Upper Limit	0.1186

$$p = 0.1 \quad p \pm Z\sqrt{\frac{p(1-p)}{n}} = 0.1 \pm \sqrt{\frac{0.1(1-0.1)}{100}}$$

$$0.0814 \leq \pi \leq 0.1186$$

(b)   Most adults have a PC/laptop and a smartphone. Some adults have a tablet computer and very few have a smart watch.

8.56   Note: All the answers are computed using PHStat. Answers computed otherwise may be slightly different due to rounding.

(a)   PHStat output:

Confidence Interval Estimate for the Mean

Data	
Sample Standard Deviation	3.5
Sample Mean	51
Sample Size	40
Confidence Level	95%

Intermediate Calculations	
Standard Error of the Mean	0.553398591
Degrees of Freedom	39
t Value	2.0227
Interval Half Width	1.1194

Confidence Interval	
Interval Lower Limit	49.88
Interval Upper Limit	52.12

$$49.88 \leq \mu \leq 52.12$$

8.56   (b)   PHStat output:
cont.

Confidence Interval Estimate for the Proportion

Data	
Sample Size	40
Number of Successes	32
Confidence Level	95%

Intermediate Calculations	
Sample Proportion	0.8000
Z Value	-1.9600
Standard Error of the Proportion	0.0632
Interval Half Width	0.1240

Confidence Interval	
Interval Lower Limit	0.6760
Interval Upper Limit	0.9240

$$0.6760 \leq \pi \leq 0.9240$$

(c) $n = \dfrac{Z^2 \cdot \sigma^2}{e^2} = \dfrac{1.96^2 \cdot 5^2}{2^2} = 24.01$ Use $n = 25$

(d) $n = \dfrac{Z^2 \cdot \pi \cdot (1-\pi)}{e^2} = \dfrac{1.96^2 \cdot (0.5) \cdot (0.5)}{(0.06)^2} = 266.7680$ Use $n = 267$

(e)   If a single sample were to be selected for both purposes, the larger of the two sample sizes ($n = 267$) should be used.

8.58   (a)   PHStat output:

Confidence Interval Estimate for the Mean

Data	
Sample Standard Deviation	7.3
Sample Mean	6.2
Sample Size	25
Confidence Level	95%

Intermediate Calculations	
Standard Error of the Mean	1.46
Degrees of Freedom	24
t Value	2.0639
Interval Half Width	3.0133

Confidence Interval	
Interval Lower Limit	3.19
Interval Upper Limit	9.21

$$3.19 \leq \mu \leq 9.21$$

8.58   (b)   PHStat output:
cont.

Confidence Interval Estimate for the Proportion

Data	
Sample Size	25
Number of Successes	13
Confidence Level	95%

Intermediate Calculations	
Sample Proportion	0.52
Z Value	-1.9600
Standard Error of the Proportion	0.0999
Interval Half Width	0.1958

Confidence Interval	
Interval Lower Limit	0.3242
Interval Upper Limit	0.7158

$$0.3241 \le \pi \le 0.7158$$

(c) $n = \dfrac{Z^2 \cdot \sigma^2}{e^2} = \dfrac{1.96^2 \cdot 8^2}{1.5^2} = 109.2682$ Use $n = 110$

(d) $n = \dfrac{Z^2 \cdot \pi \cdot (1-\pi)}{e^2} = \dfrac{1.645^2 \cdot (0.5) \cdot (0.5)}{(0.075)^2} = 120.268$ Use $n = 121$

(e)   If a single sample were to be selected for both purposes, the larger of the two sample sizes ($n = 121$) should be used.

8.60   (a) $p \pm Z \cdot \sqrt{\dfrac{p(1-p)}{n}} = 0.31 \pm 1.645 \cdot \sqrt{\dfrac{0.31(0.69)}{200}}$ $0.2562 \le \pi \le 0.3638$

(b) $\bar{X} \pm t \cdot \dfrac{S}{\sqrt{n}} = 3.5 \pm 1.9720 \cdot \dfrac{2}{\sqrt{200}}$ $3.22 \le \mu \le 3.78$

(c) $\bar{X} \pm t \cdot \dfrac{S}{\sqrt{n}} = 18000 \pm 1.9720 \cdot \dfrac{3000}{\sqrt{200}}$ $\$17,581.68 \le \mu \le \$18,418.32$

8.62   (a) $\bar{X} \pm t \cdot \dfrac{S}{\sqrt{n}} = \$38.54 \pm 2.0010 \cdot \dfrac{\$7.26}{\sqrt{60}}$ $\$36.66 \le \mu \le \$40.42$

(b) $p \pm Z \cdot \sqrt{\dfrac{p(1-p)}{n}} = 0.30 \pm 1.645 \cdot \sqrt{\dfrac{0.30(0.70)}{60}}$ $0.2027 \le \pi \le 0.3973$

(c) $n = \dfrac{Z^2 \sigma^2}{e^2} = \dfrac{1.96^2 \cdot 8^2}{1.5^2} = 109.27$ Use $n = 110$

(d) $n = \dfrac{Z^2 \cdot \pi \cdot (1-\pi)}{e^2} = \dfrac{1.645^2 \cdot (0.5) \cdot (0.5)}{(0.04)^2} = 422.82$ Use $n = 423$

(e)   If a single sample were to be selected for both purposes, the larger of the two sample sizes ($n = 423$) should be used.

8.64   (a)

Confidence Interval Estimate for the Proportion	

Data	
Sample Size	90
Number of Successes	51
Confidence Level	95%

Intermediate Calculations	
Sample Proportion	0.566666667
Z Value	-1.9600
Standard Error of the Proportion	0.0522
Interval Half Width	0.1024

Confidence Interval	
Interval Lower Limit	0.4643
Interval Upper Limit	0.6690

$$p \pm Z \cdot \sqrt{\frac{p(1-p)}{n}} = 0.5667 \pm 1.96 \cdot \sqrt{\frac{0.5667(1-0.5667)}{90}}$$

$$0.4643 \leq \pi \leq 0.6690$$

(b)

Confidence Interval Estimate for the Mean	

Data	
Sample Standard Deviation	1103.6491
Sample Mean	563.38
Sample Size	51
Confidence Level	95%

Intermediate Calculations	
Standard Error of the Mean	154.5417855
Degrees of Freedom	50
t Value	2.0086
Interval Half Width	310.4063

Confidence Interval	
Interval Lower Limit	252.97
Interval Upper Limit	873.79

$$\bar{X} \pm t \cdot \frac{S}{\sqrt{n}} = 563.38 \pm 2.0086 \left(\frac{1103.6491}{\sqrt{51}} \right) \qquad \$252.97 \leq \mu \leq \$873.79$$

8.66   (a)   MiniTab Output

One-Sample T: Answer Time (seconds)

Descriptive Statistics

N	Mean	StDev	SE Mean	95% CI for μ
50	14.980	5.557	0.786	(13.401, 16.559)

μ: mean of Answer Time (seconds)

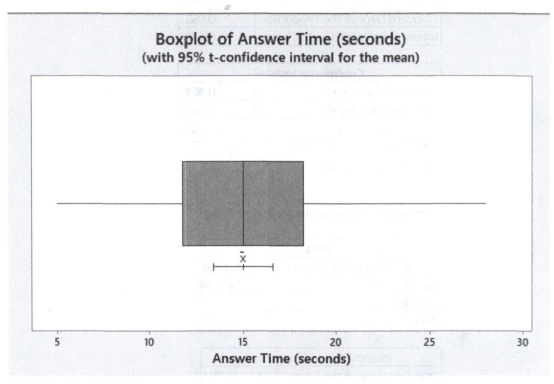

Boxplot of Answer Time (seconds)
(with 95% t-confidence interval for the mean)

$13.4001 \leq \mu \leq 16.559$

   (b)   With 95% confidence, the population mean answer time is somewhere between 13.40 and 16.56 seconds.

   (c)   The assumption is valid as the answer time is approximately normally distributed.

8.68   (a) $\bar{X} \pm t \cdot \dfrac{S}{\sqrt{n}} = 0.2641 \pm 1.9741 \cdot \dfrac{0.1424}{\sqrt{170}}$ $0.2425 \leq \mu \leq 0.2856$

   (b) $\bar{X} \pm t \cdot \dfrac{S}{\sqrt{n}} = 0.218 \pm 1.9772 \cdot \dfrac{0.1227}{\sqrt{140}}$ $0.1975 \leq \mu \leq 0.2385$

8.68   (c)
cont.

Normal Probability Plot

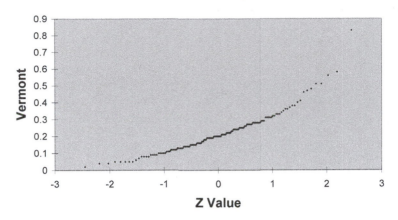

(c)

Normal Probability Plot

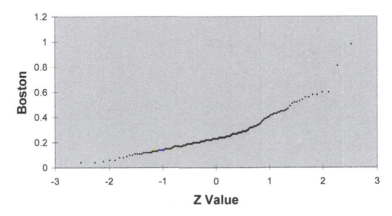

The amount of granule loss for both brands are skewed to the right but the sample sizes are large enough so the violation of the normality assumption is not critical.

(d)   Because the two confidence intervals do not overlap, you can conclude that the mean granule loss of Boston shingles is higher than that of Vermont shingles

CHAPTER 9

9.2   Decision rule: Reject H_0 if $Z_{STAT} < -1.96$ or $Z_{STAT} > +1.96$.
Decision: Since $Z_{STAT} = +2.21$ is greater than the upper critical value of $+1.96$, reject H_0.

9.4   Decision rule: Reject H_0 if $Z_{STAT} < -2.58$ or $Z_{STAT} > +2.58$.

9.6 p-value $= 2(1 - .9772) = 0.0456$

9.8 p-value $= 0.1676$

9.10   Under the French judicial system, unlike ours in the United States, the null hypothesis assumes the defendant is guilty, the alternative hypothesis assumes the defendant is innocent. A Type I error would be not convicting a guilty person and a Type II error would be convicting an innocent person.

9.12 H_0: $\mu = 20$ minutes. 20 minutes is adequate travel time between classes.
          H_1: $\mu \neq 20$ minutes. 20 minutes is not adequate travel time between classes.

9.14   (a)   Minitab Output:

One-Sample Z

Descriptive Statistics

N	Mean	SE Mean	95% CI for μ
64	49875	188	(49508, 50242)

μ: mean of Sample
Known standard deviation = 1500

Test

Null hypothesis	H_0: μ = 50000
Alternative hypothesis	H_1: μ ≠ 50000

Z-Value	P-Value
-0.67	0.505

H_0: $\mu = 50,000$. The mean life of a large shipment of LEDs is equal to 50,000 hours.
H_1: $\mu \neq 50,000$. The mean life of a large shipment of LEDs differs from 50,000 hours.
Decision rule: Reject H_0 if $|Z_{STAT}| > 1.96$

Test statistic: $Z_{STAT} = \dfrac{\overline{X} - \mu}{\dfrac{\sigma}{\sqrt{n}}} = -0.67$

Decision: Since $-1.96 < Z_{STAT} = -0.67 < 1.96$, do not reject H_0. There is not enough evidence to conclude that the mean life of a large shipment of LEDs differs from 50,000 hours.

(b) p-value $= 0.505$. If the population mean life of a large shipment of LEDs is indeed equal to 50,000 hours, there is a 50.5% chance of observing a test statistic at least as contradictory to the null hypothesis as the sample result.

9.14   (c) $\overline{X} \pm Z_{a/2}\dfrac{\sigma}{\sqrt{n}} = 49875 \pm 1.96\dfrac{1500}{\sqrt{64}}$ $49508 \le \mu \le 50242$

cont.   (d)   Because the interval includes the hypothesized value of 50000 hours, you do not reject the null hypothesis. There is insufficient evidence that the mean life of a large shipment of LEDs differs from 50,000 hours. The same decision was reached using the two-tailed hypothesis test.

9.16   (a)   PHStat output:

Data	
Null Hypothesis μ =	1
Level of Significance	0.01
Population Standard Deviation	0.02
Sample Size	50
Sample Mean	0.995
Intermediate Calculations	
Standard Error of the Mean	0.002828427
Z Test Statistic	-1.767766953
Two-Tail Test	
Lower Critical Value	-2.575829304
Upper Critical Value	2.575829304
p-Value	0.077099872
Do not reject the null hypothesis	

H_0: $\mu = 1$. The mean amount of water is 1 gallon.

H_1: $\mu \ne 1$. The mean amount of water differs from 1 gallon.

Decision rule: Reject H_0 if $|Z_{STAT}| > 2.5758$

Test statistic: $Z_{STAT} = \dfrac{\overline{X} - \mu}{\dfrac{\sigma}{\sqrt{n}}} = \dfrac{.995 - 1}{\dfrac{.02}{\sqrt{50}}} = -1.7678$

Decision: Since $|Z_{STAT}| < 2.5758$, do not reject H_0. There is not enough evidence to conclude that the mean amount of water contained in 1-gallon bottles purchased from a nationally known water bottling company is different from 1 gallon.

(b)   p-value = 0.0771. If the population mean amount of water contained in 1-gallon bottles purchased from a nationally known water bottling company is actually 1 gallon, the probability of obtaining a test statistic that is more than 1.7678 standard error units away from 0 is 0.0771.

9.16   (c)   PHStat output:
cont.

Data	
Population Standard Deviation	0.02
Sample Mean	0.995
Sample Size	50
Confidence Level	99%
Intermediate Calculations	
Standard Error of the Mean	0.002828427
Z Value	-2.5758293
Interval Half Width	0.007285545
Confidence Interval	
Interval Lower Limit	0.987714455
Interval Upper Limit	1.002285545

$$\overline{X} \pm Z_{a/2}\frac{\sigma}{\sqrt{n}} = .995 \pm 2.5758\frac{.02}{\sqrt{50}} \qquad 0.9877 \le \mu \le 1.0023$$

You are 99% confident that population mean amount of water contained in 1-gallon bottles purchased from a nationally known water bottling company is somewhere between 0.9877 and 1.0023 gallons.

(d)   Since the 99% confidence interval does contain the hypothesized value of 1, you will not reject H_0. The conclusions are the same.

9.18 $t_{STAT} = \dfrac{\overline{X} - \mu}{\dfrac{S}{\sqrt{n}}} = \dfrac{56 - 50}{\dfrac{12}{\sqrt{16}}} = 2.00$

9.20   For a two-tailed test with a 0.05 level of confidence, the critical values are ± 2.1315.

9.22   No, you should not use the t test to test the null hypothesis that $\mu = 60$ on a population that is left-skewed because the sample size ($n = 16$) is less than 30. The t test assumes that, if the underlying population is not normally distributed, the sample size is sufficiently large to enable the test to be valid. If sample sizes are small ($n < 30$), the t test should not be used because the sampling distribution does not meet the requirements of the Central Limit Theorem.

9.24   PHStat output:

t Test for Hypothesis of the Mean	
Data	
Null Hypothesis $\mu =$	3.7
Level of Significance	0.05
Sample Size	64
Sample Mean	3.57
Sample Standard Deviation	0.8
Intermediate Calculations	
Standard Error of the Mean	0.1
Degrees of Freedom	63
t Test Statistic	-1.3
Two-Tail Test	
Lower Critical Value	-1.9983405
Upper Critical Value	1.9983405
***p*-Value**	0.1983372
Do not reject the null hypothesis	

(a) $H_0 : \mu = 3.7$ $H_1 : \mu \neq 3.7$

Decision rule: Reject H_0 if $|t_{STAT}| > 1.9983$ $d.f. = 63$

Test statistic: $t_{STAT} = \dfrac{\overline{X} - \mu}{\dfrac{S}{\sqrt{n}}} = \dfrac{3.57 - 3.7}{\dfrac{0.8}{\sqrt{64}}} = -1.3$

Decision: Since $|t_{STAT}| < 1.9983$, do not reject H_0. There is not enough evidence to conclude that the population mean waiting time is different from 3.7 minutes at the 0.05 level of significance.

(b)   The sample size of 64 is large enough to apply the Central Limit Theorem and, hence, you do not need to be concerned about the shape of the population distribution when conducting the *t*-test in (a). In general, the *t* test is appropriate for this sample size except for the case where the population is extremely skewed or bimodal.

9.26   PHStat output:

t Test for Hypothesis of the Mean

Data	
Null Hypothesis μ=	1475
Level of Significance	0.05
Sample Size	100
Sample Mean	1500
Sample Standard Deviation	200

Intermediate Calculations	
Standard Error of the Mean	20.0000
Degrees of Freedom	99
t Test Statistic	1.2500

Two-Tail Test	
Lower Critical Value	-1.9842
Upper Critical Value	1.9842
p-Value	0.2142
Do not reject the null hypothesis	

(a) $H_0 : \mu = \$1,475$ $H_1 : \mu \neq \$1,475$

Decision rule: Reject H_0 if p-value < 0.05

Test statistic: $t_{STAT} = \dfrac{\overline{X} - \mu}{\dfrac{S}{\sqrt{n}}} = 1.2500$

p-value = 0.2142

Decision: Since the p-value of 0.2142 > 0.05, do not reject H_0. There is not enough evidence to conclude that the population mean amount spent on Amazon.com by Amazon Prime member shoppers is different from $1,475.

(b)   The p-value is 0.2142. If the population mean is indeed $1,475, the probability of obtaining a test statistic that is more than 1.25 standard error units away from 0 in either direction is 0.2142.

9.28   PHStat output:

t Test for Hypothesis of the Mean

Data	
Null Hypothesis $\mu=$	6.5
Level of Significance	0.05
Sample Size	15
Sample Mean	7.09
Sample Standard Deviation	1.406031226

Intermediate Calculations	
Standard Error of the Mean	0.3630
Degrees of Freedom	14
t Test Statistic	1.6344

Two-Tail Test	
Lower Critical Value	-2.1448
Upper Critical Value	2.1448
p-Value	0.1245
Do not reject the null hypothesis	

(a) $H_0 : \mu = \$6.50 \qquad H_1 : \mu \neq \$6.50$

Decision rule: Reject H_0 if $|t_{STAT}| > 2.1448$ or *p*-value < 0.05

Test statistic: $t_{STAT} = \dfrac{\overline{X} - \mu}{\dfrac{S}{\sqrt{n}}} = 1.6344$

Decision: Since $|t_{STAT}| < 2.1448$, do not reject H_0. There is not enough evidence to conclude that the mean amount spent for lunch is different from $6.50.

(b)   The *p*-value is 0.1245. If the population mean is indeed $6.50, the probability of obtaining a test statistic that is more than 1.6344 standard error units away from 0 in either direction is 0.4069.

(c)   That the distribution of the amount spent on lunch is normally distributed.

(d)   With a sample size of 15, it is difficult to evaluate the assumption of normality. However, the distribution may be fairly symmetric because the mean and the median are close in value. Also, the boxplot appears only slightly skewed so the normality assumption does not appear to be seriously violated.

9.30   (a) $H_0 : \mu = 2 \qquad H_1 : \mu \neq 2 \qquad d.f. = 49$

Decision rule: Reject H_0 if $|t_{STAT}| > 2.0096$

Test statistic: $t_{STAT} = \dfrac{\overline{X} - \mu}{\dfrac{S}{\sqrt{n}}} = \dfrac{2.0007 - 2}{\dfrac{0.0446}{\sqrt{50}}} = 0.1143$

Decision: Since $|t_{STAT}| < 2.0096$, do not reject H_0. There is not enough evidence to conclude that the mean amount of soft drink filled is different from 2.0 liters.

(b)   *p*-value = 0.9095. If the population mean amount of soft drink filled is indeed 2.0 liters, the probability of observing a sample of 50 soft drinks that will result in a sample mean amount of fill more different from 2.0 liters is 0.9095.

9.30
cont.
(c)

Normal Probability Plot

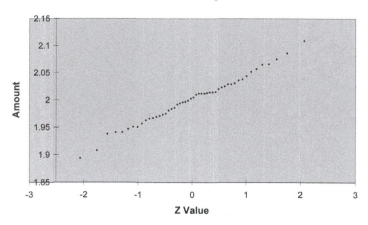

(d)   The normal probability plot suggests that the data are rather normally distributed. Hence, the results in (a) are valid in terms of the normality assumption.

(e)

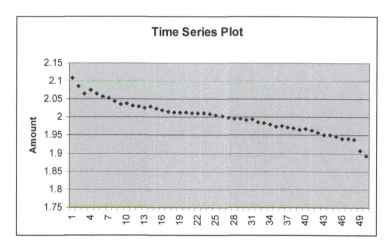

The time series plot of the data reveals that there is a downward trend in the amount of soft drink filled. This violates the assumption that data are drawn independently from a normal population distribution because the amount of fill in consecutive bottles appears to be closely related. As a result, the *t* test in (a) becomes invalid.

9.32   (a) $H_0 : \mu = 8.46$ $H_1 : \mu \neq 8.46$

Decision rule: Reject H_0 if $|t_{STAT}| > 2.0106$ $d.f. = 48$

Test statistic: $t_{STAT} = \dfrac{\overline{X} - \mu}{\dfrac{S}{\sqrt{n}}} = \dfrac{8.4209 - 8.46}{\dfrac{0.0461}{\sqrt{49}}} = -5.9355$

Decision: Since $|t_{STAT}| > 2.0106$, reject H_0. There is enough evidence to conclude that mean widths of the troughs is different from 8.46 inches.

(b)   The population distribution needs to be normal.

9.32   (c)
cont.

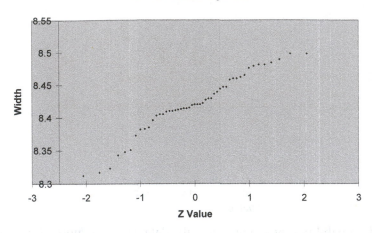

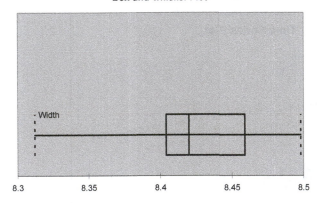

(d)   The normal probability plot and the boxplot indicate that the distribution is skewed to the left. Even though the population distribution is not normally distributed, the result obtained in (a) should still be valid due to the Central Limit Theorem as a result of the relatively large sample size of 49.

9.34   (a) $H_0 : \mu = 5.5$ $H_1 : \mu \neq 5.5$

Decision rule: Reject H_0 if $|t_{STAT}| > 2.680$ $d.f. = 49$

Test statistic: $t_{STAT} = \dfrac{\overline{X} - \mu}{\dfrac{S}{\sqrt{n}}} = \dfrac{5.5014 - 5.5}{\dfrac{0.1058}{\sqrt{50}}} = 0.0935$

Decision: Since $|t_{STAT}| < 2.680$, do not reject H_0. There is not enough evidence to conclude that the mean amount of tea per bag is different from 5.5 grams.

(b) $\overline{X} \pm t \cdot \dfrac{s}{\sqrt{n}} = 5.5014 \pm 2.6800 \cdot \dfrac{0.1058}{\sqrt{50}}$ $5.46 < \mu < 5.54$

With 99% confidence, you can conclude that the population mean amount of tea per bag is somewhere between 5.46 and 5.54 grams.

(c)   The conclusions are the same.

9.36   *p*-value = 1 − 0.9772 = 0.0228

9.38   *p*-value = 0.0838

9.40   *p*-value = $P(Z < 1.38) = 0.9162$

9.42   *t* = 2.7638

9.44   *t* = -2.5280

9.46   (a)

One-Sample T

Descriptive Statistics

N	Mean	StDev	SE Mean	95% Lower Bound for μ
64	8210.0	625.0	78.1	8079.6

μ: mean of Sample

Test

Null hypothesis	Ho: μ = 8000
Alternative hypothesis	H₁: μ > 8000

T-Value	P-Value
2.69	0.005

$H_0 : \mu \leq 8000 \qquad H_1 : \mu > 8000$

Decision rule: Reject H_0 if *p*-value < 0.05   *d.f.* = 63

Test statistic: $t_{STAT} = \dfrac{\overline{X} - \mu}{\dfrac{S}{\sqrt{n}}} = 2.69$

p-value = 0.005

Decision: t_{STAT} = 2.69 > 1.6694, reject H_0. There is evidence to conclude that the population mean bus miles is more than 8000 bus miles.

(b)   The *p*-value is 0.005 < 0.05. The probability of getting a t_{STAT} statistic greater than 2.69 given that the null hypothesis is true, is 0.005.

9.48   (a)   Minitab Output:

One-Sample T

Descriptive Statistics

N	Mean	StDev	SE Mean	99% Upper Bound for μ
860	24.050	16.500	0.563	25.361

μ: mean of Sample

Test

Null hypothesis	H_0: $\mu = 30$
Alternative hypothesis	H_1: $\mu < 30$

T-Value	P-Value
-10.58	0.000

$H_0 : \mu \geq 30$ $H_1 : \mu < 30$

Decision rule: Reject H_0 if p-value < 0.01 $d.f. = 859$

Test statistic: $t_{STAT} = \dfrac{\overline{X} - \mu}{\dfrac{S}{\sqrt{n}}} = $ -10.58

p-value $= 0.000$

Decision: $t_{STAT} = -10.58 < $ -2.3307, reject H_0. p-value $= 0.000 < 0.01$, reject H_0. There is evidence to conclude that the population mean wait time is less than 30 minutes.

   (b)   The probability of getting a sample mean of 24 minutes or less if the population mean is 30 minutes is 0.000.

9.50   (a)   Minitab Output:

One-Sample T

Descriptive Statistics

N	Mean	StDev	SE Mean	99% Lower Bound for μ
133	87.000	9.000	0.780	85.162

μ: mean of Sample

Test

Null hypothesis	H_0: $\mu = 85.5$
Alternative hypothesis	H_1: $\mu > 85.5$

T-Value	P-Value
1.92	0.028

9.50   (a) $H_0 : \mu \le 85.5$ $H_1 : \mu > 85.5$
cont.   Decision rule: Reject H_0 if p-value < 0.01 $d.f. = 132$

Test statistic: $t_{STAT} = \dfrac{\overline{X} - \mu}{\dfrac{S}{\sqrt{n}}} = 1.92$

p-value = 0.028

Decision: $t_{STAT} = 1.92 < 2.35493$, do not reject H_0. p-value = 0.028 > 0.01, do not reject H_0. There is insufficient evidence to conclude that the population mean one-time gift donation is greater than $85.50.

(b)   The probability of getting a sample mean of $87 or more if the population mean is $85.5 is 0.028.

9.52 $p = \dfrac{X}{n} = \dfrac{88}{400} = 0.22$

9.54 H_0: $\pi = 0.20$
H_1: $\pi \ne 0.20$
Decision rule: If $Z < -1.96$ or $Z > 1.96$, reject H_0.

Test statistic: $Z_{STAT} = \dfrac{p - \pi}{\sqrt{\dfrac{\pi(1-\pi)}{n}}} = \dfrac{0.22 - 0.20}{\sqrt{\dfrac{0.20(0.8)}{400}}} = 1.00$

Decision: Since $Z = 1.00$ is between the critical bounds of ± 1.96, do not reject H_0.

9.56   (a)   Minitab Output:

Test and CI for One Proportion

Method

p: event proportion
Normal approximation method is used for this analysis.

Descriptive Statistics

N	Event	Sample p	95% Lower Bound for p
100	60	0.600000	0.519419

Test

Null hypothesis	H_0: p = 0.5643
Alternative hypothesis	H_1: p > 0.5643

Z-Value	P-Value
0.72	0.236

H_0: $\pi \le 0.5643$
H_1: $\pi > 0.5643$

9.56   (a)   Decision rule: p-value < 0.05, reject H_0.

cont.   Test statistic: $Z_{STAT} = \dfrac{p - \pi}{\sqrt{\dfrac{\pi(1-\pi)}{n}}} = 0.72$ p-value $= 0.236$

Decision: Since p-value $= 0.236 > 0.05$, Do not reject H_0. There is not enough evidence that the proportion of Chrome web browser users at your university is greater than 0.5643

(b)   Minitab Output:

Test and CI for One Proportion

Method

p: event proportion
Normal approximation method is used for this analysis.

Descriptive Statistics

N	Event	Sample p	95% Lower Bound for p
600	360	0.600000	0.567103

Test

Null hypothesis	H_0: p = 0.5643
Alternative hypothesis	H_1: p > 0.5643

Z-Value	P-Value
1.76	0.039

H_0: $\pi \leq 0.5643$
H_1: $\pi > 0.5643$
Decision rule: p-value < 0.05, reject H_0.

Test statistic: $Z_{STAT} = \dfrac{p - \pi}{\sqrt{\dfrac{\pi(1-\pi)}{n}}} = 1.76$ p-value $= 0.039$

Decision: Since p-value $= 0.039 < 0.05$, Reject H_0. There is evidence that the proportion of Chrome web browser users at your university is greater than 0.5643.

(c)   The sample size had a major effect on being able to reject the null hypothesis.

(d)   You would be very unlikely to reject the null hypothesis with a sample of 20.

9.58   (a)   Minitab Output:

Test and CI for One Proportion

Method

p: event proportion
Normal approximation method is used for this analysis.

Descriptive Statistics

N	Event	Sample p	95% CI for p
703	464	0.660028	(0.625012, 0.695045)

Test

Null hypothesis	H_0: p = 0.6
Alternative hypothesis	H_1: p ≠ 0.6

Z-Value	P-Value
3.25	0.001

(b) H_0: $\pi = 0.60$
H_1: $\pi \neq 0.60$
Decision rule: p-value < 0.05, reject H_0.

Test statistic: $Z_{STAT} = \dfrac{p - \pi}{\sqrt{\dfrac{\pi(1-\pi)}{n}}} = 3.25$ p-value $= 0.001$

Decision: Since p-value $= 0.001 < 0.05$, reject H_0. There is evidence that the proportion of all talent acquisition professionals who report competition is the biggest obstacle to attracting the best talent at their company is different from 0.60.

9.60   (a) H_0: $\pi \geq 0.294$. H_1: $\pi < 0.294$.

9.60   (b)   Minitab Output:
cont.

Test and CI for One Proportion

Method

p: event proportion
Normal approximation method is used for this analysis.

Descriptive Statistics

N	Event	Sample p	95% Upper Bound for p
100	27	0.270000	0.343025

Test

Null hypothesis	H_0: p = 0.294
Alternative hypothesis	H_1: p < 0.294

Z-Value	P-Value
-0.53	0.299

H_0: $\pi \geq 0.294$
H_1: $\pi < 0.294$
Decision rule: p-value < 0.05, reject H_0 or $Z_{STAT} < -1.645$, reject H_0

Test statistic: $Z_{STAT} = \dfrac{p - \pi}{\sqrt{\dfrac{\pi(1-\pi)}{n}}} = -0.53$ p-value = 0.299

Decision: Because $Z_{STAT} = -0.53 > -1.645$ or p-value = 0.299 > 0.05, Do not reject H_0.
There is not enough evidence that the proportion is less than 0.294.

9.62   A Type I error represents rejecting a true null hypothesis, while a Type II error represents not rejecting a false null hypothesis.

9.64   In a one-tailed test for a mean or proportion, the entire rejection region is contained in one tail of the distribution. In a two-tailed test, the rejection region is split into two equal parts, one in the lower tail of the distribution, and the other in the upper tail.

9.66   Assuming a two-tailed test is used, if the hypothesized value for the parameter does not fall into the confidence interval, then the null hypothesis can be rejected.

9.68   The following are the 5-step p-value approach to hypothesis testing: (1) State the null hypothesis, H_0, and the alternative hypothesis, H_1. (2) Choose the level of significance, α, and the sample size, n. (3) Determine the appropriate test statistic and the sampling distribution. (4) Collect the sample data, compute the value of the test statistic, and compute the p-value. (5) Make the statistical decision and state the managerial conclusion. If the p-value is greater than or equal to α, you do not reject the null hypothesis, H_0. If the p-value is less than α, you reject the null hypothesis.

9.70   (a)   A Type I error occurs when a firm is predicted to be a bankrupt firm when it will not.
      (b)   A Type II error occurs when a firm is predicted to be a non-bankrupt firm when it will go bankrupt.
      (c)   The executives are trying to avoid a Type I error by adopting a very stringent decision criterion. Only firms that show significant evidence of being in financial stress will be predicted to go bankrupt within the next two years at the chosen level of the possibility of making a Type I error.
      (d)   If the revised model results in more moderate or large Z scores, the probability of committing a Type I error will increase. Many more of the firms will be predicted to go bankrupt than will go bankrupt. On the other hand, the revised model that results in more moderate or large Z scores will lower the probability of committing a Type II error because few firms will be predicted to go bankrupt than will actually go bankrupt.

9.72   (a)   PHStat output:

t Test for Hypothesis of the Mean

Data	
Null Hypothesis $\mu=$	6.5
Level of Significance	0.05
Sample Size	60
Sample Mean	7.25
Sample Standard Deviation	1.75

Intermediate Calculations	
Standard Error of the Mean	0.2259
Degrees of Freedom	59
t Test Statistic	3.3197

Two-Tail Test	
Lower Critical Value	-2.0010
Upper Critical Value	2.0010
p-Value	0.0015
Reject the null hypothesis	

H_0: μ = \$6.50
H_1: $\mu \neq$ \$6.50

Decision rule: $d.f.$ = 59. If p-value < 0.05, reject H_0.

Test statistic: $t_{STAT} = \dfrac{\overline{X} - \mu}{\dfrac{S}{\sqrt{n}}} = = 3.3197$ p-value = 0.0015

Decision: Since p-value < 0.05, reject H_0. There is enough evidence to conclude that the mean amount spent differs from \$6.50
      (b) p-value = 0.0015.
Note: The-p value was found using Excel.

9.72   (c)   PHStat output:
cont.

Z Test of Hypothesis for the Proportion	
Data	
Null Hypothesis $\pi =$	0.5
Level of Significance	0.05
Number of Items of Interest	31
Sample Size	60

Intermediate Calculations	
Sample Proportion	0.516666667
Standard Error	0.0645
Z Test Statistic	0.2582

Upper-Tail Test	
Upper Critical Value	1.6449
p-Value	0.3981
Do not reject the null hypothesis	

H_0: $\pi \leq 0.50$.

H_1: $\pi > 0.50$.

Decision rule: If *p*-value < 0.05, reject H_0.

Test statistic: $Z_{STAT} = \dfrac{p - \pi}{\sqrt{\dfrac{\pi(1-\pi)}{n}}} = \, = 0.2582$ *p*-value $= 0.3981$

Decision: Since *p*-value > 0.05, do not reject H_0. There is not sufficient evidence to conclude that more than 50% of customers say they "definitely will" recommend the specialty coffee shop to family and friends.

(d)   PHStat output:

t Test for Hypothesis of the Mean	
Data	
Null Hypothesis $\mu =$	6.5
Level of Significance	0.05
Sample Size	60
Sample Mean	6.25
Sample Standard Deviation	1.75

Intermediate Calculations	
Standard Error of the Mean	0.2259
Degrees of Freedom	59
t Test Statistic	-1.1066

Two-Tail Test	
Lower Critical Value	-2.0010
Upper Critical Value	2.0010
p-Value	0.2730
Do not reject the null hypothesis	

9.72 (d)
cont.

H_0: μ = $6.50

H_1: $\mu \ne$ $6.50

Decision rule: d.f. = 59. If p-value < 0.05, reject H_0.

Test statistic: $t = \dfrac{\overline{X} - \mu}{\dfrac{S}{\sqrt{n}}} = \dfrac{6.25 - 6.5}{\dfrac{1.75}{\sqrt{60}}} = -1.1066$ p-value = 0.2730

Decision: Since the p-value > 0.05, do not reject H_0. There is not enough evidence to conclude that the mean amount spent differs from $6.50.

(e)   PHStat output:

Z Test of Hypothesis for the Proportion

Data	
Null Hypothesis π =	0.5
Level of Significance	0.05
Number of Items of Interest	39
Sample Size	60

Intermediate Calculations	
Sample Proportion	0.65
Standard Error	0.0645
Z Test Statistic	2.3238

Upper-Tail Test	
Upper Critical Value	1.6449
p-Value	0.0101
Reject the null hypothesis	

H_0: $\pi \le 0.50$.

H_1: $\pi > 0.50$.

Decision rule: If p-value < 0.05, reject H_0.

Test statistic: $Z_{STAT} = \dfrac{p - \pi}{\sqrt{\dfrac{\pi(1-\pi)}{n}}} = = 2.3238$ p-value = 0.0101

Decision: Since p-value < 0.05, reject H_0. There is sufficient evidence to conclude that more than 50% of customers say they "definitely will" recommend the specialty coffee shop to family and friends.

9.74 (a)

H_0: $\mu \ge$ 5 minutes. The mean waiting time at a bank branch in a commercial district of the city is at least 5 minutes during the 12:00 p.m. to 1 p.m. peak lunch period.
H_1: $\mu <$ 5 minutes. The mean waiting time at a bank branch in a commercial district of the city is less than 5 minutes during the 12:00 p.m. to 1 p.m. peak lunch period.
Decision rule: d.f. = 14. If $t_{STAT} < -1.7613$, reject H_0.

Test statistic: $t_{STAT} = \dfrac{\overline{X} - \mu}{\dfrac{S}{\sqrt{n}}} = \dfrac{4.28\overline{66} - 5.0}{\dfrac{1.637985}{\sqrt{15}}} = -1.6867$

9.74   (a)   Decision: Since $t_{STAT} = -1.6867$ is greater than the critical bound of -1.7613, do not reject
cont. H_0. There is not enough evidence to conclude that the mean waiting time at a bank branch
                in a commercial district of the city is less than 5 minutes during the 12:00 p.m. to 1 p.m.
                peak lunch period.

        (b)   To perform the t-test on the population mean, you must assume that the observed
                sequence in which the data were collected is random and that the data are approximately
                normally distributed.

        (c)   Normal probability plot:

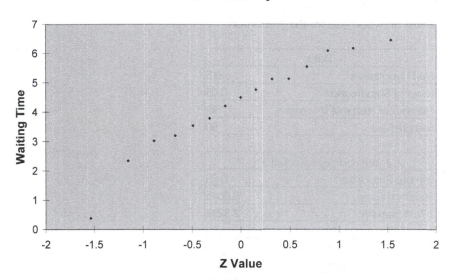

Normal Probability Plot

        (d)   With the exception of one extreme point, the data are approximately normally distributed.
        (e)   Based on the results of (a), the manager does not have enough evidence to make that
                statement.

9.76   (a) $H_0 : \mu \geq 0.35$ $H_1 : \mu < 0.35$

                Decision rule: Reject H_0 if $t_{STAT} < -1.690$ $d.f. = 35$

                Test statistic: $t_{STAT} = \dfrac{\bar{X} - \mu}{\dfrac{S}{\sqrt{n}}} = \dfrac{0.3167 - 0.35}{\dfrac{0.1357}{\sqrt{36}}} = -1.4735$

                Decision: Since $t_{STAT} > -1.690$, do not reject H_0.

                There is not enough evidence to conclude that the mean moisture content for Boston
                shingles is less than 0.35 pounds per 100 square feet.

        (b) p-value $= 0.0748$. If the population mean moisture content is in fact no less than 0.35
                pounds per 100 square feet, the probability of observing a sample of 36 shingles that will
                result in a sample mean moisture content of 0.3167 pounds per 100 square feet or less is
                .0748.

        (c) $H_0 : \mu \geq 0.35$ $H_1 : \mu < 0.35$

                Decision rule: Reject H_0 if $t_{STAT} < -1.6973$ $d.f. = 30$

                Test statistic: $t_{STAT} = \dfrac{\bar{X} - \mu}{\dfrac{S}{\sqrt{n}}} = \dfrac{0.2735 - 0.35}{\dfrac{0.1373}{\sqrt{31}}} = -3.1003$

9.76   (c)   Decision: Since $t_{STAT} < -1.6973$, reject H_0. There is enough evidence to conclude that the
cont.   mean moisture content for Vermont shingles is less than 0.35 pounds per 100 square feet.
        (d) p-value = 0.0021. If the population mean moisture content is in fact no less than 0.35
                pounds per 100 square feet, the probability of observing a sample of 31 shingles that will
                result in a sample mean moisture content of 0.2735 pounds per 100 square feet or less is
                .0021.
        (e)   In order for the t test to be valid, the data are assumed to be independently drawn from a
                population that is normally distributed. Since the sample sizes are 36 and 31,
                respectively, which are considered quite large, the t distribution will provide a good
                approximation to the sampling distribution of the mean as long as the population
                distribution is not very skewed.
        (f)

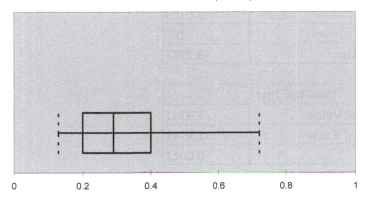

Box-and-whisker Plot (Boston)

        (f)

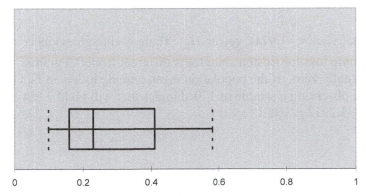

Box-and-whisker Plot (Vermont)

                Both boxplots suggest that the data are skewed slightly to the right, more so for the
                Boston shingles. However, the very large sample sizes mean that the results of the t test
                are relatively insensitive to the departure from normality.

9.78   (a) $H_0 : \mu = 0.3$ $H_1 : \mu \neq 0.3$

t Test for Hypothesis of the Mean	
Data	
Null Hypothesis μ=	0.3
Level of Significance	0.05
Sample Size	170
Sample Mean	0.26
Sample Standard Deviation	0.142382504

Intermediate Calculations	
Standard Error of the Mean	0.0109
Degrees of Freedom	169
t Test Statistic	-3.2912

Two-Tail Test	
Lower Critical Value	-1.9741
Upper Critical Value	1.9741
p-Value	0.0012
Reject the null hypothesis	

Decision rule: Reject H_0 if $|t_{STAT}| > 1.9741$ $d.f. = 169$

Test statistic: $t_{STAT} = \dfrac{\overline{X} - \mu}{\dfrac{S}{\sqrt{n}}} = -3.2912$, p-value $= 0.0012$

Decision: Since $t_{STAT} < -1.9741$, reject H_0. There is enough evidence to conclude that the mean granule loss for Boston shingles is different from 0.3 grams.

(b) p-value is virtually zero. If the population mean granule loss is in fact 0.3 grams, the probability of observing a sample of 170 shingles that will yield a test statistic more extreme than -3.2912 is 0.0012.

9.78   (c) $H_0 : \mu = 0.5$ $H_1 : \mu \neq 0.5$

cont.

t Test for Hypothesis of the Mean	
Data	
Null Hypothesis μ=	0.3
Level of Significance	0.05
Sample Size	140
Sample Mean	0.22
Sample Standard Deviation	0.122698672
Intermediate Calculations	
Standard Error of the Mean	0.0104
Degrees of Freedom	139
t Test Statistic	-7.9075
Two-Tail Test	
Lower Critical Value	-1.9772
Upper Critical Value	1.9772
p-Value	0.0000
Reject the null hypothesis	

Decision rule: Reject H_0 if $|t_{STAT}| > 1.9772$ $d.f. = 139$

Test statistic: $t_{STAT} = \dfrac{\overline{X} - \mu}{\dfrac{S}{\sqrt{n}}} = -7.9075$

Decision: Since $t_{STAT} < -1.977$, reject H_0. There is enough evidence to conclude that the mean granule loss for Vermont shingles is different from 0.3 grams.

   (d)   *p*-value is virtually zero. The probability of observing a sample of 140 shingles that will yield a test statistic more extreme than -1.977 is virtually zero if the population mean granule loss is in fact 0.3 grams.

   (e)   In order for the *t* test to be valid, the data are assumed to be independently drawn from a population that is normally distributed. Both normal probability plots indicate that the data are slightly right-skewed. Since the sample sizes are 170 and 140, respectively, which are considered large enough, the *t* distribution will provide a good approximation to the sampling distribution of the mean even if the population is not normally distributed.

CHAPTER 10

10.2 (a) $$S_p^2 = \frac{(n_1-1)\cdot S_1^2 + (n_2-1)\cdot S_2^2}{(n_1-1)+(n_2-1)} = \frac{(7)\cdot 4^2 + (14)\cdot 5^2}{7+14} = 22$$

$$t_{STAT} = \frac{\left(\overline{X}_1 - \overline{X}_2\right) - \left(\mu_1 - \mu_2\right)}{\sqrt{S_p^2\left(\frac{1}{n_1}+\frac{1}{n_2}\right)}} = \frac{(42-34)-0}{\sqrt{22\left(\frac{1}{8}+\frac{1}{15}\right)}} = 3.8959$$

(b) $d.f. = (n_1 - 1) + (n_2 - 1) = 7 + 14 = 21$

(c) Decision rule: $d.f. = 21$. If $t_{STAT} > 2.5177$, reject H_0.

(d) Decision: Since $t = 3.8959$ is greater than the critical bound of 2.5177, reject H_0. There is enough evidence to conclude that the first population mean is larger than the second population mean.

10.4 $\left(\overline{X}_1 - \overline{X}_2\right) \pm t\sqrt{S_p^2\left(\frac{1}{n_1}+\frac{1}{n_2}\right)} = (42-34) \pm 2.0796\sqrt{22\left(\frac{1}{8}+\frac{1}{15}\right)}$ $3.7296 \le \mu_1 - \mu_2 \le 12.2704$

10.6 PHStat output:

Data	
Hypothesized Difference	0
Level of Significance	0.01
Population 1 Sample	
Sample Size	5
Sample Mean	42
Sample Standard Deviation	4
Population 2 Sample	
Sample Size	4
Sample Mean	34
Sample Standard Deviation	5

Intermediate Calculations	
Population 1 Sample Degrees of Freedom	4
Population 2 Sample Degrees of Freedom	3
Total Degrees of Freedom	7
Pooled Variance	19.85714
Difference in Sample Means	8
t Test Statistic	2.676242

Upper-Tail Test	
Upper Critical Value	2.997949
p-Value	0.015856
Do not reject the null hypothesis	

10.6 $H_0: \mu_1 \le \mu_2$ $H_1: \mu_1 > \mu_2$

cont.   Test statistic: $t_{STAT} = \dfrac{\left(\overline{X}_1 - \overline{X}_2\right) - \left(\mu_1 - \mu_2\right)}{\sqrt{S_p^2\left(\dfrac{1}{n_1} + \dfrac{1}{n_2}\right)}} = 2.6762$

Decision: Since $t_{STAT} = 2.6762$ is smaller than the upper critical bounds of 2.9979, do not reject H_0. There is not enough evidence of a difference in the means of the two populations.

10.8   (a)   Because $t_{STAT} = 2.8990 > 1.6620$ or p-value $= 0.0024 < 0.05$, reject H_0. There is evidence that the mean amount of Walker Crisps eaten by children who watched a commercial featuring a long-standing sports celebrity endorser is higher than for those who watched a commercial for an alternative food snack.

      (b) $3.4616 \le \mu_1 - \mu_2 \le 18.5384$

      (c)   The results cannot be compared because (a) is a one-tail test and (b) is a confidence interval that is comparable only to the results of a two-tail test.

      (d)   You would choose the commercial featuring a long-standing celebrity endorser.

10.10 (a)

Two-Sample T-Test and CI: Number of Partners, Region

Method

μ_1: mean of Number of Partners when Region = Gulf Coast
μ_2: mean of Number of Partners when Region = Southeast
Difference: $\mu_1 - \mu_2$

Equal variances are assumed for this analysis.

Descriptive Statistics: Number of Partners

Region	N	Mean	StDev	SE Mean
Gulf Coast	18	33.3	47.3	11
Southeast	17	36.4	37.4	9.1

Estimation for Difference

Difference	Pooled StDev	95% CI for Difference
-3.0	42.8	(-32.4, 26.4)

Test

Null hypothesis $H_0: \mu_1 - \mu_2 = 0$
Alternative hypothesis $H_1: \mu_1 - \mu_2 \ne 0$

T-Value	DF	P-Value
-0.21	33	0.836

10.10 (a)   The results from a pooled variance t test revealed that there is no evidence at the .05 level
cont.   of significance that there is a difference between the Southeast region accounting firms
            and the Gulf Coast accounting firms with respect to the mean number of partners.
            Because $t_{STAT} = -0.21$ or p-value $= 0.836$, do not reject H_0.

(b)   The p-value was 0.836, well above the .05 level. This means that the probability of
      obtaining an equal or larger value than the observed test statistic, when H_0 is true, is
      83.6%.

(c)   The pooled variance t test assumes that the variance associated with the two populations
      of accounting firms are equal and that the number of partners data are approximately
      normally distributed for the two populations.

10.12 (a) $H_0 : \mu_1 = \mu_2$ Mean waiting times of Bank 1 and Bank 2 are the same.
            $H_1 : \mu_1 \neq \mu_2$ Mean waiting times of Bank 1 and Bank 2 are different.

      PHStat output:

t Test for Differences in Two Means	
Data	
Hypothesized Difference	0
Level of Significance	0.05
Population 1 Sample	
Sample Size	15
Sample Mean	4.286667
Sample Standard Deviation	1.637985
Population 2 Sample	
Sample Size	15
Sample Mean	7.114667
Sample Standard Deviation	2.082189
Intermediate Calculations	
Population 1 Sample Degrees of Freedom	14
Population 2 Sample Degrees of Freedom	14
Total Degrees of Freedom	28
Pooled Variance	3.509254
Difference in Sample Means	−2.828
t-Test Statistic	−4.13431
Two-Tailed Test	
Lower Critical Value	−2.04841
Upper Critical Value	2.048409
p-Value	0.000293
Reject the null hypothesis	

      Since the p-value of 0.000293 is less than the 5% level of significance, reject the null
      hypothesis. There is enough evidence to conclude that the mean waiting time is different
      in the two banks.

(b) p-value $= 0.000293$. The probability of obtaining a sample that will yield a t test statistic
      more extreme than -4.13431 is 0.000293 if, in fact, the mean waiting times of Bank 1 and
      Bank 2 are the same.

(c)   We need to assume that the two populations are normally distributed.

(d) $$\left(\overline{X}_1 - \overline{X}_2\right) + t \sqrt{S_p^2 \left(\frac{1}{n_1} + \frac{1}{n_2}\right)} = \left(4.2867 - 7.1147\right) + 2.0484 \sqrt{3.5093 \left(\frac{1}{15} + \frac{1}{15}\right)}$$

      $$-4.2292 \leq \mu_1 - \mu_2 \leq -1.4268$$

10.12
cont.
You are 95% confident that the difference in mean waiting time between Bank 1 and Bank 2 is between −4.2292 and −1.4268 minutes.

10.14   (a)   Because $t_{STAT} = 2.7349 > 2.0484$, reject H_0. There is evidence of a difference in the mean time to start a business between developed and emerging countries.

   (b) p-value $= 0.0107$. The probability that two samples have a mean difference of 14.62 or more is 0.0107 if there is no difference in the mean time to start a business between developed and emerging countries.

   (c)   You need to assume that the population distribution of the time to start a business of both developed and emerging countries is normally distributed.

   (d) $3.6700 \le \mu_1 - \mu_2 \le 25.5700$

10.16   (a)   Because $t_{STAT} = -2.1554 < -2.0017$ or p-value $= 0.03535 < 0.05$, reject H_0. There is evidence of a difference in the mean time per day accessing the Internet via a mobile device between males and females.

   (b)   You must assume that each of the two independent populations is normally distributed.

10.18   The degrees of freedom is $20 - 1$, or 19.

10.20   (a) $t_{STAT} = \dfrac{(-1.5566)}{\left(\dfrac{1.424}{\sqrt{9}} \right)} = -3.2772$.   Because $t_{STAT} = -3.2772 < -2.306$ or

   p-value $= 0.0112 < 0.05$, reject H_0. There is enough evidence of a difference in the mean summated ratings between the two brands.

   (b)   You must assume that the distribution of the differences between the two ratings is approximately normal.

   (c) p-value $= 0.0112$. The probability of obtaining a mean difference in ratings that results in a test statistic that deviates from 0 by 3.2772 or more in either direction is 0.0112 if there is no difference in the mean summated ratings between the two brands.

   (d) $-2.6501 \le \mu_D \le -0.4610$. You are 95% confident that the mean difference in summated ratings between brand A and brand B is somewhere between −2.6501 and −0.4610.

10.22   (a)   Because $t_{STAT} = -6.9984 < 2.0423$ reject H_0. There is evidence to conclude that the mean download speed at AT&T is lower than at Verizon Wireless.

   (b)   You must assume that the distribution of the differences between the ratings is approximately normal.

10.22   (c)
cont.

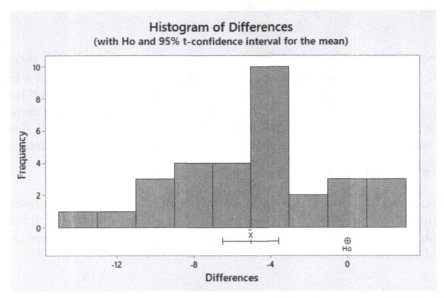

Although a histogram of differences reveals slight skewness to the left, there does not appear to be a substantial violation of the normality assumption.

(d)   The confidence interval is from –6.477 to –3.551.

Estimation for Paired Difference

Mean	StDev	SE Mean	95% CI for μ_difference
-5.014	3.989	0.716	(-6.477, -3.551)

μ_difference: mean of (AT&T (Mbps) - Verizon (Mbps))

10.24   (a)   Define the difference in bone marrow microvessel density as the density before the transplant minus the density after the transplant and assume that the difference in density is normally distributed.

$$H_0 : \mu_D \leq 0 \quad \text{vs.} \quad H_1 : \mu_D > 0$$

Excel output:

t-Test: Paired Two Sample for Means

	Before	After
Mean	312.1429	226
Variance	15513.14	4971
Observations	7	7
Pearson Correlation	0.295069	
Hypothesized Mean Difference	0	
df	6	
t Stat	1.842455	
P(T<=t) one-tail	0.057493	
t Critical one-tail	1.943181	
P(T<=t) two-tail	0.114986	
t Critical two-tail	2.446914	

10.24   (a)
cont.

Test statistic: $t_{STAT} = \dfrac{\bar{D} - \mu_D}{\dfrac{S_D}{\sqrt{n}}} = 1.8425$

Decision: Since $t_{STAT} = 1.8425$ is less than the critical value of 1.943, do not reject H_0. There is not enough evidence to conclude that the mean bone marrow microvessel density is higher before the stem cell transplant than after the stem cell transplant.

(b) p-value = 0.0575. The probability of obtaining a mean difference in density that gives rise to a t test statistic that deviates from 0 by 1.8425 or more is .0575 if the mean density is not higher before the stem cell transplant than after the stem cell transplant.

(c) $\bar{D} \pm t \dfrac{S_D}{\sqrt{n}} = 86.1429 \pm 2.4469 \dfrac{123.7005}{\sqrt{7}}$ $-28.26 \le \mu_D \le 200.55$

You are 95% confident that the mean difference in bone marrow microvessel density before and after the stem cell transplant is somewhere between –28.26 and 200.55.

(d)   You must assume that the distribution of differences between the mean density of before and after stem cell transplant is approximately normal.

10.26   (a)

H_0: $\mu_{\bar{D}} \ge 0$

H_1: $\mu_{\bar{D}} < 0$

Decision rule: $d.f. = 39$. If $t_{STAT} < -2.4258$, reject H_0.

Test statistic: $t_{STAT} = \dfrac{\bar{D} - \mu_D}{\dfrac{S_D}{\sqrt{n}}} = -9.372$

Decision: Since $t_{STAT} = -9.372$ is less than the critical bound of -2.4258, reject H_0. There is enough evidence to conclude that the mean strength is lower at two days than at seven days.

(b)   You must assume that the distribution of the differences between the mean strength of the concrete is approximately normal.

(c) p-value is virtually 0. The probability of obtaining a mean difference that gives rise to a test statistic that is -9.372 or less when the null hypothesis is true is virtually 0.

10.28   (a) $p_1 = \dfrac{X_1}{n_1} = \dfrac{45}{100} = 0.45$, $p_2 = \dfrac{X_2}{n_2} = \dfrac{25}{50} = 0.50$, and $\bar{p} = \dfrac{X_1 + X_2}{n_1 + n_2} = \dfrac{45 + 25}{100 + 50} = 0.467$

H_0: $\pi_1 = \pi_2$ H_1: $\pi_1 \ne \pi_2$

Decision rule: If $Z < -2.58$ or $Z > 2.58$, reject H_0.

$Z_{STAT} = \dfrac{(p_1 - p_2) - (\pi_1 - \pi_2)}{\sqrt{\bar{p}(1 - \bar{p})\left(\dfrac{1}{n_1} + \dfrac{1}{n_2}\right)}} = \dfrac{(0.45 - 0.50) - 0}{\sqrt{0.467(1 - 0.467)\left(\dfrac{1}{100} + \dfrac{1}{50}\right)}} = -0.58$

Decision: Since $Z_{STAT} = -0.58$ is between the critical bound of ± 2.58, do not reject H_0. There is insufficient evidence to conclude that the population proportion differs for group 1 and group 2

(b) $(p_1 - p_2) \pm Z \sqrt{\left(\dfrac{p_1(1 - p_1)}{n_1} + \dfrac{p_2(1 - p_2)}{n_2}\right)} = -0.05 \pm 2.5758 \sqrt{\left(\dfrac{.45(.55)}{100} + \dfrac{.5(.5)}{50}\right)}$

$-0.2727 \le \pi_1 - \pi_2 \le 0.1727$

10.30   (a) H_0: $\pi_1 \leq \pi_2$ H_1: $\pi_1 > \pi_2$
Population 1 = following VOD D+4 viewing, 2 = general TV viewing
        (b)   PHStat output:

Z Test for Differences in Two Proportions	
Data	
Hypothesized Difference	0
Level of Significance	0.05
Group 1	
Number of Items of Interest	147
Sample Size	250
Group 2	
Number of Items of Interest	35
Sample Size	201

Intermediate Calculations	
Group 1 Proportion	0.588
Group 2 Proportion	0.174129353
Difference in Two Proportions	0.413870647
Average Proportion	0.4035
Z Test Statistic	8.9045

Upper-Tail Test	
Upper Critical Value	1.6449
p-Value	0.0000
Reject the null hypothesis	

        (b)   Decision rule: If $Z_{STAT} > 1.6449$, reject H_0.
Test statistic:

$$Z_{STAT} = \frac{(p_1 - p_2) - (\pi_1 - \pi_2)}{\sqrt{\bar{p}(1-\bar{p})\left(\dfrac{1}{n_1} + \dfrac{1}{n_2}\right)}} = 8.9045 \quad p\text{-value is essentially 0.}$$

Decision: Since p-value < 0.05, reject H_0. There is sufficient evidence to conclude that the population proportion of those who viewed the brand on VOD D4 were more likely to visit the brand website.
        (c)   Yes, the result in (b) make it appropriate to claim that ad impact is stronger following VOD D4+ than following general TV viewing.

10.32   (a)   PHStat output:

Z Test for Differences in Two Proportions	
Data	
Hypothesized Difference	0
Level of Significance	0.01
Group 1	
Number of Items of Interest	930
Sample Size	1000
Group 2	
Number of Items of Interest	230
Sample Size	1000
Intermediate Calculations	
Group 1 Proportion	0.93
Group 2 Proportion	0.23
Difference in Two Proportions	0.7
Average Proportion	0.58
Z Test Statistic	31.71351646
Two-Tail Test	
Lower Critical Value	-2.5758
Upper Critical Value	2.5758
p-Value	0.0000
Reject the null hypothesis	

Confidence Interval Estimate of the Difference Between Two Proportions	
Data	
Confidence Level	99%
Intermediate Calculations	
Z Value	-2.5758
Std. Error of the Diff. between two Proporti	0.0156
Interval Half Width	0.0401
Confidence Interval	
Interval Lower Limit	0.6599
Interval Upper Limit	0.7401

(a) H_0: $\pi_1 = \pi_2$ H_1: $\pi_1 \neq \pi_2$

Population: 1 = Superbanked; 2 = Unbanked.

Decision rule: If $|Z_{STAT}| > 2.5758$ or p-value < 0.05, reject H_0.

Test statistic:

$$Z_{STAT} = \frac{(p_1 - p_2) - (\pi_1 - \pi_2)}{\sqrt{\bar{p}(1-\bar{p})\left(\frac{1}{n_1} + \frac{1}{n_2}\right)}} = 31.7135$$

Decision: Since p-value < 0.05, reject H_0. There is evidence of a difference in the proportion of Superbanked and Unbanked with respect to the proportion that use credit cards.

(b) p-value is virtually 0. The probability of obtaining a difference in proportions that gives rise to a test statistic below -31.7135 or above $+31.7135$ is 0.0000 if there is no difference in the proportion of Superbanked and Unbanked who use credit cards.

(c) $$(p_1 - p_2) \pm Z \sqrt{\left(\frac{p_1(1-p_1)}{n_1} + \frac{p_2(1-p_2)}{n_2}\right)} = 0.7 \pm 2.5758 \sqrt{\left(\frac{0.93(1-0.93)}{1000} + \frac{0.2391 - 0.23}{1000}\right)}$$

$$0.6599 \leq \pi_1 - \pi_2 \leq 0.7401$$

You are 99% confident that the difference in the proportion of Superbanked and Unbanked who use credit cards is between 0.6599 and 0.7401.

10.34 (a) $H_0: \pi_1 = \pi_2$ $H_1: \pi_1 \neq \pi_2$ Where Population: 1 = Co-browsing,
2 = Non-co-browsing

Z Test for Differences in Two Proportions

Data	
Hypothesized Difference	0
Level of Significance	0.05
Group 1	
Number of Items of Interest	81
Sample Size	129
Group 2	
Number of Items of Interest	65
Sample Size	176

Intermediate Calculations	
Group 1 Proportion	0.627906977
Group 2 Proportion	0.369318182
Difference in Two Proportions	0.258588795
Average Proportion	0.4787
Z Test Statistic	4.4662

Two-Tail Test	
Lower Critical Value	-1.9600
Upper Critical Value	1.9600
p-Value	0.0000
Reject the null hypothesis	

Decision rule: If p-value < 0.05, reject H_0.
Decision: Since p-value = 0.0000 < 0.05, reject H_0. There is sufficient evidence of a difference between co-browsing organizations and non-co-browsing organizations in the proportion that use skills-based routing to match the caller with the right agent.

(b) p-value is 0.0000. The probability of obtaining a difference in proportions that gives rise to a test statistic that deviates from 0 by 4.4662 or more in either direction is 0.0000 if there is not a difference between co-browsing organizations and non-co-browsing organizations in the proportion that use skills-based routing to match the caller with the right agent.

10.36 (a) 2.20
(b) 2.57
(c) 3.50

10.38 (a) Population B: $S^2 = 25$
(b) 1.5625

10.40 $df_{numerator} = 24$, $df_{denominator} = 24$,

10.42 Because $F_{STAT} = 1.2109 < 2.27$, do not reject H_0.

10.44 (a)   Because $F_{STAT} = 1.2995 < 3.18$, do not reject H_0.

(b)   Because $F_{STAT} = 1.2995 < 2.62$, do not reject H_0.

10.46

F Test for Differences in Two Variances	
Data	
Level of Significance	0.05
Larger-Variance Sample	
Sample Size	18
Sample Variance	2236.353
Smaller-Variance Sample	
Sample Size	17
Sample Variance	1395.493
Intermediate Calculations	
F Test Statistic	1.6026
Population 1 Sample Degrees of Freedom	17
Population 2 Sample Degrees of Freedom	16
Two-Tail Test	
Upper Critical Value	2.7380
p-Value	0.3516
Do not reject the null hypothesis	

10.46
cont.

Test and CI for Two Variances: Number of Partners vs Region

Method

σ_1: standard deviation of Number of Partners when Region = Gulf Coast
σ_2: standard deviation of Number of Partners when Region = Southeast
Ratio: σ_1/σ_2
F method was used. This method is accurate for normal data only.

Descriptive Statistics

Region	N	StDev	Variance	95% CI for σ
Gulf Coast	18	47.290	2236.353	(35.486, 70.895)
Southeast	17	37.356	1395.493	(27.822, 56.854)

Ratio of Standard Deviations

Estimated Ratio	95% CI for Ratio using F
1.26592	(0.765, 2.079)

Test

Null hypothesis	H_0: $\sigma_1 / \sigma_2 = 1$
Alternative hypothesis	H_1: $\sigma_1 / \sigma_2 \neq 1$
Significance level	$\alpha = 0.05$

Method	Test Statistic	DF1	DF2	P-Value
F	1.60	17	16	0.352

At the .05 level, there is no evidence that there is a difference between the variances of the two types of cell providers. One would fail to reject the null hypothesis. The F_{STAT} of 1.60 is below the upper critical value. Because $F_{STAT} = 1.6026$ or p-value $= 0.3516$, do not reject H_0.

The p-value is 0.3516, which means that the probability of obtaining an equal or larger value than the observed test statistic, when H_0 is true, is 35.16%.

To justify the use of the F test, it was assumed that the rating data from both populations were normally distributed.

Because the results from (a) and (b) revealed that there was no significant difference between the two types of cell provides, one would use the pooled variance t test.

10.48

F Test for Differences in Two Variances	
Data	
Level of Significance	0.05
Larger-Variance Sample	
Sample Size	17
Sample Variance	1.108814
Smaller-Variance Sample	
Sample Size	40
Sample Variance	0.674493
Intermediate Calculations	
F Test Statistic	1.6439
Population 1 Sample Degrees of Freedom	16
Population 2 Sample Degrees of Freedom	39
Two-Tail Test	
Upper Critical Value	2.1637
p-Value	0.2050
Do not reject the null hypothesis	

Test and CI for Two Variances: 60 Second Ads, 30 Second Ads

Method

σ_1: standard deviation of 60 Second Ads
σ_2: standard deviation of 30 Second Ads
Ratio: σ_1/σ_2
F method was used. This method is accurate for normal data only.

Descriptive Statistics

Variable	N	StDev	Variance	95% CI for σ
60 Second Ads	17	1.053	1.109	(0.784, 1.603)
30 Second Ads	40	0.821	0.674	(0.673, 1.055)

Ratio of Standard Deviations

Estimated Ratio	95% CI for Ratio using F
1.28216	(0.872, 2.033)

Test

Null hypothesis	H_0: $\sigma_1 / \sigma_2 = 1$
Alternative hypothesis	H_1: $\sigma_1 / \sigma_2 \neq 1$
Significance level	$\alpha = 0.05$

Method	Test Statistic	DF1	DF2	P-Value
F	1.64	16	39	0.205

10.48
cont.
At the .05 level, there is no evidence that there is a difference between the variances in the rating scores between the 30 second and 60 second ads. The F_{STAT} of 1.64 is below the upper critical value. Because $F_{STAT}= 1.6439$ or p-value $= 0.2050$, do not reject H_0.

The p-value is 0.205, which means that the probability of obtaining an equal or larger value than the observed test statistic, when H_0 is true, is a 20.50%. The p-value is well above .05 indicating that F_{STAT} is not statistically significant at the .05 level.

To justify the use of the F test, it was assumed that the rating data from both groups were normally distributed.

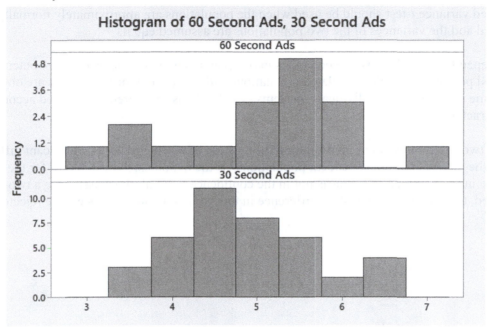

Descriptive Statistics: 60 Second Ads, 30 Second Ads

Statistics

Variable	N	N*	Mean	SE Mean	StDev	Minimum	Q1	Median	Q3	Maximum
60 Second Ads	17	23	5.105	0.255	1.053	3.220	4.460	5.300	5.880	6.910
30 Second Ads	40	0	4.899	0.130	0.821	3.550	4.370	4.805	5.303	6.640

Variable	Skewness
60 Second Ads	-0.53
30 Second Ads	0.44

Ratings for the 60 second ads were skewed to the left while the 30 second ads were skewed somewhat to the right.

Because the results from (a) revealed that there was no significant difference between the two types of ads, one would use the pooled variance t test.

10.50   (a)   Because $F_{STAT} = 69.50001 > 1.9811$ or p-value $= 0.0000 < 0.05$, reject H_0. There is evidence of a difference in the variance of the delay times between the two drivers.

(b)   You assume that the delay times are normally distributed.

(c)   From the boxplot and the normal probability plots, the delay times appear to be approximately normally distributed.

(d)   Because there is a difference in the variance of the delay times between the two drivers, you should use the separate variance t-test to determine whether there is evidence of a difference in the mean delay time between the two drivers.

10.52   The pooled variance t-test should be used when the populations are approximately normally distributed and the variances of the two populations are assumed equal.

10.54   With independent populations, the outcomes in one population do not depend on the outcomes in the second population. With two related populations, either repeated measurements are obtained on the same set of items or individuals, or items or individuals are paired or matched according to some characteristic.

10.56   They are two different ways of investigating the concern of whether there is significant difference between the means of two independent populations. If the hypothesized value of 0 for the difference in two population means is not in the confidence interval, then, assuming a two-tailed test is used, the null hypothesis of no difference in the two population means can be rejected.

10.58

Test and CI for Two Variances

Method

σ_1: standard deviation of Sample 1
σ_2: standard deviation of Sample 2
Ratio: σ_1/σ_2
F method was used. This method is accurate for normal data only.

Descriptive Statistics

Sample	N	StDev	Variance	95% CI for σ^2
Sample 1	39	28086.000	7.88823E+08	(5.26848E+08, 1.31020E+09)
Sample 2	109	24120.000	5.81774E+08	(4.53165E+08, 7.74428E+08)

Ratio of Variances

Estimated Ratio	95% CI for Ratio using F
1.35589	(0.826, 2.380)

Test

Null hypothesis	$H_0: \sigma_1^2 / \sigma_2^2 = 1$
Alternative hypothesis	$H_1: \sigma_1^2 / \sigma_2^2 \neq 1$
Significance level	$\alpha = 0.05$

Method	Test Statistic	DF1	DF2	P-Value
F	1.36	38	108	0.228

(a)   At the .05 level, there is insufficient evidence that there is a statistically difference in variances for the two types of jobs. Because $F_{STAT} = 1.36$ or p-value = 0.228, do not reject H_0.

10.58   (b)   Based on the results from (a), one would fail to reject the null hypothesis and would
cont.   choose the pooled variance t test.

Two-Sample T-Test and CI

Method

μ_1: mean of Sample 1
μ_2: mean of Sample 2
Difference: $\mu_1 - \mu_2$

Equal variances are assumed for this analysis.

Descriptive Statistics

Sample	N	Mean	StDev	SE Mean
Sample 1	109	98445	24120	2310
Sample 2	39	79749	28086	4497

Estimation for Difference

Difference	Pooled StDev	95% CI for Difference
18696	25212	(9399, 27993)

Test

Null hypothesis	$H_0: \mu_1 - \mu_2 = 0$
Alternative hypothesis	$H_1: \mu_1 - \mu_2 \neq 0$

T-Value	DF	P-Value
3.97	146	0.000

(c)   At the .05 level, there is evidence that the mean salary for Black belt jobs are
significantly higher than the mean salary for Green belt jobs. The t_{STAT} of 3.97 is above
the critical value. The *p*-value is 0.000. Because $t_{STAT} = 3.97$ or *p*-value = 0.000, reject H_0.

10.60   (a)

Test and CI for Two Variances

Method

σ₁: standard deviation of Sample 1
σ₂: standard deviation of Sample 2
Ratio: σ₁/σ₂
F method was used. This method is accurate for normal data only.

Descriptive Statistics

Sample	N	StDev	Variance	95% CI for σ^2
Sample 1	100	70.000	4900.000	(3777.391, 6612.498)
Sample 2	100	60.000	3600.000	(2775.226, 4858.162)

Ratio of Variances

Estimated Ratio	95% CI for Ratio using F
1.36111	(0.916, 2.023)

Test

Null hypothesis	H_0: $\sigma_1^2 / \sigma_2^2 = 1$
Alternative hypothesis	H_1: $\sigma_1^2 / \sigma_2^2 \neq 1$
Significance level	$\alpha = 0.05$

Method	Test Statistic	DF1	DF2	P-Value
F	1.36	99	99	0.127

Using a .01 level of significance, there is insufficient evidence that there is a difference in the variances in time spent online between males and females. Because $F_{STAT} = 1.36$ or p-value = 0.127, do not reject H_0.

10.60 (b) It is most appropriate to use the pooled-variance t test to test for differences in mean
cont. online time between males and females.

Two-Sample T-Test and CI

Method

μ_1: mean of Sample 1
μ_2: mean of Sample 2
Difference: $\mu_1 - \mu_2$

Equal variances are assumed for this analysis.

Descriptive Statistics

Sample	N	Mean	StDev	SE Mean
Sample 1	100	1254.0	60.0	6.0
Sample 2	100	1344.0	70.0	7.0

Estimation for Difference

Difference	Pooled StDev	95% CI for Difference
-90.00	65.19	(-108.18, -71.82)

Test

Null hypothesis	$H_0: \mu_1 - \mu_2 = 0$
Alternative hypothesis	$H_1: \mu_1 - \mu_2 \neq 0$

T-Value	DF	P-Value
-9.76	198	0.000

10.60 (b)
cont.

At the .01 significance level, the t_{STAT} of -9.76 is well below the lower critical value. Because $t_{STAT} = -9.76$ or p-value $= 0.000$, one would reject the null hypothesis that there is no difference between the mean online time between males and females. The results indicate that men spent significantly more time online compared to women.

Test and CI for Two Variances

Method

σ_1: standard deviation of Sample 1
σ_2: standard deviation of Sample 2
Ratio: σ_1/σ_2
F method was used. This method is accurate for normal data only.

Descriptive Statistics

Sample	N	StDev	Variance	95% CI for σ^2
Sample 1	100	20.000	400.000	(308.358, 539.796)
Sample 2	100	15.000	225.000	(173.452, 303.635)

Ratio of Variances

Estimated Ratio	95% CI for Ratio using F
1.77778	(1.196, 2.642)

Test

Null hypothesis	$H_0: \sigma_1^2 / \sigma_2^2 = 1$
Alternative hypothesis	$H_1: \sigma_1^2 / \sigma_2^2 \neq 1$
Significance level	$\alpha = 0.05$

Method	Test Statistic	DF1	DF2	P-Value
F	1.78	99	99	0.005

10.60   (c)   Using a .01 level of significance, there is evidence that there is a difference in the
cont.   variances in time spent playing online games between males and females. Because
                   $F_{STAT} = 1.78$ or p-value $= 0.005$, reject H_0.

Two-Sample T-Test and CI

Method

μ_1: mean of Sample 1
μ_2: mean of Sample 2
Difference: $\mu_1 - \mu_2$

Equal variances are not assumed for this analysis.

Descriptive Statistics

Sample	N	Mean	StDev	SE Mean
Sample 1	100	360.0	20.0	2.0
Sample 2	100	294.0	15.0	1.5

Estimation for Difference

Difference	95% CI for Difference
66.00	(61.07, 70.93)

Test

Null hypothesis	H_0: $\mu_1 - \mu_2 = 0$
Alternative hypothesis	H_1: $\mu_1 - \mu_2 \neq 0$

T-Value	DF	P-Value
26.40	183	0.000

(d)   A separate variance t test revealed that at the .01 significance level, there is evidence that
men and women differ significantly in amount of time spent playing online games. Men
spent significantly more time playing online games than women. Because $F_{STAT} = 26.40$
or p-value $= 0.000$, reject H_0.

10.62   (a) H_0: $\mu \leq 10$ minutes. Introductory computer students required no more than a mean of 10
minutes to write and run a program in VB.NET.
              H_1: $\mu > 10$ minutes. Introductory computer students required more than a mean of 10
minutes to write and run a program in VB.NET.
Decision rule: $d.f. = 8$. If $t_{STAT} > 1.8595$, reject H_0.

Test statistic: $t_{STAT} = \dfrac{\overline{X} - \mu}{\dfrac{S}{\sqrt{n}}} = \dfrac{12 - 10}{\dfrac{1.8028}{\sqrt{9}}} = 3.3282$

10.62   (a)   Decision: Since t_{STAT} = 3.3282 is greater than the critical bound of 1.8595, reject H_0.
cont.   There is enough evidence to conclude that the introductory computer students required
               more than a mean of 10 minutes to write and run a program in VB.NET.

        (b) H_0: $\mu \leq 10$ minutes. Introductory computer students required no more than a mean of 10
               minutes to write and run a program in VB.NET.
               H_1: $\mu > 10$ minutes. Introductory computer students required more than a mean of 10
               minutes to write and run a program in VB.NET.
               Decision rule: $d.f.$ = 8. If $t_{STAT} > 1.8595$, reject H_0.

               Test statistic: $t_{STAT} = \dfrac{\overline{X} - \mu}{\dfrac{S}{\sqrt{n}}} = \dfrac{16 - 10}{\dfrac{13.2004}{\sqrt{9}}} = 1.3636$

               Decision: Since t_{STAT} = 1.3636 is less than the critical bound of 1.8595, do not reject H_0.
               There is not enough evidence to conclude that the introductory computer students
               required more than a mean of 10 minutes to write and run a program in VB.NET.

        (c)   Although the mean time necessary to complete the assignment increased from 12 to 16
               minutes as a result of the increase in one data value, the standard deviation went from 1.8
               to 13.2, which in turn brought the t-value down because of the increased denominator.

        (d) H_0: $\sigma_{IC}^2 = \sigma_{CS}^2$ H_1: $\sigma_{IC}^2 \neq \sigma_{CS}^2$
               Decision rule: If $F_{STAT} > 3.8549$, reject H_0.

               Test statistic: $F_{STAT} = \dfrac{S_{CS}^2}{S_{IC}^2} = \dfrac{2.0^2}{1.8028^2} = 1.2307$

               Decision: Since F_{STAT} = 1.2307 is lower than the critical bound 3.8549, do not reject H_0.
               There is not enough evidence to conclude that the population variances are different for
               the Introduction to Computers students and computer majors. Hence, the pooled variance
               t test is a valid test to see whether computer majors can write a VB.NET program (on
               average) in less time than introductory students, assuming that the distributions of the
               time needed to write a VB.NET program for both the Introduction to Computers students
               and the computer majors are approximately normal.

        (d) H_0: $\mu_{IC} \leq \mu_{CS}$ The mean amount of time needed by Introduction to Computers students
               is not greater than the mean amount of time needed by computer majors.
               H_1: $\mu_{IC} > \mu_{CS}$ The mean amount of time needed by Introduction to Computers students
               is greater than the mean amount of time needed by computer majors.

10.62   (d)   PHStat output:
cont.

Pooled-Variance *t* Test for the Difference Between Two Means	
(assumes equal population variances)	
Data	
Hypothesized Difference	0
Level of Significance	0.05
Population 1 Sample	
Sample Size	9
Sample Mean	12
Sample Standard Deviation	1.802776
Population 2 Sample	
Sample Size	11
Sample Mean	8.5
Sample Standard Deviation	2
Intermediate Calculations	
Population 1 Sample Degrees of Freedom	8
Population 2 Sample Degrees of Freedom	10
Total Degrees of Freedom	18
Pooled Variance	3.666667
Difference in Sample Means	3.5
t Test Statistic	4.066633
Upper-Tail Test	
Upper Critical Value	1.734064
p-Value	0.000362
Reject the null hypothesis	

Decision rule: $d.f. = 18$. If $t_{STAT} > 1.7341$, reject H_0.
Test statistic:

$$S_p{}^2 = \frac{(n_{IC} - 1) \cdot S_{IC}{}^2 + (n_{CS} - 1) \cdot S_{CS}{}^2}{(n_{IC} - 1) + (n_{CS} - 1)} = \frac{9 \cdot 1.8028^2 + 11 \cdot 2.0^2}{8 + 10} = 3.6667$$

$$t_{STAT} = \frac{\left(\bar{X}_{IC} - \bar{X}_{CS}\right) - \left(\mu_{IC} - \mu_{CS}\right)}{\sqrt{S_p{}^2 \left(\frac{1}{n_{IC}} + \frac{1}{n_{CS}}\right)}} = \frac{12.0 - 8.5}{\sqrt{3.6667 \left(\frac{1}{9} + \frac{1}{11}\right)}} = 4.0666$$

Decision: Since $t_{STAT} = 4.0666$ is greater than 1.7341, reject H_0. There is enough evidence to support a conclusion that the mean time is higher for Introduction to Computers students than for computer majors.

(e)   *p*-value = 0.0052. If the true population mean amount of time needed for Introduction to Computer students to write a VB.NET program is indeed no more than 10 minutes, the probability for observing a sample mean greater than the 12 minutes in the current sample is 0.0052, which means it will be a quite unlikely event. Hence, at a 95% level of confidence, you can conclude that the population mean amount of time needed for Introduction to Computer students to write a VB.NET program is more than 10 minutes.

10.62   (e)   As illustrated in part (d) in which there is not enough evidence to conclude that the
cont.   population variances are different for the Introduction to Computers students and
              computer majors, the pooled variance *t* test performed is a valid test to determine whether
              computer majors can write a VB.NET program in less time than in introductory students,
              assuming that the distributions of the time needed to write a VB.NET program for both
              the Introduction to Computers students and the computer majors are approximately
              normal.

10.64   Because an F test for the ratio of two variances revealed no significant differences between the
      variances of the two manufacturers, a pooled-variance t test is appropriate for these data.

Test and CI for Two Variances: man2, man1

Method

σ_1: standard deviation of man2
σ_2: standard deviation of man1
Ratio: σ_1/σ_2
F method was used. This method is accurate for normal data only.

Descriptive Statistics

Variable	N	StDev	Variance	95% CI for σ
man2	40	969.014	938987.436	(793.778, 1244.248)
man1	40	943.052	889346.410	(772.511, 1210.912)

Ratio of Standard Deviations

Estimated Ratio	95% CI for Ratio using F
1.02753	(0.747, 1.413)

Test

Null hypothesis	H_0: $\sigma_1 / \sigma_2 = 1$
Alternative hypothesis	H_1: $\sigma_1 / \sigma_2 \neq 1$
Significance level	$\alpha = 0.05$

Method	Test Statistic	DF1	DF2	P-Value
F	1.06	39	39	0.866

10.64
cont.

Two-Sample T-Test and CI: Length of Life, Manufacturer

Method

μ_1: mean of Length of Life when Manufacturer = 1
μ_2: mean of Length of Life when Manufacturer = 2
Difference: $\mu_1 - \mu_2$

Equal variances are assumed for this analysis.

Descriptive Statistics: Length of Life

Manufacturer	N	Mean	StDev	SE Mean
1	40	49097	943	149
2	40	50184	969	153

Estimation for Difference

Difference	Pooled StDev	95% CI for Difference
-1087	956	(-1513, -661)

Test

Null hypothesis	H_0: $\mu_1 - \mu_2 = 0$
Alternative hypothesis	H_1: $\mu_1 - \mu_2 \neq 0$

T-Value	DF	P-Value
-5.08	78	0.000

The mean length of life was significantly longer for Manufacturer 2 compared to Manufacturer 1. Because $t_{STAT} = -5.08$ or p-value = 0.000, one would reject the null hypothesis that the mean length of bulb life is the same for the two manufacturers.

10.66 H_0: $\pi_1 = \pi_2$ H_1: $\pi_1 \neq \pi_2$ where Populations: 1 = Males, 2 = Females
Decision rule: If p-value < 0.05, reject H_0.

Gender:

10.66
cont.

PHStat output:

Z Test for Differences in Two Proportions	
Data	
Hypothesized Difference	0
Level of Significance	0.05
Group 1	
Number of Items of Interest	50
Sample Size	300
Group 2	
Number of Items of Interest	96
Sample Size	330

Intermediate Calculations	
Group 1 Proportion	0.166666667
Group 2 Proportion	0.290909091
Difference in Two Proportions	-0.12424242
Average Proportion	0.2317
Z Test Statistic	-3.6911

Two-Tail Test	
Lower Critical Value	-1.9600
Upper Critical Value	1.9600
p-Value	0.0002
Reject the null hypothesis	

Decision: Since the p-value is smaller than 0.05, reject H_0. There is enough evidence of a difference between males and females in the proportion who order dessert.

10.66   **Beef Entrée:**
cont.   PHStat output:

Z Test for Differences in Two Proportions	
Data	
Hypothesized Difference	0
Level of Significance	0.05
Group 1	
Number of Items of Interest	74
Sample Size	197
Group 2	
Number of Items of Interest	68
Sample Size	433
Intermediate Calculations	
Group 1 Proportion	0.375634518
Group 2 Proportion	0.15704388
Difference in Two Proportions	0.218590638
Average Proportion	0.2254
Z Test Statistic	6.0873
Two-Tail Test	
Lower Critical Value	-1.9600
Upper Critical Value	1.9600
p-Value	0.0000
Reject the null hypothesis	

Decision: Since the p-value = 0.0000 is smaller than 0.05, reject H_0. There is enough evidence of a difference in the proportion who order dessert based on whether a beef entrée has been ordered.

10.68   The normal probability plots suggest that the two populations are not normally distributed. An F test is inappropriate for testing the difference in the two variances. The sample variances for Boston and Vermont shingles are 0.0203 and 0.015, respectively. Because $t_{STAT} = 3.015 > 1.967$ or p-value = 0.0028 < α = 0.05, reject H_0. There is sufficient evidence to conclude that there is a difference in the mean granule loss of Boston and Vermont shingles.

10.70   An analysis of the data in 10.67 revealed that a pallet of Vermont shingles weighed significantly more than a pallet of Boston shingles. Assuming that a heavier weight shingle is associated with higher quality, the Vermont shingle might be perceived as a higher quality shingle compared to the Boston shingle. The below figure shows the results from a separate variance t-test.

10.70
cont.

Descriptive Statistics

Sample	N	Mean	StDev	SE Mean
Boston	368	3124.2	34.7	1.8
Vermont	330	3704.0	46.7	2.6

Estimation for Difference

Difference	95% CI for Difference
-579.83	(-586.01, -573.65)

Test

Null hypothesis	$H_0: \mu_1 - \mu_2 = 0$
Alternative hypothesis	$H_1: \mu_1 - \mu_2 \neq 0$

T-Value	DF	P-Value
-184.32	602	0.000

An analysis of the data in 10.68 revealed that the Vermont shingles were associated with less granule loss compared to the Boston shingles following accelerated-life testing. Shingles with less weight loss are assumed to have a longer life expectancy. Both shingles would be expected to outperform the length of the warranty period because their weight losses were well below the .8 gram threshold. However, the Vermont shingles would be expected to have a longer life expectancy given that they loss less weight relative to the Boston shingles. The below figure shows the results from a pooled-variance t-test.

Descriptive Statistics

Sample	N	Mean	StDev	SE Mean
Boston	170	0.264	0.142	0.011
Vermont	140	0.218	0.123	0.010

Estimation for Difference

Difference	Pooled StDev	95% CI for Difference
0.0461	0.1339	(0.0160, 0.0761)

Test

Null hypothesis	$H_0: \mu_1 - \mu_2 = 0$
Alternative hypothesis	$H_1: \mu_1 - \mu_2 \neq 0$

T-Value	DF	P-Value
3.01	308	0.003

Taken together, the results from 10.67 and 10.68 suggest that the Vermont shingle may be a higher quality shingle based on pallet weight and life expectancy as determined by granule loss associated with accelerated-life testing. These conclusions suggest that the manufacturer may be able to charge more for the Vermont shingle compared to the Boston shingle.

CHAPTER 11

11.2   (a) $SSW = SST - SSA = 210 - 60 = 150$

      (b) $MSA = \dfrac{SSA}{c-1} = \dfrac{60}{5-1} = 15$

      (c) $MSW = \dfrac{SSW}{n-c} = \dfrac{150}{35-5} = 5$

      (d) $F_{STAT} = \dfrac{MSA}{MSW} = \dfrac{15}{5} = 3$

11.4   (a) $df\, A = c - 1 = 3 - 1 = 2$
      (b) $df\, W = n - c = 21 - 3 = 18$
      (c) $df\, T = n - 1 = 21 - 1 = 20$

11.6   (a)   Decision rule: If $F_{STAT} > 2.95$, reject H_0.
      (b)   Since $F_{STAT} = 4$ is greater than the critical bound of 2.95, reject H_0.
      (c)   There are $c = 4$ degrees of freedom in the numerator and $n - c = 32 - 4 = 28$ degrees of freedom in the denominator. The table does not have 28 degrees of freedom in the denominator so use the next larger critical value, $Q_\alpha = 3.90$.
      (d)   To perform the Tukey-Kramer procedure, the critical range is

$$Q_\alpha \sqrt{\dfrac{MSW}{2}\left(\dfrac{1}{n_j} + \dfrac{1}{n_{j'}}\right)} = 3.90\sqrt{\dfrac{20}{2}\left(\dfrac{1}{8} + \dfrac{1}{8}\right)} = 6.166.$$

11.8

One-way ANOVA: Cost to import (US$) versus Region

Method

Null hypothesis	All means are equal
Alternative hypothesis	Not all means are equal
Significance level	$\alpha = 0.05$

Equal variances were assumed for the analysis.

Factor Information

Factor	Levels	Values
Region	4	East Asia & Pacific, Eastern Europe & Central Asia, Latin American & Carribbean, Middle East & North Africa

Analysis of Variance

Source	DF	Adj SS	Adj MS	F-Value	P-Value
Region	3	1151016	383672	4.66	0.007
Error	36	2961835	82273		
Total	39	4112852			

Model Summary

S	R-sq	R-sq(adj)	R-sq(pred)
286.833	27.99%	21.98%	11.09%

Means

Region	N	Mean	StDev	95% Upper Bound
East Asia & Pacific	10	380.1	176.7	533.2
Eastern Europe & Central Asia	10	334	334	487
Latin American & Carribbean	10	755	383	908
Middle East & North Africa	10	594.4	199.3	747.5

Pooled StDev = 286.833

11.8   (a)   At the .05 level of significance, there is evidence there are differences in import costs
cont.   among the four regions. Because $F_{STAT} = 4.66$ OR p-value $= 0.007$, reject H_0. The
                ANOVA F_{STAT} indicates that there is a difference among the four regions. However, it
                does not indicate which groups differ from one another.

Means

Region	N	Mean	StDev	95% Upper Bound
East Asia & Pacific	10	380.1	176.7	533.2
Eastern Europe & Central Asia	10	334	334	487
Latin American & Carribbean	10	755	383	908
Middle East & North Africa	10	594.4	199.3	747.5

Pooled StDev = 286.833

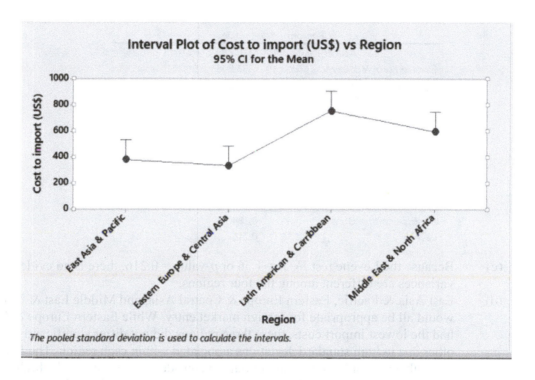

Tukey Pairwise Comparisons

Grouping Information Using the Tukey Method and 95% Confidence

Region	N	Mean	Grouping	
Latin American & Carribbean	10	755	A	
Middle East & North Africa	10	594.4	A	B
East Asia & Pacific	10	380.1		B
Eastern Europe & Central Asia	10	334		B

Means that do not share a letter are significantly different.

11.8   (b)   Pairwise comparisons with the Tukey test revealed that the Latin American & Caribbean
cont.   region had higher import costs compared to the East Asia & Pacific and Eastern Europe
               & Central Asia regions. The Latin American & Caribbean region and the Middle East &
               North Africa did not differ significantly in import costs. There were no other pairwise
               differences among the Middle East & North Africa, East Asia & Pacific and Eastern
               Europe & Central Asia regions.

Test for Equal Variances: Cost to import (US$) versus Region

Method

Null hypothesis	All variances are equal
Alternative hypothesis	At least one variance is different
Significance level	$\alpha = 0.05$

95% Bonferroni Confidence Intervals for Standard Deviations

Region	N	StDev	CI
East Asia & Pacific	10	176.739	(60.618, 686.85)
Eastern Europe & Central Asia	10	333.606	(99.291, 1494.05)
Latin American & Carribbean	10	383.221	(187.382, 1044.66)
Middle East & North Africa	10	199.262	(90.062, 587.64)

Individual confidence level = 98.75%

Tests

Method	Test Statistic	P-Value
Multiple comparisons	—	0.284
Levene	1.56	0.216

(c)   Because the Levene test $F_{STAT} = 1.56$ or p-value = 0.216, there is no evidence that the
       variances are different among the four regions.

(d)   East Asia & Pacific, Eastern Europe & Central Asia, and Middle East & North Africa
       would all be appropriate for foreign market entry. While Eastern Europe & Central Asia
       had the lowest import costs, these three regions did not differ significantly from each
       other due to high standard deviations associated within each region. The Latin American
       & Caribbean would be less appropriate to consider because it had the highest import costs
       that were significantly different compared to the East Asia & Pacific and Eastern Europe
       & Central Asia regions.

11.10   (a) $H_0: \mu_A = \mu_B = \mu_C = \mu_D = \mu_E$ H_1: At least one mean is different.

PHStat output:

ANOVA

Source of Variation	SS	df	MS	F	P-value	F crit
Between Groups	377.8667	4	94.46667	12.56206	9.74E-06	2.758711
Within Groups	188	25	7.52			
Total	565.8667	29				

Since the p-value is essentially zero, reject H_0. There is evidence of a difference in the
mean rating of the five advertisements.

11.10   (b)
cont.

Tukey Kramer Multiple Comparisons							
Group	Sample Mean	Sample Size	Comparison	Absolute Difference	Std. Error of Difference	Critical Range	Results
1	18	6	Group 1 to Group 2	0.333333	1.11952371	4.668	Means are not different
2	17.66667	6	Group 1 to Group 3	6.666667	1.11952371	4.668	Means are different
3	11.33333	6	Group 1 to Group 4	9	1.11952371	4.668	Means are different
4	9	6	Group 1 to Group 5	2.666667	1.11952371	4.668	Means are not different
5	15.33333	6	Group 2 to Group 3	6.333333	1.11952371	4.668	Means are different
			Group 2 to Group 4	8.666667	1.11952371	4.668	Means are different
Other Data			Group 2 to Group 5	2.333333	1.11952371	4.668	Means are not different
Level of significance	0.05		Group 3 to Group 4	2.333333	1.11952371	4.668	Means are not different
Numerator d.f.	5		Group 3 to Group 5	4	1.11952371	4.668	Means are not different
Denominator d.f.	25		Group 4 to Group 5	6.333333	1.11952371	4.668	Means are different
MSW	7.52						
Q Statistic	4.17						

There is a difference in the mean rating between advertisement A and C, between A and D, between B and C, between B and D and between D and E.

(c) $H_0: \sigma_A^2 = \sigma_B^2 = \sigma_C^2 = \sigma_D^2 = \sigma_E^2$ H_1: At least one variance is different.

ANOVA output for Levene's test for homogeneity of variance:

ANOVA

Source of Variation	SS	df	MS	F	P-value	F crit
Between Groups	14.13333	4	3.533333	1.927273	0.137107	2.758711
Within Groups	45.83333	25	1.833333			
Total	59.96667	29				

Since the p-value = 0.137 > 0.05, do not reject H_0. There is not enough evidence to conclude there is a difference in the variation in rating among the five advertisements.

(d)   There is no significant difference between advertisements A and B, and they have the highest mean rating among the five and should be used. There is no significant difference between advertisements C and D, and they are among the lowest in mean rating and should be avoided.

11.12   (a)

Source	Degrees of Freedom	Sums of Squares	Mean Squares	F
Among groups	2	12,463,043,330	6,231,521,665.00	2.78448714
Within groups	46	102,945,347,500.00	2,237,942,336.96	
Total	48	115,408,390,800.00		

11.12 (b)   Because $F_{STAT} = 2.784 < 3.23$, do not reject H_0. There is insufficient evidence that there
cont.   are significant differences in mean brand value among the financial institution,
                 technology, and telecom sectors.

       (c)   Because the results in (b) indicated that there were no differences in mean brand value
                 among the three sectors, it would not be appropriate to use the Tukey-Kramer procedure.

11.14

One-way ANOVA: Asia, Europe, North America, South America

Method

Null hypothesis	All means are equal
Alternative hypothesis	Not all means are equal
Significance level	$\alpha = 0.05$

Equal variances were assumed for the analysis.

Factor Information

Factor	Levels	Values
Factor	4	Asia, Europe, North America, South America

Analysis of Variance

Source	DF	Adj SS	Adj MS	F-Value	P-Value
Factor	3	1172	390.83	6.23	0.002
Error	36	2259	62.76		
Total	39	3432			

Model Summary

S	R-sq	R-sq(adj)	R-sq(pred)
7.92202	34.17%	28.68%	18.72%

Means

Factor	N	Mean	StDev	95% Upper Bound
Asia	10	49.20	5.98	53.43
Europe	10	40.60	3.86	44.83
North America	10	37.90	11.08	42.13
South America	10	34.60	8.81	38.83

Pooled StDev = 7.92202

       (a)   At the .05 level of significance, there is evidence there are differences in congestion
                 levels among the four continents. Because $F_{STAT} = 6.23$ OR p-value $= 0.002$, reject H_0.
                 The ANOVA F_{STAT} indicates that there are differences in congestion levels among the
                 four continents. However, it does not indicate which groups differ from one another.

11.14   (a)
cont.

Tukey Pairwise Comparisons

Grouping Information Using the Tukey Method and 95% Confidence

Factor	N	Mean	Grouping	
Asia	10	49.20	A	
Europe	10	40.60	A	B
North America	10	37.90		B
South America	10	34.60		B

Means that do not share a letter are significantly different.

(b)   Because the results from (a) revealed a significant difference in congestion levels among the four continents, the Tukey-Kramer procedure is appropriate. This test revealed that Asia had significantly higher congestion levels than North America and South America. There is no significant difference in congestion level between Asia and Europe. There are no significant differences in pairwise comparisons among Europe, North America, and South America.

(c)   The ANOVA F test assumes randomness and independence of samples, normally distributed data in all groups, and equal variances among groups.

Test for Equal Variances: Asia, Europe, North America, South America

Method

Null hypothesis	All variances are equal
Alternative hypothesis	At least one variance is different
Significance level	$\alpha = 0.05$

95% Bonferroni Confidence Intervals for Standard Deviations

Sample	N	StDev	CI
Asia	10	5.9777	(2.34648, 20.2984)
Europe	10	3.8644	(1.10956, 17.9395)
North America	10	11.0800	(2.90555, 56.3195)
South America	10	8.8091	(5.47314, 18.8987)

Individual confidence level = 98.75%

Tests

Method	Test Statistic	P-Value
Multiple comparisons	—	0.131
Levene	1.52	0.226

(d)   Because the Levene test $F_{STAT} = 1.52$ or p-value $= 0.226$, there is no evidence that the variances are different among the four regions.

11.16   (a) $SSE = SST - SSA - SSBL = 210 - 60 - 75 = 75$

(b) $MSA = \dfrac{SSA}{c-1} = \dfrac{60}{4} = 15$

11.16 (b)
$$MSBL = \frac{SSBL}{r-1} = \frac{75}{6} = 12.5$$

cont.
$$MSE = \frac{SSE}{(r-1)\cdot(c-1)} = \frac{75}{6\cdot 4} = 3.125$$

(c)
$$F_{STAT} = \frac{MSA}{MSE} = \frac{15}{3.125} = 4.80$$

(d)
$$F_{STAT} = \frac{MSBL}{MSE} = \frac{12.5}{3.125} = 4.00$$

11.18 (a) There are 5 degrees of freedom in the numerator and 24 degrees of freedom in the denominator.

(b) $Q_\alpha = 4.17$

(c) critical range $= Q_\alpha \sqrt{\dfrac{MSE}{r}} = 4.17 \sqrt{\dfrac{3.125}{7}} = 2.786$

11.20 (a)
$$MSE = \frac{MSA}{F} = \frac{18}{6} = 3$$
$SSE = (MSE)(df\,E) = (3)(12) = 36$

(b) $SSBL = (F)(MSE)(df\,BL) = (4)(3)(6) = 72$

(c) $SST = SSA + SSBL + SSE = 36 + 72 + 36 = 144$

(d) Since $F_{STAT} = 6 < F_{0.01,2,12} = 6.9266$, do not reject the null hypothesis of no treatment effect. There is not enough evidence to conclude there is a treatment effect.
Since $F_{STAT} = 4.0 < F_{0.01,6,12} = 4.821$, do not reject the null hypothesis of no block effect. There is not enough evidence to conclude there is a block effect.

11.22 (a) Decision rule: If $F_{STAT} > 3.07$, reject H_0.
Decision: Since $F_{STAT} = 5.185$ is greater than the critical bound 3.07, reject H_0. There is enough evidence to conclude that the treatment means are not all equal.

(b) Decision rule: If $F_{STAT} > 2.49$, reject H_0.
Decision: Since $F_{STAT} = 5.000$ is greater than the critical bound 2.49, reject H_0. There is enough evidence to conclude that the block means are not all equal.

11.24 (a) H_0: There is no interaction between filling time and mold temperature. H_1: There is an interaction between filling time and mold temperature.

Because $F_{STAT} = \dfrac{0.1136}{0.05} = 2.27 < 2.9277$ or the p-value $= 0.1018 > 0.05$, do not reject H_0.
There is insufficient evidence of interaction between filling time and mold temperature.

(b) $F_{STAT} = 9.0222 > 3.5546$, reject H_0. There is evidence of a difference in the warpage due to the filling time.

(c) $F_{STAT} = 4.2305 > 3.5546$, reject H_0. There is evidence of a difference in the warpage due to the mold temperature.

(e) The warpage for a three-second filling time seems to be much higher at 60°C and 72.5°C but not at 85°C.

11.26 (a) $F_{STAT} = 0.8325$, p-value $= 0.3725 > 0.05$, do not reject H_0.
There is not enough evidence to conclude that there is an interaction between zone lower and zone 3 upper.

(b) $F_{STAT} = .3820$, p-value is $0.5481 > 0.05$, do not reject H_0. There is insufficient evidence to conclude that there is an effect due to zone 1 lower.

(c) $F_{STAT} = 0.1048$, p-value $= 0.7517 > 0.05$, do not reject H_0. There is inadequate evidence to conclude that there is an effect due to zone 3 upper.

(d)   A large difference at a zone 3 upper of 695°C but only a small difference at zone 3 upper of 715°C.

(e)   Because this difference appeared on the cell means plot but the interaction was not statistically significant because of the large *MSE*, further testing should be done with larger sample sizes.

11.28 (a) H_0: $\mu_1 = \mu_2 = \mu_3$ where 1 = 2 days, 2 = 7 days, 3 = 28 days
H_1: At least one mean differs.
Decision rule: If $F_{STAT} > 3.114$, reject H_0.

ANOVA

Source of Variation	SS	df	MS	F	P-value	F crit
Rows	21.17006	39	0.542822	5.752312	2.92E-11	1.553239
Columns	50.62835	2	25.31417	268.2556	1.09E-35	3.113797
Error	7.360538	78	0.094366			
Total	79.15894	119				

Test statistic: $F = 268.26$
Decision: Since $F_{STAT} = 268.26$ is greater than the critical bound 3.114, reject H_0. There is enough evidence to conclude that there is a difference in the mean compressive strength after 2, 7 and 28 days.

(b)   From Table E.10, $Q_\alpha = 3.4$.

critical range $= Q_\alpha \sqrt{\dfrac{MSE}{r}} = 3.4 \sqrt{\dfrac{0.0944}{40}} = 0.1651$

$\left| \bar{X}_1 - \bar{X}_2 \right| = 0.5531*$ $\left| \bar{X}_1 - \bar{X}_3 \right| = 1.5685*$ $\left| \bar{X}_2 - \bar{X}_3 \right| = 1.0154*$

At the 0.05 level of significance, all of the comparisons are significant. This is consistent with the results of the F-test indicating that there is significant difference in the mean compressive strength after 2, 7 and 28 days.

(c) $RE = \dfrac{(r-1)MSBL + r(c-1)MSE}{(rc-1)MSE} = \dfrac{39 \cdot 0.5428 + 40 \cdot 2 \cdot 0.0943}{119 \cdot 0.0943} = 2.558$

11.28 (d)
cont.

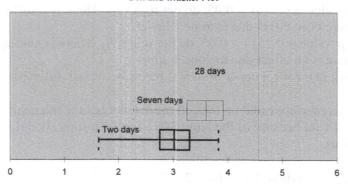

Box-and-whisker Plot

28 days

Seven days

Two days

0   1   2   3   4   5   6

(e)   The compressive strength of the concrete increases over the 3 time periods.

11.30

Source	df	SS	MS	F
Factor A	2	120	(b) $120 \div 2 = 60$	$60 \div 10 = 6$
Factor B	2	110	(b) $110 \div 2 = 55$	$55 \div 10 = 5.5$
Interaction, AB	4	(a) $540 - 120 - 110 - 270 = 40$	(c) $40 \div 4 = 10$	$10 \div 10 = 1$
Error, E	27	270	(d) $270 \div 27 = 10$	
Total, T	35	540		

11.32 $F_{(2, 27)} = 3.35$ $F_{(4, 27)} = 2.73$

(a)   Decision: Since $F_{STAT} = 6.00$ is greater than the critical bound of 3.35, reject H_0. There is evidence of a difference among factor A means.

(b)   Decision: Since $F_{STAT} = 5.50$ is greater than the critical bound of 3.35, reject H_0. There is evidence of a difference among factor B means.

(c)   Decision: Since $F_{STAT} = 1.00$ is less than the critical bound of 2.73, do not reject H_0. There is insufficient evidence to conclude there is an interaction effect.

11.34

Source	df	SS	MS	F
Factor A	2	$2 \times 80 = 160$	80	$80 \div 5 = 16$
Factor B	$8 \div 2 = 4$	220	$220 \div 4 = 55$	11
Interaction, AB	8	$8 \times 10 = 80$	10	$10 \div 5 = 2$
Error, E	30	$30 \times 5 = 150$	$55 \div 11 = 5$	
Total, T	44	$160+220+80+150 = 610$		

11.36   Excel Two-way ANOVA output:

ANOVA						
Source of Variation	SS	df	MS	F	P-value	F crit
Sample	214.2635	1	214.2635	1.8496	0.1890	4.3512
Columns	1095.2557	1	1095.2557	9.4549	0.0060	4.3512
Interaction	394.2272	1	394.2272	3.4032	0.0799	4.3512
Within	2316.8107	20	115.8405			
Total	4020.5571	23				
					Level of significance	0.05

11.36   (a) H_0: There is no interaction between die temperature and die diameter.
cont. H_1: There is an interaction between die temperature and die diameter.
              Decision: Since $F_{STAT} = 3.4032 < 4.3512$, do not reject H_0. There is insufficient evidence
              to conclude that there is any interaction between die temperature and die diameter.

        (b) H_0: $\mu_{145..} = \mu_{155..}$ H_1: $\mu_{145} \neq \mu_{155}$
              Decision: Since $F_{STAT} = 1.8496 < 4.3512$, do not reject H_0. There is insufficient evidence
              to conclude that there is an effect due to die temperature.

        (c) H_0: $\mu_{3mm.} = \mu_{4mm.}$ H_1: $\mu_{3mm} \neq \mu_{4mm}$
              Decision: Since $F_{STAT} = 9.4549 > 4.3512$, reject H_0. There is sufficient evidence to
              conclude that there is an effect due to die diameter.

        (d)   Excel output:

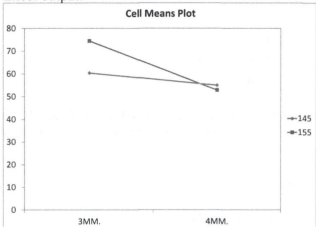

        (e)   At 5% level of significance, die diameter has an effect on the density while the die
              temperature does not have any impact on the density. There is no significant interaction
              between die diameter and die temperature.

11.38   Excel Two-way ANOVA output:

Source of Variation	SS	df	MS	F	P-value	F crit
Sample	24274.85	1	24274.85	1986.507	7.07E-20	4.413863
Columns	356.0027	2	178.0014	14.56656	0.000173	3.554561
Interaction	506.3104	2	253.1552	20.7167	2.14E-05	3.554561
Within	219.9576	18	12.21986			
Total	25357.12	23				

        (a) H_0: There is no interaction between brand and water temperature.
              H_1: There is an interaction between brand and water temperature.

$$MSAB = \frac{SSAB}{(r-1)(c-1)} = \frac{506.3104}{(1)(2)} = 253.1552$$

$$F = \frac{MSAB}{MSE} = \frac{253.1552}{12.2199} = 20.7167$$

$$F_{0.05,2,18} = 3.555$$

              Since $F_{STAT} = 20.7167 > 3.555$ or the p-value = 2.14E-05 < 0.05, reject H_0. There is
              evidence of an interaction between brand of pain-reliever and temperature of the water.

        (b)   Since there is an interaction between brand and the temperature of the water, it is
              inappropriate to analyze the main effect due to brand.

11.38 (c)
cont.

Since there is an interaction between brand and the temperature of the water, it is inappropriate to analyze the main effect due to water temperature.

(d) Excel output:

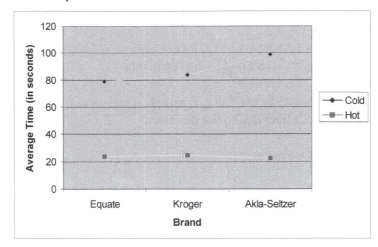

(e) The difference in the mean time a tablet took to dissolve in cold and hot water depends on the brand with Alka-Seltzer having the largest difference and Equate with the smallest difference.

11.40 (a) H_0: There is no interaction between the brake discs and the gauges.
H_1: There is an interaction between the brake discs and the gauges.
Decision rule: If p-value < 0.05, reject H_0.
Test statistic: $F_{STAT} = 0.1523$, p-value $= 0.9614$
Decision: Since p-value $= 0.9614 > 0.05$, do not reject H_0. There is not enough evidence to conclude that there is an interaction between the brake discs and the gauges.

Excel output:

ANOVA

Source of Variation	SS	df	MS	F	P-value	F crit
Sample	72207.55	4	18051.89	7.770119	3.06E-05	2.502656
Columns	340.3125	1	340.3125	0.146482	0.70308	3.977779
Interaction	1415	4	353.75	0.152265	0.96138	2.502656
Within	162627.1	70	2323.245			
Total	236590	79				

(b) H_0: $\mu_{1..} = \mu_{2..} = \mu_{3..} = \mu_{4..} = \mu_{5..}$ H_1: At least one mean differs.
Decision rule: If p-value < 0.05, reject H_0.
Test statistic: $F_{STAT} = 7.7701$, p-value is virtually 0.
Decision: Since p-value < 0.05, reject H_0. There is sufficient evidence to conclude that there is an effect due to brake discs.

(c) H_0: $\mu_{.1.} = \mu_{.2.}$ H_1: At least one mean differs.
Decision rule: If p-value < 0.05, reject H_0.
Test statistic: $F_{STAT} = 0.1465$, p-value $= 0.7031$.
Decision: Since p-value $= 0.7031 > 0.05$, do not reject H_0. There is inadequate evidence to conclude that there is an effect due to the gauges.

11.40   (d)
cont.

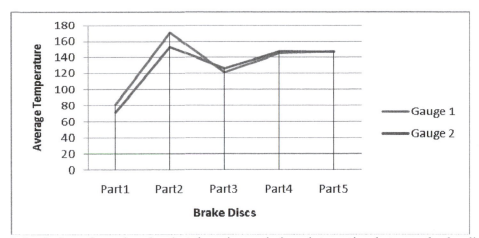

(e)   It is obvious from the plot that there is no obvious interaction between brake discs and gauges. There is no obvious difference in average temperature across the gauges either. It appears that Part 1 has the lowest, Part 3 the second lowest while Part 2 has the highest average temperature.

11.42   The completely randomized design evaluates one factor of interest, in which sample observations are randomly and independently drawn. The randomized block design also evaluates one factor of interest, but sample observations are divided into blocks according to common characteristics to reduce within group variation.

CHAPTER 12

12.2   (a)   For $df = 1$ and $\alpha = 0.05$, $\chi^2 = 3.841$.

      (b)   For $df = 1$ and $\alpha = 0.025$, $\chi^2 = 5.024$.

      (c)   For $df = 1$ and $\alpha = 0.01$, $\chi^2 = 6.635$.

12.4   (a)

Observed Freq	Expected Freq	Observed Freq	Expected Freq	Total Obs, Row 1
20	25	30	25	50
chi-sq contrib=	1.00	chi-sq contrib=	1.00	
Observed Freq	Expected Freq	Observed Freq	Expected Freq	Total Obs, Row 2
30	25	20	25	50
chi-sq contrib=	1.00	chi-sq contrib=	1.00	
Total Obs, Col 1		Total Obs, Col 2		GRAND TOTAL
50		50		100

      (b)   Decision rule: If $\chi^2 > 3.841$, reject H_0.

Test statistic: $\chi^2_{STAT} = \sum\limits_{\text{All Cells}} \dfrac{(f_0 - f_e)^2}{f_e} = 1.00 + 1.00 + 1.00 + 1.00 = 4$

Decision: Since $\chi^2_{STAT} = \sum\limits_{\text{All Cells}} \dfrac{(f_0 - f_e)^2}{f_e} = 4$ is greater than the critical value of 3.841, it is significant at the 5% level of significance.

12.6   PHStat output:

Chi-Square Test

	Observed Frequencies		
	Correctly Recall the Brand		
Arrival Method	Yes	No	Total
Recommendation	407	150	557
Browsing	193	91	284
Total	600	241	841

	Expected Frequencies		
	Correctly Recall the Brand		
Arrival Method	Yes	No	Total
Recommendation	397.3840666	159.6159334	557
Browsing	202.6159334	81.38406659	284
Total	600	241	841

Data	
Level of Significance	0.05
Number of Rows	2
Number of Columns	2
Degrees of Freedom	1

Results	
Critical Value	3.841458821
Chi-Square Test Statistic	2.404523655
p-Value	0.120984946
Do not reject the null hypothesis	

(a) $H_0: \pi_1 = \pi_2$ $H_1: \pi_1 \neq \pi_2$

(b)   Decision rule: $df = 1$. If $\chi^2_{STAT} > 3.8415$ or p-value < 0.05, reject H_0.

Test statistic: $\chi^2_{STAT} = 2.4045$

Decision: Since χ^2 STAT $= 2.4045$ is less than the upper critical bound of 3.8415, do not reject H_0. There is not enough evidence a difference in brand recall between viewers who arrived by following a social media recommendation and those who arrived by web browsing.

(c)   You should not compare the results in (a) to those of Problem 10.30 part (b) because Problem 10.30 was a one-tail test.

12.8   (a) $H_0: \pi_1 = \pi_2$. $H_1: \pi_1 \neq \pi_2$.

Because $\chi^2_{STAT} = (326 - 339.0878)^2/339.0878 + (97 - 83.9122)^2/83.9122 +$
$(167 - 153.9122)^2/153.9122 + (25 - 38.0878)^2/38.0878 = 8.1566 > 6.635$, reject H_0.
There is evidence of a difference in the proportion of organizations with 500 to 2,499 employees and organizations with 2,500+ employees with respect to the proportion that have employee recognition programs.

12.8   (b) p-value = 0.0043. The probability of obtaining a difference in proportions that gives rise
cont.   to a test statistic above 8.1566 is 0.0043 if there is no difference in the proportion in the
               two groups.
        (c)   The results of (a) and (b) are exactly the same as those of Problem 10.32.
               The χ^2 in (a) and the Z in Problem 10.32 (a) satisfy the relationship that

               $\chi^2 = 8.1566 = Z^2 = (-2.856)^2$, and the p-value in (b) is exactly the same as the
               p-value computed in Problem 10.32 (b).

12.10   (a)   <<missing answer>>
        (b)   Because $\chi^2_{STAT} = 19.9467 > 3.841$, reject H_0. There is evidence that there is a significant
               difference between the proportion of co-browsing organizations and non-co-browsing
               organizations that use skills-based routing to match the caller with the *right* agent.
        (c) p-value is virtually zero. The probability of obtaining a test statistic of 19.9467 or larger
               when the null hypothesis is true is 0.0000.
        (d)   The results are identical because $(4.4662)^2 = 19.9467$.

12.12   (a)   The expected frequencies in the first row are 20, 30, and 40.
               The expected frequencies in the second row are 30, 45, and 60.
        (b) $\chi^2_{STAT} = 12.500$. The critical value with 2 degrees of freedom and $\alpha = 0.05$ is 5.991. The
               result is deemed significant.

12.14   (a)   Because the calculated test statistic 46.4046 is greater than the critical value of 7.8147,
               you reject H_0 and conclude that there is evidence of a difference among the age groups in
               the proportion smartphone owners who have reached the maximum amount of data they
               are allowed to use as part of their plan, at least on occasion.
        (b) p-value = 0.0000. The probability of obtaining a data set that gives rise to a test statistic
               of 46.4046 or more is 0.0000 if there is no difference in the proportion who have reached
               the maximum amount of data they are allowed to use as part of their plan, at least on
               occasion.
        (c)   There is a significant difference between 18- to 29-year-olds and 50- to 64-years-olds and
               those 65 and older. There is a significant difference between 30- to 49-year-olds and 50-
               to 64-years-olds and those 65 and older.

12.16   (a) H_0: $\pi_1 = \pi_2 = \pi_3$. H_1: At least one proportion differs.

| Compensation | Observed Frequencies | | | |
| value | Group | | | |
	BE	HR	Employees	Total
Yes	28	76	66	170
No	172	124	134	430
Total	200	200	200	600

12.16 (a)
cont.

| | Expected Frequencies | | | |
| | Global Region | | | |
Investing?	NA	E	A	Total
Yes	56.6667	56.6667	56.6667	170
No	143.3333	143.3333	143.3333	430
Total	200	200	200	600

Data	
Level of Significance	0.05
Number of Rows	2
Number of Columns	3
Degrees of Freedom	2

Results	
Critical Value	5.9915
Chi-Square Test Statistic	31.5841
p-Value	0.0000
Reject the null hypothesis	

Because $31.5841 > 5.9915$, reject H_0.
There is a significant difference among business groups with respect to the proportion that say compensation (pay and rewards) makes for a unique and compelling EVP.

(b) p-value = 0.0000. The probability of a test statistic greater than 31.5841 is 0.0000.

(c)

Level of Significance	0.05
Square Root of Critical Value	2.4477

Sample Proportions	
Group 1	0.14
Group 2	0.638
Group 3	0.33

| | Marascuilo Table | | |
Proportions	Absolute Differences	Critical Range	
| Group 1 – Group 2 |	0.124	0.1033	Significant
| Group 1 – Group 3 |	0.19	0.1011	Significant
| Group 2 – Group 3 |	0.05	0.1170	Not significant

Business executives are different from HR leaders and from employees.

12.18 (a) Because $\chi^2_{STAT} = 31.6888 > 5.9915$, reject H_0. There is evidence of a difference in the percentage who use their device to check social media while watching TV between the groups.

(b) *p*-value = 0.0000.

(c) Cellphone versus computer 0.1616 > 0.0835. Significant. Cellphone versus tablet: 0.1805 > 0.0917. Significant. Computer versus tablet: 0.0188 < 0.0998. Not significant. The smartphone group is different from the computer and tablet groups.

12.20 $df = (r-1)(c-1) = (3-1)(4-1) = 6$

12.22 H_0: There is no relationship between type of dessert and type of entrée.
H_1: There is a relationship between type of dessert and type of entrée.

$$\text{Test statistic: } \chi^2_{STAT} = \sum_{\text{All cells}} \frac{(f_0 - f_e)^2}{f_e} \quad 92.1028$$

Decision: Since the calculated test statistic 92.1028 is larger than the critical value of 16.9190, you reject H_0 and conclude that there is enough evidence of a relationship between type of dessert and type of entrée.

12.24 H_0: There is no relationship between the frequency of posting on Facebook and age.
H_1: There is a relationship between the frequency of posting on Facebook and age.

Chi-Square Test
Observed Frequencies
Age Group

Frequency	16–17	18–29	30–49	50–64	65+	Total
Several	36	322	353	147	64	922
Once a day	4	69	135	100	48	356
A few times week	20	55	90	74	27	266
Every few weeks	4	11	8	25	7	55
Less often	4	14	21	25	11	75
Total	68	471	607	371	157	1,674

Chi-Square Test
Observed Frequencies
Age Group

Frequency	16–17	18–29	30–49	50–64	65+	Total
Several	37.453	259.416	334.321	204.338	86.472	922
Once a day	14.461	100.165	129.087	78.898	33.388	356
A few times week	10.805	74.84	96.453	58.952	24.947	266
Every few weeks	2.234	15.475	19.943	12.189	5.1583	55
Less often	3.0466	21.102	21	27.195	7.034	75
Total	68	471	607	371	157	1,674

12.24
cont.

Data	
Level of Significance	0.01
Number of Rows	5
Number of Columns	5
Degrees of Freedom	16

Results	
Critical Value	31.99993
Chi-Square Test Statistic	119.7494
p-Value	6.14E-18
Reject the null hypothesis	
Expected frequency assumption is met.	

Decision: Because $\chi^2_{STAT} = 119.7494 > 31.9999$ reject H_0. There is evidence to conclude that there is a relationship between the frequency of Facebook posts and age.

12.26   Because $\chi^2_{STAT} = 81.6061 > 47.3999$ reject H_0. There is evidence of a relationship between identified main opportunity and geographic region.

12.28   (a)   The lower critical value is 31.
        (b)   The lower critical value is 29.
        (c)   The lower critical value is 27.
        (d)   The lower critical value is 25.

12.30   The lower and upper critical values are 40 and 79, respectively.

12.32   (a)   The ranks for Sample 1 are 1, 2, 4, 5, and 10, respectively.
               The ranks for Sample 2 are 3, 6.5, 6.5, 8, 9, and 11, respectively.
        (b) $T_1 = 1 + 2 + 4 + 5 + 10 = 22$
        (c) $T_2 = 3 + 6.5 + 6.5 + 8 + 9 + 11 = 44$
        (d) $T_1 + T_2 = \dfrac{n(n+1)}{2} = \dfrac{11(12)}{2} = 66$ $T_1 + T_2 = 22 + 44 = 66$

12.34   Decision: Since $T_1 = 22$ is greater than the lower critical bound of 20, do not reject H_0.

12.36   (a)   The data are ordinal.
        (b)   The two-sample t-test is inappropriate because the data are ordinal, the sample size is small and the distribution of the ordinal data is not normally distributed.
        (c) H_0: $M_1 = M_2$ where Populations: 1 = California,   2 = Washington
               H_1: $M_1 \neq M_2$

12.36 (c)   PHStat output:
cont.

Data	
Level of Significance	0.05
Population 1 Sample	
Sample Size	8
Sum of Ranks	47
Population 2 Sample	
Sample Size	8
Sum of Ranks	89
Intermediate Calculations	
Total Sample Size n	16
T1 Test Statistic	47
T1 Mean	68
Standard Error of *T1*	9.521905
Z Test Statistic	–2.20544
Two-Tailed Test	
Lower Critical Value	**–1.95996**
Upper Critical Value	**1.959964**
***p*-value**	**0.027423**
Reject the null hypothesis	

$$\mu_{T1} = \frac{n_1(n+1)}{2} = \frac{8(16+1)}{2} = 68$$

$$\sigma_{T_1} = \sqrt{\frac{n_1 n_2 (n+1)}{12}} = \sqrt{\frac{8(8)(16+1)}{12}} = 9.5219$$

$$Z_{STAT} = \frac{T_1 - \mu_{T_1}}{\sigma_{T_1}} = -2.2054$$

Decision: Since $Z_{STAT} = -2.2054$ is lower than the lower critical bounds of -1.96, reject H_0. There is enough evidence of a significant difference in the median rating of California Cabernets and Washington Cabernets.

12.38 (a) $H_0: M_1 = M_2$, where Populations: $1 =$ Wing A, $2 =$ Wing B.
$H_1: M_1 \neq M_2$.
Population 1 sample: Sample size 20, sum of ranks 561
Population 2 sample: Sample size 20, sum of ranks 259

$$\mu_{T_1} = \frac{n_1(n+1)}{2} = \frac{20(40+1)}{2} = 410$$

$$\sigma_{T_1} = \sqrt{\frac{n_1 n_2 (n+1)}{12}} = \sqrt{\frac{20(20)(40+1)}{12}} = 36.9685$$

$$Z_{STAT} = \frac{T_1 - \mu_{T_1}}{S_{T_1}} = \frac{561 - 410}{36.9685} = 4.0846$$

Decision: Because $Z_{STAT} = 4.0846 > 1.96$ (or p-value $= 0.0000 < 0.05$), reject H_0. There is sufficient evidence of a difference in the median delivery time in the two wings of the hotel.

(b)   The results of (a) are consistent with the results of Problem 10.65.

12.40 (a)   Because $Z_{STAT} = 2.1342 > 1.96$, reject H_0. There is evidence to conclude that there is a difference in the median brand value between the two sectors.

(b)   You must assume approximately equal variability in the two populations.

(c)   Using the pooled-variance t test you rejected the null hypothesis and the separate-variance t test rejected the null hypothesis so you conclude in Problem 10.17 that the mean brand value is different between the two sectors. In this test, using the Wilcoxon rank sum test with large-sample Z approximation you rejected the null hypothesis and concluded that the median brand value differs between the two sectors.

12.42 (a)   Because $-1.96 < Z_{STAT} = 1.1687 < 1.96$ (or the p-value $= 0.2425 > 0.05$), do not reject H_0. There is not enough evidence to conclude that there is a difference in the median rating of 60-second and 30-second ads.

(b)   You must assume approximately equal variability in the two populations.

(c)   Using the pooled-variance t-test, you do not reject the null hypothesis ($t = -2.0040 < t_{STAT} = 0.7949 < 2.0040$; p-value $= 0.4301 > 0.05$) and conclude that there is insufficient evidence of a difference in the mean rating of 60-second and 30-second ads in Problem 10.11 (a).

12.44 (a)   Decision rule: If $H > \chi_\alpha^2 = 15.086$, reject H_0.

(b)   Decision: Since $H_{calc} = 13.77$ is less than the critical bound of 15.086, do not reject H_0.

12.46 PHStat output of Kruskal-Wallis rank test:

Data	
Level of Significance	0.05
Group 1	
Sum of Ranks	640
Sample Size	15
Group 2	
Sum of Ranks	291
Sample Size	15
Group 3	
Sum of Ranks	468
Sample Size	15
Group 4	
Sum of Ranks	431
Sample Size	15
Intermediate Calculations	
Sum of Squared Ranks/Sample Size	59937.73
Sum of Sample Sizes	60
Number of groups	4
H Test Statistic	13.51716
Test Result	
Critical Value	7.814728
p-Value	0.003642
Reject the null hypothesis	

(a) H_0: $M_{main} = M_{Sat1} = M_{Sat2} = M_{Sat3}$ H_1: At least one of the medians differs. Since the p-value $= 0.0036$ is lower than 0.05, reject H_0. There is sufficient evidence of a difference in the median waiting time in the four locations.

(b)   The results are consistent with those of Problem 11.9.

12.48   PHStat output of Kruskal-Wallis rank test:

Data	
Level of Significance	0.05
Intermediate Calculations	
Sum of Squared Ranks/Sample Size	8705.333
Sum of Sample Sizes	30
Number of Groups	5
Test Result	
H Test Statistic	19.32688
Critical Value	9.487729
p-Value	0.000678
Reject the null hypothesis	

(a) H_0: $M_A = M_B = M_C = M_D = M_E$ H_1: At least one of the medians differs.
Since the p-value = $0.0007 < 0.05$, reject H_0. There is sufficient evidence of a difference in the median rating of the five advertisements.

(b)   In (a), you conclude that there is evidence of a difference in the median rating of the five advertisements, while in problem 11.10 (a), you conclude that there is evidence of a difference in the mean rating of the five advertisements.

(c)   Since the combined scores are not true continuous variables, the nonparametric Kruskal-Wallis rank test is more appropriate because it does not require the scores to be normally distributed.

12.50   (a)   Because $H = 13.0522 > 7.815$ or the p-value is 0.0045, reject H_0. There is sufficient evidence of a difference in the median cost associated with importing a standardized cargo of goods by sea transport across the global regions.

(b)   The results are the same.

12.52   The Chi-square test can be used for c populations as long as all expected frequencies are at least one.

12.54   The Wilcoxon rank sum test should be used when you are unable to assume that each of two independent populations are normally distributed.

12.56   (a) H_0: There is no relationship between a student's gender and his/her pizzeria selection.
H_1: There is a relationship between a student's gender and his/her pizzeria selection.
Decision rule: $d.f. = 1$.   If $\chi^2_{STAT} > 3.841$, reject H_0.   Test statistic: $\chi^2_{STAT} = 0.412$
Decision: Since the $\chi^2_{STAT} = 0.412$ is smaller than the critical bound of 3.841, do not reject H_0. There is not enough evidence to conclude that there is a relationship between a student's gender and his/her pizzeria selection.

(b)   Test statistic: $\chi^2_{STAT} = 2.624$
Decision: Since the $\chi^2_{STAT} = 2.624$ is less than the critical bound of 3.841, do not reject H_0. There is not enough evidence to conclude that there is a relationship between a student's gender and his/her pizzeria selection.

(c) H_0: There is no relationship between price and pizzeria selection.
H_1: There is a relationship between price and pizzeria selection.
Decision rule: $d.f. = 2$.   If $\chi^2_{STAT} > 5.991$, reject H_0.   Test statistic: $\chi^2_{STAT} = 4.956$

12.56   (c)   Decision: Since the $\chi^2_{STAT} = 4.956$ is smaller than the critical bound of 5.991, do not reject
cont. H_0. There is not enough evidence to conclude that there is a relationship between price
                 and pizzeria selection.

         (d) p-value = 0.0839. The probability of obtaining a sample that gives a test statistic equal to
                 or greater than 4.956 is 0.0839 if the null hypothesis of no relationship between price and
                 pizzeria selection is true.

12.58   (a)   Because $\chi^2_{STAT} = 7.4298 < 9.4877$; p-value = 0.1148 > 0.05 do not reject H_0. There is not
                 enough evidence to conclude that there is evidence of a difference in the proportion of
                 organizations that have embarked on digital transformation on the basis of industry
                 sector.

         (b)   Because $\chi^2_{STAT} = 38.09 > 21.0261$; p-value = 0.0001 < 0.05 reject H_0. There is evidence of
                 a relationship between digital transformation progress and industry sector.

CHAPTER 13

13.2 (a) yes
     (b) no
     (c) no
     (d) yes

13.4 (a)

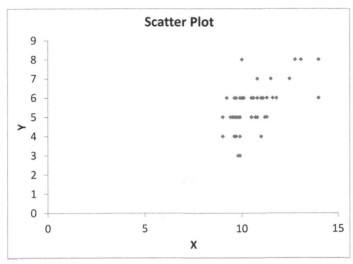

The scatter plot shows a positive linear relationship.

(b) For each % increase in alcohol content, there is an expected increase in quality of an estimated 0.5624.

(c) $\hat{Y} = -0.3529 + 0.5624X = -0.3529 + 0.5624(10) = 5.2715$

(d) There appears to be a positive linear relationship between quality and % alcohol content. For each % increase in alcohol content, there is an expected increase in quality of an estimated 0.5624.

13.6   (a)

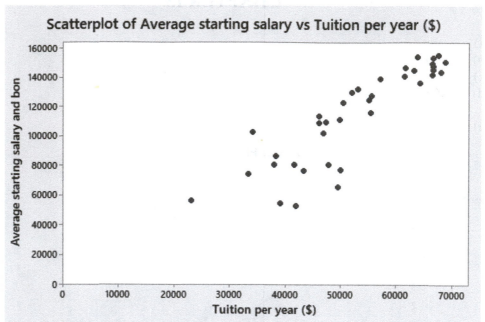

(b) $b_0 = -13,130.6592$, $b_1 = 2.4218$.

(c)   For each increase of $1,000 in tuition, the mean starting salary is predicted to increase by $2,421.80.

(d) $109,047.01

(e)   Starting salary seems higher for those schools that have a higher tuition.

13.8   (a)

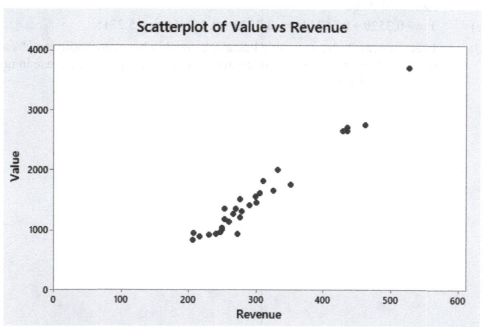

(b) $b_0 = -1,039.5317$, $b_1 = 8.5816$.

(c)   For each additional million dollar increase in revenue, the mean value is predicted to increase by an estimated $8.5816 million. Literal interpretation of b0 is not meaningful because an operating franchise cannot have zero revenue.

13.8 (d) $1,105.864 million.
cont. (e) That the value of the franchise can be expected to increase as revenue increases.

13.10 (a)

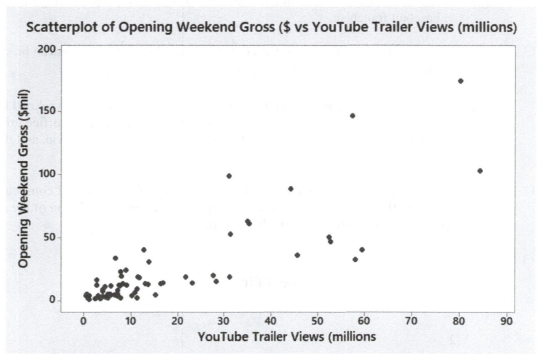

(b) $b_0 = -0.7744$, $b_1 = 1.4030$.
(c) For each increase of million YouTube trailer views, the predicted weekend box office gross is estimated to increase by $1.4030 million.
(d) $27.2847 million.
(e) You can conclude that the mean predicted increase in weekend box office gross is $1.4030 million for each million increase in YouTube trailer views.

13.12 $SST = 40$ and $r^2 = 0.90$. So, 90% of the variation in the dependent variable can be explained by the variation in the independent variable.

13.14 $r^2 = 0.75$. So, 75% of the variation in the dependent variable can be explained by the variation in the independent variable.

13.16 (a) $r^2 = \dfrac{SSR}{SST} = 0.3417$. So, 34.17% of the variation in wine quality can be explained by the variation in alcohol content.

(b) $S_{YX} = \sqrt{\dfrac{SSE}{n-2}} = \sqrt{\dfrac{\sum\limits_{i=1}^{n}\left(Y_i - \hat{Y}_i\right)^2}{n-2}} = 0.9369$

(c) Based on (a) and (b), the model should be moderately useful for predicting wine quality.

13.18 (a) $r^2 = 0.7665$. 76.65% of the variation in starting salary can be explained by the variation in tuition.
(b) $S_{YX} = 15{,}944.3807$.
(c) Based on (a) and (b), the model should be very useful for predicting the starting salary.

13.20   (a) $r^2 = 0.9612$, 96.12% of the variation in the value of a baseball franchise can be explained by the variation in its annual revenue.

(b) $S_{YX} = 140.8188$

(c)   Based on (a) and (b), the model should be very useful for predicting the value of a baseball franchise.

13.22   (a) $r^2 = 0.6676$, 66.76% of the variation in weekend box office gross can be explained by the variation in YouTube trailer views.

(b) $S_{YX} = 19.4447$.

(c)   Based on (a) and (b), the model should be useful for predicting weekend box office gross.

(d)   Other variables that might explain the variation in weekend box office gross could be the amount spent on advertising, the timing of the release of the movie, and the type of movie.

13.24   A residual analysis of the data indicates a pattern, with sizable clusters of consecutive residuals that are either all positive or all negative. This pattern indicates a violation of the assumption of linearity. A curvilinear model should be investigated.

13.26

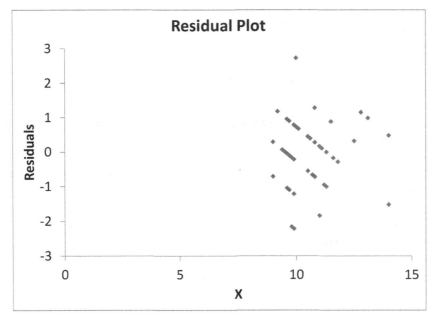

Based on the residual plot, there does not appear to be a pattern in the residual plot. The linearity and equal variance assumptions appear to be holding up.

13.26
cont.

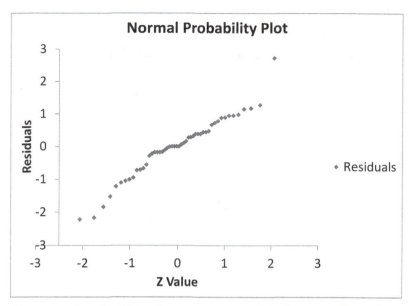

The normal probability plot suggests possible departure from the normality assumption.

13.28   Based on the residual plot, the assumption of equal variance may be violated.

13.30   Based on the residual plot, there is no evidence of a pattern.

13.32   (a)

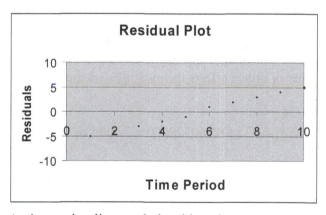

An increasing linear relationship exists.

(b)   There appears to be strong positive autocorrelation among the residuals.

13.34   (a)   No, it is not necessary to compute the Durbin-Watson statistic since the data have been collected for a single period for a set of bags.

(b)   If a single bag-sealing equipment was studied over a period of time and the amount of plate gap varied over time, computation of the Durbin-Watson statistic would be necessary.

13.36 (a) $b_1 = \dfrac{SSXY}{SSX} = \dfrac{201399.05}{12495626} = 0.0161$

$b_0 = \bar{Y} - b_1\bar{X} = 71.2621 - 0.0161(4393) = 0.458$

(b) $\hat{Y} = 0.458 + 0.0161X = 0.458 + 0.0161(4500) = 72.908$ or $72,908

(c)

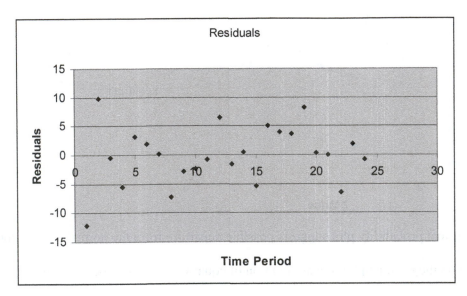

(d) $D = \dfrac{\sum\limits_{i=2}^{n}(e_i - e_{i-1})^2}{\sum\limits_{i=1}^{n} e_i^2} = \dfrac{1243.2244}{599.0683} = 2.08 > 1.45.$

There is no evidence of positive autocorrelation among the residuals.

(e) Based on a residual analysis, the model appears to be adequate.

(f) It appears that the number of orders affects the monthly distribution costs.

13.38 (a) $b_0 = -2.535$, $b_1 = 0.060728$

(b) $\hat{Y} = -2.535 + 0.060728X = -2.535 + 0.060728(83) = 2.5054$ or $2505.40

(c)

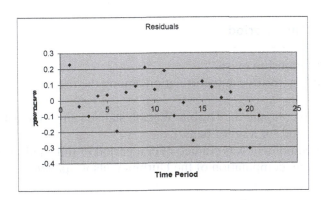

13.38 (d) $D = 1.64 > 1.42$. There is no evidence of positive autocorrelation among the residuals.

cont. (e) The plot of the residuals versus time period shows some clustering of positive and negative residuals for intervals in the domain, suggesting a nonlinear model might be better. Otherwise, the model appears to be adequate.

(f) There appears to be a positive relationship between sales and atmospheric temperature.

13.40 (a) $H_0 : \beta_1 = 0 \qquad H_1 : \beta_1 \neq 0$

Test statistic: $t_{STAT} = (b_1 - 0) / s_{b_1} = 4.5 / 1.5 = 3.00$

(b) With $n = 18$, df $= 18 - 2 = 16$, $t_{0.05/2} = \pm 2.1199$.

(c) Reject H_0. There is evidence that the fitted linear regression model is useful.

(d) $b_1 - t_{0.05/2} s_{b_1} \leq \beta_1 \leq b_1 + t_{0.05/2} s_{b_1}$

$4.5 - 2.1199(1.5) \leq \beta_1 \leq 4.5 + 2.1199(1.5)$

$1.32 \leq \beta_1 \leq 7.68$

13.42 (a) $H_0 : \beta_1 = 0 \qquad H_1 : \beta_1 \neq 0$

	Coefficients	Standard Error	t Stat	P-value	Lower 95%	Upper 95%
Intercept	-0.3529	1.2000	-0.2941	0.7700	-2.7656	2.0599
alcohol	0.5624	0.1127	4.9913	0.0000	0.3359	0.7890

$t_{STAT} = \dfrac{b_1 - \beta_1}{S_{b_1}} = 4.9913$ with a p-value $= 0.0000 < 0.05$. Reject H_0. There is enough

evidence to conclude that the fitted linear regression model is useful.

(b) $b_1 \pm t_{\alpha/2} S_{b_1} \qquad 0.3359 \leq \beta_1 \leq 0.7890$

13.44 (a) $t_{STAT} = 10.7174 > 2.0301$; p-value $= 0.0000\ 6\ 0.05$ reject H_0. There is evidence of a linear relationship between tuition and starting salary.

(b) $1.963 \leq \beta_1 \leq 2.8805$

13.46 (a) $t_{STAT} = 26.3347 > 2.0484$ or because the p-value is 0.0000, reject H_0 at the 5% level of significance. There is evidence of a linear relationship between annual revenue and franchise value.

(b) $7.9141 \leq \beta_1 \leq 9.2491$

13.48 (a) $t_{STAT} = 11.3381 > 1.9977$ or because the p-value $= 0.0000 < 0.05$; reject H_0. There is evidence of a linear relationship between YouTube trailer views and weekend box office gross.

(b) $1.1558 \leq \beta_1 \leq 1.6501$

13.50 (a) (% daily change in SPUU) $= b_0 + 2.0$ (% daily change in S&P 500 index).

(b) If the S&P 500 gains 10% in a year, SPUU is expected to gain an estimated 20%.

(c) If the S&P 500 loses 20% in a year, SPUU is expected to lose an estimated 40%.

(d) Risk takers will be attracted to leveraged funds, and risk-averse investors will stay away.

13.52 (a) **First weekend gross and the U. S. gross**

$r = 0.7284$. There appears to be a strong positive linear relationship.

First weekend gross and the worldwide gross

$r = 0.8233$. There appears to be a strong positive linear relationship.

13.52   (a)   **U. S. gross, and worldwide gross**
cont. $r = 0.9642$ There appears to be a very strong positive linear relationship.

        (b)   **First weekend gross and the U. S. gross**
              Since $t_{stat} = 2.6042 > 2.4469$ and p-value $= 0.0404 < 0.05$, reject H_0. At the 0.05 level of
              significance, there is evidence of a linear relationship between first weekend sales and
              U.S. gross.
              First weekend gross and the worldwide gross
              Since $t_{stat} = 3.5532 > 2.4469$ and p-value $= 0.0120 < 0.05$, reject H_0. At the 0.05 level of
              significance, there is evidence of a linear relationship between first weekend sales and
              worldwide gross.
              U. S. gross, and worldwide gross
              Since $t_{stat} = 8.9061 > 2.4469$ and p-value $= 0.0001 < 0.05$, reject H_0. At the 0.05 level of
              significance, there is evidence of a linear relationship between U.S. gross and worldwide
              gross.

13.54   (a) $r = 0.3002$. There is an insignificant linear relationship between social media networking
              and the GDP per capita.

        (b) $t_{STAT} = 1.6048$, p-value $= 0.1206 > 0.05$. Do not reject H_0. At the 0.05 level of
              significance, there is insufficient evidence of a linear relationship between social media
              networking and the GDP per capita.

        (c)   There does not appear to be a linear relationship.

13.56   (a)   When $X = 4$, $\hat{Y} = 5 + 3X = 5 + 3(4) = 17$

              $$h = \frac{1}{n} + \frac{(X_i - \bar{X})^2}{\sum_{i=1}^{n}(X_i - \bar{X})^2} = \frac{1}{20} + \frac{(4-2)^2}{20} = 0.25$$

              95% confidence interval: $\hat{Y} \pm t_{0.05/2} s_{YX} \sqrt{h} = 17 \pm 2.1009 \cdot 1 \cdot \sqrt{0.25}$
              $15.95 \leq \mu_{Y|X=4} \leq 18.05$

        (b)   95% prediction interval: $\hat{Y} \pm t_{0.05/2} s_{YX} \sqrt{1+h} = 17 \pm 2.1009 \cdot 1 \cdot \sqrt{1.25}$
              $14.651 \leq Y_{X=4} \leq 19.349$

        (c)   The intervals in this problem are wider because the value of X is farther from $\bar{X}$.

13.58   (a) $4.9741 \leq \mu_{Y|X=10} \leq 5.568984094$

        (b) $3.3645 \leq Y_{X=10} \leq 7.178609919$

        (c)   Part (b) provides a prediction interval for the individual response given a specific value of
              the independent variable, and part (a) provides an interval estimate for the mean value,
              given a specific value of the independent variable. Because there is much more variation
              in predicting an individual value than in estimating a mean value, a prediction interval is
              wider than a confidence interval estimate.

13.60   (a) $\$103,638.95 \leq \mu_{Y|X=50,450} \leq \$114,455.06$

        (b) $\$76,229.52 \leq Y_{X=50,450} \leq \$141,864.49$

        (c)   You can estimate a mean more precisely than you can predict a single observation.

13.62 (a) $1,043.1911 \le \mu_{Y|X=250} \le 1,168.5370$

(b) $810.6799 \le Y_{X=250} \le 1,401.0480$

(c) Because there is much more variation in predicting an individual value than in estimating a mean, the prediction interval is wider than the confidence interval.

13.64 The slope of the line, b_1, represents the estimated expected change in Y per unit change in X. It represents the estimated mean amount that Y changes (either positively or negatively) for a particular unit change in X. The Y intercept b_0 represents the estimated mean value of Y when X equals 0.

13.66 The unexplained variation or error sum of squares (SSE) will be equal to zero only when the regression line fits the data perfectly and the coefficient of determination equals 1.

13.68 Unless a residual analysis is undertaken, you will not know whether the model fit is appropriate for the data. In addition, residual analysis can be used to check whether the assumptions of regression have been seriously violated.

13.70 The normality of error assumption can be evaluated by obtaining a histogram, boxplot, and/or normal probability plot of the residuals. The homoscedasticity assumption can be evaluated by plotting the residuals on the vertical axis and the X variable on the horizontal axis. The independence of errors assumption can be evaluated by plotting the residuals on the vertical axis and the time order variable on the horizontal axis. This assumption can also be evaluated by computing the Durbin-Watson statistic.

13.72 The confidence interval for the mean response estimates the mean response for a given X value. The prediction interval estimates the value for a single item or individual.

13.74 (a) $b_0 = 24.84$, $b_1 = 0.14$

(b) 24.84 is the portion of estimated mean delivery time that is not affected by the number of cases delivered. For each additional case, the estimated mean delivery time increases by 0.14 minutes.

(c) $\hat{Y} = 24.84 + 0.14 \quad X = 24.84 + 0.14(150) = 45.84$

(d) No, 500 cases is outside the relevant range of the data used to fit the regression equation.

(e) $r^2 = 0.972$. So, 97.2% of the variation in delivery time can be explained by the variation in the number of cases.

(f) Based on a visual inspection of the graphs of the distribution of residuals and the residuals versus the number of cases, there is no pattern. The model appears to be adequate.

(g) $t = 24.88 > t_{0.05/2} = 2.1009$ with 18 degrees of freedom for $\alpha = 0.05$. Reject H_0. There is evidence that the fitted linear regression model is useful.

(h) $44.88 \le \mu_{Y|X=150} \le 46.80$

$41.56 \le Y_{X=150} \le 50.12$

13.76 (a) $b_0 = 326.5935$, $b_1 = 0.0835$.

(b) For each additional square foot of living space in the house, the mean asking price is predicted to increase by \$83.50. The estimated asking price of a house with 0 living space is 326.5935 thousand dollars. However, this interpretation is not meaningful because the living space of the house cannot be 0.

13.76 (c) $\hat{Y} = 493.6769$ thousand dollars.

cont. (d) $r^2 = 0.3979$. So 39.79% of the variation in asking price is explained by the variation in living space.

(e)   Neither the residual plot nor the normal probability plot reveals any potential violation of the linearity, equal variance, and normality assumptions.

(f) $t_{STAT} = 6.2436 > 2.0010$, p-value is 0.0000. Because p-value < 0.05, reject H_0. There is evidence of a linear relationship between asking price and living space.

(g) $0.0568 \le \beta_1 \le 0.1103$

(h)   The living space in the house is somewhat useful in predicting the asking price, but because only 39.79% of the variation in asking price is explained by variation in living space, other variables should be considered.

13.78 (a) $b_0 = 21.2034$, $b_1 = -0.1517$.

(b)   For each additional point on the efficiency ratio, the predicted mean tangible common equity (ROATCE) is estimated to decrease by 0.1517. For an efficiency of 0, the predicted mean tangible common equity (ROATCE) is 21.2034.

(c)   12.0989.

(d) $r^2 = 0.1882$.

(e)   There is no obvious pattern in the residuals, so the assumptions of regression are met. The model appears to be adequate.

(f) $t_{STAT} = -4.7662 < -1.9845$; reject H_0. There is evidence of a linear relationship between efficiency ratio and tangible common equity (ROATCE).

(g) $11.4060 \le \mu_{Y|X=60} \le 12.7918$, $5.1534 \le Y_{X=60} \le 19.0444$

(h) $-0.2149 \le \beta_1 \le -0.0886$ (i) There is a small relationship between efficiency ratio and tangible common equity (ROATCE).

13.80 (a)

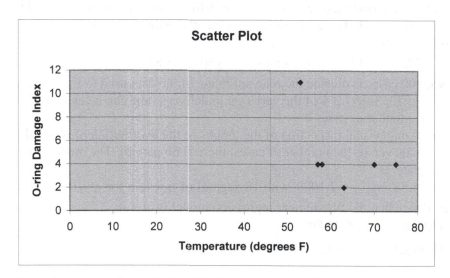

There is not any clear relationship between atmospheric temperature and O-ring damage from the scatter plot.

13.80   (b)
cont.

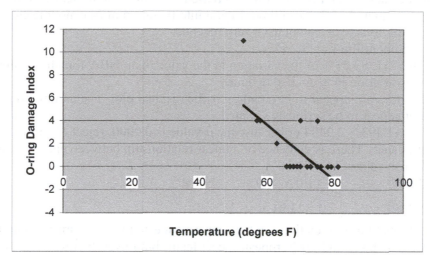

(c)   In (b), there are 16 observations with an O-ring damage index of 0 for a variety of temperatures. If one concentrates on these observations with no O-ring damage, there is obviously no relationship between O-ring damage index and temperature. If all observations are used, the observations with no O-ring damage will bias the estimated relationship. If the intention is to investigate the relationship between the degrees of O-ring damage and atmospheric temperature, it makes sense to focus only on the flights in which there was O-ring damage.

(d)   Prediction should not be made for an atmospheric temperature of 31 ^{0}F because it is outside the range of the temperature variable in the data. Such prediction will involve extrapolation, which assumes that any relationship between two variables will continue to hold outside the domain of the temperature variable.

(e) $\hat{Y} = 18.036 - 0.240X$

(g)   A nonlinear model is more appropriate for these data.

(h)

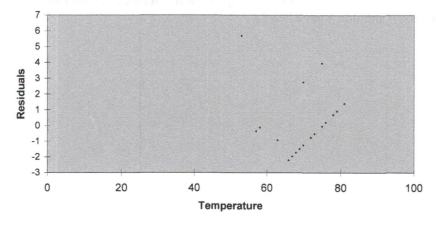

The string of negative residuals and positive residuals that lie on a straight line with a positive slope in the lower-right corner of the plot is a strong indication that a nonlinear model should be used if all 23 observations are to be used in the fit.

13.82 (a) $b_0 = -893.4994$, $b_1 = 12.3871$.

      (b)   For each additional million-dollar increase in revenue, the franchise value will increase by an estimated 12.3871 million. Literal interpretation of b_0 is not meaningful because an operating franchise cannot have zero revenue.

      (c) $964.5599 million.

      (d) $r^2 = 0.8251$. 82.51% of the variation in the value of an NBA franchise can be explained by the variation in its annual revenue.

      (e)   There does not appear to be a pattern in the residual plot. The assumptions of regression do not appear to be seriously violated.

      (f) $t_{STAT} = 11.493 > 2.0484$ or because the p-value is 0.0000, reject H_0 at the 5% level of significance. There is evidence of a linear relationship between annual revenue and franchise value.

      (g) $852.6812 \le \mu_{Y|X=150} \le 1{,}076.439$

      (h) $405.1897 \le Y_{X=150} \le 1{,}523.93$

      (i)   The strength of the relationship between revenue and value is approximately the same for NBA franchises and for European soccer teams but lower than for Major League Baseball teams.

13.84 (a) $b_0 = -2{,}629.222$, $b_1 = 82.472$.

      (b)   For each additional centimeter in circumference, the weight is estimated to increase by 82.472 grams.

      (c)   2,319.08 grams.

      (d)   Yes, because circumference is a very strong predictor of weight.

      (e) $r^2 = 0.937$.

      (f)   There appears to be a nonlinear relationship between circumference and weight.

      (g) p-value is virtually $0 < 0.05$; reject H_0.

      (h) $72.7875 \le \beta_1 \le 92.156$.

13.86 (a)   The correlation between compensation and stock performance is 0.0550.

      (b) $t_{STAT} = 0.7757$; p-value $= 0.4388 > 0.05$. The correlation between compensation and stock performance is not significant, only 0.3% of the variation in compensation can be explained by return.

      (c)   The small correlation between compensation and stock performance was surprising (or maybe it shouldn't have been!).

CHAPTER 14

14.2 (a) Holding constant the effect of X_2, for each increase of one unit in X_1, the response variable Y is estimated to decrease an average of 2 units. Holding constant the effect of X_1, for each increase of one unit in X_2, the response variable Y is estimated to increase an average of 7 units.

(b) The Y-intercept 50 is the estimate of the mean value of Y if X_1 and X_2 are both 0.

14.4 (a) $\hat{Y} = 1.3960 - 0.0117X_1 + 0.0286X_2$

(b) For a given capital adequacy, for each increase of 1% in efficiency ratio, ROAA decreases by 0.0117%. For a given efficiency ratio, for each increase of 1% in capital adequacy, ROAA increases by 0.0286%

(c) $\hat{Y} = 1.1214$

(d) $1.0798 \le \mu_{Y|X} \le 1.1629$

(e) $0.5679 \le Y_X \le 1.6749$

(f) The interval in (e) is narrower because it is estimating the mean value, not an individual value.

(g) The model uses both the efficiency ratio and capital adequacy to predict ROA. This may produce a better model than if only one of these independent variables is included.

14.6 (a) $\hat{Y} = 301.78 + 3.4771X_1 + 41.041X_2$

(b) For a given amount of voluntary turnover, for each increase of $1 billion in worldwide revenue, the mean number of full-time jobs added is predicted to increase by 3.4771. For a given $1 billion in worldwide revenue, for each increase of 1% in voluntary turnover, the mean number of full-time jobs added is predicted to increase by 41.041.

(c) The Y intercept has no meaning in this problem.

(d) Holding the other independent variable constant, voluntary turnover has a higher slope than worldwide revenue.

14.8 (a) $\hat{Y} = 532.2883 + 407.1346X_1 - 2.8257X_2$ where $X_1 =$ Land, $X_2 =$ Age

(b) For a given age, each increase by one acre in land area is estimated to result in a mean increase in fair market value of $407.1346 thousands. For a given acreage, each increase of one year in age is estimated to result in the mean decrease in fair market value of $2.8257 thousands.

(c) The interpretation of b_0 has no practical meaning here because it would have meant the estimated mean fair market value of a new house that has no land area.

(d) $\hat{Y} = 532.2883 + 407.1346(.25) - 2.8257(55) = \$478.6577$ thousands.

(e) $446.8367 \le \mu_{Y|X} \le 510.4788$

(f) $307.2577 \le Y_X \le 650.0577$

14.10 (a) $MSR = SSR / k = 30 / 2 = 15$
$MSE = SSE / (n - k - 1) = 120 / 10 = 12$

(b) $F_{STAT} = MSR / MSE = 15 / 12 = 1.25$

(c) $F_{STAT} = 1.25 < F_{U(2,13-2-1)} = 4.103$. Do not reject H_0. There is not sufficient evidence of a significant linear relationship.

14.10 (d) $$r^2 = \frac{SSR}{SST} = \frac{30}{150} = 0.2$$

cont. (e) $$r_{adj}^2 = 1 - \left[\left(1 - r_{Y.12}^2 \right) \frac{n-1}{n-k-1} \right] = 0.04$$

14.12 p-value for revenue is $0.0395 < 0.05$ and the p-value for efficiency is less than $0.0001 < 0.05$. Reject H_0 for each of the independent variables. There is evidence of a significant linear relationship with each of the independent variables.

14.14 (a) $F_{STAT} = 37.8384 > 3.00$; reject H_0.
 (b) p-value = 0.0000. The probability of obtaining an F_{STAT} value > 37.8384 if the null hypothesis is true is 0.0000.
 (c) $r^2 = 0.2785$. 27.85% of the variation in ROA can be explained by variation in efficiency ratio and variation in risk-based capital.
 (d) $r_{adj}^2 = 0.2712$

14.16 (a) $F_{STAT} = 1.95 < 3.15$; Do not reject H_0. There is insufficient evidence of a significant linear relationship.
 (b) p-value = 0.1512. The probability of obtaining an F_{STAT} value > 1.95 if the null hypothesis is true is 0.1512.
 (c) $r^2 = 0.0610$. 6.10% of the variation in full-time jobs added can be explained by variation in worldwide revenue and variation in full-time voluntary turnover.
 (d) $r_{adj}^2 = 0.0297$

14.18 (a)–(e) Based on a residual analysis, there is no evidence of a violation of the assumptions of regression.

14.20 (a) There is no evidence of a violation of the assumptions
 (b) Because the data are not collected over time, the Durbin-Watson test is not appropriate.
 (c) They are valid

14.22 (a)

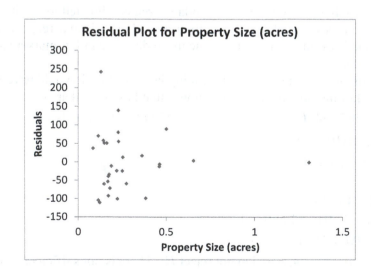

14.22   (a)
cont.

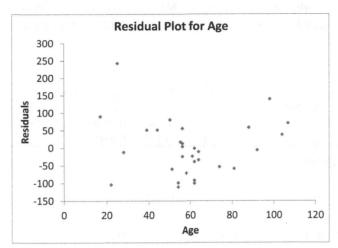

The residual analysis reveals no patterns.

(b)   Since the data set is cross-sectional, the Durbin-Watson test is not appropriate.

(c)   There are no apparent violations of the assumptions.

14.24   (a)   The slope of X_2 in terms of the t statistic is 3.75 which is larger than the slope of X_1 in terms of the t statistic which is 3.33.

(b)   95% confidence interval on β_1: $b_1 \pm t_{n-k-1} s_{b_1}$, $4 \pm 2.1098(1.2)$

$1.46824 \leq \beta_1 \leq 6.53176$

(c)   For X_1: $t_{STAT} = \dfrac{b_1}{s_{b_1}} = \dfrac{4}{1.2} = 3.33 > t_{17} = 2.1098$ with 17 degrees of freedom for $\alpha = 0.05$.

Reject H_0. There is evidence that the variable X_1 contributes to a model already containing X_2.

For X_2: $t_{STAT} = \dfrac{b_2}{s_{b_2}} = \dfrac{3}{0.8} = 3.75 > t_{17} = 2.1098$ with 17 degrees of freedom for $\alpha = 0.05$.

Reject H_0. There is evidence that the variable X_2 contributes to a model already containing X_1. Both variables X_1 and X_2 should be included in the model.

14.26   (a)   95% confidence interval on β_1: $b_1 \pm t S_{b_1}$, $-0.0117 \pm 1.98(0.0022)$,

$-0.0161 \leq \beta_1 \leq -0.0074$

(b)   For X_1 : $t_{STAT} = \dfrac{b_1}{S_{b_1}} = \dfrac{-0.0177}{0.0022} = -5.3415 < -1.98$.   Reject H_0. There is evidence that X_1

contributes to a model already containing X_2.

For X_2 : $t_{STAT} = \dfrac{b_2}{S_{b_2}} = \dfrac{0.0286}{0.0054} = 5.2992 > 1.98$. Reject H_0.

There is evidence that X_2 contributes to a model already containing X_1. Both X_1 (efficiency ratio) and X_2 (total risk-based capital) should be included in the model.

14.28   (a) $-5.8682 \leq \beta_1 \leq 12.8225$

(b)   For X_1 : $t_{STAT} = 0.7443 < 2.0003$. Don't reject H_0. There is insufficient evidence that X_1 contributes to a model already containing X_2.

14.28 (b) cont.

For X_2: $t_{STAT} = 1.8835 < 2.0003$. Do not reject H_0. There is insufficient evidence that X_2 contributes to a model already containing X_1. Neither variable contributes to a model that includes the other variable. You should consider using only a simple linear regression model.

14.30 (a)

	Coefficients	Standard Error	t Stat	P-value	Lower 95%	Upper 95%
Intercept	532.2883	48.6661	10.9376	0.0000	432.4338	632.1428
Property Size (acres	407.1346	64.8028	6.2827	0.0000	274.1702	540.0990
Age	-2.8257	0.6813	-4.1475	0.0003	-4.2236	-1.4278

$274.1702 \le \beta_1 \le 540.0990$

(b) For X_1: $t_{STAT} = \dfrac{b_1}{s_{b_1}} = 6.2827$ and p-value $= 0.0000$. Since p-value < 0.05, reject H_0.

There is evidence that the variable X_1 contributes to a model already containing X_2.

For X_2: $t_{STAT} = \dfrac{b_2}{s_{b_2}} = -4.1475$ and p-value $= 0.0003$. Since p-value < 0.05, reject H_0.

There is evidence that the variable X_2 contributes to a model already containing X_1. Both variables X_1 and X_2 should be included in the model.

14.32 (a) For X_1: $SSR(X_1|X_2) = SSR(X_1 \text{ and } X_2) - SSR(X_2) = 30 - 15 = 15$

$$F_{STAT} = \frac{SSR(X_1|X_2)}{MSE} = \frac{15}{120/10} = 1.25 < F_{U(1,10)} = 4.965 \text{ with 1 and 10 degrees of freedom}$$

and $\alpha = 0.05$. Do not reject H_0. There is not sufficient evidence that the variable X_1 contributes to a model already containing X_2.

For X_2: $SSR(X_2|X_1) = SSR(X_1 \text{ and } X_2) - SSR(X_1) = 30 - 20 = 10$

$$F_{STAT} = \frac{SSR(X_2|X_1)}{MSE} = \frac{10}{120/10} = 0.833 < F_{U(1,10)} = 4.965 \text{ with 1 and 10 degrees of}$$

freedom and $\alpha = 0.05$. Do not reject H_0. There is not sufficient evidence that the variable X_2 contributes to a model already containing X_1.

Neither independent variable X_1 nor X_2 makes a significant contribution to the model in the presence of the other variable. Also the overall regression equation involving both independent variables is not significant:

$$F_{STAT} = \frac{MSR}{MSE} = \frac{30/2}{120/10} = 1.25 < F_{U(2,10)} = 4.103$$

Neither variable should be included in the model and other variables should be investigated.

(b) $$r^2_{Y1.2} = \frac{SSR(X_1|X_2)}{SST - SSR(X_1 \text{ and } X_2) + SSR(X_1|X_2)} = \frac{15}{150 - 30 + 15} = 0.1111.$$

Holding constant the effect of variable X_2, 11.11% of the variation in Y can be explained by the variation in variable X_1.

$$r^2_{Y2.1} = \frac{SSR(X_2|X_1)}{SST - SSR(X_1 \text{ and } X_2) + SSR(X_2|X_1)} = \frac{10}{150 - 30 + 10} = 0.0769.$$

Holding constant the effect of variable X_1, 7.69% of the variation in Y can be explained by the variation in variable X_2.

14.34   (a)   For X_1:
$$SSR(X_1 | X_2) = SSR(X_1 \text{ and } X_2) - SSR(X_2) = 3368.087 - 3246.062 = 122.025$$

$$F_{STAT} = \frac{SSR(X_1 | X_2)}{MSE} = \frac{122.025}{477.043 / 21} = 5.37 > F_{U(1,21)} = 4.325 \text{ with 1 and 21 degrees of}$$

freedom and $\alpha = 0.05$. Reject H_0. There is evidence that the variable X_1 contributes to a model already containing X_2.

For X_2:
$$SSR(X_2 | X_1) = SSR(X_1 \text{ and } X_2) - SSR(X_1) = 3368.087 - 2726.822 = 641.265$$

$$F_{STAT} = \frac{SSR(X_2 | X_1)}{MSE} = \frac{641.265}{477.043 / 21} = 28.23 > F_{U(1,21)} = 4.325 \text{ with 1 and 21 degrees of}$$

freedom and $\alpha = 0.05$. Reject H_0. There is evidence that the variable X_2 contributes to a model already containing X_1.

Since each independent variable, X_1 and X_2, makes a significant contribution to the model in the presence of the other variable, the most appropriate regression model for this data set should include both variables.

(b) $$r_{Y1.2}^2 = \frac{SSR(X_1 | X_2)}{SST - SSR(X_1 \text{ and } X_2) + SSR(X_1 | X_2)}$$

$$= \frac{122.025}{3845.13 - 3368.087 + 122.025} = 0.2037. \text{ Holding constant the effect of the number of}$$

orders, 20.37% of the variation in Y can be explained by the variation in sales.

$$r_{Y2.1}^2 = \frac{SSR(X_2 | X_1)}{SST - SSR(X_1 \text{ and } X_2) + SSR(X_2 | X_1)}$$

$$= \frac{641.265}{3845.13 - 3368.087 + 641.265} = 0.5734. \text{ Holding constant the effect of sales, 57.34%}$$

of the variation in Y can be explained by the variation in the number of orders.

14.36   (a)   For X_1: $F_{STAT} = 0.554 < 4.00$; Don't reject H_0. There is insufficient evidence that X_1 contributes to a model containing X_2. For X_2: $F_{STAT} = 3.5476 < 4.00$. Do not reject H_0. There is insufficient evidence that X_2 contributes to a model already containing X_1. Because only X_1 makes a significant contribution to the model in the presence of the other variable, only X_1 should be included in the model.

(b) $r_{Y1.2}^2 = 0.0091$. Holding constant the effect of full-time voluntary turnover, 0.91% of the variation in full-time jobs added be explained by the variation in total worldwide revenue. $r_{Y2.1}^2 = 0.0558$. Holding constant the effect of total worldwide revenue, 5.58% of the variation in full-time jobs created can be explained by the variation in full-time voluntary turnover.

14.38   (a)   Holding constant the effect of X_2, the estimated mean value of the dependent variable will increase by 4 units for each increase of one unit of X_1.

(b)   Holding constant the effects of X_1, the presence of the condition represented by $X_2 = 1$ is estimated to increase the mean value of the dependent variable by 2 units.

(c) $t = 3.27 > t_{17} = 2.1098$. Reject H_0. The presence of X_2 makes a significant contribution to the model.

14.40 (a) $\hat{Y} = 243.7371 + 9.2189X_1 + 12.6967X_2$, where X_1 = number of rooms and X_2 = neighborhood (east = 0).

(b) Holding constant the effect of neighborhood, for each additional room, the selling price is estimated to increase by a mean of 9.2189 thousands of dollars, or $9218.9. For a given number of rooms, a west neighborhood is estimated to increase mean selling price over an east neighborhood by 12.6967 thousands of dollars, or $12,696.7.

(c) $\hat{Y} = 243.7371 + 9.2189(9) + 12.6967(0) = 326.70758$ or $326,707.58

$309,560.04 \le Y_{X=X_i} \le $343,855.11 \quad $321,471.44 \le \mu_{Y|X=X_i} \le $331,943.71$

(d)

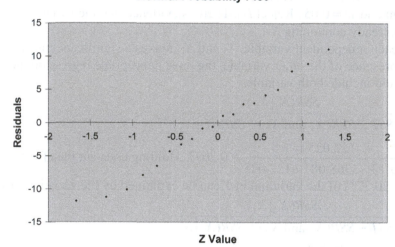

Normal Probability Plot

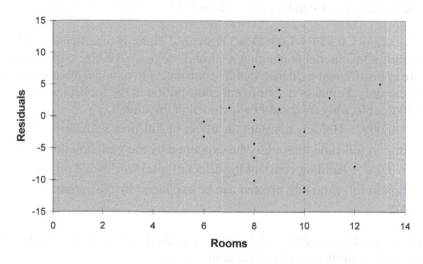

Rooms Residual Plot

Based on a residual analysis, the model appears adequate.

(e) F_{STAT} = 55.39, p-value is virtually 0. Since p-value < 0.05, reject H_0. There is evidence of a significant relationship between selling price and the two independent variables (rooms and neighborhood).

(f) For X_1: t_{STAT} = 8.9537, p-value is virtually 0. Reject H_0. Number of rooms makes a significant contribution and should be included in the model.

14.40   (f)   For X_2: $t_{STAT} = 3.5913$, p-value = $0.0023 < 0.05$. Reject H_0. Neighborhood makes a
cont.   significant contribution and should be included in the model.
                  Based on these results, the regression model with the two independent variables should
                  be used.

       (g) $7.0466 \le \beta_1 \le 11.3913$,

       (h) $5.2378 \le \beta_2 \le 20.1557$

       (i) $r_{adj}^2 = 0.851$

       (j) $r_{Y1.2}^2 = 0.825$. Holding constant the effect of neighborhood, 82.5% of the variation in
              selling price can be explained by variation in number of rooms. $r_{Y2.1}^2 = 0.431$. Holding
              constant the effect of number of rooms, 43.1% of the variation in selling price can be
              explained by variation in neighborhood.

       (k)   The slope of selling price with number of rooms is the same regardless of whether the
              house is located in an east or west neighborhood.

       (l) $\hat{Y} = 253.95 + 8.032X_1 - 5.90X_2 + 2.089X_1X_2$.

              For $X_1 X_2$: the p-value is 0.330. Do not reject H_0. There is no evidence that the interaction
              term makes a contribution to the model.

       (m)   The two-variable model in (f) should be used.

       (n)   The real estate association can conclude that the number of rooms and the neighborhood
              both significantly affect the selling price, but the number of rooms has a greater effect.

14.42   (a) $\hat{Y} = 8.0100 + 0.0052X_1 - 2.1052X_2$, where X_1 = depth (in feet) and X_2 = type of drilling
              (wet = 0, dry = 1).

       (b)   Holding constant the effect of type of drilling, for each foot increase in depth of the hole,
              the additional drilling time is estimated to increase by a mean of 0.0052 minute . For a
              given depth, a dry drilling is estimated to reduce mean additional drilling time over wet
              drilling by 2.1052 minutes.

       (c)   Dry drilling: $\hat{Y} = 8.0101 + 0.0052(100) - 2.1052 = 6.4276$ minutes.

              $6.2096 \le \mu_{Y|X=X_i} \le 6.6457$, $4.9230 \le Y_{X=X_i} \le 7.9322$

       (d)

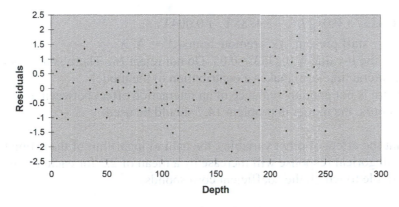

Depth Residual Plot

Based on a residual analysis, the model appears adequate.

       (e) $F_{STAT} = 111.109$ with 2 and 97 degrees of freedom, $F_{2,97} = 3.09$ using Excel. p-value is
              virtually 0. Reject H_0 at 5% level of significance. There is evidence of a relationship
              between additional drilling time and the two dependent variables.

14.42   (f)   For X_1: $t_{STAT} = 5.0289 > t_{97} = 1.9847$. Reject H_0. Depth of the hole makes a significant
cont.   contribution and should be included in the model.
                 For X_2: $t_{STAT} = -14.0331 < t_{97} = -1.9847$. Reject H_0. Type of drilling makes a significant
                 contribution and should be included in the model.
                 Based on these results, the regression model with the two independent variables should
                 be used.

        (g) $0.0032 \le \beta_1 \le 0.0073$

        (h) $-2.4029 \le \beta_2 \le -1.8075$

        (i) $r^2_{adj} = 0.6899$

        (j) $r^2_{Y1.2} = 0.2068$. Holding constant the effect of type of drilling, 20.68% of the variation in
                 additional drilling time can be explained by variation in depth of the hole. $r^2_{Y2.1} = 0.6700$.
                 Holding constant the effect of the depth of the hole, 67% of the variation in additional
                 drilling time can be explained by variation in type of drilling.

        (k)   The slope of additional drilling time with depth of the hole is the same regardless of
                 whether it is a dry drilling hole or a wet drilling hole.

        (l) $\hat{Y} = 7.9120 + 0.0060X_1 - 1.9091X_2 - 0.0015X_1X_2$.
                 For X_1X_2: the p-value is $0.4624 > 0.05$. Do not reject H_0. There is not evidence that the
                 interaction term makes a contribution to the model.

        (m)   The two-variable model in (a) should be used.

        (n)   Both variables affect the drilling time. Dry drilling holes should be used to reduce the
                 drilling time.

14.44   (a) $\hat{Y} = 1.1079 - 0.0070X_1 + 0.0448X_2 - 0.0003X_1X_2$, where X_1 = efficiency ratio,
                 X_2 = total risk-based capital, p-value $= 0.4593 > 0.05$. Do not reject H_0. There is not
                 enough evidence that the interaction term makes a contribution to the model.

        (b)   Because there is insufficient evidence of any interaction effect between efficiency ratio
                 and total risk-based capital, the model in Problem 14.4 should be used.

14.46   (a)   The p-value of the interaction term $= 0.1650 < 0.05$, so the term is not significant and
                 should be not included in the model.

        (b)   Use the model developed Problem 14.6.

14.48   (a) $\hat{Y} = 250.4237 + 0.0127X_1 - 1.4785X_2 + 0.004X_3$.
                 where X_1 = staff present, X_2 = remote hours, $X_3 = X_1 X_2$
                 For X_1X_2: the p-value is $0.2353 > 0.05$. Do not reject H_0. There is not enough evidence
                 that the interaction term makes a contribution to the model.

        (b)   Since there is not enough evidence of an interaction effect between total staff present and
                 remote hours, the model in problem 14.7 should be used.

14.50   Holding constant the effect of other variables, the natural logarithm of the estimated odds ratio for
        the dependent categorical response will increase by a mean of 2.2 for each unit increase in the
        independent variable to which the coefficient corresponds.

14.52   Estimated Probability of Success $= \dfrac{\text{Estimated Odds Ratio}}{(1 + \text{Estimated Odds Ratio})} = \dfrac{0.75}{(1 + 0.75)} = 0.4286$

14.54 (a)   ln(estimated odds ratio) $= -6.94 + 0.13947X_1 + 2.774X_2$
$$= -6.94 + 0.13947(36) + 2.774(0) = -1.91908$$
Estimated odds ratio $= e^{-1.91908} = 0.1467$
Estimated Probability of the Event of Interest $=$
$$\frac{\text{Estimated Odds Ratio}}{(1 + \text{Estimated Odds Ratio})} = \frac{0.1467}{(1 + 0.1467)} = 0.1280$$

(b)   From the text discussion of the example, 70.16% of the individuals who charge $36,000 per annum and possess additional cards can be expected to purchase the premium card. Only 12.80% of the individuals who charge $36,000 per annum and do not possess additional cards can be expected to purchase the premium card. For a given amount of money charged per annum, the likelihood of purchasing a premium card is substantially higher among individuals who already possess additional cards than for those who do not possess additional cards.

(c)   ln(estimated odds ratio) $= -6.94 + 0.13947X_1 + 2.774X_2$
$$= -6.94 + 0.13947(18) + 2.774(0) = -4.42954$$
Estimated odds ratio $= e^{-4.42954} = 0.0119$

(c)   Estimated Probability of the Event of Interest $=$
$$\frac{\text{Estimated Odds Ratio}}{(1 + \text{Estimated Odds Ratio})} = \frac{0.0119}{(1 + 0.0119)} = 0.01178$$

(d)   Among individuals who do not purchase additional cards, the likelihood of purchasing a premium card diminishes dramatically with a substantial decrease in the amount charged per annum.

14.56 (a)   PHStat output:

Binary Logistic Regression

Predictor	Coefficients	SE Coef	Z	p-Value
Intercept	-47.4821	12.0173	-3.9512	0.0001
fixed acidity	1.310179398	0.4139	3.1656	0.0015
chlorides	90.57937563	22.643	4.0003	0.0001
pH	9.779258829	2.9743	3.288	0.0010
Deviance	54.45564087			

(b)   Holding constant the effects of chlorides and pH, for each increase of one unit of fixed acidity, ln(odds) increases by an estimate of 1.3102. Holding constant the effects of fixed acidity and pH, for each increase of one unit in chlorides, ln(odds) increases by an estimate of 90.5794. Holding constant the effects of fixed acidity and chlorides, for each increase of one unit in pH, ln(odds) increases by an estimate of 9.7793.

(c)   ln(estimated odds ratio) $= -47.4821 + 1.3102X_1 + 90.5794X_2 + 9.7793X_3 = -0.4603$
Estimated odds ratio $= e^{-0.4603} = 0.6311$
Estimated Probability of the Event of Interest $=$
$$\frac{\text{Estimated Odds Ratio}}{(1 + \text{Estimated Odds Ratio})} = \frac{0.6311}{(1 + 0.6311)} = 0.3869$$

(d)   The deviance statistic is 54.4556, which has a p-value of 0.9998. Do not reject H_0. The model is a good fitting model.

(e)   For fixed acidity: $Z_{STAT} = 3.1656$ with a p-value $= 0.0015$. Reject H_0. There is sufficient evidence that fixed acidity makes a significant contribution to the model.

14.56 (e) For chlorides: $Z_{STAT} = 4.0003$ with a p-value $= 0.0001$. Reject H_0. There is sufficient
cont. evidence that the amount of chlorides makes a significant contribution to the model.
For pH: $Z_{STAT} = 3.2880$ with a p-value $= 0.0010$. Reject H_0. There is sufficient evidence
that pH makes a significant contribution to the model.

(f) Based on the p-values corresponding to the Z-values for the variable coefficients in the
logistic regression equation and corresponding to the deviance statistics, the model that
includes fixed acidity, chlorides and pH should be used to predict whether the wine is
red.

14.58 (a) PHStat output:

Predictor	Coefficients	SE Coef	Z	p-Value
Intercept	-0.6048	0.4194	-1.4421	0.1493
claims/year	0.093769442	0.5029	0.1865	0.8521
new business (1=yes, 0=no):1	1.810770296	0.8134	2.2261	0.0260
Deviance	119.4353239		p-value	0.0457

(b) Holding constant the effects of whether the policy is new, for each increase of the number
of claims submitted per year by the policy holder, ln(odds) increases by an estimate of
0.0938. Holding constant the number of claims submitted per year by the policy holder,
ln(odds) is estimated to be 1.8108 higher when the policy is new as compared to when
the policy is not new.

(c) ln(estimated odds ratio) $= -0.6048 + 0.0938(1) + 1.8108(1) = 1.2998$

Estimated odds ratio $= e^{1.2998} = 3.6684$

$$\text{Estimated Probability of the Event of Interest} = \frac{\text{Estimated Odds Ratio}}{(1 + \text{Estimated Odds Ratio})} = 0.7858$$

(d) The deviance statistic is 119.4353 with a χ^2 distribution of 95 d.f. and p-value $= 0.0457$
< 0.05. Reject H_0. The model is not a good fitting model.

(e) For claims/year: $Z_{STAT} = 0.1865$, p-value $= 0.8521 > 0.05$. Do not eject H_0. There is not
sufficient evidence that the number of claims submitted per year by the policy holder
makes a significant contribution to the logistic model.
For new business: $Z_{STAT} = 2.2261$, p-value $= 0.0260 < 0.05$. Reject H_0. There is sufficient
evidence that whether the policy is new makes a significant contribution to the logistic
model.

(f) PHStat output:

Predictor	Coefficients	SE Coef	Z	p-Value
Intercept	-1.0125	0.3888	-2.6042	0.0092
claims/year	0.992742206	0.3367	2.9481	0.0032
Deviance	125.0102452		p-value	0.0250

(g) PHStat output:

Predictor	Coefficients	SE Coef	Z	p-Value
Intercept	-0.5423	0.2515	-2.1563	0.0311
new business	1.928618927	0.5211	3.7008	0.0002
Deviance	119.4701921		p-value	0.0526

14.58   (h)   The deviance statistic for (f) is 125.0102 with a χ^2 distribution of 96 d.f. and
cont. p-value $= 0.0250 < 0.05$. Reject H_0. The model is not a good fitting model.
                   The deviance statistic for (g) is 119.4702 with a χ^2 distribution of 96 d.f. and
                   p-value $= 0.0526 > 0.05$. Do not reject H_0. The model is a good fitting model.
                   The model in (g) should be used to predict a fraudulent claim.

14.60   (a)   ln(estimated odds) $= 1.252 - 0.0323$ Age $+ 2.2165$ subscribes to the wellness newsletters.
         (b)   Holding constant the effect of subscribes to the wellness newsletters, for each increase of
                one year in age, ln(estimated odds) decreases by an estimate of 0.0323. Holding constant
                the effect of age, for a customer who subscribes to the wellness newsletters, ln(estimated
                odds) increases by an estimate of 2.2165.
         (c)   0.912
         (d)   Deviance $= 102.8762$, p-value $= 0.3264$. Do not reject H_0 so model is adequate.
         (e)   For Age: $Z = -1.8053 > -1.96$, Do not reject H_0. For subscribes to the wellness
                newsletters: $Z = 4.3286 > 1.96$, Reject H_0.
         (f)   Only subscribes to wellness newsletters is useful in predicting whether a customer will
                purchase organic food.

14.62   In the case of the simple linear regression model, the slope b_1 represents the change in the
         estimated mean of Y per unit change in X and does not take into account any other variables. In
         the multiple linear regression model, the slope b_1 represents the change in the estimated mean of
         Y per unit change in X_1, taking into account the effect of all the other independent variables.

14.64   The coefficient of partial determination measures the proportion of variation in Y explained by a
         particular X variable holding constant the effect of the other independent variables in the model.
         The coefficient of multiple determination measures the proportion of variation in Y explained by
         all the X variables included in the model.

14.66   You test whether the interaction of the dummy variable and each of the independent variables in
         the model make a significant contribution to the regression model.

14.68   It is assumed that the slope of the dependent variable Y with an independent variable X is the
         same for each of the two levels of the dummy variable.

14.70   In least squares regression the dependent variable is numerical. The use of categorical variables in
         least squares regression would violate the normality assumption and would not be appropriate
         with this method. Logistic regression allows one to predict a categorical dependent variable
         utilizing the odds ratio. The least squares regression uses a numerical dependent variable while
         logistic regression uses a categorical dependent variable.

14.72   (a) $\hat{Y} = -3.9152 + 0.0319 X_1 + 4.2228 X_2$, where X_1 = number cubic feet moved and
                X_2 = number of pieces of large furniture.
         (b)   Holding constant the number of pieces of large furniture, for each additional cubic foot
                moved, the mean labor hours are estimated to increase by 0.0319. Holding constant the
                amount of cubic feet moved, for each additional piece of large furniture, the mean labor
                hours are estimated to increase by 4.2228.
         (c) $\hat{Y} = 20.4926$

14.72   (d)   Based on a residual analysis, the errors appear to be normally distributed.
cont.   The equal-variance assumption might be violated because the variances appear to be larger around the center region of both independent variables. There might also be violation of the linearity assumption. A model with quadratic terms for both independent variables might be fitted.

(e) $F_{STAT} = 228.80$, p-value is virtually $0 < 0.05$, reject H_0. There is evidence of a significant relationship between labor hours and the two independent variables (the amount of cubic feet moved and the number of pieces of large furniture).

(f)   The p-value is virtually 0. The probability of obtaining a test statistic of 228.80 or greater is virtually 0 if there is no significant relationship between labor hours and the two independent variables (the amount of cubic feet moved and the number of pieces of large furniture).

(g) $r^2 = 0.9327$. 93.27% of the variation in labor hours can be explained by variation in the number of cubic feet moved and the number of pieces of large furniture.

(h) $r^2_{adj} = 0.9287$

(i)   For X_1: $t_{STAT} = 6.9339$, the p-value is virtually 0. Reject H_0. The number of cubic feet moved makes a significant contribution and should be included in the model. For X_2: $t_{STAT} = 4.6192$, the p-value is virtually 0. Reject H_0. The number of pieces of large furniture makes a significant contribution and should be included in the model. Based on these results, the regression model with the two independent variables should be used.

(j)   For X_1: $t_{STAT} = 6.9339$, the p-value is virtually 0. The probability of obtaining a sample that will yield a test statistic greater than 6.9339 is virtually 0 if the number of cubic feet moved does not make a significant contribution, holding the effect of the number of pieces of large furniture constant. For X_2: $t_{STAT} = 4.6192$, the p-value is virtually 0. The probability of obtaining a sample that will yield a test statistic greater than 4.6192 is virtually 0 if the number of pieces of large furniture does not make a significant contribution, holding the effect of the amount of cubic feet moved constant.

(k) $0.0226 \leq \beta_1 \leq .0413$

(l) $r^2_{Y1.2} = 0.5930$. Holding constant the effect of the number of pieces of large furniture, 59.3% of the variation in labor hours can be explained by variation in the amount of cubic feet moved. $r^2_{Y2.1} = 0.3927$. Holding constant the effect of the number of cubic feet moved, 39.27% of the variation in labor hours can be explained by variation in the number of pieces of large furniture.

(m)   Both the number of cubic feet moved and the number of large pieces of furniture are useful in predicting the labor hours, but the cubic feet moved is more important.

14.74   (a) $\hat{Y} = 360.2158 + 0.0775X_1 - 0.4122X_2$, where X_1 = house size and X_2 = age.

(b)   Holding constant the age, for each additional square foot in the size of the house, the mean asking price is estimated to increase by 77.50 thousand dollars. Holding constant the living space of the house, for each additional year in age, the asking price is estimated to decrease by 0.4122 thousand dollars.

(c) $\hat{Y} = 492.5316$ thousand dollars.

(d)   Based on a residual analysis, the model appears to be adequate.

(e) $F_{STAT} = 19.4909$, the p-value $= 0.0000 < 0.05$, reject H_0. There is evidence of a significant relationship between asking price and the two independent variables (size of the house and age).

14.74   (f)   The *p*-value is 0.0000. The probability of obtaining a test statistic of 19.4909 or greater is
cont.   virtually 0 if there is no significant relationship between asking price and the two
                    independent variables (living space of the house and age).

         (g) $r^2 = 0.4019$. 40.19% of the variation in asking price can be explained by variation in the
                    size of the house and age.

         (h) $r^2_{adj} = 0.3813$.

         (i)   For X_1: $t_{STAT} = 4.6904$, the *p*-value is 0.0000. Reject H_0. The living space of the house
                    makes a significant contribution and should be included in the model.
                    For X_2: $t_{STAT} = -0.6304$, *p*-value $= 0.5309 > 0.05$. Do not reject H_0. Age does not make a
                    significant contribution and should not be included in the model. Based on these results,
                    the regression model with only the size of the house should be used.

         (j)   For X_1: $t_{STAT} = 4.6904$. The probability of obtaining a sample that will yield a test statistic
                    farther away than 4.6904 is 0.0000 if the living space does not make a significant
                    contribution, holding age constant. For X_2: $t_{STAT} = -0.6304$. The probability of obtaining a
                    sample that will yield a test statistic farther away than 0.6304 is 0.5309 if the age does
                    not make a significant contribution holding the effect of the living space constant.

         (k) $0.0444 \le \beta_1 \le 0.1106$ You are 95% confident that the asking price will increase by an
                    amount somewhere between $44.40 thousand and $110.60 thousand for each additional
                    thousand square foot increase in living space, holding constant the age of the house. In
                    Problem 13.76, you are 95% confident that the assessed value will increase by an amount
                    somewhere between $56.8 thousand and $110.30 thousand for each additional 1,000
                    square foot increase in living space, regardless of the age of the house.

         (l) $r^2_{Y1.2} = 0.2750$. Holding constant the effect of the age of the house, 27.50% of the
                    variation in asking price can be explained by variation in the living space of the house.
                    $r^2_{Y2.1} = 0.0068$. Holding constant the effect of the size of the house, 0.68% of the variation
                    in asking price can be explained by variation in the age of the house.

         (m)   Only the living space of the house should be used to predict asking price.

14.76   (a) $\hat{Y} = -90.2166 + 9.2169X_1 + 2.5069X_2$, where $X_1 =$ asking price and $X_2 =$ age.

         (b)   Holding age constant, for each additional $1,000 in asking price, the taxes are estimated
                    to increase by a mean of $9.2169 thousand. Holding asking price constant, for each
                    additional year, the taxes are estimated to increase by $2.5069

         (c) $\hat{Y} = \$3,721.90$

         (d)   Based on a residual analysis, the errors appear to be normally distributed. The equal-
                    variance assumption appears to be valid. However, there is one very large residual that is
                    from the house that is 107 years old. Removing this point, still leaves a residual for the
                    house that has an asking price of $550,000 and is 52 years old. However, because this
                    model is an almost perfect fit, you may want to use this model. In this model, age is no
                    longer significant.

         (e) $F_{STAT} = 1,677.8619$, *p*-value $= 0.0000 < 0.05$, reject H_0. There is evidence of a significant
                    relationship between taxes and the two independent variables (asking price and age).

         (f)   *p*-value $= 0.0000$. The probability of obtaining an F_{STAT} test statistic of 1,677.8619 or
                    greater is virtually 0 if there is no significant relationship between taxes and the two
                    independent variables (asking price and age).

         (g) $r^2 = 0.9830$, 98.30% of the variation in taxes can be explained by variation in asking price
                    and age.

         (h) $r^2_{adj} = 0.9824$

14.76   (i)   For X_1: t_{STAT} = 53.7184, p-value = 0.0000 < 0.05. Reject H_0. The asking price makes a
cont.   significant contribution and should be included in the model. For X_2: t_{STAT} = 2.7873,
                 p-value = 0.0072 < 0.05. Reject H_0. The age of a house makes a significant contribution
                 and should be included in the model. Based on these results, the regression model with
                 asking price and age should be used.

         (j)   For X_1: p-value = 0.0000. The probability of obtaining a sample that will yield a test
                 statistic greater than 53.7184 is 0.0000 if the asking price does not make a significant
                 contribution, holding age constant. For X_2: p-value = 0.0072. The probability of obtaining
                 a sample that will yield a test statistic greater than 2.7873 is 0.0072 if the age of a house
                 does not make a significant contribution, holding the effect of the asking price constant.

         (k) $8.8735 \leq \beta_1 \leq 9.5604$. You are 95% confident that the mean taxes will increase by an
                 amount somewhere between $8.87 and $9.56 for each additional $1,000 increase in the
                 asking price, holding constant the age. In Problem 13.77, you are 95% confident that the
                 mean taxes will increase by an amount somewhere between $5.968 and $11.03 for each
                 additional $1,000 increase in asking price, regardless of the age.

         (l) $r^2_{Y1.2} = 0.9803$. Holding constant the effect of age, 98.03% of the variation in taxes can be
                 explained by variation in the asking price. $r^2_{Y2.1} = 0.1181$. Holding constant the effect of
                 the asking price, 11.81% of the variation in taxes can be explained by variation in the
                 age.

         (m)   Based on your answers to (b) through (k), the age of a house has an effect on its taxes.
                 However, given the results when the 107-year-old house is not included, the assessor can
                 state that for houses that are not that old, that age does not have an effect on taxes.

14.78   (a) $\hat{Y} = 160.6120 - 18.7181X_1 - 2.8903X_2$, where X_1 = ERA and X_2 = league (American = 0
                 National = 1).

         (b)   Holding constant the effect of the league, for each additional earned run, the number of
                 wins is estimated to decrease by 18.7181. For a given ERA, a team in the National
                 League is estimated to have 2.8903 fewer wins than a team in the American League.

         (c)   76.3803 wins.

         (d)   Based on a residual analysis, there is no pattern in the errors. There is no apparent
                 violation of other assumptions.

         (e) F_{STAT} = 24.306 > 3.35, p-value = 0.0000 < 0.05, reject H_0. There is evidence of a
                 significant relationship between wins and the two independent variables (ERA and
                 league).

         (f)   For X_1: t_{STAT} = –6.9184 < –2.0518, the p-value = 0.0000. Reject H_0. ERA makes a
                 significant contribution and should be included in the model.
                 For X_2: t_{STAT} = –1.1966 > –2.0518, p-value = 0.2419 > 0.05. Do not reject H_0. The league
                 does not make a significant contribution and should not be included in the model. Based
                 on these results, the regression model with only the ERA as the independent variable
                 should be used.

         (g) $-24.2687 \leq \beta_1 \leq -13.1676$

         (h) $-7.8464 \leq \beta_2 \leq 2.0639$

         (i) $r^2_{adj} = 0.6165$ 61.65% of the variation in wins can be explained by the variation in ERA
                 and league after adjusting for number of independent variables and sample size.

         (j) $r^2_{Y1.2} = 0.6394$ Holding constant the effect of league, 63.94% of the variation in number of
                 wins can be explained by the variation in ERA. $r^2_{Y2.1} = 0.0504$ Holding constant the effect
                 of ERA, 5.04% of the variation in number of wins can be explained by the variation in
                 league.

14.78   (k)   The slope of the number of wins with ERA is the same, regardless of whether the team
cont.   belongs to the American League or the National League.

       (l)   For X_1X_2: $t_{STAT} = 1.175 < 2.0555$ the p-value is $0.2506 > 0.05$. Do not reject H_0. There is
no evidence that the interaction term makes a contribution to the model.

       (m)   The model with one independent variable (ERA) should be used.

14.80   The multiple regression model is
Predicted base salary = 48,091.7853 + 8,249.2156 (gender) + 1,061.4521 (age).
Holding constant the age of the person, the mean base salary is predicted to be $8,249.22 higher
for males than for females. Holding constant the gender of the person, for each addition year of
age, the mean base salary is predicted to be $1,061.45 higher. The regression model with the two
independent variables has $F = 118.0925$ and a p-value $= 0.0000$. So, you can conclude that at
least one of the independent variable makes a significant contribution to the model to predict base
pay. Each independent variable makes a significant contribution to the regression model given
that the other variable is included. ($t_{STAT} = 3.9937$, p-value $= 0.0001$ for gender and
$t_{STAT} = 14.8592$, p-value $= 0.0000$ for age). Both independent variables should be included in the
model. 37.01% of the variation in base salary can be explained by gender and age. There is no
pattern in the residuals and no other violations of the assumptions, so the model appears to be
appropriate. Including an interaction term of gender and age does not significantly improve the
model (t_{STAT} -0.2371, p-value $= 0.8127 > 0.05$). You can conclude that females are paid less than
males holding constant the age of the person. Perhaps other variables such as department,
seniority, and score on a performance evaluation can be included in the model to see if the model
is improved.

14.82 $b_0 = 18.2892$ (die temperature), $b_1 = 0.5976$, (die diameter), $b_2 = -13.5108$. The r^2 of the multiple
regression model is 0.3257 so 32.57% of the variation in unit density can be explained by the
variation of die temperature and die diameter. The F test statistic for the combined significance of
die temperature and die diameter is 5.0718 with a p-value of 0.0160. Hence, at a 5% level of
significance, there is enough evidence to conclude that die temperature and die diameter affect
unit density. The p-value of the t test for the significance of die temperature is 0.2117, which is
greater than 5%. Hence, there is insufficient evidence to conclude that die temperature affects unit
density holding constant the effect of die diameter. The p-value of the t test for the significance of
die diameter is 0.0083, which is less than 5%. There is enough evidence to conclude that die
diameter affects unit density at the 5% level of significance holding constant the effect of die
temperature. After removing die temperature from the model, $b_0 = 107.9267$ (die diameter),
$b_1 = -13.5108$. The r^2 of the multiple regression is 0.2724. So 27.24% of the variation in unit
density can be explained by the variation of die diameter. The p-value of the t test for the
significance of die diameter is 0.0087, which is less than 5%. There is enough evidence to
conclude that die diameter affects unit density at the 5% level of significance. There is some lack
of equality in the residuals and some departure from normality.

CHAPTER 15

15.2 (a)

GPA	Predicted HOCS	GPA	Predicted HOCS
2	2.8600	3	3.9900
2.1	3.0342	3.1	4.0282
2.2	3.1948	3.2	4.0528
2.3	3.3418	3.3	4.0638
2.4	3.4752	3.4	4.0612
2.5	3.5950	3.5	4.0450
2.6	3.7012	3.6	4.0152
2.7	3.7938	3.7	3.9718
2.8	3.8728	3.8	3.9148
2.9	3.9382	3.9	3.8442
		4	3.7600

(b)

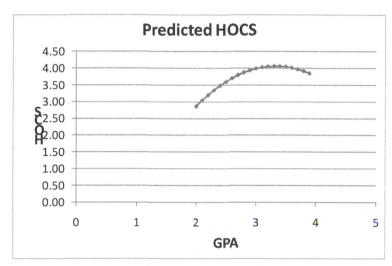

(c) The curvilinear relationship suggests that HOCS increases at a decreasing rate. It reaches its maximum value of 4.0638 at GPA = 3.3 and declines after that as GPA continues to increase.

(d) An r^2 of 0.07 and an adjusted r^2 of 0.06 tell you that GPA has very low explanatory power in explaining the variation in HOCS. You can tell that the individual HOCS scores will have scattered quite widely around the curvilinear relationship plotted in (b) and discussed in (c).

15.4 (a) $\hat{Y} = -5.48730 - 21.5105X_1 + 3.9633X_2$ where X_1 = alcohol % and X_2 = carbohydrates. F_{STAT} = 2,258.7579 p-value = 0.0000 < 0.05, so reject H_0. At the 5% level of significance, the linear terms are significant together.

(b) $\hat{Y} = 10.0421 + 15.0776X_1 + 4.5851X_2 + 0.4874X_1^2 - 0.0209X_2^2$, where X_1 = alcohol % and X_2 = carbohydrates.

(c) F_{STAT} = 1,154.1043 p-value = 0.0000 < 0.05, so reject H_0. At the 5% level of significance, the model with quadratic terms are significant. t_{STAT} = 2.2414, and the p-value = 0.0264. Reject H_0. There is enough evidence that the quadratic term for alcohol % is significant at the 5% level of significance. t_{STAT} = -1.2313, p-value = 0.2201. Do not reject H_0.

15.4
cont.
(c)   There is insufficient evidence that the quadratic term for carbohydrates is significant at the 5% level of significance. Hence, because the quadratic term for alcohol is significant, the model in (b) that includes this term is better.

(d)   The number of calories in a beer depends quadratically on the alcohol percentage but linearly on the number of carbohydrates. The alcohol percentage and number of carbohydrates explain about 96.79% of the variation in the number of calories in a beer.

15.6   (a)

(b)   price = 18,029.9837 – 1,812.9389 age + 63.2116 age2.

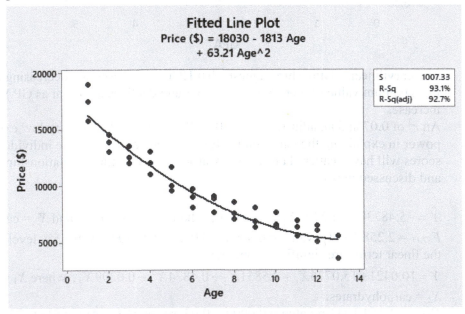

(c)   18,029.9837 – 1,812.9389(5) + 63.2116(5)2 = $10,545.58.
(d)   There are no patterns in any of the residual plots.
(e) F_{STAT} = 243.5061 > 3.27. Reject H_0. There is a significant quadratic relationship between age and price.

15.6 (f) p-value = 0.0000. The probability of F_{STAT} = 243.5061 or higher is 0.0000, given the null
cont.   hypothesis is true.
      (g) t_{STAT} = 4.8631 > 2.0281. Reject H_0.
      (h)   The probability of $t_{STAT} < -4.8631$ or > 4.8631 is 0.0000, given the null hypothesis is true.
      (i) $r^2 = 0.9312$. 93.12% of the variation in price can be explained by the quadratic
          relationship between age and price.
      (j)   adjusted $r^2 = 0.9273$.
      (k)   There is a strong quadratic relationship between age and price.

15.8 (a) $\log \hat{Y} = \log(3.07) + 0.9\log(8.5) + 1.41\log(5.2) = 2.33318$

$$\hat{Y} = 10^{2.33318} = 215.37$$

      (b)   Holding constant the effects of X_2, for each additional unit of the logarithm of X_1, the
          logarithm of Y is estimated to increase by a mean of 0.9. Holding constant the effects of
          X_1, for each additional unit of the logarithm of X_2, the logarithm of Y is estimated to
          increase by a mean of 1.41.

15.10 (a) $\sqrt{\hat{Y}} = 6.2417 + 0.7768X_1 + 0.1683X_2$, where X_1 = alcohol % and X_2 = carbohydrates.
      (b)   The normal probability plot of the linear model showed departure from a normal
          distribution, so a square-root transformation of calories was done. F_{STAT} = 1,720.6801.
          Because the p-value is 0.0000, reject H_0 at the 5% level of significance. There is evidence
          of a significant linear relationship between the square root of calories and the percentage
          of alcohol and the number of carbohydrates.
      (d) $r^2 = 0.9569$. So 95.69% of the variation in the square root of calories can be explained by
          the variation in the percentage of alcohol and the number of carbohydrates.
      (e)   Adjusted $r^2 = 0.9563$.
      (f)   The model in Problem 15.4 is slightly better because it has a higher r^2.

15.12 (a)   Predicted ln(Price) = 9.7771 – 0.10622 Age.
      (b) $10,573.4350.
      (c)   The model is adequate.
      (d) $t_{STAT} = -19.4814 < -2.0262$; reject H_0.
      (e)   91.12%. 91.12% of the variation in the natural log of price can be explained by the age of
          the auto.
      (f)   90.88%.
      (g)   Choose the model from Problem 15.6. That model has a higher adjusted r^2 of 92.73%.

15.14 $VIF = \dfrac{1}{1-0.2} = 1.25$

15.16 $R_1^2 = 0.0634$, $VIF_1 = \dfrac{1}{1-0.0634} = 1.0677$, $R_2^2 = 0.0634$,, $VIF_2 = \dfrac{1}{1-0.0634} = 1.0677$.
         There is no evidence of collinearity because both VIFs are < 5.

15.18 $VIF = 1.0066 < 5$. There is no evidence of collinearity.

15.20 $VIF = \dfrac{1}{1-0.0104} = 1.0105$. There is no reason to suspect the existence of collinearity.

15.22   (a) $C_p = \dfrac{(1-R_k^2)(n-T)}{1-R_T^2} - [n-2(k+1)] = \dfrac{(1-0.274)(40-7)}{1-0.653} - [40-2(2+1)] = 35.04$

(b) C_p overwhelmingly exceeds $k+1 = 3$, the number of parameters (including the Y-intercept), so this model does not meet the criterion for further consideration as the best model.

15.24   Let Y = asking price, X_1 = lot size, X_2 = living space, and X_3 = number of bedrooms. X_4 = number of bathrooms, X_5 = age, and X_6 = fireplace (0 = No, 1 = Yes). Based on a full regression model involving all of the variables, all the VIF values (1.3953, 2.1175, 2.0878, 2.3537, 1.7807, and 1.0939, respectively) are less than 5. There is no reason to suspect the existence of collinearity. Based on a best-subsets regression and examination of the resulting C_p values, the best model appear to be a model with variables X_2 and X_6, which has $C_p = 0.8701$. Models that add other variables do not change the results very much. Based on a stepwise regression analysis with all the original variables, only variables X_2 and X_6 make a significant contribution to the model at the 0.05 level. Thus, the best model is the model using the living area of the house (X_2) and fireplace X_6 should be included in the model. This was the model developed in Section 14.6.

15.26   In order to evaluate whether independent variables are intercorrelated, you can compute the Variance Inflationary Factor (VIF).

15.28   One way to choose among models that meet these criteria is to determine whether the models contain a subset of variables that are common, and then test whether the contribution of the additional variables is significant.

15.30   An analysis of the linear regression model using PHStat with all of the three possible independent variables does not reveal any variable with $VIF > 5.0$.
A best subsets regression produces only one model that has C_p values less than or equal to $k+1$.

Partial PHStat output

Model	Cp	k+1	R Square	Adj. R Square	Std. Error	Consider This Model?
X2X3	2.4959	3	0.4816	0.3873	9.1710	Yes
X1X2X3	4.0000	4	0.5061	0.3579	9.3886	Yes

where X_1 = Temperature, X_2 = Pressure, X_3 = Cost (1 if low and 0 otherwise)
The model with the highest adjusted r^2 and contain all the three variables yields the following:

	Coefficients	Standard Error	t Stat	P-value
Intercept	-44.5795	40.3144	-1.1058	0.2947
Temperature	0.0849	0.1205	0.7042	0.4974
Pressure	0.8004	0.6027	1.3280	0.2137
Cost	-12.4788	5.1683	-2.4145	0.0364

The p-values for temperature and pressure are both > 0.05. Dropping temperature which has the largest p-value yields the following:

	Coefficients	Standard Error	t Stat	P-value
Intercept	-18.4899	15.5245	-1.1910	0.2587
Pressure	0.7879	0.5885	1.3389	0.2076
Cost	-13.1029	4.9737	-2.6345	0.0232

15.30
cont.
The p-value for pressure is still > 0.05. Dropping pressure yields the following:

Regression Statistics	
Multiple R	0.6301
R Square	0.3971
Adjusted R Square	0.3468
Standard Error	9.4690
Observations	14

Note:
This worksheet does not recalculate.
If regression data changes, rerun procedure
to create an updated version of this worksheet.

ANOVA

	df	SS	MS	F	Significance F
Regression	1	708.5829	708.5829	7.9028	0.0157
Residual	12	1075.9514	89.6626		
Total	13	1784.5343			

	Coefficients	Standard Error	t Stat	P-value	Lower 95%	Upper 95%
Intercept	1.7714	3.5790	0.4950	0.6296	-6.0265	9.5693
Cost	-14.2286	5.0614	-2.8112	0.0157	-25.2564	-3.2007

The best linear model is determined to be:

$\hat{Y} = 1.7714 - 14.2286X_3$.

The overall model has $F = 7.9028$ (1 and 12 degrees of freedom) with a p-value $= 0.0157 < 0.05$.
$r^2 = 0.3971$, $r^2_{adj} = 0.3468$.

A residual analysis does not reveal any strong patterns. The errors appear to be normally distributed.

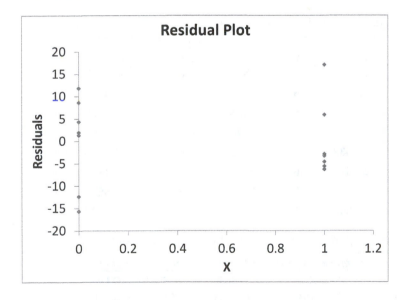

15.30
cont.

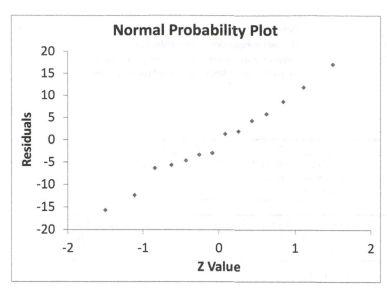

15.32–15.34

Let Y = fair market value, X_1 = land area, X_2 = interior size, X_3 = age, X_4 = number of rooms, X_5 = number of bathrooms, X_6 = garage size.

(a)   **Glencove:**

Based on a full regression model involving all of the variables:

All *VIF*s are less than 5. So there is no reason to suspect collinearity between any pair of variables.

The best-subset approach yielded the following models to be considered:

Model	Cp	k+1	R Square	Adj. R Square	Std. Error	Consider This Model?
X1X2X3	2.1558	4	0.8424	0.8242	60.5007	Yes
X1X2X3X4	4.1117	5	0.8427	0.8175	61.6425	Yes
X1X2X3X5	3.2400	5	0.8484	0.8241	60.5180	Yes
X1X2X3X6	3.8887	5	0.8442	0.8192	61.3567	Yes
X1X2X3X4X5	5.1832	6	0.8488	0.8173	61.6903	Yes
X1X2X3X4X6	5.7825	6	0.8449	0.8125	62.4827	Yes
X1X2X3X5X6	5.1038	6	0.8493	0.8179	61.5846	Yes
X1X2X3X4X5X6	7.0000	7	0.8500	0.8108	62.7677	Yes

The stepwise regression approach reveals the following best model:

	Coefficients	Standard Error	t Stat	P-value
Intercept	260.6791	66.3288	3.9301	0.0006
Property Size (acres)	362.8318	48.6233	7.4621	0.0000
House Size (square feet)	0.1109	0.0228	4.8682	0.0000
Age	-1.7543	0.5483	-3.1996	0.0036

The *p*-value of the individual slope coefficients indicate that all the remaining independent variables are significant individually.

Combining the results of both approaches, the most appropriate multiple regression model for predicting fair market value in Glencove is

$$\hat{Y} = 260.6791 + 362.8318X_1 + 0.1109X_2 - 1.7543X_3$$

15.32–15.34
cont.   (a)   **Roslyn:**
Based on a full regression model involving all of the variables:
All *VIF*s are less than 5. So there is no reason to suspect collinearity between any pair of variables.

The best-subset approach yielded the following models to be considered:

Model	Cp	k+1	R Square	Adj. R Square	Std. Error	Consider This Model?
X1X2	0.5528	3	0.9113	0.9047	97.3426	Yes
X1X2X3	1.5185	4	0.9151	0.9053	97.0851	Yes
X1X2X4	2.4581	4	0.9117	0.9015	99.0055	Yes
X1X2X5	2.4425	4	0.9117	0.9015	98.9740	Yes
X1X2X6	1.3027	4	0.9158	0.9061	96.6386	Yes
X1X2X3X4	3.4720	5	0.9152	0.9017	98.9099	Yes
X1X2X3X5	3.5164	5	0.9151	0.9015	99.0034	Yes
X1X2X3X6	3.0817	5	0.9166	0.9033	98.0841	Yes
X1X2X4X5	4.3936	5	0.9119	0.8978	100.8330	Yes
X1X2X4X6	3.2095	5	0.9162	0.9028	98.3553	Yes
X1X2X5X6	3.3019	5	0.9158	0.9024	98.5508	Yes
X1X2X3X4X5	5.4718	6	0.9152	0.8976	100.9491	Yes
X1X2X3X4X6	5.0164	6	0.9169	0.8995	99.9650	Yes
X1X2X3X5X6	5.0793	6	0.9166	0.8993	100.1014	Yes
X1X2X4X5X6	5.2051	6	0.9162	0.8987	100.3739	Yes
X1X2X3X4X5X6	7.0000	7	0.9169	0.8953	102.0786	Yes

The stepwise regression approach reveals the following best model:

	Coefficients	Standard Error	t Stat	P-value
Intercept	-168.9968	56.0905	-3.0129	0.0056
House Size (square feet)	0.2559	0.0226	11.3482	0.0000
Property Size (acres)	1094.5706	193.7733	5.6487	0.0000

The *p*-value of X_3, X_4, X_5, X_6 are all greater than 0.05 in the regression model with X_1, X_2, X_3, X_4, X_5, and X_6. Combing the results of both approaches, the most appropriate multiple regression model for predicting fair market value in Roslyn is
$$\hat{Y} = -168.9968 + 1094.5706X_1 + 0.2559X_2$$

Freeport:
Based on a full regression model involving all of the variables:
All *VIF*s are less than 5. So there is no reason to suspect collinearity between any pair of variables.

15.32–15.34
cont.   (a)   The best-subset approach yielded the following models to be considered:

Model	Cp	k+1	R Square	Adj. R Square	Std. Error	Consider This Model?
X1X2	2.5499	3	0.8638	0.8538	27.2314	Yes
X1X2X3	3.8212	4	0.8676	0.8523	27.3666	Yes
X1X2X5	2.5555	4	0.8741	0.8595	26.6875	Yes
X1X2X6	2.0625	4	0.8766	0.8624	26.4182	Yes
X1X2X3X5	4.4527	5	0.8746	0.8545	27.1590	Yes
X1X2X3X6	3.9052	5	0.8774	0.8578	26.8532	Yes
X1X2X4X5	4.2508	5	0.8756	0.8557	27.0466	Yes
X1X2X4X6	3.9937	5	0.8770	0.8573	26.9029	Yes
X1X2X5X6	3.5681	5	0.8791	0.8598	26.6632	Yes
X1X2X3X4X6	5.6740	6	0.8786	0.8533	27.2741	Yes
X1X2X3X5X6	5.3826	6	0.8801	0.8551	27.1057	Yes
X1X2X4X5X6	5.4360	6	0.8798	0.8548	27.1366	Yes
X1X2X3X4X5X6	7.0000	7	0.8820	0.8513	27.4612	Yes

The p-value of the t-test for individual coefficient shows that X_1 is not significant at the 5% level of significance.

	Coefficients	Standard Error	t Stat	P-value
Intercept	145.1217	15.1661	9.5688	0.0000
Property size (acres	149.9337	86.1028	1.7413	0.0930
House Size (square	0.0913	0.0120	7.5956	0.0000

The stepwise regression approach reveals that the following best model:

	Coefficients	Standard Error	t Stat	P-value
Intercept	142.7398	15.6428	9.1249	0.0000
House Size (square feet)	0.1066	0.0085	12.5252	0.0000

Combining the results of both approaches, the most appropriate multiple regression model for predicting fair market value in Freeport is
$$\hat{Y} = 142.7398 + 0.1066 X_2$$

(b)   The adjusted r^2 for the best model in 15.32(a), 15.33(a), and 15.34(a) are, respectively, 0.8242, 0.9047 and 0.8431. The model in 15.33(a) has the highest explanatory power after adjusting for the number of independent variables and sample size.

15.36   Let $Y =$ fair market value, $X_1 =$ land area, $X_2 =$ interior size, $X_3 =$ age, $X_4 =$ number of rooms, $X_5 =$ number of bathrooms, $X_6 =$ garage size, $X_7 = 1$ if GlenCove and 0 otherwise, $X_8 = 1$ if Roslyn and 0 otherwise.
        (a)   Based on a full regression model involving all of the variables:
        The VIF of X_2, X_3 and X_7 are greater than 5.
        Dropping X_2 with the largest VIF, X_3 still has a VIF greater than 5.
        After dropping X_2 and X_3, all remaining VIFs are less than 5. So there is no reason to suspect collinearity between any pair of variables.

15.36   (a)
cont.

Now let Y = fair market value, X_1 = land area, X_2 = number of rooms, X_3 = number of bathrooms, X_4 = garage size, X_5 = 1 if GlenCove and 0 otherwise, X_6 = 1 if Roslyn and 0 otherwise.

The best-subset approach yielded the following models to be considered:

Model	Cp	k+1	R Square	Adj. R Square	Std. Error	Consider This Model?
X1X3X4X6	4.3211	5	0.6958	0.6815	145.4771	Yes
X1X2X3X4X6	5.3213	6	0.6994	0.6815	145.4702	Yes
X1X2X3X4X5X6	7.0000	7	0.7005	0.6789	146.0615	Yes

The p-value of X_2, X_4 and X_5 are all greater than 0.05 in the regression model with X_1, X_2, X_3, X_4, X_5, and X_6.

	Coefficients	Standard Error	t Stat	P-value
Intercept	-19.7877	76.9121	-0.2573	0.7976
Property Size (acres)	551.1974	103.5799	5.3215	0.0000
Rooms	11.3359	10.7931	1.0503	0.2966
Baths	101.7208	26.0074	3.9112	0.0002
Garage	48.1114	29.1443	1.6508	0.1026
Glen Cove	23.1968	40.9252	0.5668	0.5724
Roslyn	226.0072	42.2948	5.3436	0.0000

The stepwise regression approach reveals the following best model:

	Coefficients	Standard Error	t Stat	P-value
Intercept	30.1063	44.6655	0.6740	0.5021
Baths	130.7788	21.7928	6.0010	0.0000
Property Size (acres)	611.6910	98.5954	6.2040	0.0000
Roslyn	214.2567	35.5299	6.0303	0.0000

Combining the results of both approaches, the most appropriate multiple regression model for predicting fair market value is
$$\hat{Y} = 30.1063 + 611.6910 X_1 + 130.7788 X_3 + 214.2567 X_6$$

(b)

The estimated mean fair market value in Roslyn is \$214.2567 thousands above Freeport for two otherwise identical properties. There is no significant difference in mean fair market value between two otherwise identical properties in Glen Cove and Freeport.

15.38   In the multiple regression model with catalyst, pH, pressure, temperature and voltage as independent variables, none of the variables have a *VIF* value of 5 or larger.

The best-subset approach yielded only the following model to be considered:

Model	Cp	k+1	R Square	Adj. R Square	Std. Error
X1X2X3X4X5	6	6	0.875922	0.861822068	1.293575

where X_1 = catalyst, X_2 = pH, X_3 = pressure, X_4 = temp, and X_5 = voltage.

15.38   Looking at the p-values of the t statistics for each slope coefficient of the model that includes X_1
cont.   through X_5 reveals that pH level is not significant at 5% level of significance.

	Coefficients	Standard Error	t Stat	P-value
Intercept	4.454255233	8.222983547	0.541683588	0.590769119
Catalyst	0.162669323	0.036277562	4.484020293	5.18724E-05
pH	0.086375011	0.080013101	1.079510851	0.286242198
Pressure	-0.043059299	0.013464369	-3.198018263	0.002564899
Temp	-0.402556214	0.069704281	-5.775200729	7.21416E-07
Voltage	0.422370024	0.028413318	14.86521277	9.13658E-19

The multiple regression model with pH level deleted shows that all coefficients are significant
individually at 5% level of significance.

	Coefficients	Standard Error	t Stat	P-value
Intercept	3.683340948	8.206951065	0.44880747	0.655724457
Catalyst	0.154754083	0.035594069	4.347749199	7.77444E-05
Pressure	-0.041971526	0.013451255	-3.120268445	0.003150939
Temp	-0.4035674	0.069825915	-5.779622062	6.62469E-07
Voltage	0.428756573	0.027841579	15.3998654	1.47975E-19

The best linear model is determined to be:
$$\hat{Y} = 3.6833 + 0.1548X_1 - 0.04197X_3 - 0.4036X_4 + 0.4288X_5.$$
The overall model has $F = 77.0793$ (4 and 45 degrees of freedom) with a p-value that is virtually
0. $r^2 = 0.8726$, $r^2_{adj} = 0.8613$.

None of the observations have a Cook's $D_i > F_\alpha = 0.8809$ with d.f. = 5 and 56.

Hence, using the Studentized deleted residuals, hat matrix diagonal elements and Cook's distance
statistic together, there is insufficient evidence for removal of any observation from the model.

The normal probability plot does not suggest possible violation of the normality assumption. A
residual analysis reveals a potential non-linear relationship in temperature.

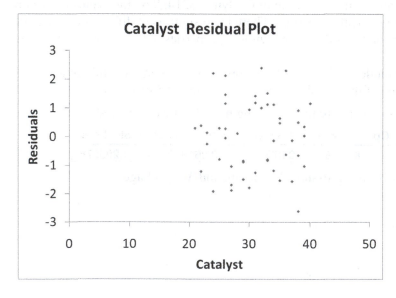

15.38
cont.

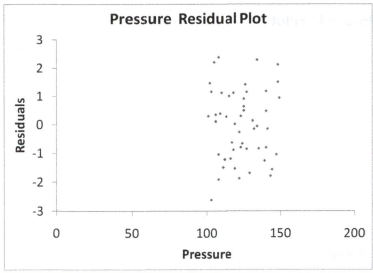

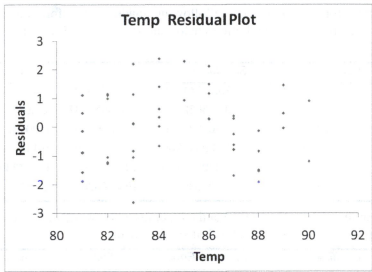

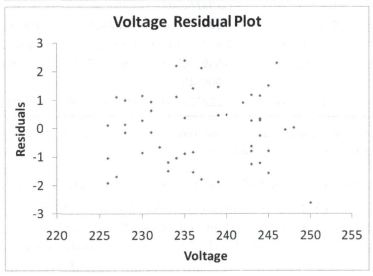

15.38
cont.

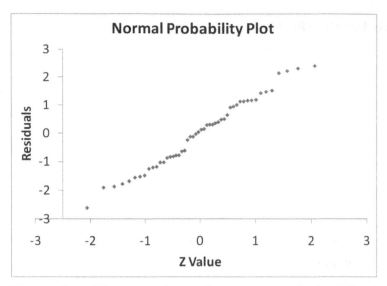

The *p*-value of the squared term for temperature in the following quadratic transformation of temperature does not support the need for a quadratic transformation at the 5% level of significance.

	Coefficients	Standard Error	t Stat	P-value
Intercept	-322.0541757	209.7341228	-1.535535426	0.131812685
Catalyst	0.16474942	0.035632189	4.623612047	3.30582E-05
Pressure	-0.044452151	0.01334035	-3.332157868	0.001753581
Temp	7.27648367	4.9417966	1.472436901	0.148020497
Temp Squared	-0.04508917	0.029010216	-1.554251433	0.127288634
Voltage	0.424662847	0.027539942	15.41988889	2.34994E-19

The *p*-value of the interaction term between pressure and temperature below indicates that there is not enough evidence of an interaction at the 5% level of significance.

	Coefficients	Standard Error	t Stat	P-value
Intercept	103.5523674	55.92763384	1.851542078	0.070809822
Catalyst	0.144935857	0.035157935	4.122422311	0.000163315
Pressure	-0.859424944	0.453254189	-1.896121349	0.064522645
Temp	-1.586885548	0.659370559	-2.406667277	0.020363651
Pressure x Temp	0.009640768	0.005343284	1.804277709	0.078035623
Voltage	0.431941042	0.027226309	15.86484039	8.10114E-20

The best model is still the one that includes catalyst, pressure, temperature and voltage which manages to explain 87.26% of the variation in thickness.

15.40   Best subset regression produced several models that had $C_p \le k + 1$. They were $X_2 X_3 = 3.9$,

$X_2 X_3 X_4 = 3.3$, and $X_1 X_2 X_3 X_4 = 4.7$. Stepwise regression produced a model that included only X_2 (median home value) and X_4 (average commuting time). Because X_2 (median home value), X_3 (violent crime rate), and average commuting time (X_4) had a low C_p, this model was chosen for

15.40
cont.
further analysis. The residual plot for all the independent variables showed only random patterns and no violations in the assumptions. The model is

$$\text{Median Average Annual Salary} = \frac{16{,}830 + 38.256 \text{ Median home value (\$000)} - 9.534 \text{ Violent crime}}{100{,}000 \text{ residents} + 1{,}053 \text{ average commuting time in minutes}}$$

The r^2 of this model is 0.847, meaning that 84.7% of the variation in Average Annual Salary can be explained by variation in median home value, variation in violent crime, and variation in average commuting time.

CHAPTER 16

Note: Chapter 15 introduced variance inflationary factor (VIF) as a measure of collinearity. It was recommended that variables with VIF values > 5 should not be used. A number of solutions in Chapter 16 include variables with VIF factors above 5. The VIF values were included because the output produced by Minitab 18 automatically produces VIF values along with the model coefficients. While adjustments can be made to time series data to reduce collinearity, such adjustments were not covered in the text. The reader should be aware that the intent of this chapter is to cover how to perform a number of time series methods. Addressing collinearity with some of the time series models, such as the quadratic and autoregressive models, is beyond the scope of this text. The purpose of this note is to explain why the VIF values in some of these solutions were not utilized to determine the appropriateness of a model.

16.2   (a)   Since you need data from four prior years to obtain the centered 9-year moving average for any given year and since the first recorded value is for 1984, the first centered moving average value you can calculate is for 1988.

         (b)   You would lose four years for the period 1984-1987 since you do not have enough past values to compute a centered moving average. You will also lose the final four years of recorded time series since you do not have enough later values to compute a centered moving average. Therefore, you will lose a total of eight years in computing a series of 9-year moving averages.

16.4   (a)

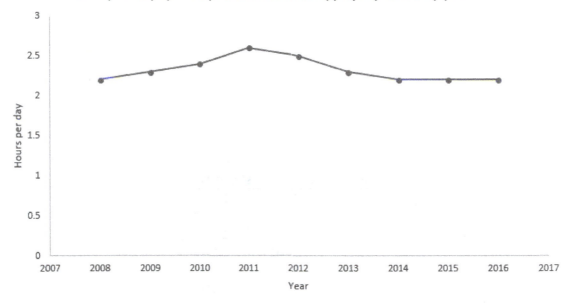

16.4   (b)
cont.

	A	B	C
1	Year	Hours	MA 3-Yr
2	2008	2.2	#N/A
3	2009	2.3	2.3000
4	2010	2.4	2.4333
5	2011	2.6	2.5000
6	2012	2.5	2.4667
7	2013	2.3	2.3333
8	2014	2.2	2.2333
9	2015	2.2	2.2000
10	2016	2.2	#N/A

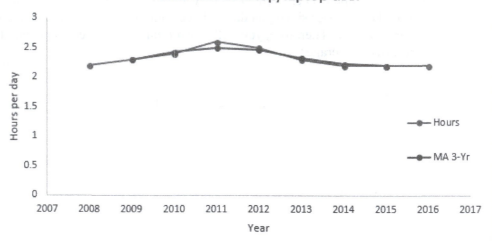

Three-Year Moving Average for Hours per day spent by American desktop/laptop user

(c), (e)

	A	B	C	D
1	Year	Hours	ES(W=0.50)	ES(W=0.25)
2	2008	2.2	2.2000	2.2000
3	2009	2.3	2.2500	2.2250
4	2010	2.4	2.3250	2.2688
5	2011	2.6	2.4625	2.3516
6	2012	2.5	2.4813	2.3887
7	2013	2.3	2.3906	2.3665
8	2014	2.2	2.2953	2.3249
9	2015	2.2	2.2477	2.2937
10	2016	2.2	2.2238	2.2702
11				

16.4
cont.

(c), (e)

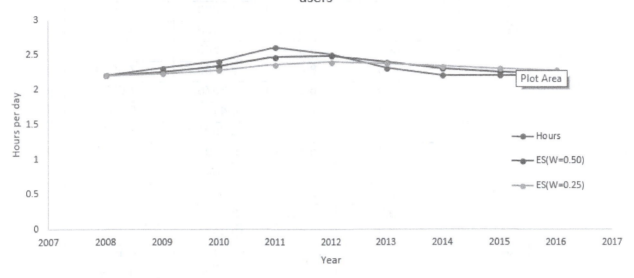

Exponentially Smoothed Hours Spent per day by American desktop/laptop users

(d) $\hat{Y}_{2017} = E_{2016} = 2.2238$

(e) $\hat{Y}_{2017} = E_{2016} = 2.2702$

(f)   The exponential smoothing with $W = 0.5$ assigns more weight to the more recent values and is better for forecasting, while the exponential smoothing with $W = 0.25$ which assigns more weight to more distant values is better suited for eliminating unwanted cyclical and irregular variations.

(g)   There is no perceptible trend in the number of hours spent per day by American desktop/laptop users from 2008-1016.

16.6   (a),(b),(c)

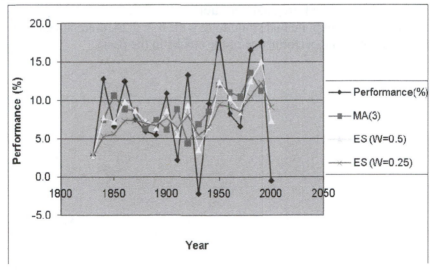

16.6   (b),(c),(e)
cont.

Decade	Performance(%)	MA(3)	ES (W=0.5)	ES (W=0.25)
1830s	2.8		2.8000	2.8000
1840s	12.8	7.4000	7.8000	5.3000
1850s	6.6	10.6333	7.2000	5.6250
1860s	12.5	8.8667	9.8500	7.3438
1870s	7.5	8.6667	8.6750	7.3828
1880s	6.0	6.3333	7.3375	7.0371
1890s	5.5	7.4667	6.4188	6.6528
1900s	10.9	6.2000	8.6594	7.7146
1910s	2.2	8.8000	5.4297	6.3360
1920s	13.3	4.4333	9.3648	8.0770
1930s	-2.2	6.9000	3.5824	5.5077
1940s	9.6	8.5333	6.5912	6.5308
1950s	18.2	12.0333	12.3956	9.4481
1960s	8.3	11.0333	10.3478	9.1611
1970s	6.6	10.5000	8.4739	8.5208
1980s	16.6	13.6000	12.5370	10.5406
1990s	17.6	11.2333	15.0685	12.3055
2000s	-0.5		7.2842	9.1041

(d) $\hat{Y}_{2010s} = E_{2000s} = 7.2842$

(e) (d) $\hat{Y}_{2010s} = E_{2000s} = 9.1041$

(f)   The exponentially smoothed forecast for 2010 with $W = 0.5$ is lower than that with $W = 0.25$. The exponential smoothing with $W = 0.5$ assigns more weight to the more recent values and is better for forecasting, while the exponential smoothing with $W = 0.25$ which assigns more weight to more distance values is better suited for eliminating unwanted cyclical and irregular variations.

(g)   According to the exponential smoothing with $W = 0.25$, there appears to be a general upward trend in the performance of the stocks in the past.

16.8   (a)

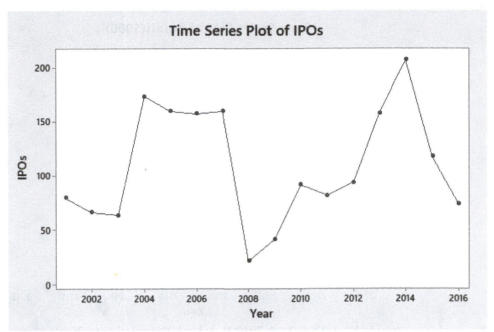

(b), (c), (e)

Year	IPOs	MA 3-Yr	ES(W = .50)	ES(W = .25)
2001	79	#N/A	79.0000	79.0000
2002	66	69.3333	72.5000	75.7500
2003	63	100.6667	67.7500	72.5625
2004	173	131.6667	120.3750	97.6719
2005	159	163.0000	139.6875	113.0039
2006	157	158.3333	148.3438	124.0029
2007	159	112.3333	153.6719	132.7522
2008	21	73.6667	87.3359	104.8141
2009	41	51.0000	64.1680	88.8606
2010	91	71.0000	77.5840	89.3955
2011	81	88.3333	79.2920	87.2966
2012	93	110.3333	86.1460	88.7224
2013	157	152.3333	121.5730	105.7918
2014	207	160.3333	164.2865	131.0939
2015	117	132.3333	140.6432	127.5704
2016	73	#N/A	106.8216	113.9278

(d) $W = 0.5$: $\hat{Y}_{2017} = E_{2016} = 106.8216$; $W = 0.25$: $\hat{Y}_{2017} = E_{2016} = 113.9278$.

(f)   The exponentially smoothed forecast for 2017 with $W = 0.5$ is lower than that with $W = 0.25$.

16.10   (a)   The Y intercept $b_0 = 4.0$ is the fitted trend value reflecting the real total revenues (in millions of dollars) during the origin, or base year, 1994.

(b)   The slope $b_1 = 1.5$ indicates that the real total revenues are increasing at an estimated rate of $1.5 million per year.

(c)   Year is 2000, $X = 2000 - 1996 = 4$, $\hat{Y}_5 = 4.0 + 1.5(4) = 10.0$ million dollars.

(d)   Year is 2017, $X = 2017 - 1996 = 21$, $\hat{Y}_{20} = 4.0 + 1.5(21) = 35.5$ million dollars.

(e)   Year is 2020, $X = 2020 - 1996 = 24$, $\hat{Y}_{23} = 4.0 + 1.5(24) = 40$ million dollars.

16.12   (a)

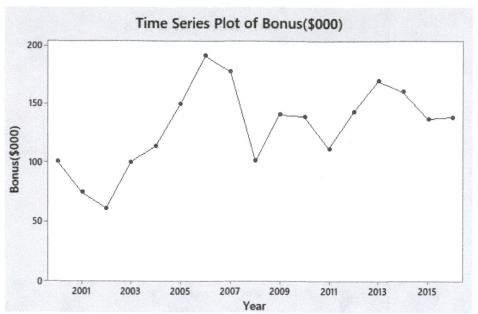

(b)   Linear trend: $\hat{Y} = 99.5412 + 3.7912X$, where X is relative to 2000.

(c)   Quadratic trend: $\hat{Y} = 75.922 + 13.2389X - 0.5905X^2$, where X is relative to 2000.

(d)   Exponential trend: $\log_{10}\hat{Y} = 1.9726 + 0.0154X$, where X is relative to 2000.

(e)   Linear trend: $\hat{Y}_{2017} = 99.5412 + 3.7912(17) = 163.9912$

$$\hat{Y}_{2018} = 99.5412 + 3.7912(18) = 167.7824$$

(e)   Quadratic trend: $\hat{Y}_{2017} = 75.9220 + 13.2389(17) - 0.5905(17)^2$

$$= 130.1338$$

$$\hat{Y}_{2018} = 75.9220 + 13.2389(18) - 0.5905(18)^2 = 122.9059$$

Exponential trend: $\hat{Y}_{2017} = 10^{1.9726+0.0154(17)} = 171.4728$

$$\hat{Y}_{2018} = 10^{1.9726+0.0154(18)} = 177.6593$$

(f)   The quadratic trend model fit the data better than the linear trend or exponential trend models and, hence, that forecast should be used.

16.14 (a)

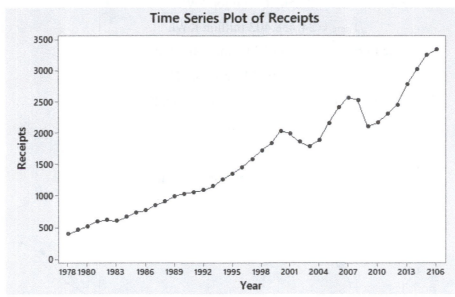

(b) $\hat{Y} = 246.7986 + 71.0028X$ where X = years relative to 1978.

(c) $X = 39$, $\hat{Y} = 3,015.907$ billion $X = 40$ $\hat{Y} = 3,086.91$ billion

(d)   There is an upward trend in federal receipts between 1978 and 2016. The trend appears to be linear.

16.16 (a)

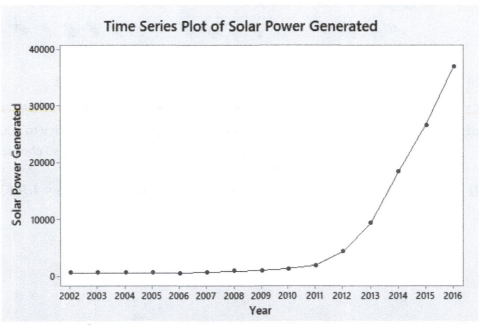

(b)   Linear trend: $\hat{Y} = -6,786.2833 + 1,952X$, where X is relative to 2002.

(c)   Quadratic trend: $\hat{Y} = 4,667.05 - 3,333.361 + 377.5824X^2$, where X is relative to 2002.

(d)   Exponential trend: $\log_{10} \hat{Y} = 2.3228 + 0.1401X$, where X is relative to 2002.

16.16   (e)   Linear trend: $\hat{Y}_{2015} = 22,505.61$ million KWh

cont. $\hat{Y}_{2018} = 24,458.402$ million KWh

Quadratic trend: $\hat{Y}_{2017} = 39,622.68$ million KWh

$\hat{Y}_{2018} = 47,994.17$ million KWh

Exponential trend: $\hat{Y}_{2017} = 26,533.8946$ million KWh

$\hat{Y}_{2018} = 36,632.706$ million KWh

16.18   (a)

(b)   Linear trend: $\hat{Y} = 1.9998 + 0.1389X$, where X is relative to 2000.

(c)   Quadratic trend: $\hat{Y} = 2.1902 + 0.0675X - 0.0042X^2$, where X is relative to 2000.

(d)   Exponential trend: $\log_{10}\hat{Y} = 0.3289 + 0.0191X$, where X is relative to 2000. The quadratic and exponential models appear to fit the data equally, so choose the quadratic model because it is simplest.

(f)   The forecast using the quadratic model is: Quadratic trend: $\hat{Y}_{2018} = 4.7663$ millions

16.20 (a)

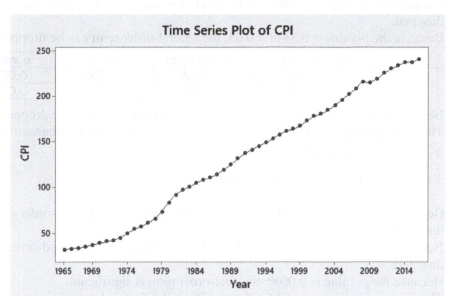

(b)   There has been an upward trend in the CPI in the United States over the 52-year period.

(c)   Linear trend: $\hat{Y} = 16.5346 + 4.4751X$.

(d)   Quadratic trend: $\hat{Y} = 18.6219 + 4.2246X + 0.0049X^2$.

(e)   Exponential trend: $\log_{10}\hat{Y} = 1.5764 + 0.0180X$.

(f)   Choose the linear model because it is simplest.

(g)   Linear trend: For 2017: $\hat{Y}_{2017} = 249.2405$

For 2018: $\hat{Y}_{2018} = 253.7156$

16.22 (a)   For Time Series I, the graph of Y versus X appears to be more linear than the graph of log Y versus X, so a linear model appears to be more appropriate. For Time Series II, the graph of log Y versus X appears to be more linear than the graph of Y versus X, so an exponential model appears to be more appropriate.

(b)   Times Series I: $\hat{Y} = 100.0731 + 14.9776X$, where X = years relative to 2005.

Times Series II: $\hat{Y} = 10^{1.9982 + 0.0609X}$, where X = years relative to 2005.

(c) $X = 12$ for year 2017 in all models. Forecasts for the year 2017:

Times Series I: $\hat{Y} = 100.0731 + 14.9776(12) = 279.8045$

Times Series II: $\hat{Y} = 10^{1.9982 + 0.0609(12)} = 535.6886$.

16.24 $t_{STAT} = \dfrac{a_3}{S_{a_3}} = \dfrac{0.24}{0.10} = 2.4$ is greater than the critical bound of 2.2281. Reject H_0. There is sufficient

evidence that the third-order regression parameter is significantly different from zero. A third-order autoregressive model is appropriate.

16.26 (a) $t_{STAT} = \dfrac{a_3}{S_{a_3}} = \dfrac{0.24}{0.15} = 1.6$ is less than the critical bound of 2.2281. Do not reject H_0. . There is

not sufficient evidence that the third-order regression parameter is significantly different than zero. A third-order autoregressive model is not appropriate.

(b)   Fit a second-order autoregressive model and test to see if it is appropriate.

16.28 (a)   Because the p-value $= 0.7509 > 0.05$ level of significance, the third-order term can be dropped.

(b)   Because the p-value $= 0.3448 > 0.05$, the second-order term can be dropped.

	Coefficients	Standard Error	t Stat	p-value
Intercept	56.5818	28.2785	2.0009	0.0652
YLag1	0.5808	0.2107	2.7564	0.0155

Because the p-value $= 0.0155 < 0.05$ the first-order term cannot be dropped.

(d)   The most appropriate model for forecasting is the first-order autoregressive model:

$$\hat{Y}_{2017} = 56.5818 + 0.5808 Y_{2016} = 136.8484.$$

$$\hat{Y}_{2018} = 56.5818 + 0.5808 \hat{Y}_{2017} = 136.0635.$$

16.30 (a)   Because the p-value $= 0.515 > 0.05$ level of significance, the third-order term can be dropped.

(b)   Because the p-value $= 0.594 > 0.05$ level of significance, the second-order term can be dropped.

(c)   Because the p-value is 0.0000, the first-order term is significant.

(d)   The most appropriate model for forecasting is the first-order autoregressive model:

$$\hat{Y}_{2018} = 0.0132 + 1.0473 Y_{2017} = \$4.9355 \text{ million}.$$

16.32 (a) $S_{YX} = \sqrt{\dfrac{\sum_{i=1}^{n} (Y_i - \hat{Y}_i)^2}{n - p - 1}} = \sqrt{\dfrac{45}{12 - 1 - 1}} = 2.121$. The standard error of the estimate is 2.121.

(b) $MAD = \dfrac{\sum_{i=1}^{n} \left| Y_i - \hat{Y}_i \right|}{n} = \dfrac{18}{12} = 1.5$. The mean absolute deviation is 1.5.

16.34 (a)   The residuals in the linear, quadratic, and exponential trend model show strings of consecutive positive and negative values.

(b), (c)

	Linear	Quadratic	Exponential	AR2
S_{yx}	7,449.3680	3,332.5112	6,481.891	1,484.3969
MAD	5,785.5073	2,612.3410	3,199.24	977.5796

(d)   The residuals in the three trend models show strings of consecutive positive and negative values. The autoregressive model performs well for the historical data and has a fairly random pattern of residuals. It has the smallest values in MAD and S_{yx}. The autoregressive model would be the best model for forecasting.

16.36   (a)   Linear:

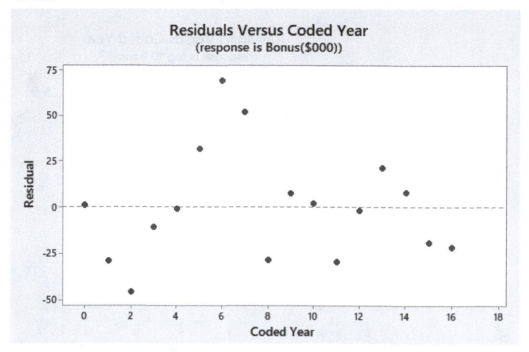

Quadratic:

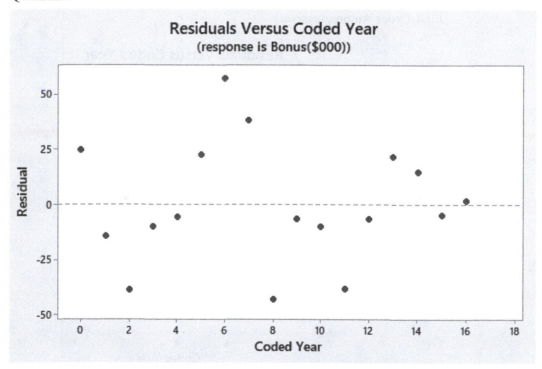

16.36   (a)   Exponential:
cont.

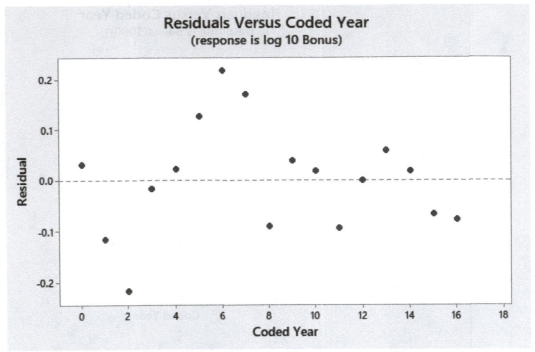

First-Order Autoregressive:

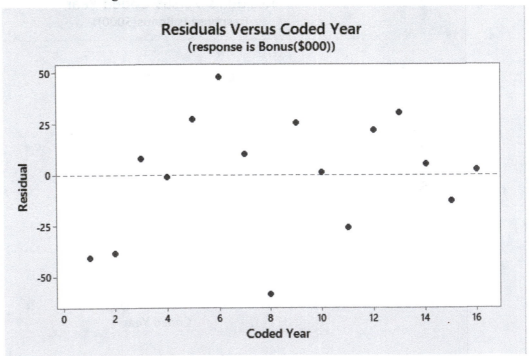

(b), (c)

	Linear	Quadratic	Exponential	AR1
S_{yx}	31.3035	29.2719	29.6198	30.1604
MAD	22.3806	21.2215	23.0246	22.3010

16.36   (d)   The residuals in the linear and exponential trend models show strings of consecutive
cont.   positive and negative values. The quadratic and autoregressive models have a fairly
                   random pattern of residuals. There is very little difference in *MAD* and S_{yx} between the
                   quadratic and autoregressive models. Either the quadratic or autoregressive model can be
                   chosen for forecasting.

16.38   (a)   Linear:

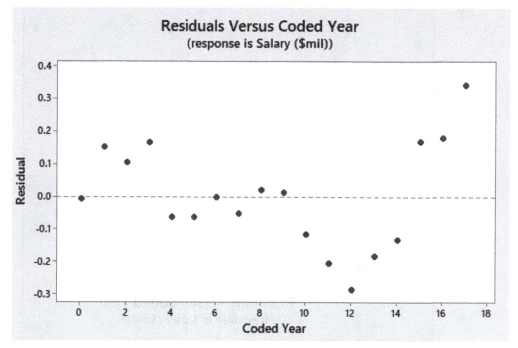

Quadratic:

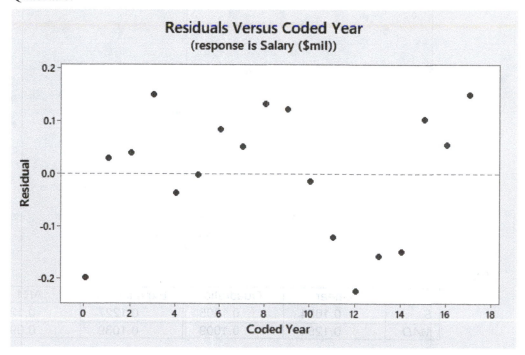

16.38
cont.
(a)   Exponential:

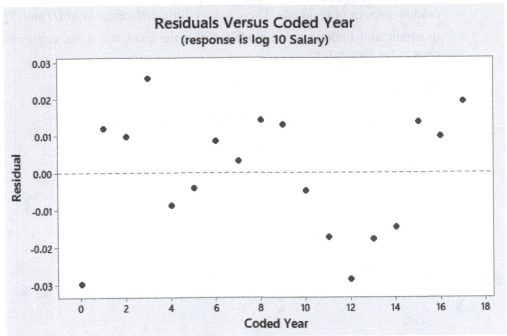

First-Order Autoregressive:

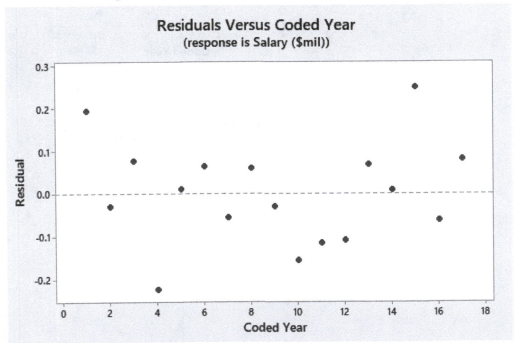

(b), (c)

	Linear	Quadratic	Exponential	AR1
S_{yx}	0.1654	0.1305	0.1227	0.1245
MAD	0.1254	0.1009	0.1039	0.0935

16.38 (d)
cont.
The residuals in the linear and exponential trend models show strings of consecutive positive and negative values. The quadratic and autoregressive models have a fairly random pattern of residuals. The *MAD* and S_{yx} values are similar in the quadratic, exponential, and autoregressive models. The quadratic or autoregressive model would be the best model for forecasting due to their fairly random pattern of residuals.

16.40 (a) $\log \hat{\beta}_0 = 2$, $\hat{\beta}_0 = 100$. This is the fitted value for January 2011 prior to adjustment with the January multiplier.

(b) $\log \hat{\beta}_1 = 0.01$, $\hat{\beta}_1 = 1.023300$. The estimated monthly compound growth rate is 2.33%.

(c) $\log \hat{\beta}_2 = 0.1$, $\hat{\beta}_2 = 1.2589$. The January values in the time series are estimated to have a mean 25.89% higher than the December values.

16.42 (a) $\log \hat{\beta}_0 = 3.0$, $\hat{\beta}_0 = 1,000$. This is the fitted value for the first quarter of 2013 prior to adjustment by the quarterly multiplier.

(b) $\log \hat{\beta}_1 = 0.1$, $\hat{\beta}_1 = 1.2589$. The estimated monthly compound growth rate is $(\hat{\beta}_1 - 1)100\% = 25.89\%$.

(c) $\log \hat{\beta}_3 = 0.2$, $\hat{\beta}_3 = 1.5849$.

16.44 (a) The retail industry is heavily subject to seasonal variation due to the holiday seasons and so are the revenues for Toys R Us.

(b) There is obvious seasonal effect in the time series.

(c) $\log_{10} \hat{Y} = 3.6522 + 0.0014X - 0.3600Q_1 - 0.3604Q_2 - 0.3390Q_3$.

(d) $\log_{10} \hat{\beta}_1 = 0.0014$. $\hat{\beta}_1 = 1.0032$. The estimated quarterly compound growth rate is $(\hat{\beta}_1 - 1)100\% = 0.32\%$.

(e) $\log_{10} \hat{\beta}_2 = -0.3600$. $\hat{\beta}_2 = 0.4365$. $(\hat{\beta}_2 - 1)100\% = -56.35\%$. The 1st quarter values in the time series are estimated to have a mean 56.35% below the 4th quarter values.

$\log_{10} \hat{\beta}_3 = -0.3604$. $\log_{10} \hat{\beta}_3 = 0.4361$. $(\hat{\beta}_3 - 1)100\% = -56.39\%$.

The 2nd quarter values in the time series are estimated to have a mean 56.39% below the 4th quarter values. $\log_{10} \hat{\beta}_4 = -0.3390$. $\log_{10} \hat{\beta}_4 = 0.4581$. $(\hat{\beta}_4 - 1)100\% = -54.19\%$.

The 3rd quarter values in the time series are estimated to have a mean 54.19% below the 4th quarter values.

(f) Forecasts for the last three quarters of 2017 and all of 2018 are 2,577.9471, 2,750.4706, 6,018.1637, 2,605.5535, 2,611.5299, 2,752.2508, and 6,026.7614 millions.

16.46   (a)

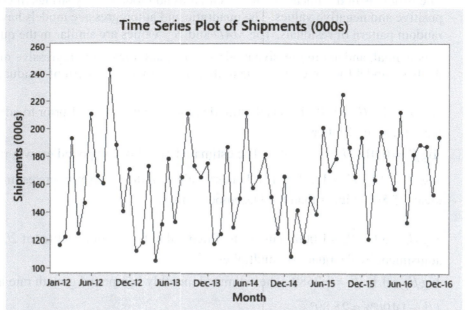

Time Series Plot of Shipments (000s)

(b) $\log 10(\text{Predicted } Y) = 2.2313 + 0.0007X - 0.1871M_1 - 0.1241M_2 - 0.0144M_3 - 0.1196M_4 - 0.0902M_5 + 0.0560M_6 - 0.0725M_7 - 0.0207M_8 + 0.0677M_9 - 0.0056M_{10} - 0.0802M_{11}.$

(c)   216.5938, 183.2386, 154.5297, 186.1607.

(e)   0.1613%

(f) $0.8463\left(\hat{\beta}_8 - 1\right)100\% = -15.37\%.$ The July values in the time series are estimated to have a mean 15.37% below the December values.

16.48   (a)

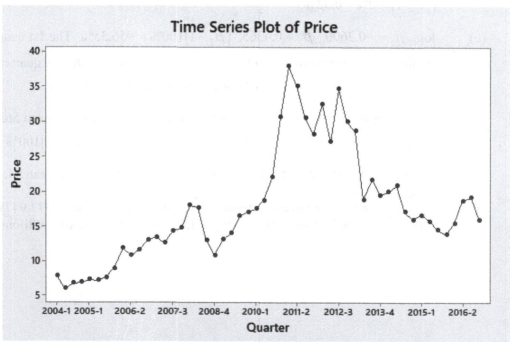

Time Series Plot of Price

(b) $\log 10(\text{Predicted } Y) = 0.9640 + 0.0087X + 0.045Q_1 + 0.0083Q_2 + 0.0130Q_3$

(c)   2.0234%, after adjusting for the seasonal component.

16.48   (d)   10.92% above the fourth-quarter values.
cont.   (e)   Last quarter, 2016: $Y = \$25.4407$.
         (f)   2017: 28.7858, 26.9885, 27.8299, 27.5524.

16.50   A time series is a set of numerical data obtained at regular periods over time.

16.52   Moving averages take into account the results of a limited number of periods of time. Exponential smoothing takes into account all the time periods but gives increased weight to more recent time periods.

16.54   The linear trend model in this chapter has the time period as the X variable.

16.56   The different methods for choosing an appropriate forecasting model are residual analysis, the sum of squared deviations, the mean absolute deviation and parsimony.

16.58   Forecasting for monthly or quarterly data uses an exponential trend model with dummy variables to represent either months or quarters.

16.60   (a)

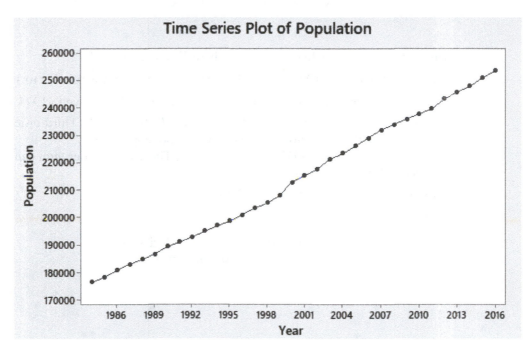

         (b)   Linear trend: $\hat{Y} = 173,789.3351 + 2,459.3332X,$ where X is relative to 1984.
         (c)   2017: $\hat{Y}_{2017} = 254,947.331$ thousands
                    2018: $\hat{Y}_{2018} = 257,406.665.$
         (d), (b) Linear trend: $\hat{Y} = 116,723.2674 + 1,435.6197X,$ where X is relative to 1984.
         (c)   2017: $\hat{Y}_{2017} = 164,098.716$ thousands.
                    2018: $\hat{Y}_{2018} = 165,534.336$ thousands.

16.62   (a)

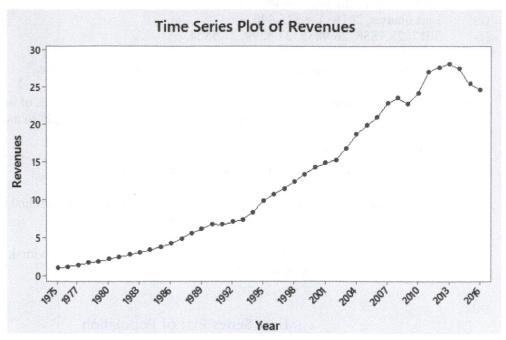

(b)   Linear trend: $\hat{Y} = -2.6364 + 0.7247X$, where X is relative to 1975.

(c)   Quadratic trend: $\hat{Y} = 0.2377 + 0.2935X + 0.0105X^2$, where X is relative to 1975.

(d)   Exponential trend: $\log_{10} \hat{Y} = 0.2115 + 0.0345X$, where X is relative to 1975.

(e)   Test of A_3: p-value = 0.14 > 0.05. Do not reject H_0 that $A_2 = 0$. Third-order term can be deleted. A third-order autoregressive model is not appropriate.
Test of A_2: p-value = 0.0042 < 0.05 Reject H_0. The second-order term cannot be deleted. The second-order model is appropriate.

AR(2): $\hat{Y}_i = 0.3681 + 1.5164Y_{i-1} - 0.5249Y_{i-2}$

(f)   Linear:

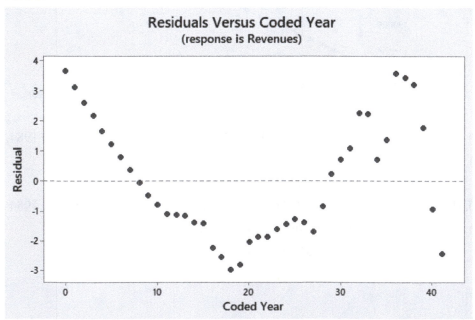

16.62   (f)   Quadratic:
cont.

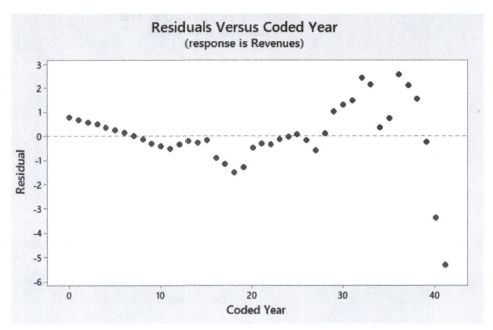

Exponential:

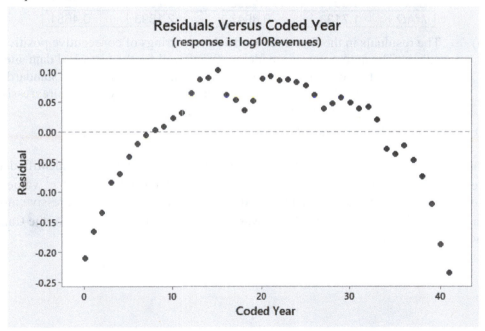

16.62 (f) Second-order Autoregressive:

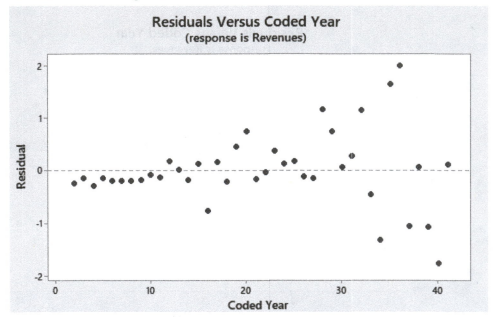

(g)

	Linear	Quadratic	Exponential	AR2
Syx	1.9955	1.4253	3.7962	0.7264
MAD	1.7133	0.8943	2.1893	0.4681

(h) The residuals in the first three models show strings of consecutive positive and negative values. The autoregressive model performs well for the historical data and has a fairly random pattern of residuals. It also has the smallest values in the standard error of the estimate and MAD. Based on the principle of parsimony, the autoregressive model would probably be the best model for forecasting.

(i) $\hat{Y}_{2015} = \$28.3149$ billions.

16.64 For each of the three currencies, a first-order autoregressive model was identified as the best model. In each case, the first-order autoregressive model had the highest r^2 value compared to the linear, quadratic, and exponential models. For the first-order autoregressive model of the Canadian dollar exchange rate, the r^2 was 0.6829. The time series plot for the Canadian dollar is shown in the below figure.

16.64
cont.

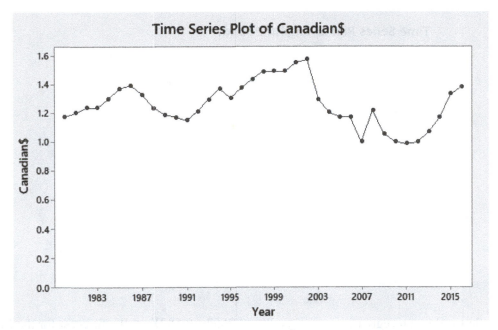

Using the first-order autoregressive equation, $\hat{Y}_i = 0.219 + 0.8301Y_{i-1}$, the forecast for the Canadian dollar is 1.36 and 1.35 for 2017 and 2018, respectively. For the Japanese yen, the first-order autoregressive model had the highest r^2 value (0.8795). The time series plot for the Japanese yen is shown in the below figure.

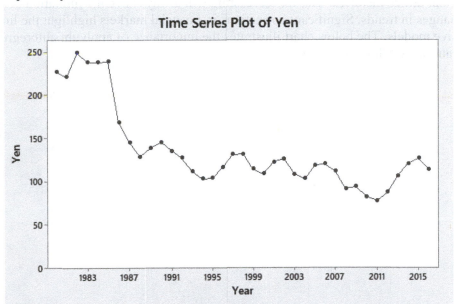

Using the first-order autoregressive equation, $\hat{Y}_i = 11.66 + 0.8911Y_{i-1}$, the forecast for the Japanese yen is 112.48 and 111.89 for 2017 and 2018, respectively. For the English pound, the first-order autoregressive model had the highest r^2 value (0.3632). The time series plot for the English pound is shown in the below figure.

16.64
cont.

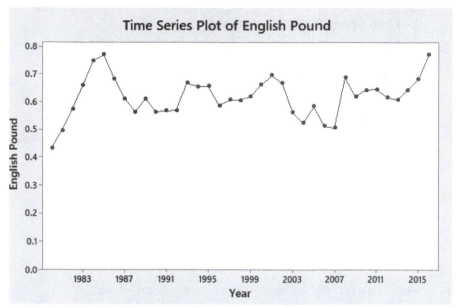

Using the first-order autoregressive equation, $\hat{Y}_i = 0.2652 + 0.582Y_{i-1}$, the forecast for the English pound is 0.71 and 0.68 for 2017 and 2018, respectively.

Residual analyses revealed no clear pattern for each of the three first-order autoregressive models.One limitation in autoregressive models is unexpected shifts in a historical trend. For example, the exchange rate for the Japanese yen was 238.47 in 1985 before dropping to 168.35 in 1986. Models that utilize historical data for forecasting will always have the limitation of unexpected changes in trends. Significant corrections in financial markets highlight the limitation of autoregressive models. The below chart illustrates the importance of applyubf autoregressive models with caution and thoughtfulness.

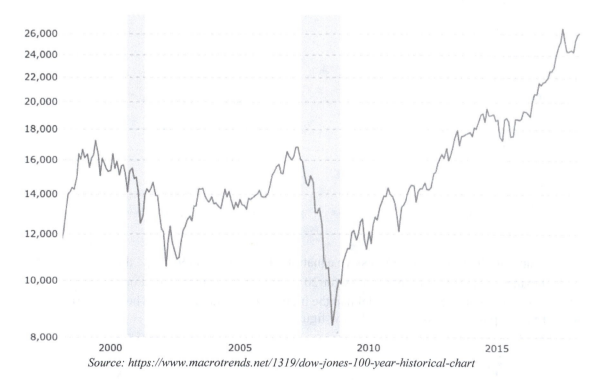

Source: https://www.macrotrends.net/1319/dow-jones-100-year-historical-chart

17.2   (a)   Bullet graph for one-year return:

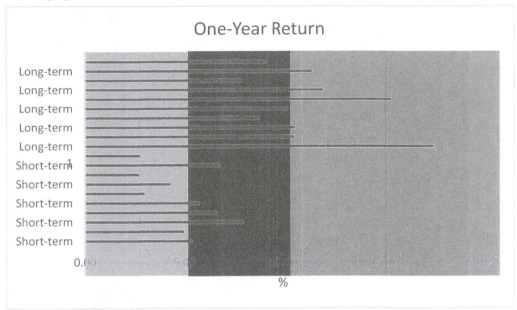

Bullet graph for three-year return:

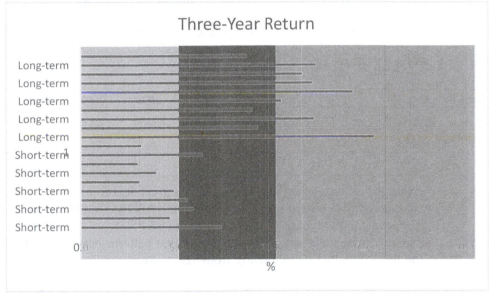

    (b)   Gauges take up too much visual space that would be needed for the 20 funds.

    (c)   The one-year return and the three-year return is much higher for the long-term funds than for the short-term funds.

17.4   (a)

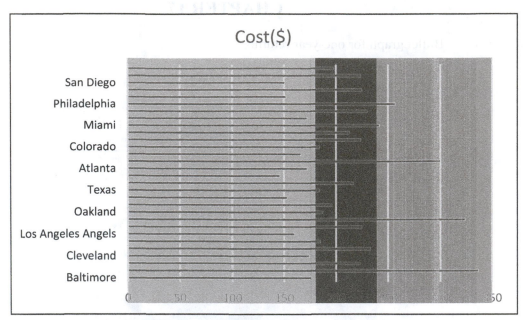

(b)   The bullet graph shows that four teams have costs considered as expensive while the stem-and-leaf display shows that the costs are concentrated between $172 and $225.

(c)   The bullet graph enables you to see the names of the individual teams and which teams are inexpensive, typical, and expensive whereas the stem-and-leaf display only shows the distribution of the costs.

(d)   The bullet graphs shows the costs for each team and which teams fall into the inexpensive, typical, and expensive categories.

17.6   (a)

Stock Indexes		2006	2007	2008	2009	2010	2011	2012
DJIA		16.3	6.4	-33.8	18.8	11.0	5.5	7.3
S&P 500		13.6	3.5	-38.5	23.5	12.8	0.0	13.4
NASDAQ		9.5	9.8	-40.5	43.9	16.9	-1.8	15.9

(b)   The rates of return of the three indices vary a great deal from year to year, but the pattern for the three indices are similar except for the NASDAQ in 2009 which had a much higher return in that year than the DJIA or the S&P500.

(c)   Unlike the three stock indices which had similar patterns between 2006–2012, the returns of the three metals differed greatly from year to year.

17.8 (a)

Fast Food Chain		1	2	3	Year 4	5	6
Burger King		178.45	171.33	178.20	162.22	173.37	160.52
Chick-Fil-A		219.39	198.81	194.80	167.21	150.57	146.38
McDonald's		177.59	167.02	169.88	170.85	162.72	156.92
Wendy's		171.30	150.29	141.73	134.67	127.21	116.22
Fast Food Chain		7	8	9	Year 10	11	12
Burger King							
Chick-Fil-A		173.19	166.10	166.00	179.90	153.06	166.85
McDonald's		163.74	168.60	191.90	194.30	175.01	167.59
Wendy's		152.52	167.90	163.90	167.10	158.77	174.22
		124.69	135.70	135.10	138.50	131.08	134.09

(b) Wendy's consistently has the fastest service time. The service time at McDonald's and Burger King are similar over the years. The service time at Chick-Fil-A was slower in the earlier and later years than the other fast food chains.

17.10 (a)

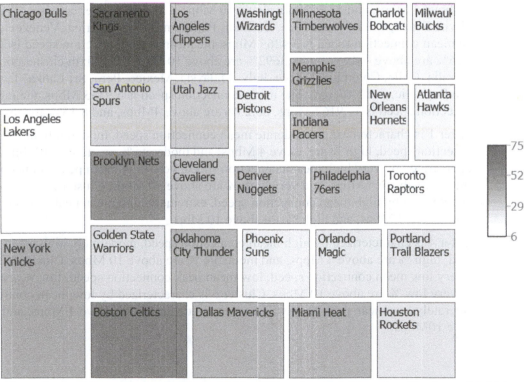

(b) The values of the teams varied from $312 million for the Milwaukee Bucks to $1,100 million for the New York Knicks. The change in values was not consistent across the teams. The two most valuable teams, the Los Angeles Lakers, and the New York Knicks had very different increases in value (11% and 41% respectively.)

17.12   The optimal number of clusters in the range between three and five is 3 (CCC = −1.4223). The first cluster consists of Russia, Poland, Lebanon, Malaysia, Argentina, Chile, Venezuela, Turkey, Brazil, and Mexico. The mean GDP per capita of this cluster is 21,085.4 and the social media usage % is 81.4. The second cluster consists of Ukraine, Jordan, Philippines, Vietnam, Peru, South Africa, Indonesia, Ghana, Kenya, Senegal, Tanzania, Uganda, Nigeria, and Ethiopia. The mean GDP per capita of this cluster is 6,613.36 and the social media usage % is 80.14. The third cluster consists of China, India, Pakistan, and Burkina Faso. The mean GDP per capita of this cluster is 6,768.75 and the social media usage % is 60. Thus, cluster 1 is characterized by high GDP and high social media usage. Cluster 2 is characterized by low GDP and high social media usage. Cluster 3 is characterized by low GDP and high social media usage.

17.14   The optimal number of clusters in the range between three and eight is 6 (CCC = 2.4411). The first cluster consists of Austria, Canada, Germany, Hungary, India, Ireland, Israel, New Zealand, Poland, Portugal, Russia, Slovakia, Spain, Taiwan, and Thailand. The mean connection speed is 10.44 Mbps, the mean peak connection speed is 54.9067 Mbps, 86% are above 4 Mbps, and 36.0667% are above 18.15 Mbps. The second cluster consists of Hong Kong and South Korea. The mean connection speed is 10.44 Mbps, the mean peak connection speed is 93.85 Mbps, 94% are above 4 Mbps, and 63.5% are above 10 Mbps. The third cluster consists only of Singapore. The mean connection speed is 12.5 Mbps, the mean peak connection speed is 13.5 Mbps, 87 % are above 4 Mbps, and 51% are above 10 Mbps.

The fourth cluster consists of Belgium, Czech Republic, Denmark, Finland, Japan, Netherlands, Norway, Rumania, Sweden, Switzerland, United Kingdom, and the United States. The mean connection speed is 14.6167 Mbps, the mean peak connection speed is 60.975 Mbps, 90.0833% are above 4 Mbps, and 52.75% are above 10 Mbps. The fifth cluster consists of Argentina, Bolivia, Brazil, China, Costa Rica, Ecuador, Philippines, South Africa, Venezuela, and VietNam. The mean connection speed is 3.4269 Mbps, the mean peak connection speed is 21.3538 Mbps, 66.25% are above 4Mbps, and 1.3692% are above 10 Mbps. The sixth cluster consists of Australia, Chile, Colombia, France, Italy, Malaysia, Mexico, Peru, Sri Lanka, Turkey, United Arab Republic, and Uruguay. The mean connection speed is 5.9333 Mbps, the mean peak connection speed is 37.9167 Mbps, 66.25% are above 4Mbps, and 8.15% are above 10 Mbps.

Cluster 1 is characterized by moderate mean connection speed, moderately high mean peak connection speed, high % are above 4 Mbps, and moderate % are above 10Mbps. Cluster 2 is characterized by very high mean connection speed, very high mean peak connection speed, very high % are above 4 Mbps, and very high % are above 10 Mbps. Cluster 3 (Singapore) is characterized by high mean connection speed, extremely high mean peak connection speed, high % are above 4 Mbps, and high % are above 10 Mbps.

Cluster 4 is characterized by high mean connection speed, moderately high mean peak connection speed, high % are above 4 Mbps, and moderate % are above 10 Mbps. Cluster 5 is characterized by very low mean connection speed, low mean peak connection speed, low % are above 4 Mbps, and very low % are above 10 Mbps. Cluster 6 is characterized by low mean connection speed, moderately low mean peak connection speed, moderate % are above 4 Mbps, and very low % are above 10Mbps.

17.16   The correspondence analysis plot shows that online guests are associated with purchasing household items while online members are strongly associated with grocery items and in-store customers more associated with hardlines and apparel than the two other categories. Positive comments are most associated with apparel items, while household items are associated with negative comments. Those that post most frequently tend to post positive comments. Managers may want to further examine the experience of online guests purchasing household items as such customers may be among the most disappointed by their shopping experience.

17.20   The highest five-year return of 12.33 is for a large cap growth fund.

17.22   The two-dimensional plot has a stress value of 0.0524. Singapore is separated from the other countries. The countries opposite Singapore low mean connection speed, moderately low mean peak connection speed, moderate % are above 4Mbps, and very low % are above 10Mbps. There appears to be a grouping of countries that have low mean connection speed, low mean peak connection speed, low % are above 4Mbps, and very low % are above 10Mbps. Many of the countries that are opposite these have moderate mean connection speed, moderately high mean peak connection speed, high % are above 4Mbps, and moderate % are above 10Mbps.

17.24   Because half the data will be used for a validation sample, the results will differ depending on which values are in the training sample and which are in the validation sample.

17.26   (a)

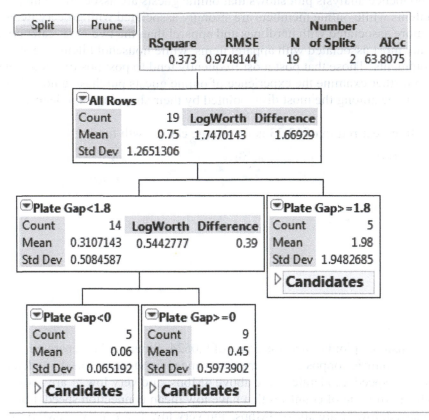

(b)   The r^2 for the regression tree model is 0.373. The first split is based on a plate gap of 1.8. For those bags with a plate gap less than 1.8, the mean tear is 0.3107. For those bags with a plate gap at least 1.8, the mean tear is 1.98. For those bags with a plate gap less than 0.0, the mean tear is 0.06. For those bags with a plate gap less than 1.8 but greater than 0, the mean tear is 0.45. Thus, you would recommend that a plate gap of less than 0 be used to minimize tears in the bag.

17.28 (a)   JMP output:

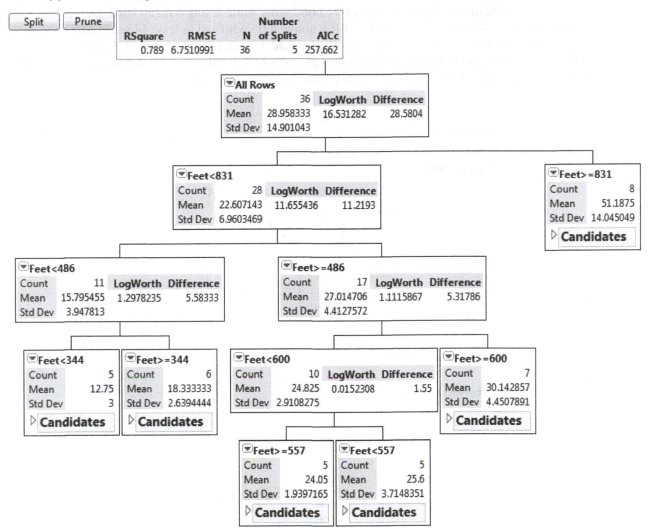

(b)   The r^2 for the regression tree model is 0.789. The first split is based on 831 square feet. Moves of at least 831 sq. ft. have a mean moving time of 51.1875 hours. Moves of less than 831 square feet have a mean moving time of 22.6071 hours. Among moves of less than 831 sq. ft., moves of less than 486 sq. ft., have a mean moving time of 15.7955 hours. Moves of less than 344 sq. ft. have a mean moving time of 12.75 hours. Moves of between 344 and 486 sq. ft. have a mean moving time of 18.3333 hours. Moves of between 486 and 830 sq. ft. have a mean moving time of 27.0147 hours. Moves between 486 and 599 sq. ft. have a mean moving time of 24.825 hours. Moves between 600 and 830 have a mean moving time of 30.1429 hours. Moves between 557 and 599 sq. ft. have a mean moving time of 24.05 hours. Moves between 486 and 557 sq. ft have a mean moving time of 25.6 hours.

17.30   The r^2 of the regression tree model is 0.731. The prime determinant of wins is the ERA Teams with an ERA below 4.05 had a mean of 91.6667 wins while teams with an ERA above 4.05 had a mean of 76.2857 wins. Teams with an ERA above 4.05 who had at least 44 saves had a mean of 83.5 wins while teams with fewer than 44 saves had a mean of 71.8461 wins. Teams with an ERA above 4.05 who had fewer than 44 saves and an ERA below 4.33 had a mean of 77.4 wins. (Those that had an ERA above 4.33 had a mean of 68.375 wins.)

17.32   (a)

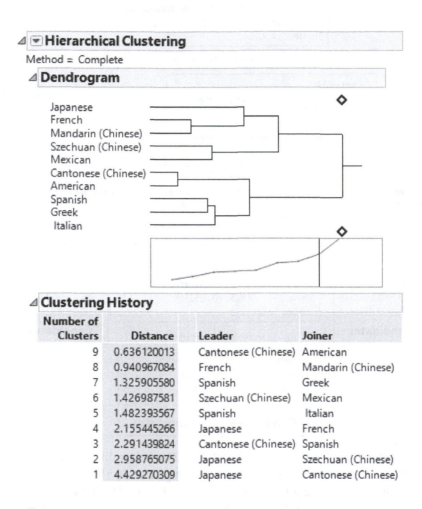

Hierarchical Clustering

Method = Complete

Dendrogram

Japanese
French
Mandarin (Chinese)
Szechuan (Chinese)
Mexican
Cantonese (Chinese)
American
Spanish
Greek
Italian

Clustering History

Number of Clusters	Distance	Leader	Joiner
9	0.636120013	Cantonese (Chinese)	American
8	0.940967084	French	Mandarin (Chinese)
7	1.325905580	Spanish	Greek
6	1.426987581	Szechuan (Chinese)	Mexican
5	1.482393567	Spanish	Italian
4	2.155445266	Japanese	French
3	2.291439824	Cantonese (Chinese)	Spanish
2	2.958765075	Japanese	Szechuan (Chinese)
1	4.429270309	Japanese	Cantonese (Chinese)

17.32 (b)
cont.

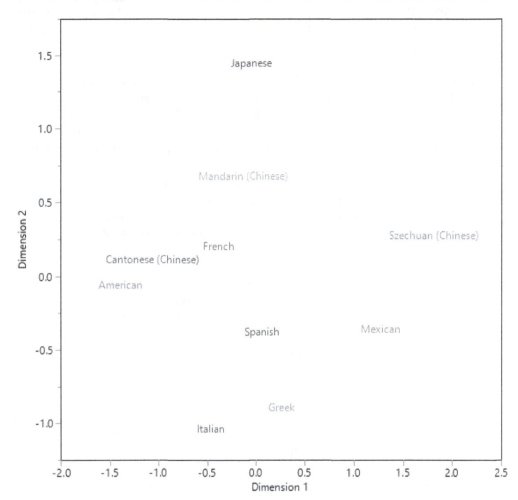

(c)   The first two foods to cluster are Cantonese and American, followed by French and
Mandarin, followed by Spanish and Greek. At the two-cluster level, the first cluster
includes Japanese, French, Mandarin, Szechuan, and Mexican. The second cluster
includes Cantonese, American, Spanish, Greek, and Italian. A two-dimensional scaling
analysis with a stress statistic of 0.3527 reveals no clearly interpretable dimensions.
American and Cantonese foods are close to each other in both dimensions. Japanese food
is separated by itself.

17.34   The r^2 of the regression tree model is 0.727. The first split is based on the living space of 2,220 square feet. Houses with a living space < 2,220 square feet have a mean asking price of $558,678.95 while houses with a living space > 2,220 square feet have a mean asking price of $ $446,854.76. Houses with a living space > 2,220 square feet that have a brick exterior have a mean asking price of $499,616.67 while those without a brick exterior have a mean asking price of $585,938.46. Houses without a brick exterior that have a lot size greater than 0.46 (acres) have a mean asking price of $634,760 while houses that have a lot size less than 0.46 (acres) have a mean asking price of $555,425.

Houses with a living space < 2,220 square feet that have a living space > 1,197 square feet have a mean asking price of $463,741.18 while those with a living space below 1,197 square feet have a mean asking price of $375,087.50. Houses with a living space < 2,220 square feet that have a living space > 1,197 square feet that have a fireplace have a mean asking price of $484,643.48 while those that do not have a fireplace have a mean asking price of $420,036.36.

Houses with a living space < 2,220 square feet that have a living space > 1,197 square feet that have a fireplace and a lot size > 0.19 acres have a mean asking price of $448,128.57 (those with a brick exterior have a mean asking price of $463,928.57 while those without a brick exterior have a mean asking price of $432,328.57) while those that have a lot size < 0.19 acres have a mean asking price of $541,444.44.

Houses with a living space < 2,220 square feet that have a living space > 1,197 square feet that do not have a fireplace and have at least three bathrooms have a mean asking price of $444,100 while those that have fewer than three bathrooms have a mean asking price of $391,160.

17.36   The optimal number of clusters in the range between three and eight is 6 (CCC = 3.97273). The first cluster consists of Stonyfield Organic Greek. The second cluster consists of the six regular yogurts. The third cluster consists of the Great Value Greek only. The fourth cluster consists of the Organic Valley Greek only. The fifth cluster consists of the Trader Joe's Plain Whole Greek only. The sixth cluster consists of Dannon Oikos, Wallaby Organic, and Chobani Greek. You can conclude that the regular yogurts are different from the Greek yogurts and that many of the Greek yogurts are different from each other.

CHAPTER 18

18.2 Let X_1 = Temp X_2 = Win% X_3 = OpWin% X_4 = Weekend X_5 = Promotion

With all the 5 independent variables in the model: None of the *VIF* is > 5.

The best-subset regression produces the following potential models:

Model	Cp	k	R Square	Adj. R Square	Std. Error	Consider This Model?
X1X2X3X4X5	6	6	0.301052	0.253826288	6442.446	Yes
X1X2X3X5	4.0174	5	0.300888	0.263602154	6400.104	Yes
X1X3X5	3.703162	4	0.284966	0.256740664	6429.852	Yes
X2X3X4X5	4.674724	5	0.29468	0.257062456	6428.46	Yes
X2X3X5	2.680286	4	0.294627	0.26678334	6386.265	Yes

Based on the smallest C_p value and the highest adjusted *r*-square, the best model is the following:

	Coefficients	Standard Error	t Stat	P-value	Lower 95%	Upper 95%
Intercept	-1669.988177	5531.248104	-0.30191887	0.763538564	-12686.43764	9346.46129
Win%	27.4932005	14.0652218	1.954693705	0.054297102	-0.520152407	55.50655341
OpWin%	10.53699651	6.324477812	1.666065851	0.099817096	-2.059308864	23.13330188
Promotion	7089.212249	1455.76966	4.869734852	5.9398E-06	4189.791975	9988.632523

Since only X_5 makes significant contribution to the regression model at 5% level of significance, the more parsimonious model includes only X_5.

$\hat{Y} = 13{,}935.703 + 6{,}813.228X_5$

	Coefficients	Standard Error	t Stat	P-value
Intercept	13935.7027	1096.695459	12.70699408	1.09284E-20
Promotion	6813.22753	1495.880191	4.554661244	1.90736E-05

The estimated mean paid attendance on a non-promotion day is 13,935.70. The estimated mean paid attendance on a promotion day will be 6,813.23 higher than when there is no promotion.

$H_0 : \beta_5 = 0$ vs $H_1 : \beta_5 \neq 0$

Since the *p*-value is virtually zero, reject H_0. At the 0.05 level of significance, promotion makes a significant contribution to the regression model.

$r^2 = 0.2101$. Hence, 21.02% of the variation in attendance can be explained by promotion.

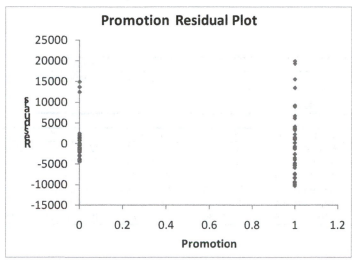

18.2
cont.

Normal Probability Plot

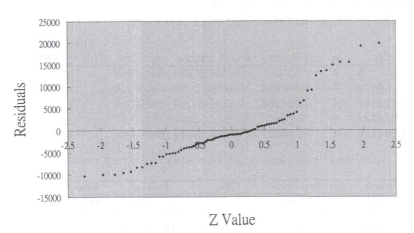

Z Value

The normal probability plot reveals non-normality in the residuals. The residual plot suggests possible violation of the homoscedasticity assumption.

18.4   Let $X_1 = $ Temp $X_2 = $ Win% $X_3 = $ OpWin% $X_4 = $ Weekend $X_5 = $ Promotion
With all the 5 independent variables in the model: None of the *VIF* is > 5.
The best-subset regression produces only one potential model:

Model	Cp	k	R Square	Adj. R Square	Std. Error	Consider This Model?
X1X2X3X4X5	6	6	0.390987	0.350386138	4320.381	Yes

The best model is the full model that includes all the independent variables.

Regression Statistics	
Multiple R	0.625289536
R Square	0.390987004
Adjusted R Square	0.350386138
Standard Error	4320.381297
Observations	81

ANOVA

	df	SS	MS	F	Significance F
Regression	5	898754711.7	179750942.3	9.630016278	3.94963E-07
Residual	75	1399927091	18665694.55		
Total	80	2298681803			

	Coefficients	Standard Error	t Stat	P-value	Lower 95%	Upper 95%
Intercept	10682.45521	6013.474857	1.776419701	0.079719211	-1297.003842	22661.91425
Temp	82.20546833	38.59788228	2.129792192	0.036469445	5.314525708	159.096411
Win%	26.26250802	12.37716144	2.121852263	0.037152917	1.60593222	50.91908383
OpWin%	7.367011607	5.929542741	1.24242491	0.217950544	-4.445246053	19.17926927
Weekend	3369.907577	1026.248391	3.283715332	0.001558126	1325.515463	5414.299691
Promotion	3129.013192	1030.12174	3.037517868	0.003280737	1076.904969	5181.121414

18.4	Since X_3 does not make significant contribution to the regression model at 5% level of
cont.	significance, it can be dropped from the model. The more parsimonious model includes X_1, X_2,

X_4 and X_5.

$\hat{Y} = 14{,}965.626 + 88.888X_1 + 23.269X_2 + 3{,}562.425X_4 + 3{,}029.087X_5$

	Coefficients	Standard Error	t Stat	P-value
Intercept	14965.62623	4944.771809	3.026555483	0.003375413
Temp	88.88797075	38.35774548	2.317340856	0.023179453
Win%	23.26917677	12.1837526	1.909853026	0.059925592
Weekend	3562.425371	1018.104525	3.499076257	0.000784145
Promotion	3029.087074	1030.643544	2.939024935	0.004358397

Since X_2 does not make significant contribution to the regression model at 5% level of significance, it can be dropped from the model. The more parsimonious model includes only X_1, X_4 and X_5.

$\hat{Y} = 22601.7676 + 108.6331X_1 + 3907.6538X_4 + 3433.9977X_5$

	Coefficients	Standard Error	t Stat	P-value
Intercept	22601.76761	2958.970207	7.638389719	5.03953E-11
Temp	108.633101	37.56787033	2.891649169	0.004978867
Weekend	3907.653774	1019.008546	3.834760553	0.000255422
Promotion	3433.997688	1025.794791	3.347645862	0.001263126

Since the non-dummy independent variable, day high temperature, is unlikely to have zero values, the intercept should be interpreted as the portion of paid attendance that varies with factors other than those already included in the model.

As the high temperature increases by one degree, the estimated mean paid attendance will increase by 108.6331 taking into consideration all the other independent variables included in the model.

The estimated mean paid attendance of a game played on a weekend will be 3907.6538 higher than when the game is played on a weekday taking into consideration all the other independent variables included in the model.

The estimated mean paid attendance on a promotion day will be 3433.9977 higher than when there is no promotion taking into consideration all the other independent variables included in the model.

$H_0 : \beta_j = 0 \qquad H_1 : \beta_j \neq 0 \qquad$ for $j = 1, 2, 4, 5$

At the 0.05 level of significance, temperature, and the weekend and promotion dummy variables make a significant contribution to the regression model individually.

Adjusted $r^2 = .3232$. Hence, 32.32% of the variation in attendance can be explained by the 3 independent variables after adjusting for the number of independent variables and the sample size.

18.4
cont.

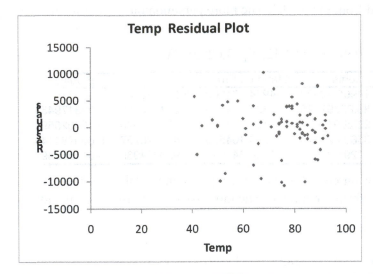

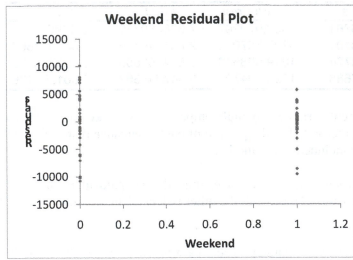

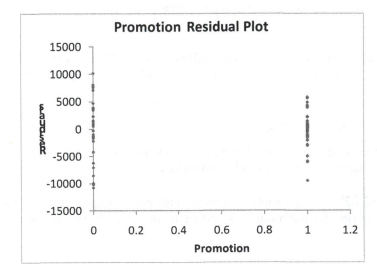

18.4
cont.

Normal Probability Plot

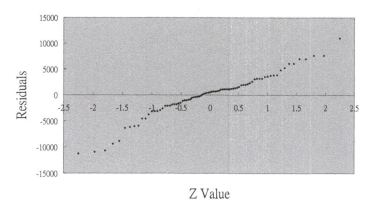

Z Value

The residual plots do not reveal any obvious pattern. The normal probability plot does not reveal departure from the normality assumption.

18.6

Descriptive Statistics: Employment in Tourism 2015, ... Establishments

Statistics

Variable	Total Count	N	N*	Mean	SE Mean	StDev	CoefVar	Minimum	Q1
Employment in Tourism 2015	28	28	0	296839	81597	431771	145.46	6084	38304
Business Travel & Tourism Spend	28	28	0	8764	3644	19284	220.04	229	525
International Visitors 2015 (00	28	28	0	15777	3937	20833	132.05	1027	2734
Tourism Establishments	28	28	0	13513	4061	21487	159.01	434	1497

Variable	Median	Q3	Maximum	Range	Skewness	Kurtosis
Employment in Tourism 2015	137591	271799	1791220	1785136	2.28	4.96
Business Travel & Tourism Spend	1933	6406	98719	98490	4.09	18.66
International Visitors 2015 (00	8035	16623	87412	86385	2.32	5.30
Tourism Establishments	4223	14030	87079	86645	2.36	5.28

Coefficients

Term	Coef	SE Coef	T-Value	P-Value	VIF
Constant	10401	23245	0.45	0.659	
Business Travel & Tourism Spend	14.04	1.37	10.23	0.000	2.09
International Visitors 2015 (00	10.08	1.07	9.46	0.000	1.47
Tourism Establishments	0.33	1.27	0.26	0.799	2.22

Because the goal of 18.6 is to predict the value of a dependent variable, employment in tourism, one would use multiple regression. As a first step in the model building process, a review of the VIFs reveals that all three independent variables have VIF values below five.

18.6
cont.

Best Subsets Regression: Employment in Tourism 2015 ... ourism Estab.

Response is Employment in Tourism 2015

Vars	R-Sq	R-Sq (adj)	R-Sq (pred)	Mallows Cp	S	Business Travel Spend	International Visits	Tourism Estab.
1	77.6	76.8	14.6	100.6	208185	X		
1	65.2	63.9	54.0	169.5	259501		X	
1	52.5	50.7	24.8	240.2	303213			X
2	95.7	95.3	92.8	2.1	93321	X	X	
2	79.6	78.0	1.9	91.4	202588	X		X
2	76.9	75.0	34.3	106.7	215815		X	X
3	95.7	95.1	91.9	4.0	95115	X	X	X

A Best Subsets analysis reveals that the model including all three independent variables has a C_p value equal to k + 1, where k is the number of independent variables. The model with two independent variables, spending on business travel and the number of international visitors, had a C_p value below k + 1. All other models have C_p values greater than k+1. The adjusted r^2 of 0.953 is slightly higher for the two variable model with spending on business travel and international visitors as the two independent variables. The adjusted r^2 for the model including all three variables is 0.951. Based on this difference and the principle of parsimony, the two variable model is the preferred model.

18.6
cont.

Regression Analysis: Employment in Tourism 2015 versus ... nal Visitors

Analysis of Variance

Source	DF	Adj SS	Adj MS	F-Value	P-Value
Regression	2	4.81578E+12	2.40789E+12	276.49	0.000
Business Travel Spend	1	1.53314E+12	1.53314E+12	176.04	0.000
International Visitors	1	9.09149E+11	9.09149E+11	104.39	0.000
Error	25	2.17722E+11	8708872636		
Total	27	5.03350E+12			

Model Summary

S	R-sq	R-sq(adj)	R-sq(pred)
93321.3	95.67%	95.33%	92.80%

Coefficients

Term	Coef	SE Coef	T-Value	P-Value	VIF
Constant	11618	22329	0.52	0.607	
Business Travel Spend	14.25	1.07	13.27	0.000	1.33
International Visitors	10.160	0.994	10.22	0.000	1.33

Regression Equation

Employment in Tourism 2015 = 11618 + 14.25 Business Travel Spend
+ 10.160 International Visitors

The F-test of the overall model reveals that the model is significant at the .05 significance level. Because $F_{STAT} = 276.49$ or p-value $= 0.000$, reject H_0. Individual t-tests on the independent variables are significant at the .05 level, which suggests that two of the independent variables should be included. The adjusted r^2 of this model is .9533. The $r^2 = .9567$ which indicates that 95.67% of the variation in tourism employment can be explained by the variation in spending on business travel and the number of international visitors.

18.6
cont.

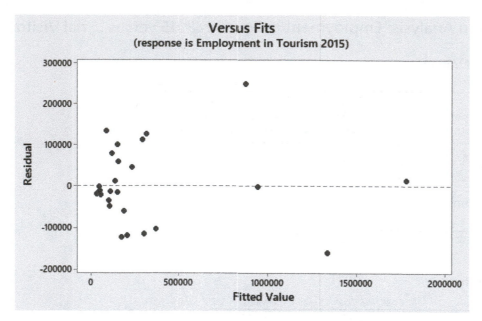

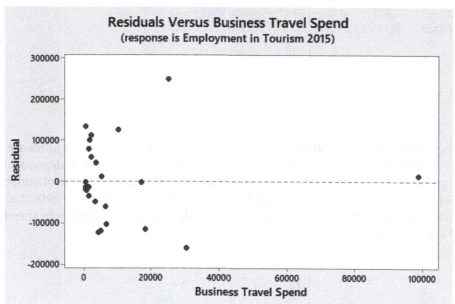

18.6
cont.

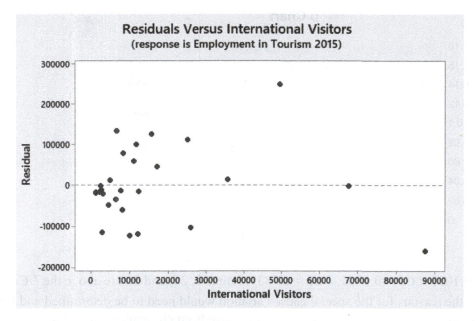

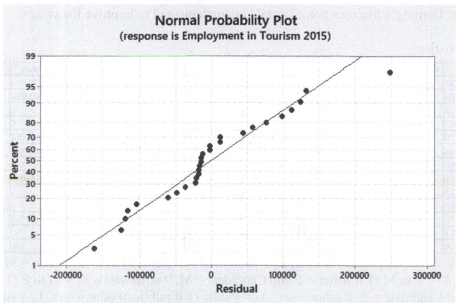

The residual plots reveal no clear pattern, indicating no evidence for violation of the equal variance or linearity assumptions. The normal probability plot suggest that there is evidence of deviation from normality as well as one outlier. Based on potential violations of normality one should consider using transformed data in this model to address the potential violation of normality.

Durbin-Watson Statistic

Durbin-Watson Statistic =   2.30671

Because the Durbin-Watson statistic of 2.30671 is above the critical value of 1.56, there is no evidence of positive autocorrelation in the model.

18.8   (a)

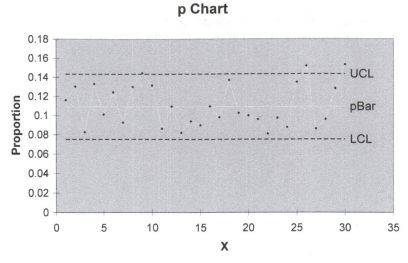

$\bar{p} = 0.1091$, $LCL = 0.0751$, $UCL = 0.1431$. Points 9, 26, and 30 are above the UCL.

(b)   First, the reasons for the special cause variation would need to be determined and local corrective action taken. Once special causes have been eliminated and the process is stable, Deming's fourteen points should be implemented to improve the system.

18.10   Summary Statistics:

	Salary	Competence Rating	M to M	F to M	M to F	Public	Biology	Chemistry	Age-Rater
Mean	29.4025	3.733333333	0.25	0.25	0.25	0.5	0.333333333	0.333333333	54.05833333
Standard Error	0.475963511	0.140394269	0.039694209	0.039694209	0.039694209	0.045834925	0.043213582	0.043213582	0.52504446
Median	28.95	4	0	0	0	0.5	0	0	55
Mode	28.3	4	0	0	0	1	0	0	56
Standard Deviation	5.213919033	1.537942166	0.434828277	0.434828277	0.434828277	0.502096445	0.473381068	0.473381068	5.751573893
Sample Variance	27.18495168	2.365266106	0.18907563	0.18907563	0.18907563	0.25210084	0.224089636	0.224089636	33.08060224
Kurtosis	3.019432897	-0.510058795	-0.643584915	-0.643584915	-0.643584915	-2.034188034	-1.512711864	-1.512711864	0.264824682
Skewness	1.085010708	0.219536333	1.169368699	1.169368699	1.169368699	0	0.716089158	0.716089158	-0.185855334
Range	31.5	6	1	1	1	1	1	1	34
Minimum	18.5	1	0	0	0	0	0	0	37
Maximum	50	7	1	1	1	1	1	1	71
Sum	3528.3	448	30	30	30	60	40	40	6487
Count	120	120	120	120	120	120	120	120	120

18.10   Let Y = Salary, X_1 = Competence Rating, X_2 = M to M (1 if Rater = M and Candidate = M,
cont.   0 otherwise), X_3 = F to M (1 if Rater = F and Candidate = M, 0 otherwise), X_4 = M to F (1 if Rater = M and Candidate = F, 0 otherwise), X_5 = Public (1 if public, 0 otherwise), X_6 = Biology (1 if Biology, 0 otherwise), X_7 = Chemistry (1 if Chemistry, 0 otherwise), X_8 = Age-Rater.

The regression with all eight potential independent variable indicates that none of the VIF is > 5. Regression output that include all eight independent variables:

18.10
cont.

Regression Statistics	
Multiple R	0.9358
R Square	0.8757
Adjusted R Square	0.8667
Standard Error	1.9035
Observations	120

ANOVA

	df	SS	MS	F	Significance F
Regression	8	2832.8317	354.1040	97.7318	0.0000
Residual	111	402.1776	3.6232		
Total	119	3235.0093			

	Coefficients	Standard Error	t Stat	P-value	Lower 95%	Upper 95%	Lower 95%
Intercept	15.7064	1.9022	8.2570	0.0000	11.9371	19.4758	11.9371
Competence Rating	2.9869	0.1159	25.7765	0.0000	2.7573	3.2166	2.7573
M to M	1.2944	0.4989	2.5946	0.0107	0.3058	2.2830	0.3058
F to M	1.7128	0.4984	3.4486	0.0008	0.7312	2.7065	0.7312
M to F	-0.8224	0.4964	-1.6567	0.1004	-1.8062	0.1613	-1.8062
Public	0.3157	0.3541	0.8917	0.3745	-0.3859	1.0174	-0.3859
Biology	-0.3072	0.4268	-0.7196	0.4733	-1.1530	0.5387	-1.1530
Chemistry	0.2041	0.4291	0.4755	0.6353	-0.6462	1.0543	-0.6462
Age-Rater	0.0847	0.0315	1.1001	0.2737	-0.0278	0.0971	-0.0278

The full-model $F_{stat} = 97.7318$ with a p-value = 0.0000. Hence, the eight independent variables as a group are significant in explaining the variation in Salary at the 5% level of significance.
The individual t test indicates that "M to F", "Public", "Biology", "Chemistry", and "Age-Rater" all have p-value > 0.05 and, hence, are not significant individually at the 5% level of significance.

Regression output after dropping "M to F," "Public," "Biology," "Chemistry," and "Age-Rater:"

Regression Statistics	
Multiple R	0.9321
R Square	0.8687
Adjusted R Square	0.8653
Standard Error	1.9134
Observations	120

ANOVA

	df	SS	MS	F	Significance F
Regression	3	2810.3354	936.7785	255.8818	0.0000
Residual	116	424.6739	3.6610		
Total	119	3235.0093			

	Coefficients	Standard Error	t Stat	P-value	Lower 95%	Upper 95%
Intercept	17.3144	0.4705	36.8036	0.0000	16.3826	18.2462
Competence Rating	2.9823	0.1161	25.6975	0.0000	2.7524	3.2122
M to M	1.6897	0.4326	3.9062	0.0002	0.8330	2.5465
F to M	2.1270	0.4332	4.9103	0.0000	1.2691	2.9849

18.10 Partial *F*-test for portion of the multiple regression model:
cont. $H_0 : \beta_4 = \beta_5 = \beta_6 = \beta_7 = \beta_8 = 0$ vs. H_1 : Not all $\beta_j = 0$ for $j = 4,5,6,7,8$

$$F_{STAT} = \frac{\left(SSR\left(X_4, X_5, X_6, X_7, X_8 \mid X_1, X_2, X_3 \right)\right)/5}{MSE\left(\text{All } Xs \right)} = \frac{\left(SSR\left(\text{All } Xs \right) - SSR\left(X_1, X_2, X_3 \right)\right)/5}{MSE\left(\text{All } Xs \right)}$$

= 1.2418 with 5 and 111 degrees of freedom.
Since *p*-value = 0.2945 > 0.05, do not reject H_0. There is not enough evidence that at least one of
"M to F", "Public", "Biology", "Chemistry", and "Age-Rater" is significant.
The best model is
Salary $= 17.3144 + 2.9823 \left(\text{Competence Rating} \right) + 1.6897 \left(\text{M to M} \right) + 2.1270 \left(\text{F to M} \right)$

The normal probability plot of the residuals:

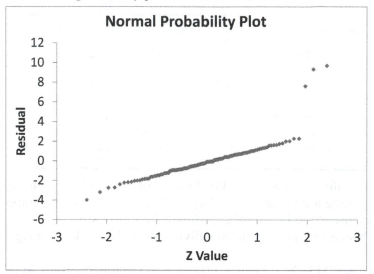

The normal probability plot suggests that the residuals are quite normally distributed except the 3
outliers in the right-tail, which could severly bias the result.

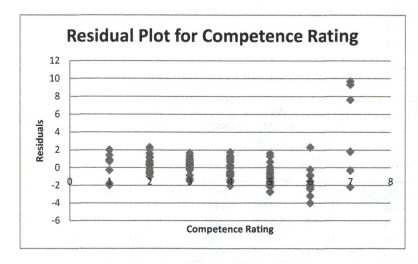

18.10
cont.

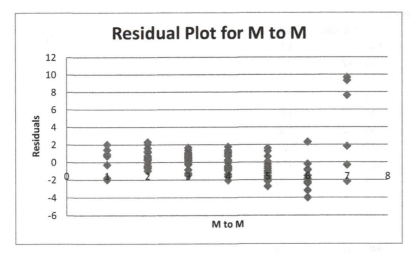

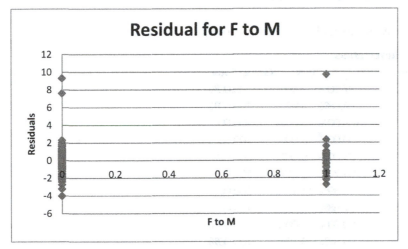

The residual plots suggest violation of the equal variance assumption. Hence, the conclusion from the regression result might not be reliable.

The best regression model suggests that after taking into consideration the other factors like competence rating that could have affected salary, the mean salary of a femal candidate is estimated to be the same regardless of the gender of the rater. The mean salary of a male candidate is estimated to be $1.6897 thousands higher than his female counterpart when rated by a male and estimated to be $2.1270 thousands higher than his female counterpart when rated by a female.

18.12   Pivital table in terms of counts (Job by Term Deposit):

Count of Job	Column Labels		
Row Labels	no	yes	Grand Total
admin.	134	4	138
blue-collar	270	17	287
entrepreneur	29		29
housemaid	8		8
management	133	7	140
retired	36	2	38
self-employed	24	3	27
services	121	3	124
student	10		10
technician	152	5	157
unemployed	19		19
unknown	2		2
Grand Total	**938**	**41**	**979**

Pivital table in terms of row totals (Job by Term Deposit):

Count of Term Deposit	Column Labels		
Row Labels	no	yes	Grand Total
admin.	97.10%	2.90%	100.00%
blue-collar	94.08%	5.92%	100.00%
entrepreneur	100.00%	0.00%	100.00%
housemaid	100.00%	0.00%	100.00%
management	95.00%	5.00%	100.00%
retired	94.74%	5.26%	100.00%
self-employed	88.89%	11.11%	100.00%
services	97.58%	2.42%	100.00%
student	100.00%	0.00%	100.00%
technician	96.82%	3.18%	100.00%
unemployed	100.00%	0.00%	100.00%
unknown	100.00%	0.00%	100.00%
Grand Total	**95.81%**	**4.19%**	**100.00%**

18.12   PHStat output for the Chi-square test for the difference in proportions:
cont.

Chi-Square Test

					Observed Frequencies								
					Column variable								
Row variable	admin.	blue-colla	entreprer	housemai	managem	retired	self-empl	services	student	techniciar	unemploy	unknown	Total
No	134	270	29	8	133	36	24	121	10	152	19	2	938
Yes	4	17			7	2	3	3		5			41
Total	138	287	29	8	140	38	27	124	10	157	19	2	979

					Expected Frequencies								
					Column variable								
Row variable	admin.	blue-collar	ntreprene	housemai	canagemer	retired	lf-employ	services	student	techniciar	nemploye	unknown	Total
No	132.2206	274.9806	27.7855	7.664964	134.1369	36.40858	25.86925	118.8069	9.581205	150.4249	18.20429	1.916241	938
Yes	5.779367	12.01941	1.214505	0.335036	5.863126	1.59142	1.130746	5.193054	0.418795	6.575077	0.79571	0.083759	41
Total	138	287	29	8	140	38	27	124	10	157	19	2	979

Data	
Level of Significance	0.05
Number of Rows	2
Number of Columns	12
Degrees of Freedom	11

Results	
Critical Value	19.67514
Chi-Square Test Statistic	10.62328
p-Value	0.475342
Do not reject the null hypothesis	

Expected frequency assumption
   is violated.

The p-value = 0.4753 > 0.05, do not reject H_0. There is not enough evidence that the proportions are different across the different type of jobs at the 5% level of significance. However, the expected frequency assumption for the chi-square test is violated.

Pivital table in terms of counts (Marital by Term Deposit):

Count of Term Deposit	Column Labels		
Row Labels	no	yes	Grand Total
divorced	120	9	129
married	572	18	590
single	246	14	260
Grand Total	938	41	979

Pivital table in terms of row totals (Marital by Term Deposit):

Count of Term Deposit	Column Labels		
Row Labels	no	yes	Grand Total
divorced	93.02%	6.98%	100.00%
married	96.95%	3.05%	100.00%
single	94.62%	5.38%	100.00%
Grand Total	95.81%	4.19%	100.00%

18.12   PHStat output for the Chi-square test for the difference in proportions: cont.

Chi-Square Test

Observed Frequencies

	Column variable			
Row variable	divorced	married	single	Total
No	120	572	246	938
Yes	9	18	14	41
Total	129	590	260	979

Expected Frequencies

	Column variable			
Row variable	divorced	married	single	Total
No	123.5975	565.2911	249.1113	938
Yes	5.402451	24.70889	10.88866	41
Total	129	590	260	979

Data	
Level of Significance	0.05
Number of Rows	2
Number of Columns	3
Degrees of Freedom	2

Results	
Critical Value	5.991465
Chi-Square Test Statistic	5.329455
p-Value	0.069618
Do not reject the null hypothesis	

Expected frequency assumption is met.

The p-value = 0.0696 > 0.05, do not reject H_0. There is not enough evidence that the proportions are different across the different marital status at the 5% level of significance.

Pivital table in terms of counts (Education by Term Deposit):

Count of Term Deposit	Column Labels		
Row Labels	no	yes	Grand Total
primary	139	10	149
secondary	576	21	597
tertiary	183	9	192
unknown	40	1	41
Grand Total	938	41	979

Pivital table in terms of row totals (Education by Term Deposit):

Count of Term Deposit	Column Labels		
Row Labels	no	yes	Grand Total
primary	93.29%	6.71%	100.00%
secondary	96.48%	3.52%	100.00%
tertiary	95.31%	4.69%	100.00%
unknown	97.56%	2.44%	100.00%
Grand Total	95.81%	4.19%	100.00%

18.12   PHStat output for the Chi-square test for the difference in proportions:
cont.

Chi-Square Test

Observed Frequencies

Row variable	primary	secondary	tertiary	unknown	Total
		Column variable			
No	139	576	183	40	938
Yes	10	21	9	1	41
Total	149	597	192	41	979

Expected Frequencies

Row variable	primary	secondary	tertiary	unknown	Total
		Column variable			
No	142.76	571.998	183.9591	39.28294	938
Yes	6.240041	25.00204	8.040858	1.717058	41
Total	149	597	192	41	979

Data	
Level of Significance	0.05
Number of Rows	2
Number of Columns	4
Degrees of Freedom	3

Results	
Critical Value	7.814728
Chi-Square Test Statistic	3.465157
p-Value	0.325309
Do not reject the null hypothesis	

Expected frequency assumption
is met.

The p-value = $0.3253 > 0.05$, do not reject H_0. There is not enough evidence that the proportions are different across the different education levels at the 5% level of significance.

Pivital table in terms of counts (Default by Term Deposit):

Count of Term Deposit	Column Labels ▼		
Row Labels ▼	no	yes	Grand Total
no	914	40	954
yes	24	1	25
Grand Total	938	41	979

Pivital table in terms of row totals (Default by Term Deposit):

Count of Term Deposit	Column Labels ▼		
Row Labels ▼	no	yes	Grand Total
no	95.81%	4.19%	100.00%
yes	96.00%	4.00%	100.00%
Grand Total	95.81%	4.19%	100.00%

18.12   PHStat output for the Chi-square test for the difference in proportions:
cont.

Chi-Square Test

	Observed Frequencies		
	Column variable		
Row variable	No	Yes	Total
No	914	24	938
Yes	40	1	41
Total	954	25	979

	Expected Frequencies		
	Column variable		
Row variable	No	Yes	Total
No	914.047	23.95301	938
Yes	39.95301	1.046987	41
Total	954	25	979

Data	
Level of Significance	0.05
Number of Rows	2
Number of Columns	2
Degrees of Freedom	1

Results	
Critical Value	3.841459
Chi-Square Test Statistic	0.002259
p-Value	0.962096
Do not reject the null hypothesis	

Expected frequency assumption
   is violated.

The p-value = 0.9621 > 0.05, do not reject H_0. There is not enough evidence that the proportions are different across whether credit is in default at the 5% level of significance. However, the expected frequency assumption needed for the chi-square test is violated.

Pivital table in terms of counts (Housing Loan by Term Deposit):

Count of Term Deposit	Column Labels ▼		
Row Labels ▼	no	yes	Grand Total
no	101	4	105
yes	837	37	874
Grand Total	938	41	979

Pivital table in terms of row totals (Housing Loan by Term Deposit):

Count of Term Deposit	Column Labels ▼		
Row Labels ▼	no	yes	Grand Total
no	96.19%	3.81%	100.00%
yes	95.77%	4.23%	100.00%
Grand Total	95.81%	4.19%	100.00%

18.12   PHStat output for the Chi-square test for the difference in proportions:
cont.

Chi-Square Test

Observed Frequencies			
	Column variable		
Row variable	No	Yes	Total
No	101	837	938
Yes	4	37	41
Total	105	874	979

Expected Frequencies			
	Column variable		
Row variable	No	Yes	Total
No	100.6027	837.3973	938
Yes	4.397344	36.60266	41
Total	105	874	979

Data	
Level of Significance	0.05
Number of Rows	2
Number of Columns	2
Degrees of Freedom	1

Results	
Critical Value	3.841459
Chi-Square Test Statistic	0.041975
p-Value	0.837667
Do not reject the null hypothesis	

*Expected frequency assumption
    is violated.*

The p-value $= 0.8377 > 0.05$, do not reject H_0. There is not enough evidence that the proportions are different across whether there is a housing loan at the 5% level of significance. However, the expected frequency assumption needed for the chi-square test is violated.

Pivital table in terms of counts (Personal Loan by Term Deposit):

Count of Term Deposit	Column Labels ▾		
Row Labels ▾	no	yes	Grand Total
no	101	4	105
yes	837	37	874
Grand Total	938	41	979

Pivital table in terms of row totals (Personal Loan by Term Deposit):

Count of Term Deposit	Column Labels ▾		
Row Labels ▾	no	yes	Grand Total
no	95.40%	4.60%	100.00%
yes	98.04%	1.96%	100.00%
Grand Total	95.81%	4.19%	100.00%

18.12   PHStat output for the Chi-square test for the difference in proportions: cont.

Chi-Square Test

Observed Frequencies

Row variable	No	Yes	Total
	Column variable		
No	788	150	938
Yes	38	3	41
Total	826	153	979

Expected Frequencies

Row variable	No	Yes	Total
	Column variable		
No	791.4076	146.5924	938
Yes	34.59244	6.407559	41
Total	826	153	979

Data

Level of Significance	0.05
Number of Rows	2
Number of Columns	2
Degrees of Freedom	1

Results

Critical Value	3.841459
Chi-Square Test Statistic	2.241695
p-Value	0.134334
Do not reject the null hypothesis	

Expected frequency assumption is met.

The p-value $= 0.1343 > 0.05$, do not reject H_0. There is not enough evidence that the proportions are different across whether there is a personal loan at the 5% level of significance.

18.14   Below are some of the summary characteristics of the variables in the data set that the students can use to write a report describing their conclusions depending on the various aspects of the variables they have chosen to analyze.

	Age	Age of Dwelling	Years at Dwelling	Bedrooms	Vehicles	Fuel Cost
Mean	45.02975255	33.79965442	9.2139474	2.120300752	1.082706767	89.85827145
Standard Error	0.705769554	1.152810723	0.342782478	0.069056259	0.039892829	0.559921397
Median	43.75442855	32.48917338	8.948247655	2	1	90.46724522
Mode	49	#N/A	1	3	1	95
Standard Deviation	11.51075308	18.80177391	5.590613026	1.126273495	0.650632352	9.132041622
Sample Variance	132.4974365	353.506702	31.254954	1.268491985	0.423322457	83.39418418
Kurtosis	0.031307707	-1.255923243	-1.219017271	-0.675904939	-0.635503488	0.555925635
Skewness	0.339425495	0.019065124	0.195702678	0.064456196	-0.082617089	-0.143141799
Range	56	63.76007056	18.83411217	5	2	63.13892164
Minimum	21	1.164978062	1	0	0	52.86107836
Maximum	77	64.92504862	19.83411217	5	2	116
Sum	11977.91418	8990.708076	2450.910008	564	288	23902.30021
Count	266	266	266	266	266	266
First Quartile	37.41105795	17.7164396	4.067588443	1	1	83.56048067
Third Quartile	52	50.94207517	13.84755467	3	2	96.34071552
Interquartile Range	14.58894205	33.22563556	9.779966227	2	1	12.78023485
CV	25.56%	55.63%	60.68%	53.12%	60.09%	10.16%

	Commuting Time (minutes)	Hours Worked	Annual Earned Income	Total Annual Income
Mean	36.13163852	37.40878791	46.15825738	49.4676592
Standard Error	1.187797971	0.723252762	1.027240886	1.085540136
Median	40.75386115	39.80193024	49.27415319	52.98579124
Mode	0	0	0	0
Standard Deviation	19.37239865	11.79589557	16.75379184	17.70462382
Sample Variance	375.2898295	139.1431523	280.6895409	313.4537046
Kurtosis	-0.454039967	4.019858826	1.406214288	1.478263003
Skewness	-0.681350273	-1.845682346	-1.132319043	-1.165455659
Range	75.4025378	63.85282643	77.25577829	82.97470766
Minimum	0	0	0	-1.1
Maximum	75.4025378	63.85282643	77.25577829	81.87470766
Sum	9611.015845	9950.737585	12278.09646	13158.39735
Count	266	266	266	266
First Quartile	28.34918331	33.74792776	37.26373866	40.75810124
Third Quartile	49.37348862	44.27061018	58.17911369	62.16256804
Interquartile Range	21.02430531	10.52268242	20.91537503	21.4044668
CV	53.62%	31.53%	36.30%	35.79%

18.14
cont.

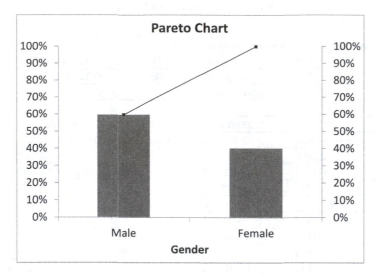

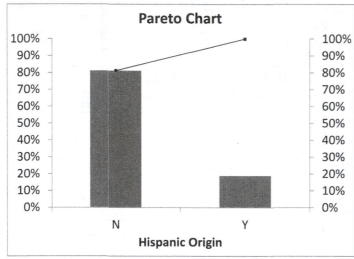

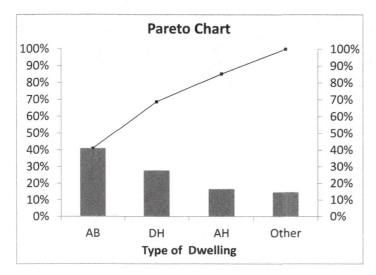

18.14
cont.

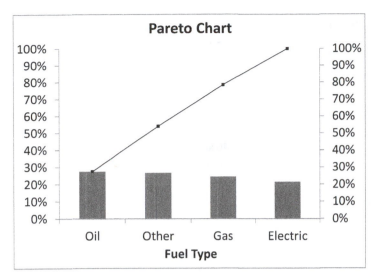

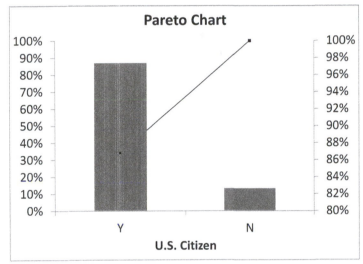

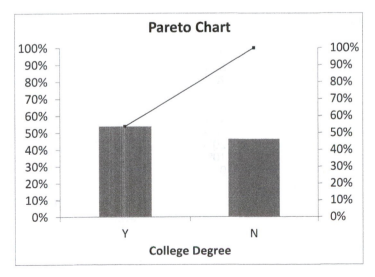

18.14
cont.

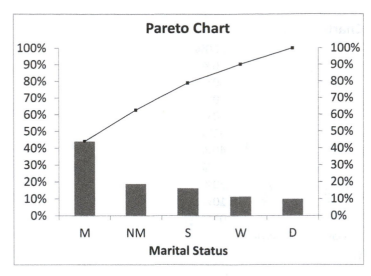

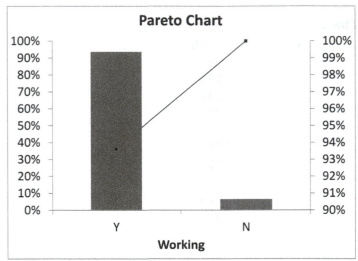

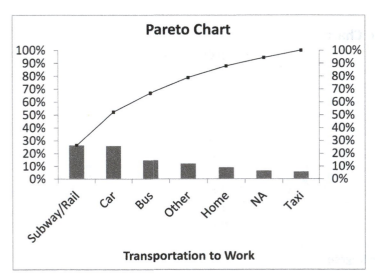

18.14
cont.

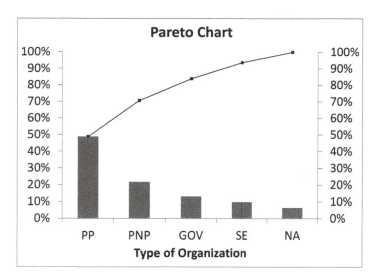

19.2 (a) Proportion of nonconformances largest on Day 4, smallest on Day 3.

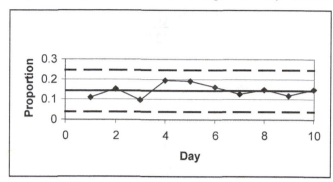

(b) $\bar{n} = 1036/10 = 103.6$, $\bar{p} = 148/1036 = 0.142857$,

$$LCL = \bar{p} - 3\sqrt{\frac{\bar{p}(1-\bar{p})}{\bar{n}}} = 0.142857 - 3\sqrt{\frac{0.142857(1-0.142857)}{103.6}} = 0.039719$$

$$UCL = \bar{p} + 3\sqrt{\frac{\bar{p}(1-\bar{p})}{\bar{n}}} = 0.142857 + 3\sqrt{\frac{0.142857(1-0.142857)}{103.6}} = 0.245995$$

(c) Proportions are within control limits, so there do not appear to be any special causes of variation.

19.4 (a) $n = 500$, $\bar{p} = 761/16000 = 0.0476$

$$LCL = \bar{p} - 3\sqrt{\frac{\bar{p}(1-\bar{p})}{n}} = 0.0476 - 3\sqrt{\frac{0.0476(1-0.0476)}{500}} = 0.0190 > 0$$

$$UCL = \bar{p} + 3\sqrt{\frac{\bar{p}(1-\bar{p})}{n}} = 0.0476 + 3\sqrt{\frac{0.0476(1-0.0476)}{500}} = 0.0761$$

p Chart

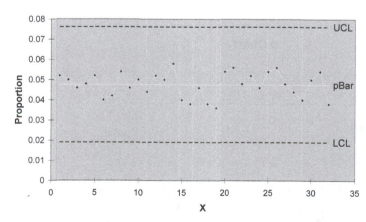

(b) Since the individual points are distributed around $\bar{p}$ without any pattern and all the points are within the control limits, the process is in a state of statistical control.

19.6   (a) $\bar{n} = 113345/22 = 5152.0455$, $\bar{p} = 1460/113345 = 0.01288$,

$$LCL = \bar{p} - 3\sqrt{\frac{\bar{p}(1-\bar{p})}{\bar{n}}} = 0.01288 - 3\sqrt{\frac{0.01288(1-0.01288)}{5152.0455}} = 0.00817$$

$$UCL = \bar{p} + 3\sqrt{\frac{\bar{p}(1-\bar{p})}{\bar{n}}} = 0.01288 + 3\sqrt{\frac{0.01288(1-0.01288)}{5152.0455}} = 0.01759$$

PHStat output:

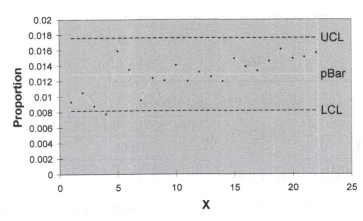

The proportion of unacceptable cans is below the LCL on Day 4. There is evidence of a pattern over time, since the last eight points are all above the mean and most of the earlier points are below the mean. Thus, the special causes that might be contributing to this pattern should be investigated before any change in the system of operation is contemplated.

(b)   Once special causes have been eliminated and the process is stable, Deming's fourteen points should be implemented to improve the system. They might also look at day 4 to see if they could identify and exploit the special cause that led to such a low proportion of defects on that day.

19.8   (a)

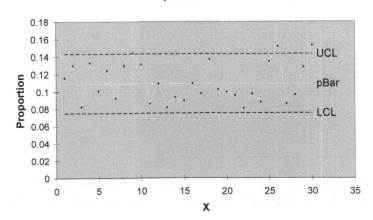

$\bar{p} = 0.1091$, $LCL = 0.0751$, $UCL = 0.1431$. Points 9, 26, and 30 are above the UCL.

19.8   (b)   First, the reasons for the special cause variation would need to be determined and local
cont.   corrective action taken. Once special causes have been eliminated and the process is
               stable, Deming's fourteen points should be implemented to improve the system.

19.10   The results will vary due to individual differences across classes. The original experiment from
        19.9 had 800 red beads in the box. Removal of red 400 beads would reduce the number of red
        beads to half of the original 800 red beads. Individual performances would be expected to be
        much lower than what was observed in 19.9. While one would still expect to observe common
        cause variation across individuals, the overall results would be expected to be lower due to
        special cause variation. A specific event, removal of 400 red beads, would be attributed to the
        improved results.

19.12   (a) $\bar{c} = 115/10 = 11.5,$ $LCL = \bar{c} - 3\sqrt{\bar{c}} = 11.5 - 3\sqrt{11.5} = 1.32651$
               $UCL = \bar{c} + 3\sqrt{\bar{c}} = 11.5 + 3\sqrt{11.5} = 21.67349$

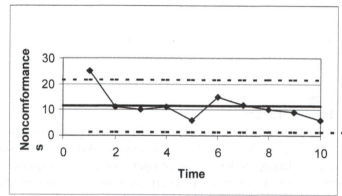

        (b)   Yes, the number of nonconformances per unit for Time Period 1 is above the upper
               control limit.

19.14   (a)   The twelve errors committed by Gina appear to be much higher than all others, and Gina
               would need to explain her performance.

        (b)

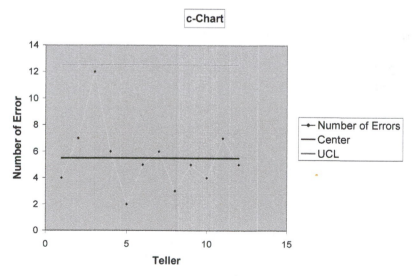

        $\bar{c} = 5.5$, $UCL = 12.56$, LCL does not exist. The number of errors is in a state of statistical
        control since none of the tellers are outside the UCL.

19.14   (c)   Since Gina is within the control limits, she is operating within the system, and should not
cont.   be singled out for further scrutiny.
        (d)   The process needs to be studied and potentially changed using principles of Six Sigma®
                management and/or Deming's 14 points for management.

19.16   (a) $\bar{c} = 3.057$
        (b)

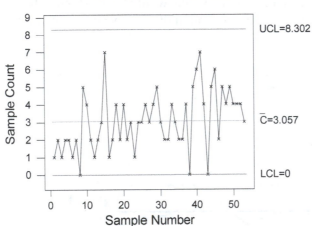

(c)   There is evidence of a pattern over time, since the first eight points are all below the
mean. Thus, the special causes that might be contributing to this pattern should be
investigated before any change in the system of operation is contemplated.

(d)   Even though weeks 15 and 41 experienced seven fire runs each, they are both below the
upper control limit. They can, therefore, be explained by chance causes.

(e)   After having identified the special causes that might have contributed to the first eight
points that are below the average, the fire department can use the c-chart to monitor the
process in future weeks in real-time and identify any potential special causes of variation
that might have arisen and could be attributed to increased arson, severe drought, or
holiday-related activities.

19.18   (a) $d_2 = 2.059$
        (b) $d_3 = 0.88$
        (c) $D_3 = 0$
        (d) $D_4 = 2.282$
        (e) $A_2 = 0.729$

19.20 (a) $\overline{R} = 0.247$, R chart: $UCL = 0.636$; LCL does not exist

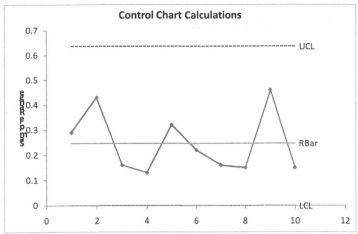

(b) According to the R-charts, the process appears to be in control with all points lying inside the control limits without any pattern and no evidence of special cause variation.

(c) $\overline{\overline{X}} = 47.998$, $\overline{X}$ chart: $UCL = 48.2507$; $LCL = 47.7453$

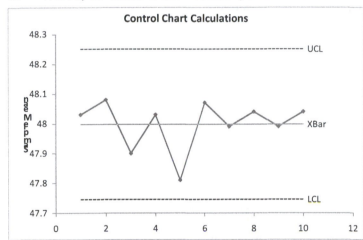

(d) According to the $\overline{X}$-chart, the process appears to be in control with all points lying inside the control limits without any pattern and no evidence of special cause variation.

19.22 (a) $\overline{R} = \dfrac{\displaystyle\sum_{i=1}^{k} R_i}{k} = 3.275$, $\overline{\overline{X}} = \dfrac{\displaystyle\sum_{i=1}^{k} \overline{X}_i}{k} = 5.9413$.

R chart:

$$UCL = D_4\overline{R} = 2.282(3.275) = 7.4736$$

LCL does not exist.

$\overline{X}$ chart:

$$UCL = \overline{\overline{X}} + A_2\overline{R} = 5.9413 + 0.729(3.275) = 8.3287$$

$$LCL = \overline{\overline{X}} - A_2\overline{R} = 5.9413 - 0.729(3.275) = 3.5538$$

19.22   (a)   **PHStat R Chart output:**
cont.

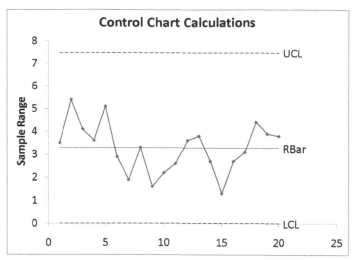

PHStat $\bar{X}$ Chart output:

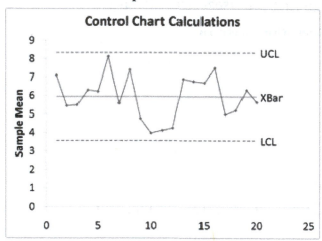

(b)   The process appears to be in control since there are no points outside the control limits and there is no evidence of a pattern in the range chart, and there are no points outside the control limits and there is no evidence of a pattern in the $\bar{X}$ chart.

19.24   (a) $\bar{R} = 0.8794$, R chart: $UCL = 2.0068$; LCL does not exist

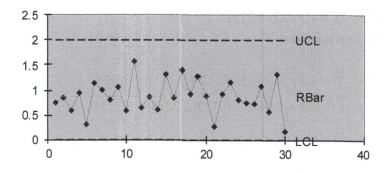

19.24   (b) $\overline{\overline{X}} = 20.1065$, $\overline{X}$ chart: $UCL = 20.7476$; $LCL = 19.4654$
cont.

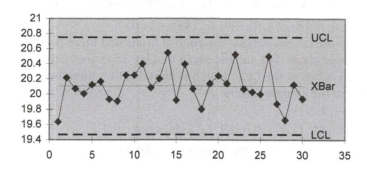

(c)   The process appears to be in control since there are no points outside the lower and upper control limits of either the R-chart and Xbar-chart, and there is no pattern in the results over time.

19.26   (a)

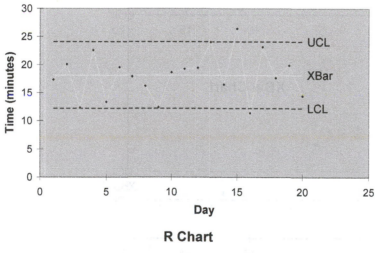

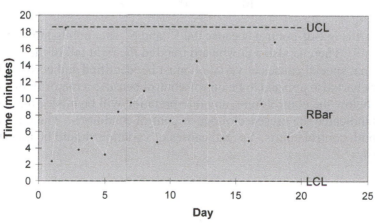

19.26 (a) $\bar{R} = 8.145$, $\bar{\bar{X}} = 18.12$.
cont.   R chart: $LCL = D_3 \bar{R} = 0\,(8.145) = 0$. *LCL* does not exist.
   $UCL = D_4 \bar{R} = (2.282)\,(8.145) = 18.58689$.
   For $\bar{X}$ chart: $LCL = \bar{\bar{X}} - A_2 \bar{R} = 18.12 - (0.729)\,(8.145) = 12.1823$
   $UCL = \bar{\bar{X}} + A_2 \bar{R} = 18.12 + (0.729)\,(8.145) = 24.0577$

   (b)   There are no sample ranges outside the control limits and there does not appear to be a pattern in the range chart. The sample mean on Day 15 is above the *UCL* and the sample mean on Day 16 is below the *LCL*, which is an indication there is evidence of special cause variation in the sample means.

19.28 (a) $\bar{R} = 0.3022$, *R* chart: $UCL = 0.6389$; *LCL* does not exist
   $\bar{\bar{X}} = 90.1317$, $\bar{X}$ chart: $UCL = 90.3060$; $LCL = 89.9573$

R Chart

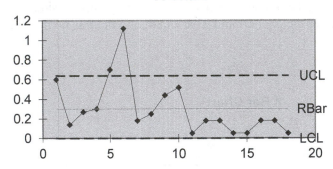

XBar Chart

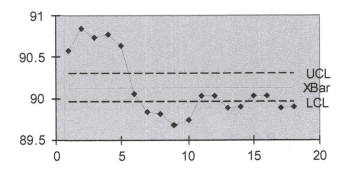

   (b)   The *R*-chart is out-of-control because the 5th and 6th data points fall above the upper control limit. There is also a downward trend in the right tail of the *R*-chart, which signifies that special causes of variation must be identified and corrected. Even though the *X*-bar chart also appears to be out-of-control because a majority of the data point fall above or below the control limit, any interpretation will be misleading because the *R*-chart has indicated the presence of out-of-control conditions. There is also a downward trend in both control charts. Special causes of variation should be investigated and eliminated.

19.30 (a) Estimate of the population mean = $\overline{\overline{X}} = 100$

Estimate of population standard deviation = $\dfrac{\overline{R}}{d_2} = \dfrac{3.386}{1.693} = 2$

$$P(98 < X < 102) = P\left(\dfrac{98-100}{2} < Z < \dfrac{102-100}{2}\right) = 0.6827$$

(b) $P(93 < X < 107.5) = P\left(\dfrac{93-100}{2} < Z < \dfrac{107.5-100}{2}\right) = .9997$

(c) $P(X > 93.8) = P\left(Z > \dfrac{93.8-100}{2}\right) = .9990$

(d) $P(X < 110) = P\left(Z < \dfrac{110-100}{2}\right) \cong 1$

19.32 (a) $P(18 < X < 22) = P\left(\dfrac{18-20.1065}{\dfrac{0.8794}{2.059}} < Z < \dfrac{22-20.1065}{\dfrac{0.8794}{2.059}}\right)$

$= P(-4.932 < Z < 4.4335) = 0.9999$

(b) $C_p = \dfrac{(USL - LSL)}{6\left(\dfrac{\overline{R}}{d_2}\right)} = \dfrac{(22-18)}{6\left(\dfrac{0.8794}{2.059}\right)} = 1.56$

$CPL = \dfrac{\left(\overline{\overline{X}} - LSL\right)}{3\left(\dfrac{\overline{R}}{d_2}\right)} = \dfrac{(20.1065-18)}{3\left(\dfrac{0.8794}{2.059}\right)} = 1.644$

$CPU = \dfrac{\left(USL - \overline{\overline{X}}\right)}{3\left(\dfrac{\overline{R}}{d_2}\right)} = \dfrac{(22-20.1065)}{3\left(\dfrac{0.8794}{2.059}\right)} = 1.4778$

$C_{pk} = \min(CPL, CPU) = 1.4778$

19.34 (a) $P(5.2 < X < 5.8) = P\left(\dfrac{5.2-5.509}{\dfrac{0.2248}{2.059}} < Z < \dfrac{5.8-5.509}{\dfrac{0.2248}{2.059}}\right)$

$= P(-2.830 < Z < 2.665) = 0.9938$

(b) According to the estimate in (a), only 99.38% of the tea bags will have weight fall between 5.2 grams and 5.8 grams. The process is, therefore, incapable of meeting the 99.7% goal.

19.36   Chance or common causes of variation represent the inherent variability that exists in a system. These consist of the numerous small causes of variability that operate randomly or by chance. Special or assignable causes of variation represent large fluctuations or patterns in the data that are not inherent to a process. These fluctuations are often caused by changes in a system that represent either problems to be fixed or opportunities to exploit.

19.38   When only common causes of variation are present, it is up to management to change the system.

19.40   Attribute control charts are used for categorical or discrete data such as the number of nonconformances. Variables control charts are used for numerical variables and are based on statistics such as the mean and standard deviation.

19.42   From the red bead experiment you learned that variation is an inherent part of any process, that workers work within a system over which they have little control, that it is the system that primarily determines their performance, and that only management can change the system.

19.44   If a process has a $C_p = 1.5$ and a $C_{pk} = 0.8$, it indicates that the process has the potential of meeting production specification limits but fails to meet the specification limits in actual performance. The process should be investigated and adjusted to increase either the *CPU* or *CPL* or both.

19.46   (a)   One the main reason that service quality is lower than product quality is because the former involves human interaction which is prone to variation. Also, the most critical aspects of a service are often timeliness and professionalism, and customers can always perceive that the service could be done quicker and with greater professionalism. For products, customers often cannot perceive a better or more ideal product than the one they are getting. For example, a new laptop is better and contains more interesting features than any laptop that he or she has ever imagined.

(b)   Both services and products are the results of processes. However, measuring services is often harder because of the dynamic variation due to the human interaction between the service provider and the customer. Product quality is often a straightforward measurement of a static physical characteristic like the amount of sugar in a can of soda. Categorical data are also more common in service quality.

(c)   Yes.

(d)   Yes.

19.48   (a)

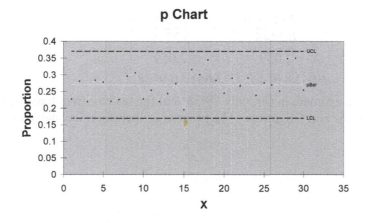

19.48   (b)   Yes, RudyBird's market share is in control before the start of the in-store promotion since
cont.   all sample proportions fall within the control limits.

        (c)

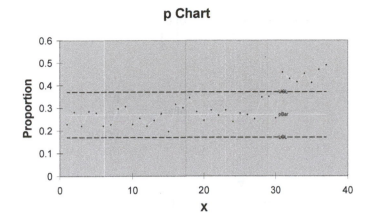

After including the data for days 31-37, there is an apparent upward trend in the p chart
during the promotion period and all the market share proportions in that period are above
the upper control limit. The process became out-of-control. This assignable-cause
variation can be attributed to the in-store promotion. The promotion was successful in
increasing the market share of RudyBird.

19.50   (a)

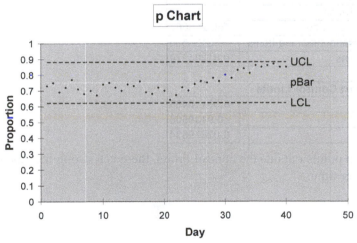

$\bar{p} = 0.75175$, $LCL = 0.62215$, $UCL = 0.88135$. Although none of the points are outside
either the LCL or UCL, there is a clear pattern over time with lower values occurring in
the first half of the sequence and higher values occurring toward the end of the sequence.

        (b)   This would explain the pattern in the results over time.
        (c)   The control chart would have been developed using the first 20 days and then, using
               those limits, the additional proportions could have been plotted.

19.52   (a) $\bar{p} = 0.1198$, $LCL = 0.0205$, $UCL = 0.2191$.
        (b)   The process is out of statistical control. The proportion of trades that are undesirable is
               below the LCL on Day 24 and are above the UCL on Day 4.
        (c)   Special causes of variation should be investigated and eliminated. Next, process
               knowledge should be improved to decrease the proportion of trades that are undesirable.

19.54   Kidney- Shift 1

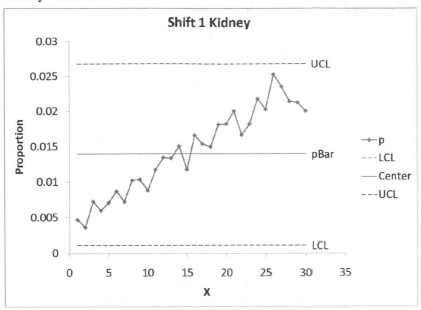

PHStat output:

Shift 1 Kidney	
Intermediate Calculations	
Sum of Subgroup Sizes	22508
Number of Subgroups Taken	30
Average Sample/Subgroup Size	750.266667
Average Proportion of Nonconforming Items	0.0139506
Three Standard Deviations	0.01284574

p Chart Control Limits	
Lower Control Limit	**0.00110486**
Center	**0.0139506**
Upper Control Limit	**0.02679634**

Although there are no points outside the control limits, there is a strong increasing trend in nonconformances over time.

19.54   Kidney- Shift 2
cont.

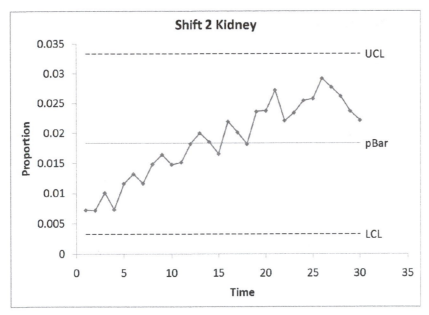

Shift 2 Kidney	
Intermediate Calculations	
Sum of Subgroup Sizes	21486
Number of Subgroups Taken	30
Average Sample/Subgroup Size	716.2
Average Proportion of Nonconforming Items	0.01829098
Three Standard Deviations	0.01502152
Preliminary Lower Control Limit	0.00326946

p Chart Control Limits	
Lower Control Limit	0.00326946
Center	0.01829098
Upper Control Limit	0.0333125

Although there are no points outside the control limits, there is a strong increasing trend in nonconformances over time.

19.54   Shift 1 Shrimp
cont.

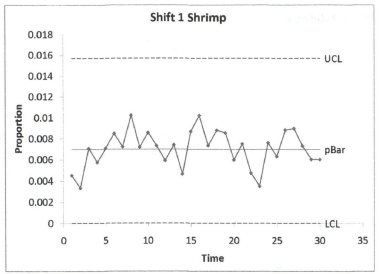

Shift 1 Shrimp	
Intermediate Calculations	
Sum of Subgroup Sizes	24732
Number of Subgroups Taken	30
Average Sample/Subgroup Size	824.4
Average Proportion of Nonconforming Items	0.00699499
Three Standard Deviations	0.00870806
Preliminary Lower Control Limit	-0.00171307

p Chart Control Limits	
Lower Control Limit	**0**
Center	**0.00699499**
Upper Control Limit	**0.01570305**

There are no points outside the control limits and there is no pattern over time.

19.54
cont.

Shift 2 Shrimp

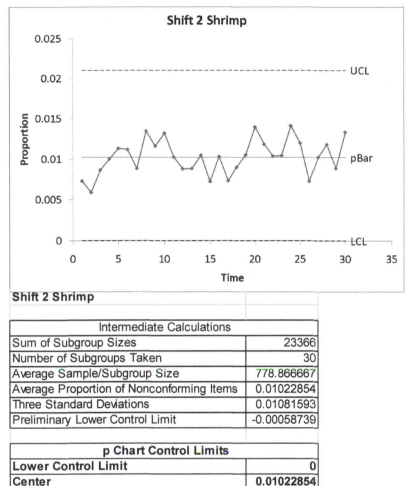

Shift 2 Shrimp

Intermediate Calculations	
Sum of Subgroup Sizes	23366
Number of Subgroups Taken	30
Average Sample/Subgroup Size	778.866667
Average Proportion of Nonconforming Items	0.01022854
Three Standard Deviations	0.01081593
Preliminary Lower Control Limit	-0.00058739

p Chart Control Limits	
Lower Control Limit	0
Center	0.01022854
Upper Control Limit	0.02104447

There are no points outside the control limits and there is no pattern over time.
The team needs to determine the reasons for the increase in nonconformances for the kidney product. The production volume for kidney is clearly decreasing for both shifts. This can be observed from a plot of the production volume over time. The team needs to investigate the reasons for this.

19.56   Results will vary due to individual differences in classes. The proposed class project is a variation of the red bead experiment described in problems 19.9 and 19.10. It would be reasonable to expect to observe an in-control process where variation across individuals would likely be due to common causes of variation. If someone's performance was outside of the system it would be reasonable to consider that the person may not have chosen the numbers according to the specified random process. Paying a bonus to the top 10% of students who had the fewest red balls would likely result in frustration for the rest of the students. The students not receiving the bonus would know that the process itself determines their performance and that they lack control of their results. Paying a bonus to the top 10% of students would likely represent tampering in that an adjustment to the process would be made as a result of misinterpreting common cause variation as special cause variation.

20.2   (a)

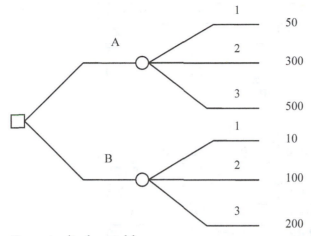

(b)   Opportunity loss table:

Event	Optimum Action	Profit of Optimum Action	Alternative Courses of Action	
			A	B
1	B	50	50 – 50 = 0	50 – 10 = 40
2	A	300	300 – 300 = 0	300 – 100 = 200
3	A	500	500 – 500 = 0	500 – 200 = 300

20.4   (a)–(b) Payoff table:

	Action			
Event	Company A		Company B	
1	$10,000 + $2 · 1,000 =	$12,000	$2,000 + $4 · 1,000 =	$6,000
2	$10,000 + $2 · 2,000 =	$14,000	$2,000 + $4 · 2,000 =	$10,000
3	$10,000 + $2 · 5,000 =	$20,000	$2,000 + $4 · 5,000 =	$22,000
4	$10,000 + $2 · 10,000 =	$30,000	$2,000 + $4 · 10,000 =	$42,000
5	$10,000 + $2 · 50,000 =	$110,000	$2,000 + $4 · 50,000 =	$202,000

(c)

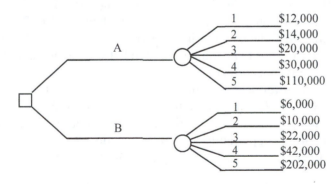

(d)   Opportunity loss table:

Event	Optimum Action	Profit of Optimum Action	Alternative Courses of Action	
			A	B
1	A	12,000	0	6,000
2	A	14,000	0	4,000
3	B	22,000	2,000	0
4	B	42,000	12,000	0
5	B	202,000	92,000	0

20.6   Excel output:

Probabilities & Payoffs Table:					
	P	**A**	**B**	
E1	0.5	50	100	
E2	0.5	200	125	
Max		200	125	
Min		50	100	
Maximax	(a)	200		
maximin			(b)	100

Statistics for:	**A**		**B**	
Expected Monetary Value	(c)	125	(c)	112.5
Variance		5625		156.25
Standard Deviation		75		12.5
Coefficient of Variation		0.6		0.111111
Return to Risk Ratio		1.666667		9

Opportunity Loss Table:					
	Optimum	Optimum		Alternatives	
	Action	Profit		A	B
E1	B	100		50	0
E2	A	200		0	75
				A	**B**
Expected Opportunity Loss				(d) 25	(d) 37.5
				EVPI	

(a)   The optimal action based on the maximax criterion is *Action A*.

(b)   The optimal action based on the maximin criterion is *Action B*.

(c) $EMV_A = 50(0.5) + 200(0.5) = 125$ $EMV_B = 100(0.5) + 125(0.5) = 112.50$

(d) $EOL_A = 50(0.5) + 0(0.5) = 25$ $EOL_B = 0(0.5) + 75(0.5) = 37.50$

(e)   Perfect information would correctly forecast which event, 1 or 2, will occur. The value of perfect information is the increase in the expected value if you knew which of the events 1 or 2 would occur prior to making a decision between actions. It allows us to select the optimum action given a correct forecast.

EMV with perfect information $= 100(0.5) + 200(0.5) = 150$

$EVPI = EMV$ with perfect information $- EMV_A = 150 - 125 = 25$

(f)   Based on (c) and (d) above, select action *A* because it has a higher expected monetary value (a) and a lower opportunity loss (b) than action *B*.

(g) $\sigma_A{}^2 = (50 - 125)^2 (0.5) + (200 - 125)^2 (0.5) = 5625$ $\sigma_A = 75$

$CV_A = \dfrac{75}{125} \cdot 100\% = 60\%$

$\sigma_B{}^2 = (100 - 112.5)^2 (0.5) + (125 - 112.5)^2 (0.5) = 156.25$ $\sigma_B = 12.5$

$CV_B = \dfrac{12.5}{112.5} \cdot 100\% = 11.11\%$

(h)   Return-to-risk ratio for $A = \dfrac{125}{75} = 1.667$

20.6   (h)   Return-to-risk ratio for $B = \dfrac{112.5}{12.5} = 9.0$

cont.   (i)   Based on (g) and (h), select action B because it has a lower coefficient of variation and a higher return-to-risk ratio.

        (j)   The best decision depends on the decision criteria. In this case, expected monetary value leads to a different decision than the return-to-risk ratio.

20.8   (a)   Rate of return $= \dfrac{\$100}{\$1,000} \cdot 100\% = 10\%$

        (b) $CV = \dfrac{\$25}{\$100} \cdot 100\% = 25\%$

        (c)   Return-to-risk ratio $= \dfrac{\$100}{\$25} = 4.0$

20.10   Select stock A because it has a higher expected monetary value while it has the same standard deviation as stock B.

20.12   PHStat output:

Expected Monetary Value				
Probabilities & Payoffs Table:				
	P	**Sell Soft Drinks**	**Sell Ice Cream**	
Cool weather	0.4	50	30	
Warm weather	0.6	60	90	
max		60	90	
min		50	30	
Maximax			90	
Maximin		50		
Statistics for:		**Sell Soft Drinks**	**Sell Ice Cream**	
Expected Monetary Value		56	66	
Variance		24	864	
Standard Deviation		4.898979	29.39388	
Coefficient of Variation		0.087482	0.445362	
Return to Risk Ratio		11.43095	2.245366	

Opportunity Loss Table:				
	Optimum	Optimum	Alternatives	
	Action	Profit	Sell Soft Drinks	Sell Ice Cream
Cool weather	Sell Soft Drinks	50	0	20
Warm weather	Sell Ice Cream	90	30	0
			Sell Soft Drinks	Sell Ice Cream
Expected Opportunity Loss			18	8
				EVPI

        (a)   The optimal action based on the maximax criterion is to sell ice cream.
        (b)   The optimal action based on the maximin criterion is to sell soft drinks.
        (c) EMV(Soft drinks) $= 50(0.4) + 60(0.6) = 56$
               EMV(Ice cream) $= 30(0.4) + 90(0.6) = 66$
        (d) EOL(Soft drinks) $= 0(0.4) + 30(0.6) = 18$
               EOL(Ice cream) $= 20(0.4) + 0(0.6) = 8$

20.12   (e)   *EVPI* is the maximum amount of money the vendor is willing to pay for the information about which event will occur.

cont.   (f)   Based on (c) and (d), choose to sell ice cream because you will earn a higher expected monetary value and incur a lower opportunity loss than choosing to sell soft drinks.

(g) $CV(\text{Soft drinks}) = \dfrac{4.899}{56} \cdot 100\% = 8.748\%$

$CV(\text{Ice cream}) = \dfrac{29.394}{66} \cdot 100\% = 44.536\%$

(h)   Return-to-risk ratio for soft drinks $= \dfrac{56}{4.899} = 11.431$

Return-to-risk ratio for ice cream $= \dfrac{66}{29.394} = 2.245$

(i)   To maximize return and minimize risk, you will choose to sell soft drinks because it has the smaller coefficient of variation and the larger return-to-risk ratio.

(j)   Ignoring the variability of the payoff in (f), you will choose to sell ice cream. However, when risk, which is measured by standard deviation, is taken into consideration as in coefficient of variation or return-to-risk ratio, you will choose to sell soft drinks because it has the lower variability per unit of expected return or the higher expected return per unit of variability.

20.14   PHStat output:

Probabilities & Payoffs Table:					
	P	A	B	C	
Economy declines	0.3	500	-2000	-7000	
No change	0.5	1000	2000	-1000	
Economy expands	0.2	2000	5000	20000	
Max		2000	5000	20000	
Min		500	-2000	-7000	
Maximax				20000	
Maximin		500			

Statistics for:	A	B	C	
Expected Monetary Value	1050	1400	1400	
Variance	272500	6240000	93240000	
Standard Deviation	522.0153	2497.999	9656.086	
Coefficient of Variation	0.497157	1.784285	6.897204	
Return to Risk Ratio	2.011435	0.560449	0.144986	

Opportunity Loss Table:

	Optimum Action	Optimum Profit	Alternatives		
			A	B	C
Economy declines	A	500	0	2500	7500
No change	B	2000	1000	0	3000
Economy expands	C	20000	18000	15000	0
			A	B	C
Expected Opportunity Loss			4100	3750	3750
				EVPI	EVPI

(a)   The optimal action based on the maximax criterion is to choose investment *C*.
(b)   The optimal action based on the maximin criterion is to choose investment *A*.

20.14 **(c)** $EMV_A = 500(0.3) + 1,000(0.5) + 2,000(0.2) = 1,050$
cont. $EMV_B = -2,000(0.3) + 2,000(0.5) + 5,000(0.2) = 1,400$
             $EMV_C = -7,000(0.3) - 1,000(0.5) + 20,000(0.2) = 1,400$

(d)   See the table above.
        $EOL_A = 0(0.3) + 1,000(0.5) + 18,000(0.2) = 4,100$
        $EOL_B = 2,500(0.3) + 0(0.5) + 15,000(0.2) = 3,750$
        $EOL_C = 7,500(0.3) + 3,000(0.5) + 0(0.2) = 3,750$

(e) EMV with perfect information $= 500(0.3) + 2,000(0.5) + 20,000(0.2) = 5,150$
        $EVPI = EMV$ with perfect information $- EMV_{B \, or \, C} = 5,150 - 1,400 = 3,750$
        The investor should not be willing to pay more than \$3,750 for a perfect forecast.

(f)   Action B and C maximize the expected monetary value and have the lower opportunity loss

(g) $\sigma_A^2 = (500 - 1,050)^2 (0.3) + (1,000 - 1,050)^2 (0.5) + (2,000 - 1,050)^2 (0.2)$
          $= 272,500$

        $\sigma_A = 522.02$

        $\sigma_B^2 = (-2,000 - 1,400)^2 (0.3) + (2,000 - 1,400)^2 (0.5) + (5,000 - 1,400)^2 (0.2)$
          $= 6,240,000$

        $\sigma_B = 2,498.00$

        $\sigma_C^2 = (-7,000 - 1,400)^2 (0.3) + (-1,000 - 1,400)^2 (0.5) + (20,000 - 1,400)^2 (0.2)$
          $= 93,240,000$

        $\sigma_C = 9656.09$

        $CV_A = \dfrac{522.02}{1050} \cdot 100\% = 49.72\%$

        $CV_B = \dfrac{2498.00}{1400} \cdot 100\% = 178.43\%$

        $CV_C = \dfrac{9656.09}{1400} \cdot 100\% = 689.72\%$

(h)   Return-to-risk ratio for $A = \dfrac{1050}{522.02} = 2.01$

        Return-to-risk ratio for $B = \dfrac{1400}{2498} = 0.56$

        Return-to-risk ratio for $C = \dfrac{1400}{9656.09} = 0.14$

(i)–(j) Action A minimizes the coefficient of variation and maximizes the investor's return-to-risk.

20.14 (k)
cont.

	(1) 0.1, 0.6, 0.3	(2) 0.1, 0.3, 0.6	(3) 0.4, 0.4, 0.2	(4) 0.6, 0.3, 0.1
(c) Max *EMV*	C: 4,700	C: 11,000	A or B: 800	A: 800
σ Max *EMV*	σ_C : 10,169	σ_C : 11,145	σ_A : 548 σ_B : 2,683	σ_A : 458
(d) Min *EOL* & (e) *EVPI*	C: 2,550	C: 1,650	A: 4,000 or B: 4,000	A: 2,100
(g) Min *CV*	A: 40.99%	A: 36.64%	A: 54.77%	A: 57.28%
(h) Max Return-to-risk	A: 2.4398	A: 2.7294	A: 1.8257	A: 1.7457
(i) Choice on (g), (h)	Choose *A*	Choose *A*	Choose *A*	Choose *A*
(j) Compare (c) and (i)	Different: (c) *C* (j) *A*	Different: (c) *C* (j) *A*	Different: (c) *A* or *B* (j) *A*	Same: *A*

20.16 PHStat output:

Probabilities & Payoffs Table:

	P	A	B	
Demand 1000	0.45	12000	6000	
Demand 2000	0.2	14000	10000	
Demand 5000	0.15	20000	22000	
Demand 10000	0.1	30000	42000	
Demand 50000	0.1	110000	202000	
Max		110000	202000	
Min		14000	10000	
Maximax			202000	
Maximin		14000		

Statistics for:	A	B	
Expected Monetary Value	25200	32400	
Variance	8.29E+08	3.32E+09	
Standard Deviation	28791.67	57583.33	
Coefficient of Variation	1.142526	1.777263	
Return to Risk Ratio	0.875253	0.562663	

Opportunity Loss Table:

	Optimum Action	Optimum Profit	Alternatives A	B	
Demand 1000	A	12000	0	6000	
Demand 2000	A	14000	0	4000	
Demand 5000	B	22000	2000	0	
Demand 10000	B	42000	12000	0	
Demand 50000	B	202000	92000	0	
			A	B	
Expected Opportunity Loss			10700	3500	
				EVPI	

(a) The optimal action based on the maximax criterion is to sign with company *B*.
(b) The optimal action based on the maximin criterion is to sign with company *A*.
(c) $EMV_A = 12,000(0.45) + 14,000(0.2) + 20,000(0.15) + 30,000(0.1)$
$+ 110,000(0.1) = 25,200$

20.16 (c)
cont.

$EMV_B = 6,000(0.45) + 10,000(0.2) + 22,000(0.15) + 42,000(0.1)$
$\qquad + 202,000(0.1) = 32,400$

(d) $EOL_A = 0(0.45) + 0(0.2) + 2,000(0.15) + 12,000(0.1) + 92,000(0.1) = 10,700$
$\qquad EOL_B = 6,000(0.45) + 4,000(0.2) + 0(0.15) + 0(0.1) + 0(0.1) = 3,500$

(e) EMV with perfect information $= 12,000(0.45) + 14,000(0.2) + 22,000(0.15)$
$\qquad + 42,000(0.1) + 202,000(0.1) = 35,900$

$EVPI = EMV,$ perfect information $- EMV_B = 35,900 - 32,400 = 3,500$

The author should not be willing to pay more than \$3,500 for a perfect forecast.

(f)   Sign with company B to maximize the expected monetary value (\$32,400) and minimize the expected opportunity loss (\$3,500).

(g) $CV_A = \dfrac{28,792}{25,200} \cdot 100\% = 114.25\% \qquad CV_B = \dfrac{57,583}{32,400} \cdot 100\% = 177.73\%$

(h)   Return-to-risk ratio for $A = \dfrac{25,200}{28,792} = 0.8752$

Return-to-risk ratio for $B = \dfrac{32,400}{57,583} = 0.5627$

(i)   Signing with company A will minimize the author's risk and yield the higher return-to-risk.

(j)   Company B has a higher EMV than A, but choosing company B also entails more risk and has a lower return-to-risk ratio than A.

(k)   (c)-(j) See the table below.

Probabilities & Payoffs Table:				
	P	A	B	
Demand 1000	0.3	12000	6000	
Demand 2000	0.2	14000	10000	
Demand 5000	0.2	20000	22000	
Demand 10000	0.1	30000	42000	
Demand 50000	0.2	110000	202000	
Max		110000	202000	
Min		14000	10000	
Maximax			202000	
Maximin		14000		
Statistics for:		A	B	
Expected Monetary Value		35400	52800	
Variance		1.42E+09	5.68E+09	
Standard Deviation		37672.8	75345.6	
Coefficient of Variation		1.064203	1.427	
Return to Risk Ratio		0.93967	0.700771	

Opportunity Loss Table:				
	Optimum	Optimum	Alternatives	
	Action	Profit	A	B
Demand 1000	A	12000	0	6000
Demand 2000	A	14000	0	4000
Demand 5000	B	22000	2000	0
Demand 10000	B	42000	12000	0
Demand 50000	B	202000	92000	0
			A	B
Expected Opportunity Loss			20000	2600
				EVPI

The author's decision is not affected by the changed probabilities.

20.18   (a) $P(E_1 | F) = \dfrac{P(F|E_1) \cdot P(E_1)}{P(F|E_1) \cdot P(E_1) + P(F|E_2) \cdot P(E_2)} = \dfrac{0.6(0.5)}{0.6(0.5) + 0.4(0.5)} = 0.6$

   $P(E_2 | F) = 1 - P(E_1 | F) = 1 - 0.6 = 0.4$

(b) $EMV_A = (0.6)(50) + (0.4)(200) = 110$
   $EMV_B = (0.6)(100) + (0.4)(125) = 110$

(c) $EOL_A = (0.6)(50) + (0.4)(0) = 30$
   $EOL_B = (0.6)(0) + (0.4)(75) = 30$

(d) $EVPI = (0.6)(100) + (0.4)(200) = 30$
   You should not be willing to pay more than \$30 for a perfect forecast.

(e)   Both have the same *EMV* and the same *EOL*.

(f) $\sigma_A^2 = (0.6)(-60)^2 + (0.4)(90)^2 = 5400$ $\sigma_A = 73.4847$

   $\sigma_B^2 = (0.6)(-10)^2 + (0.4)(15)^2 = 150$ $\sigma_B = 12.2474$

   $CV_A = \dfrac{73.4847}{110} \cdot 100\% = 66.8\%$ $CV_B = \dfrac{12.2474}{110} \cdot 100\% = 11.1\%$

(g)   Return-to-risk ratio for $A = \dfrac{110}{73.4847} = 1.497$

   Return-to-risk ratio for $B = \dfrac{110}{12.2474} = 8.981$

(h)   Action *B* has a better return-to-risk ratio.

(i)   Both have the same *EMV*, but action *B* has a better return-to-risk ratio.

20.20   (a) $P(\text{forecast cool} \mid \text{cool weather}) = 0.80$
   $P(\text{forecast warm} \mid \text{warm weather}) = 0.70$

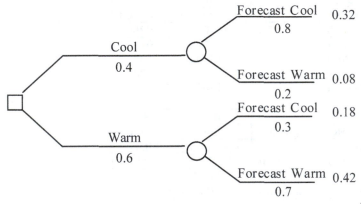

	Forecast Cool	Forecast Warm	Totals
Cool	0.32	0.08	0.4
Warm	0.18	0.42	0.6
Totals	0.5	0.5	

Revised probabilities: $P(\text{cool} \mid \text{forecast cool}) = \dfrac{0.32}{0.5} = 0.64$

   $P(\text{warm} \mid \text{forecast cool}) = \dfrac{0.18}{0.5} = 0.36$

20.20   (a)
cont.

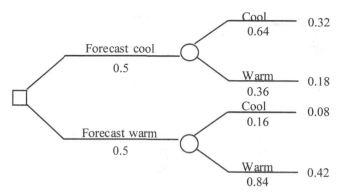

(b)   *EMV*(Soft drinks) = 50(0.64) + 60(0.36) = 53.6
EMV(Ice cream) = 30(0.64) + 90(0.36) = 51.6
EOL(Soft drinks) = 0(0.64) + 30(0.36) = 10.8
EOL(Ice cream) = 20(0.64) + 0(0.36) = 12.8
EMV with perfect information = 50(0.64) + 90(0.36) = 64.4
EVPI = *EMV,* perfect information – *EMV$_A$* = 64.4 – 53.6 = 10.8
The vendor should not be willing to pay more than \$10.80 for a perfect forecast of the weather.
The vendor should sell soft drinks to maximize value and minimize loss.

$$CV(\text{Soft drinks}) = \frac{4.8}{53.6} \cdot 100\% = 8.96\%$$

$$CV(\text{Ice cream}) = \frac{28.8}{51.6} \cdot 100\% = 55.81\%$$

$$\text{Return-to-risk ratio for soft drinks} = \frac{53.6}{4.8} = 11.1667$$

$$\text{Return-to-risk ratio for ice cream} = \frac{51.6}{28.8} = 1.7917$$

Based on these revised probabilities, the vendor's decision changes because of the increased likelihood of cool weather given a forecast for cool. Under these conditions, she should sell soft drinks to maximize the expected monetary value and also to minimize her expected opportunity loss, as well as minimizing risk and maximizing return.

20.22   (a)   *P*(favorable | 1,000) = 0.01   *P*(favorable | 2,000) = 0.01
P(favorable | 5,000) = 0.25   *P*(favorable | 10,000) = 0.60
P(favorable | 50,000) = 0.99

P(favorable *and* 1,000)   = 0.01(0.45) = 0.0045
P(favorable *and* 2,000)   = 0.01(0.20) = 0.0020
P(favorable *and* 5,000)   = 0.25(0.15) = 0.0375
P(favorable *and* 10,000) = 0.60(0.10) = 0.0600
P(favorable *and* 50,000) = 0.99(0.10) = 0.0990

20.22 (a) Joint probability table:
cont.

	Favorable	Unfavorable	Totals
1,000	0.0045	0.4455	0.45
2,000	0.0020	0.1980	0.20
5,000	0.0375	0.1125	0.15
10,000	0.0600	0.0400	0.10
50,000	0.0990	0.0010	0.10
Totals	0.2030	0.7970	

Given an unfavorable review, the revised conditional probabilities are:

$P(1,000 \mid \text{unfavorable}) = 0.4455/0.7970 = 0.5590$

$P(2,000 \mid \text{unfavorable}) = 0.1980/0.7970 = 0.2484$

$P(5,000 \mid \text{unfavorable}) = 0.1125/0.7970 = 0.1412$

$P(10,000 \mid \text{unfavorable}) = 0.0400/0.7970 = 0.0502$

$P(50,000 \mid \text{unfavorable}) = 0.0010/0.7970 = 0.0013$

(b) Payoff table, given unfavorable review:

	Pr	A	B
1,000	0.5590	12,000	6,000
2,000	0.2484	14,000	10,000
5,000	0.1412	20,000	22,000
10,000	0.0502	30,000	42,000
50,000	0.0013	110,000	202,000
	EMV	14,658.60	11,315.4
	σ^2	31,719,333.50	126877326.67
	σ	5,631.99	11263.98
	CV	38.42%	99.55%
	Return-to-risk	2.6027	1.0046

Opportunity loss table:

	Pr	A	B
Event 1	0.5590	0	6,000
Event 2	0.2484	0	4,000
Event 3	0.1412	2,000	0
Event 4	0.0502	12,000	0
Event 5	0.0013	92,000	0
	EOL	1,004.40	4,347.60

(c) The author's decision is affected by the changed probabilities. Under the new circumstances, signing with company A maximizes the expected monetary value ($14,658.60), minimizes the expected opportunity loss ($1,004.40), minimizes risk with a smaller coefficient of variation and yields a higher return-to-risk than choosing company B.

20.24 The expected monetary value does not take into consideration the variability of payoffs for various alternative courses of actions across different events. An expected monetary value (EMV) approach may not be appropriate when the EMV associated with an action is high but the return-to-risk ratio (RTTR) is low. Problems 20.3, 20.4, and 20.5 do not include calculations for the EMV because the probability associated with the various events are not provided. However, the EMV approach may not be appropriate given that there is considerable variation in payoff across the different events for each of these problems.

20.24
cont.
For 20.12, the action with the highest EMV has a much lower RTTR. The EMV approach may not be appropriate in this case. For 20.13, the action with the highest EMV also has the highest RTTR. In this case, the EMV or risk-neutral approach would be appropriate. Problem 20.13 has a second part where the calculations were based on a different cost for the product (clams) was changed. In this case, two of the actions had the same EMV, which was higher than a third action. One of the two actions with the same EMV had the highest RTTR. The EMV approach would be appropriate for this action. However, the EMV would not be appropriate for the action with the same EMV but lower RTTR. Problem 20.13 has a third part where the calculations were based on different probabilities for the occurrence of the various events. The action with the highest EMV also had the highest RTTR. It would be appropriate to utilize the EMV approach for this action.

For 20.14, two of the actions had the same EMV, which was higher than a third action. Both of these actions had lower RTTRs compared the action that had a lower EMV. The EMV approach may not be appropriate in this case. Problem 20.14 includes four different sets of calculations of EMVs and RTTRs based on various probability of event scenarios. The appropriateness of using the EMV approach is discussed for each scenario.

Scenario 1: 0.1, 0.6, and 0.3. The action with the highest EMV had a lower RTTR than an action with a lower EMV. It may not be appropriate to utilize an EMV approach in this case.

Scenario 2: 0.1, 0.3, and 0.6. The action with the highest EMV had a lower RTTR than an action with a lower EMV. It may not be appropriate to utilize an EMV approach in this case.

Scenario 3: 0.4, 0.4, and 0.2. Two actions had the same EMV, which was higher than the EMV of a third action. One of the two action with the higher EMV had the highest RTTR. It would be appropriate to utilize the EMV approach for this action. The other action with the same EMV had a lower RTTR. It may not be appropriate to utilize the EMV approach for this action.

Scenario 4: 0.6, 0.3, and 0.1. The action with the highest EMV had the highest RTTR. It would be appropriate to utilize the EMV approach for this action.

20.26
A payoff table presents the alternatives in a tabular format, while the decision tree organizes the alternatives and events visually.

20.28
Since it is the difference between the *highest* possible profit for an event and the actual profit obtained for an action taken. It can never be negative.

20.30
The expected value of perfect information represents the maximum amount you would pay to obtain perfect information. It represents the alternative course of action with the smallest expected opportunity loss. It is also equal to the expected profit under certainty minus the expected monetary value of the best alternative course of action.

20.32
Expected monetary value measures the mean return or profit of an alternative course of action over the long run without regard for the variability in the payoffs under different events. The return-to-risk ratio considers the variability in the payoffs in evaluating which alternative course of action should be chosen.

20.34
A risk averter attempts to reduce risk, while a risk seeker looks for increased return usually associated with greater risk.

20.36 (a) For the payoff table, each sell event was multiplied by the $2.99 supermarket price and excess loafs were multiplied by the $1 thrift shop price. The $1.50 purchase price was used to determine the cost of each course of action.

Event	Alternative Course of Action			
	A = Buy 6,000	B = Buy 8,000	C = Buy 10,000	D = Buy 12,000
Sell 6,000	8,940	7,940	6,940	5,940
Sell 8,000	8,940	11,920	10,920	9,920
Sell 10,000	8,940	11,920	14,900	13,900
Sell 12,000	8,940	11,920	14,900	17,880

(b)

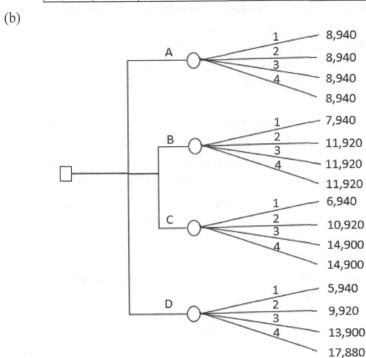

Event 1 = sell 6,000 loafs, event 2 = sell 8,000 loafs, event 3 = sell 10,000 loafs, and event 4 = sell 12,000 loafs.

(c)

Event	P	Alternative Course of Action			
		A = Buy 6,000	B = Buy 8,000	C = Buy 10,000	D = Buy 12,000
Sell 6,000	0.10	8,940(0.1) = 894	7,940(0.1) = 794	6,940(0.1) = 694	5,940(0.1) = 594
Sell 8,000	0.50	8,940(0.5) = 4,470	11,920(0.5) = 5,960	10,920(0.5) = 5,460	9,920(0.5) = 4,960
Sell 10,000	0.30	8,940(0.3) = 2,682	11,920(0.3) = 3,576	14,900(0.3) = 4,470	13900(0.3) = 4,170
Sell 12,000	0.10	8,940(0.1) = 894	11,920(0.1) = 1,192	14,900(0.1) = 1,490	17,880(0.1) = 1,788
		EMV(A)= 8,940	EMV(B)=11,522	EMV(C) = 12,114	EMV(D) = 11,512

(d)

Event	P	Optimum Action	Alternative Course of Action			
			A = Buy 6,000 LP	B = Buy 8,000 LP	C = Buy 10,000 LP	D = Buy 12,000 LP
Sell 6,000	.1	8,940	0	100	200	300
Sell 8,000	.5	11,920	1,490	0	500	1,000
Sell 10,000	.3	14,900	1,788	894	0	300
Sell 12,000	.1	17,880	894	596	298	0
			EOL(A) = 4,172	EOL(B) = 1,590	EOL(C) = 998	EOL(D) = 1,600

12.36   (e) $0.1(8,940) + 0.5(11,920) + 0.3(14,900) + 0.1(17,880) = 13,112$.
cont.   The EVPI = 13,112 - 12,114 = 998. The EVPI of 998 represents the maximum amount
                   that one would be willing to pay for certainty.
        (f)   One would choose to buy 10,000 loaves because this action had the highest expected
                   monetary value and lowest expected opportunity loss.
        (g), (h)

Action A: Buy 6,000 loaves

Event	P	Payoff	Payoff - EMV	$(Payoff - EMV)^2$	$(Payoff - EMV)^2(P)$
Sell 6,000	0.1	8,940	0	0	0
Sell 8,000	0.5	8,940	0	0	0
Sell 10,000	0.3	8,940	0	0	0
Sell 12,000	0.1	8,940	0	0	0
					0
EMV(A)				SD_A	0
8,940				CV_A	0
				RTTR(A)	#DIV/0!

Action B: Buy 8,000 loaves

Event	P	Payoff	Payoff - EMV	$(Payoff - EMV)^2$	$(Payoff - EMV)^2(P)$
Sell 6,000	0.1	7,940.0000	-3,582.0000	12,830,724.0000	1,283,072.4000
Sell 8,000	0.5	11,920.0000	398.0000	158,404.0000	79,202.0000
Sell 10,000	0.3	11,920.0000	398.0000	158,404.0000	47,521.2000
Sell 12,000	0.1	11,920.0000	398.0000	158,404.0000	15,840.4000
					1,425,636.0000
EMV(B)				SD_B	1,194.0000
11,522				CV_B	10.3628
				RTTR(B)	9.6499

Action C: Buy 10,000 loaves

Event	P	Payoff	Payoff - EMV	$(Payoff - EMV)^2$	$(Payoff - EMV)^2(P)$
Sell 6,000	0.1	6,940.0000	-5,174.0000	26,770,276.0000	2,677,027.6000
Sell 8,000	0.5	10,920.0000	-1,194.0000	1,425,636.0000	712,818.0000
Sell 10,000	0.3	14,900.0000	2,786.0000	7,761,796.0000	2,328,538.8000
Sell 12,000	0.1	14,900.0000	2,786.0000	7,761,796.0000	776,179.6000
					6,494,564.0000
EMV(C)				SD_C	2,548.4434
12,114				CV_C	21.0372
				RTTR(C)	4.7535

12.36 (g), (h)
cont.

Action D: Buy 12,000 loaves

Event	P	Payoff	Payoff - EMV	(Payoff - EMV)^2	(Payoff - EMV)^2(P)
Sell 6,000	0.1	5,940.0000	-5,572.0000	31,047,184.0000	3,104,718.4000
Sell 8,000	0.5	9,920.0000	-1,592.0000	2,534,464.0000	1,267,232.0000
Sell 10,000	0.3	13,900.0000	2,388.0000	5,702,544.0000	1,710,763.2000
Sell 12,000	0.1	17,880.0000	6,368.0000	40,551,424.0000	4,055,142.4000
					10,137,856.0000
EMV(D)				SD$_D$	3,184.0000
11,512				CV$_D$	27.6581
				RTTR(D)	3.6156

(i)   Because there was no variation in the payoff for the 6,000 loafs action, CV=0. This would be the best option if one did not want to take any risk. If one was willing to take some risk, the 8,000 loafs purchase represents the best option because it had the lowest coefficient of variation and the highest RTTR among the three actions that involved some risk.

(j)   The conclusion reached in (f) was to purchase 10,000 loaves. The conclusion reached in (i) was to choose the 6,000 loafs action if one did not want to take any risk. If one was willing to take some risk, the best option was to purchase 8,000 loafs.

(k-c)

		Alternative Course of Action			
Event	P	A = Buy 6,000	B = Buy 8,000	C = Buy 10,000	D = Buy 12,000
1	0.30	8,940(0.3) = 2,682	7,940(0.3) = 2,382	6,940(0.3) = 2,082	5,940(0.3) = 1,782
2	0.40	8,940(0.4) = 3,676	11,920(0.4) = 4,768	10,920(0.4) = 4,368	9,920(0.4) = 3,968
3	0.20	8,940(0.2) = 1,788	11,920(0.2) = 2,384	1,4900(0.2) = 2,980	13,900(0.2) = 2,780
4	0.10	8,940(0.1) = 894	11,920(0.1) = 1,192	1,4900(0.1) = 1,490	17,880(0.1) = 1,788
		EMV(A) = 8,940	EMV(B) = 10,726	EMV(C) = 10,920	EMV(D) = 10,318

Event 1 = sell 6,000 loafs, event 2 = sell 8,000 loafs, event 3 = sell 10,000 loafs, and event 4 = sell 12,000 loafs.

(k-d)

			Alternative Course of Action			
Event	P	Optimum Action	A = Buy 6,000 LP	B = Buy 8,000 LP	C = Buy 10,000 LP	D = Buy 12,000 LP
1	0.3	8,940	0(0.3) = 0	1,000(0.3) = 300	2,000(.3) = 600	3,000(0.3) = 900
2	0.4	11,920	2,980(0.4) = 1,192	0(0.4) = 0	1,000(0.4) = 400	2,000(0.4) = 800
3	0.2	14,900	5,960(0.2) = 1,192	2,980(0.2) = 596	0(0.2) = 0	1,000(0.2) = 200
4	0.1	17,880	8,940(0.1) = 894	5,960(0.1) = 596	2,980(0.1) = 298	0(0.1) = 0
			EOL(A) = 3,278	EOL(B) = 1,492	EOL(C) = 1,298	EOL(D) = 1,900

Event 1 = sell 6,000 loafs, event 2 = sell 8,000 loafs, event 3 = sell 10,000 loafs, and event 4 = sell 12,000 loafs.

(k-e)   0.3(8,940) + 0.4(11,920) + 0.2(14,900) + 0.1(17,880) = 12,218. The EVPI = 12,218 – 10,920 = 1,298. The EVPI of 1,298 represents the maximum amount that one would be willing to pay for certainty.

(k-f)   One would choose to buy 10,000 loaves because this action had the highest expected monetary value and lowest expected opportunity loss.

12.36   (k-g,h)
cont.

Action A: Buy 6,000 loaves

Event	P	Payoff	Payoff - EMV	(Payoff - EMV)^2	(Payoff - EMV)^2(P)
Sell 6,000	0.3	8,940	0	0	0
Sell 8,000	0.4	8,940	0	0	0
Sell 10,000	0.2	8,940	0	0	0
Sell 12,000	0.1	8,940	0	0	0
					0
EMV(A)				SD$_A$	0
8,940				CV$_A$	0
				RTTR(A)	#DIV/0!

Action B: Buy 8,000 loaves

Event	P	Payoff	Payoff - EMV	(Payoff - EMV)^2	(Payoff - EMV)^2(P)
Sell 6,000	0.3	7,940.0000	-2,786.0000	7,761,796.0000	2,328,538.8000
Sell 8,000	0.4	11,920.0000	1,194.0000	1,425,636.0000	570,254.4000
Sell 10,000	0.2	11,920.0000	1,194.0000	1,425,636.0000	285,127.2000
Sell 12,000	0.1	11,920.0000	1,194.0000	1,425,636.0000	142,563.6000
					3,326,484.0000
EMV(B)				SD$_B$	1,823.8651
10,726				CV$_B$	17.0041
				RTTR(B)	5.8809

Action C: Buy 10,000 loaves

Event	P	Payoff	Payoff - EMV	(Payoff - EMV)^2	(Payoff - EMV)^2(P)
Sell 6,000	0.3	6,940.0000	-3,980.0000	15,840,400.0000	4,752,120.0000
Sell 8,000	0.4	10,920.0000	0.0000	0.0000	0.0000
Sell 10,000	0.2	14,900.0000	3,980.0000	15,840,400.0000	3,168,080.0000
Sell 12,000	0.1	14,900.0000	3,980.0000	15,840,400.0000	1,584,040.0000
					9,504,240.0000
EMV(C)				SD$_C$	3,082.8947
10,920				CV$_C$	28.2316
				RTTR(C)	3.5421

Action D: Buy 12,000 loaves

Event	P	Payoff	Payoff - EMV	(Payoff - EMV)^2	(Payoff - EMV)^2(P)
Sell 6,000	0.3	5,940.0000	-4,378.0000	19,166,884.0000	5,750,065.2000
Sell 8,000	0.4	9,920.0000	-398.0000	158,404.0000	63,361.6000
Sell 10,000	0.2	13,900.0000	3,582.0000	12,830,724.0000	2,566,144.8000
Sell 12,000	0.1	17,880.0000	7,562.0000	57,183,844.0000	5,718,384.4000
					14,097,956.0000
EMV(D)				SD$_D$	3,754.7245
10,318				CV$_D$	36.3900
				RTTR(D)	2.7480

12.36   (k-i)   Because there was no variation in the payoff for the 6,000 loafs action, CV = 0.
cont.   This would be the best option if one did not want to take any risk. If one was willing to take some risk, the 8,000 loafs purchase would be the best action among the three actions that had some risk. The 8,000 loafs purchase had the lowest CV and the highest RTTR.

   (k-j)   The 10,000 loafs purchase was the best option in (k-f)) If one did not want to take any risk, the 6,000 loaf purchase was the best option in (k-i). If one was willing to take some risk, the 8,000 loaf purchase was the best option.

20.38   (a)

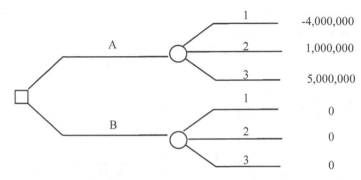

(c), (f) Payoff table:

Event		Pr	New	Old
1	Weak	0.3	− 4,000,000	0
2	Moderate	0.6	1,000,000	0
3	Strong	0.1	5,000,000	0
		EMV	− 100,000	0
		σ	2,808,914	0
		CV	− 2,808.94%	undefined
		Return-to-risk	− 0.0356	undefined

(b), (d), (e) Opportunity loss table:

	Pr	New	Old
Weak	0.3	4,000,000	0
Moderate	0.6	0	1,000,000
Strong	0.1	0	5,000,000
	EOL	1,200,000	1,100,000

EVPI = $1,100,000. The product manager should not be willing to pay more than $1,100,000 for a perfect forecast.

   (g)   The product manager should continue to use the old packaging to maximize expected monetary value and to minimize expected opportunity loss and risk.

20.38   (h)
cont.

(c), (f) Payoff table:

	Pr	New	Old
Weak	0.6	– 4,000,000	0
Moderate	0.3	1,000,000	0
Strong	0.1	5,000,000	0
	EMV	– 1,600,000	0
	σ	3,136,877	0
	CV	– 196.05%	undefined
	Return-to-risk	– 0.5101	undefined

(b), (d), (e) Opportunity loss table:

	Pr	New	Old
Weak	0.6	4,000,000	0
Moderate	0.3	0	1,000,000
Strong	0.1	0	5,000,000
	EOL	2,400,000	800,000

$EVPI = \$800,000$. The product manager should not be willing to pay more than $800,000 for a perfect forecast.

(g) The product manager should continue to use the old packaging to maximize expected monetary value and to minimize expected opportunity loss and risk.

(i)   (c), (f) Payoff table:

	Pr	New	Old
Weak	0.1	– 4,000,000	0
Moderate	0.3	1,000,000	0
Strong	0.6	5,000,000	0
	EMV	2,900,000	0
	σ	2,913,760.457	0
	CV	100.47%	undefined
	Return-to-risk	0.9953	undefined

(b), (d), (e) Opportunity loss table:

	Pr	New	Old
Weak	0.1	4,000,000	0
Moderate	0.3	0	1,000,000
Strong	0.6	0	5,000,000
	EOL	400,000	3,300,000

$EVPI = \$400,000$. The product manager should not be willing to pay more than $400,000 for a perfect forecast.

(g) The product manager should use the new packaging to maximize expected monetary value and to minimize expected opportunity loss.

(j) $P(\text{Sales decreased} \mid \text{weak response}) = 0.6$
$P(\text{Sales stayed same} \mid \text{weak response}) = 0.3$
$P(\text{Sales increased} \mid \text{weak response}) = 0.1$
$P(\text{Sales decreased} \mid \text{moderate response}) = 0.2$
$P(\text{Sales stayed same} \mid \text{moderate response}) = 0.4$
$P(\text{Sales increased} \mid \text{moderate response}) = 0.4$
$P(\text{Sales decreased} \mid \text{strong response}) = 0.05$
$P(\text{Sales stayed same} \mid \text{strong response}) = 0.35$
$P(\text{Sales increased} \mid \text{strong response}) = 0.6$

20.38 (j)
cont.

P(Sales decreased *and* weak response) $= 0.6(0.3) = 0.18$
P(Sales stayed same *and* weak response) $= 0.3(0.3) = 0.09$
P(Sales increased *and* weak response) $= 0.1(0.3) = 0.03$
P(Sales decreased *and* moderate response) $= 0.2(0.6) = 0.12$
P(Sales stayed same *and* moderate response) $= 0.4(0.6) = 0.24$
P(Sales increased *and* moderate response) $= 0.4(0.6) = 0.24$
P(Sales decreased *and* strong response) $= 0.05(0.1) = 0.005$
P(Sales stayed same *and* strong response) $= 0.35(0.1) = 0.035$
P(Sales increased *and* strong response) $= 0.6(0.1) = 0.06$

Joint probability table:

	Pr	Sales Decrease	Sales Stay Same	Sales Increase
Weak	0.3	0.180	0.090	0.030
Moderate	0.6	0.120	0.240	0.240
Strong	0.1	0.005	0.035	0.060
	Total	0.305	0.365	0.330

Given the sales stayed the same, the revised conditional probabilities are:

$$P(\text{weak response} \mid \text{sales stayed same}) = \frac{.09}{.365} = 0.2466$$

$$P(\text{moderate response} \mid \text{sales stayed same}) = \frac{.24}{.365} = 0.6575$$

$$P(\text{strong response} \mid \text{sales stayed same}) = \frac{.035}{.365} = 0.0959$$

(k)   (c), (f) Payoff table:

	Pr	New	Old
Weak	0.2466	− 4,000,000	0
Moderate	0.6575	1,000,000	0
Strong	0.0959	5,000,000	0
	EMV	150,600	0
	σ	2,641,575.219	0
	CV	1,754.03%	undefined
	Return-to-risk	0.0570	undefined

(b), (d), (e) Opportunity loss table:

	Pr	New	Old
Weak	0.2466	4,000,000	0
Moderate	0.6575	0	1,000,000
Strong	0.0959	0	5,000,000
	EOL	986,400	1,137,000

$EVPI = \$986,400$. The product manager should not be willing to pay more than $986,400 for a perfect forecast.

(g) The product manager should use the new packaging to maximize expected monetary value and to minimize expected opportunity loss.

(l)   Given the sales decreased, the revised conditional probabilities are:

$$P(\text{weak response} \mid \text{sales decreased}) = \frac{.18}{.305} = 0.5902$$

$$P(\text{moderate response} \mid \text{sales decreased}) = \frac{.12}{.305} = 0.3934$$

12.38   (l) $P(\text{strong response} \mid \text{sales decreased}) = \dfrac{.005}{.305} = 0.0164$

cont.

(m)   (c), (f) Payoff table:

	Pr	New	Old
Weak	0.5902	– 4,000,000	0
Moderate	0.3934	1,000,000	0
Strong	0.0164	5,000,000	0
EMV		– 1,885,400	0
σ		2,586,864.287	0
CV		– 137.21%	undefined
Return-to-risk		– 0.7288	undefined

(b), (d), (e) Opportunity loss table:

	Pr	New	Old
Weak	0.5902	4,000,000	0
Moderate	0.3934	0	1,000,000
Strong	0.0164	0	5,000,000
EOL		2,360,800	475,400

$EVPI = \$475,400$. The product manager should not be willing to pay more than \$475,400 for a perfect forecast.

(g) The product manager should continue to use the old packaging to maximize expected monetary value and minimize expected opportunity loss.

20.40   (a)

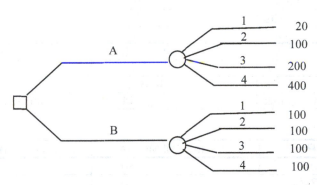

(c), (e), (f) Payoff table:*

Event		Pr	A: Do Not Call Mechanic	B: Call Mechanic
1	Very low	0.25	20	100
2	Low	0.25	100	100
3	Moderate	0.25	200	100
4	High	0.25	400	100
	EMV		180	100
	σ		142	0
	CV		78.96%	0
	Return-to-risk		1.2665	undefined

*Note: The payoff here is cost and not profit. The opportunity cost is therefore calculated as the difference between the payoff and the minimum in the same row.

20.40 (b), (d) Opportunity loss table:
cont.

	Pr	A: Do Not Call Mechanic	B: Call Mechanic
Very low	0.25	80	0
Low	0.25	0	0
Moderate	0.25	0	100
High	0.25	0	300
	EOL	20	100

(e) *EVPI* = $20. The manufacturer should not be willing to pay more than $20 for the information about which event will occur.

(g) We want to minimize the expected monetary value because it is a cost. To minimize the expected monetary value, call the mechanic.

(h) Given 2 defectives out of 15, the binomial probabilities and their related revised conditional probabilities are:

	Pr	Binomial Probabilities	Revised Conditional Probabilities
Very low	0.01	0.0092	0.0092/0.6418 = 0.0143
Low	0.05	0.1348	0.1348/0.6418 = 0.2100
Moderate	0.10	0.2669	0.2669/0.6418 = 0.4159
High	0.20	0.2309	0.2309/0.6418 = 0.3598
		0.6418	

(i) (c), (e), (f) Payoff table:

	Pr	A: Do Not Call Mechanic	B: Call Mechanic
Very low	0.0143	20	100
Low	0.2100	100	100
Moderate	0.4159	200	100
High	0.3598	400	100
	EMV	248.3860	100
	σ	121	0
	CV	48.68%	0
	Return-to-risk	2.0544	undefined

(b), (d) Opportunity loss table:

	Pr	A: Do Not Call Mechanic	B: Call Mechanic
Very low	0.0143	80	0
Low	0.2100	0	0
Moderate	0.4159	0	100
High	0.3598	0	300
	EOL	1.1440	149.53

(e) *EVPI* = $1.14. The manufacturer should not be willing to pay more than $1.14 for the information about which event will occur.

(g) We want to minimize the expected monetary value because it is a cost. To minimize the expected monetary value, call the mechanic.

Chapter 5

5.66 You can use the Poisson distribution to approximate the binomial distribution when n is large and π is very small. The approximation gets better as n gets larger and p gets smaller.

5.68

Poisson Probabilities						
Data						
Mean/Expected number of events of interest:		1				
Poisson Probabilities Table						
	X	P(X)	P(<=X)	P(<X)	P(>X)	P(>=X)
	0	0.3679	0.3679	0.0000	0.6321	1.0000
	1	0.3679	0.7358	0.3679	0.2642	0.6321
	2	0.1839	0.9197	0.7358	0.0803	0.2642

(a) $P(X = 0) = 0.3679$
(b) $P(X = 1) = 0.3679$
(c) $P(X = 2) = 0.1839$
(d) $P(X \le 2) = 0.9197$
(e) $P(X > 2) = 0.0803$

5.70

Binomial Probabilities						
Data						
Sample size	20					
Probability of an event of interest	0.01					
Statistics						
Mean	0.2					
Variance	0.198					
Standard deviation	0.4450					
Binomial Probabilities Table						
	X	P(X)	P(<=X)	P(<X)	P(>X)	P(>=X)
	0.0000	0.8179	0.8179	0.0000	0.1821	1.0000
	1.0000	0.1652	0.9831	0.8179	0.0169	0.1821
	2.0000	0.0159	0.9990	0.9831	0.0010	0.0169

5.70
cont.

$P(X \geq 1) = 0.1821$

Poisson Probabilities						
Data						
Mean/Expected number of events of interest:			0.2			
Poisson Probabilities Table						
	X	P(X)	P(<=X)	P(<X)	P(>X)	P(>=X)
	0	0.8187	0.8187	0.0000	0.1813	1.0000
	1	0.1637	0.9825	0.8187	0.0175	0.1813
	2	0.0164	0.9989	0.9825	0.0011	0.0175

$P(X \geq 1) = 0.1813$

The probability of 0.1813 obtained using a Poisson approximation is quite close to the exact binomial probability of 0.1821.

5.72 Since $n = 10,000$ is large and $\pi = 0.002$ is quite small, you can use the Poisson distribution to approximate the binomial distribution.

Poisson Probabilities						
Data						
Mean/Expected number of events of interest:			20			
Poisson Probabilities Table						
	X	P(X)	P(<=X)	P(<X)	P(>X)	P(>=X)
	0	0.0000	0.0000	0.0000	1.0000	1.0000
	5	0.0001	0.0001	0.0000	0.9999	1.0000
	10	0.0058	0.0108	0.0050	0.9892	0.9950
	20	0.0888	0.5591	0.4703	0.4409	0.5297

(a) $P(X = 0)$ is virtually 0

(b) $P(X \leq 5) = 0.0001$

(c) $P(X \leq 10) = 0.0108$

(d) $P(X \leq 20) = 0.5591$

Chapter 6

6.56 $n = 100, p = 0.40.$ $n\pi = 40 \geq 5$ and $n(1-\pi) = 60 \geq 5$

$\mu = n\pi = 40$ $\sigma = \sqrt{n\pi(1-\pi)} = 4.8990$

(a)

Probability for a Range	
From X Value	39.5
To X Value	40.5
Z Value for 39.5	-0.102062
Z Value for 40.5	0.102062
P(X<=39.5)	0.4594
P(X<=40.5)	0.5406
P(39.5<=X<=40.5)	0.0813

$P(X = 40) \cong P(39.5 \leq X \leq 40.5) = P(-0.1021 \leq Z \leq 0.1021) = 0.0813$

(b)

Probability for X >	
X Value	40.5
Z Value	0.1020616
P(X>40.5)	0.4594

$P(X > 40) = P(X \geq 41) \cong P(X \geq 40.5) = P(Z \geq 0.1021) = 0.4594$

(c)

Probability for X <=	
X Value	40.5
Z Value	0.1020616
P(X<=40.5)	0.5406461

$P(X \leq 40) \cong P(X \leq 40.5) = P(Z \leq 0.1021) = 0.5406$

(d)

Probability for X <=	
X Value	39.5
Z Value	-0.102062
P(X<=39.5)	0.4593539

$P(X < 40) = P(X \leq 39) \cong P(X \leq 39.5) = P(Z \leq -0.1021) = 0.4594$

6.58 $\pi = \dfrac{1}{3} = 0.3333$, $n = 150$, $n\pi$. $n\pi = 50 > 5$, $n(1-\pi) = 100 > 5$

(a) $P(X \geq 0) = P\left(\dfrac{X - n\pi}{\sqrt{n\pi(1-\pi)}} = \dfrac{59.5 - 150(0.3333)}{\sqrt{150(0.3333)(1-0.3333)}} \right)$

   $= P(Z > 1.6454) = 0.0499$

(b) $P(X = 60) = P(\ 59.5 \leq X_a \leq 60.5) = P(1.6454 \leq Z \leq 1.8187) = 0.0155$

(c) $P(X < 60) = P(\ X_a \leq 59.5) = P(Z \leq 1.6454) = 0.9501$

(d) $P(X = 71) = P(\ 70.5 \leq X_a \leq 71.5) = P(3.5507 \leq Z \leq 3.7239) = 0.0001$

Chapter 7

7.36 $\sqrt{\dfrac{N-n}{N-1}} = \sqrt{\dfrac{400-100}{400-1}} = 0.8671$ $\qquad$ $\sqrt{\dfrac{N-n}{N-1}} = \sqrt{\dfrac{900-200}{900-1}} = 0.8824$

A sample of size 100 selected without replacement from a population a population of size 400 has a greater effect in reducing the standard error.

7.38 $\mu = 1.30$, $\sigma = 0.04$

Since $\dfrac{n}{N} = \dfrac{16}{200} > 0.05$ and the sample is selected without replacement, we need to perform the finite population correction.

$\mu_{\bar{X}} = \mu = 1.3$ $\qquad$ $\sigma_{\bar{X}} = \dfrac{\sigma}{\sqrt{n}}\sqrt{\dfrac{N-n}{N-1}} = 0.0096$

PHstat output:

Common Data	
Mean	1.3
Standard Deviation	0.0096
Probability for a Range	
From X Value	1.31
To X Value	1.33
Z Value for 1.31	1.041667
Z Value for 1.33	3.125
P(X<=1.31)	0.8512
P(X<=1.33)	0.9991
P(1.31<=X<=1.33)	0.1479

$P(1.31 < \bar{X} < 1.33) = P(1.0417 < Z < 3.125) = 0.1479$

7.40 $\pi = .10$

Since $\dfrac{n}{N} = \dfrac{400}{5000} > 0.05$ and the sample is selected without replacement, we need to perform the finite population correction.

$\mu_p = .1$ $\qquad$ $\sigma_p = \sqrt{\dfrac{\pi(1-\pi)}{n}}\sqrt{\dfrac{N-n}{N-1}} = 0.0144$

PHstat output:

Common Data			Probability for a Range	
Mean	0.1		From X Value	0.09
Standard Deviation	0.0144		To X Value	0.1
			Z Value for 0.09	-0.694444
Probability for X <=			Z Value for 0.1	0
X Value	0.08		P(X<=0.09)	0.2437
Z Value	-1.388889		P(X<=0.1)	0.5000
P(X<=0.08)	0.0824333		P(0.09<=X<=0.1)	0.2563

(a) $\quad$ $P(0.09 < p < 0.10) = P(-0.6944 < Z < 0) = 0.2563$

(b) $\quad$ $P(p < .08) = P(Z < -1.3889) = 0.0824$

Chapter 8

8.70 $N \cdot \overline{X} \pm N \cdot t \cdot \dfrac{S}{\sqrt{n}} \sqrt{\dfrac{N-n}{N-1}} = 500 \cdot 25.7 \pm 500 \cdot 2.7969 \cdot \dfrac{7.8}{\sqrt{25}} \cdot \sqrt{\dfrac{500-25}{500-1}}$

$\$10{,}721.53 \leq$ Population Total $\leq \$14{,}978.47$

8.72 (a) $p + Z \cdot \sqrt{\dfrac{p(1-p)}{n}} \sqrt{\dfrac{(N-n)}{(N-1)}} = 0.04 + 1.2816 \cdot \sqrt{\dfrac{0.04(1-0.04)}{300}} \sqrt{\dfrac{(5000-300)}{(5000-1)}}$ $\pi < 0.05406$

  (b) $p + Z \cdot \sqrt{\dfrac{p(1-p)}{n}} \sqrt{\dfrac{(N-n)}{(N-1)}} = 0.04 + 1.645 \cdot \sqrt{\dfrac{0.04(1-0.04)}{300}} \sqrt{\dfrac{(5000-300)}{(5000-1)}}$ $\pi < 0.05804$

  (c) $p + Z \cdot \sqrt{\dfrac{p(1-p)}{n}} \sqrt{\dfrac{(N-n)}{(N-1)}} = 0.04 + 2.3263 \cdot \sqrt{\dfrac{0.04(1-0.04)}{300}} \sqrt{\dfrac{(5000-300)}{(5000-1)}}$ $\pi < 0.06552$

8.74 $N \cdot \overline{X} \pm N \cdot t \cdot \dfrac{S}{\sqrt{n}} \sqrt{\dfrac{N-n}{N-1}} = 3000 \cdot \$261.40 \pm 3000 \cdot 1.8331 \cdot \dfrac{\$138.8046}{\sqrt{10}} \cdot \sqrt{\dfrac{3000-10}{3000-1}}$

$\$543{,}176.96 \leq$ Population Total $\leq \$1{,}025{,}223.04$

8.76 $N \cdot \overline{D} \pm N \cdot t \cdot \dfrac{S_D}{\sqrt{n}} \sqrt{\dfrac{N-n}{N-1}} = 4000 \cdot \$7.45907 \pm 4000 \cdot 2.6092 \cdot \dfrac{\$29.5523}{\sqrt{150}} \cdot \sqrt{\dfrac{4000-150}{4000-1}}$

$\$5{,}126.26 \leq$ Total Difference in the Population $\leq \$54{,}546.28$

Note: The *t*-value of 2.6092 for 99% confidence and d.f. = 149 was derived on Excel.

8.78 (a) $p + Z \cdot \sqrt{\dfrac{p(1-p)}{n}} \sqrt{\dfrac{N-n}{N-1}} = 0.0367 + 1.645 \cdot \sqrt{\dfrac{0.0367(1-0.0367)}{300}} \sqrt{\dfrac{10000-300}{10000-1}}$

$\pi < 0.0542$

  (b) Since the upper bound is higher than the tolerable exception rate of 0.04, the auditor should request a larger sample.

8.80 $\overline{X} \pm t_{n-1} \dfrac{S}{\sqrt{n}} \sqrt{\dfrac{N-n}{N-1}} = 75 \pm 2.0301 \dfrac{24}{\sqrt{36}} \sqrt{\dfrac{200-36}{200-1}}$ $67.63 \leq \mu \leq 82.37$

8.82 (a) $\overline{X} \pm Z \dfrac{\sigma}{\sqrt{n}} \sqrt{\dfrac{N-n}{N-1}} = 350 \pm 1.96 \dfrac{100}{\sqrt{50}} \sqrt{\dfrac{2000-50}{2000-1}}$ $322.6238 \leq \mu \leq 377.3762$

8.82 (b) $n_0 = \dfrac{Z^2 \sigma^2}{e^2} = \dfrac{1.96^2 (100)^2}{20^2} = 96.0364$

$n = \dfrac{n_0 N}{n_0 + (N-1)} = \dfrac{96.0364(2000)}{96.0364 + (2000-1)} = 91.6799$ Use $n = 92$

  (c) (a) $\overline{X} \pm Z \dfrac{\sigma}{\sqrt{n}} \sqrt{\dfrac{N-n}{N-1}} = 350 \pm 1.96 \dfrac{100}{\sqrt{50}} \sqrt{\dfrac{1000-50}{1000-1}}$ $322.9703 \leq \mu \leq 377.0297$

8.82   (c)   (b) $n_0 = \dfrac{Z^2\sigma^2}{e^2} = \dfrac{1.96^2(100)^2}{20^2} = 96.0364$

cont.

$$n = \dfrac{n_0 N}{n_0 + (N-1)} = \dfrac{96.0364(1000)}{96.0364 + (1000-1)} = 87.7015 \qquad \text{Use } n = 88$$

8.84   (a) $p \pm Z\sqrt{\dfrac{p(1-p)}{n}}\sqrt{\dfrac{N-n}{N-1}} = 0.3 \pm 1.6449\sqrt{\dfrac{0.3(1-0.3)}{100}}\sqrt{\dfrac{1000-100}{1000-1}} \qquad 0.2285 \le \pi \le 0.3715$

       (b) $n_0 = \dfrac{Z^2 p(1-p)}{e^2} = \dfrac{1.6449^2(0.3)(1-0.3)}{0.05^2} = 227.2656$

$$n = \dfrac{n_0 N}{n_0 + (N-1)} = \dfrac{227.2656(1000)}{227.2656 + (1000-1)} = 185.3315 \qquad \text{Use } n = 186$$

       (c)   (a) $p \pm Z\sqrt{\dfrac{p(1-p)}{n}}\sqrt{\dfrac{N-n}{N-1}} = 0.3 \pm 1.6449\sqrt{\dfrac{0.3(1-0.3)}{100}}\sqrt{\dfrac{2000-100}{2000-1}}$

$$0.2265 \le \pi \le 0.3735$$

            (b) $n_0 = \dfrac{Z^2 p(1-p)}{e^2} = \dfrac{1.6449^2(0.3)(1-0.3)}{0.05^2} = 227.2656$

$$n = \dfrac{n_0 N}{n_0 + (N-1)} = \dfrac{227.2656(2000)}{227.2656 + (2000-1)} = 204.1676 \qquad \text{Use } n = 205$$

8.86   (a) $\bar{X} \pm Z\dfrac{\sigma}{\sqrt{n}}\sqrt{\dfrac{N-n}{N-1}} = 1.99 \pm 1.96\dfrac{0.05}{\sqrt{100}}\sqrt{\dfrac{2000-100}{2000-1}} \qquad 1.9804 \le \mu \le 2.0000$

       (b) $n_0 = \dfrac{Z^2\sigma^2}{e^2} = \dfrac{1.96^2(0.05)^2}{0.01^2} = 96.0364$

$$n = \dfrac{n_0 N}{n_0 + (N-1)} = \dfrac{96.0364(2000)}{96.0364 + (2000-1)} = 91.6799 \qquad \text{Use } n = 92$$

       (c)   (a) $\bar{X} \pm Z\dfrac{\sigma}{\sqrt{n}}\sqrt{\dfrac{N-n}{N-1}} = 1.99 \pm 1.96\dfrac{0.05}{\sqrt{100}}\sqrt{\dfrac{1000-100}{1000-1}} \qquad 1.9807 \le \mu \le 1.9993$

            (b) $n_0 = \dfrac{Z^2\sigma^2}{e^2} = \dfrac{1.96^2(0.05)^2}{0.01^2} = 96.0364$

$$n = \dfrac{n_0 N}{n_0 + (N-1)} = \dfrac{96.0364(1000)}{96.0364 + (1000-1)} = 87.7015 \qquad \text{Use } n = 88$$

Chapter 9

9.80 $H_0 : \mu \geq 7$, $H_1 : \mu < 7$, $\alpha = 0.05$, $n = 16$, $\sigma = 0.2$

Lower critical value: $Z_L = -1.6449$, $\bar{X}_L = \mu + Z_L \left(\dfrac{\sigma}{\sqrt{n}} \right) = 7 - 1.6449 \left(\dfrac{.2}{\sqrt{16}} \right) = 6.9178$

(a) $Z_{STAT} = \dfrac{\bar{X}_L - \mu_1}{\dfrac{\sigma}{\sqrt{n}}} = \dfrac{6.9178 - 6.9}{\dfrac{.2}{\sqrt{16}}} = 0.3551$

power $= 1 - \beta = P\left(\bar{X} < \bar{X}_L \right) = P\left(Z < 0.3551 \right) = 0.6388$

$\beta = 1 - 0.6388 = 0.3612$

(b) $Z_{STAT} = \dfrac{\bar{X}_L - \mu_1}{\dfrac{\sigma}{\sqrt{n}}} = \dfrac{6.9178 - 6.8}{\dfrac{.2}{\sqrt{16}}} = 2.3551$

power $= 1 - \beta = P\left(\bar{X} < \bar{X}_L \right) = P\left(Z < 2.3551 \right) = 0.9907$

$\beta = 1 - 0.9907 = 0.0093$

9.82 $H_0 : \mu \geq 7$, $H_1 : \mu < 7$, $\alpha = 0.05$, $n = 25$, $\sigma = 0.2$

Lower critical value: $Z_L = -1.6449$, $\bar{X}_L = \mu + Z_L \left(\dfrac{\sigma}{\sqrt{n}} \right) = 7 - 1.6449 \left(\dfrac{.2}{\sqrt{25}} \right) = 6.9342$

(a) $Z_{STAT} = \dfrac{\bar{X}_L - \mu_1}{\dfrac{\sigma}{\sqrt{n}}} = \dfrac{6.9342 - 6.9}{\dfrac{.2}{\sqrt{25}}} = 0.8551$

power $= 1 - \beta = P\left(\bar{X} < \bar{X}_L \right) = P\left(Z < 0.8551 \right) = 0.8038$

$\beta = 1 - 0.8038 = 0.1962$

(b) $Z_{STAT} = \dfrac{\bar{X}_L - \mu_1}{\dfrac{\sigma}{\sqrt{n}}} = \dfrac{6.9342 - 6.8}{\dfrac{.2}{\sqrt{25}}} = 3.3551$

power $= 1 - \beta = P\left(\bar{X} < \bar{X}_L \right) = P\left(Z < 3.3551 \right) = 0.9996$

$\beta = 1 - 0.9996 = 0.0004$

(c)   Holding everything else constant, the larger the sample size, the higher the power of the test will be and the lower the probability of committing a Type II error will be.

9.84 $H_0 : \mu \geq 25{,}000$ vs. $H_1 : \mu < 25{,}000$, $\alpha = 0.01$, $n = 100$, $\sigma = 3500$

Lower critical value: $Z_L = -2.3263$,

$\bar{X}_L = \mu + Z_L \left(\dfrac{\sigma}{\sqrt{n}} \right) = 25{,}000 - 2.3263 \left(\dfrac{3{,}500}{\sqrt{100}} \right) = 24{,}185.7786$

(a) $Z_{STAT} = \dfrac{\bar{X}_L - \mu_1}{\dfrac{\sigma}{\sqrt{n}}} = \dfrac{24{,}185.7786 - 24{,}000}{\dfrac{3500}{\sqrt{100}}} = 0.5308$

9.84   (a)   power $= 1-\beta = P\left(\bar{X} < \bar{X}_L\right) = P\left(Z < 0.5308\right) = 0.7022$

cont. $\beta = 1 - 0.7022 = 0.2978$

          (b) $Z_{STAT} = \dfrac{\bar{X}_L - \mu_1}{\dfrac{\sigma}{\sqrt{n}}} = \dfrac{24{,}185.7786 - 24{,}900}{\dfrac{3500}{\sqrt{100}}} = -2.0406$

                  power $= 1-\beta = P\left(\bar{X} < \bar{X}_L\right) = P\left(Z < -2.0406\right) = 0.0206$

                  $\beta = 1 - 0.0206 = 0.9794$

          (c)   Holding everything else constant, the greater the distance between the true mean and the hypothesized mean, the higher the power of the test will be and the lower the probability of committing a Type II error will be. Holding everything else constant, the smaller the level of significance, the lower the power of the test will be and the higher the probability of committing a Type II error will be.

9.86 $H_0 : \mu = 25{,}000$, $H_1 : \mu \neq 25{,}000$, $\alpha = 0.05$, $n = 100$, $\sigma = 3500$

          Critical values: $Z_L = -1.960$, $Z_U = 1.960$

          $\bar{X}_L = \mu + Z_L\left(\dfrac{\sigma}{\sqrt{n}}\right) = 25{,}000 - 1.960\left(\dfrac{3{,}500}{\sqrt{100}}\right) = 24{,}314.0130$

          $\bar{X}_U = \mu + Z_U\left(\dfrac{\sigma}{\sqrt{n}}\right) = 25{,}000 + 1.960\left(\dfrac{3{,}500}{\sqrt{100}}\right) = 25{,}685.9870$

          (a) $\beta = P\left(\bar{X}_L < \bar{X} < \bar{X}_U\right) = P\left(0.8972 < Z < 4.8171\right) = 0.1848$

                  power $= 1-\beta = 1 - 0.1848 = 0.8152$

          (b) $\beta = P\left(\bar{X}_L < \bar{X} < \bar{X}_U\right) = P\left(-1.6742 < Z < 2.2457\right) = 0.9406$

                  power $= 1-\beta = 1 - 0.9406 = 0.0594$

          (c)   A one-tail test is more powerful than a two-tail test, holding everything else constant.

Chapter 12

12.60 (a) $H_0 : \pi_1 = \pi_2$ $\qquad$ $H_1 : \pi_1 \neq \pi_2$ $\qquad$ where 1 = group1, 2 = group2

Decision rule: If $Z_{STAT} < -1.96$ or $Z_{STAT} > 1.96$, reject H_0.

Test statistic: $Z_{STAT} = \dfrac{B - C}{\sqrt{B + C}} = \dfrac{25 - 16}{\sqrt{25 + 16}} = 1.4056$

Decision: Since $Z_{STAT} = 1.4056$ is between the critical bounds of -1.96 and the upper critical bound of 1.96, do not reject H_0. There is not enough evidence of a difference between group 1 and group 2.

12.62 (a) $H_0 : \pi_1 = \pi_2$ $\qquad$ $H_1 : \pi_1 \neq \pi_2$ $\qquad$ where 1 = prior, 2 = after

Decision rule: If $Z < -2.5758$ or $Z > 2.5758$, reject H_0.

Test statistic: $Z_{STAT} = \dfrac{B - C}{\sqrt{B + C}} = \dfrac{21 - 36}{\sqrt{21 + 36}} = -1.9868$

Decision: Since $Z_{STAT} = -1.9868$ is in between the two critical bounds, do not reject H_0. There is not enough evidence to conclude there is a difference in the proportion of voters who favored Candidate A prior to and after the debate.

(b) p-value = 0.0469. The probability of obtaining a sample which gives rise to a test statistic that differs from 0 by -1.9868 or more in either direction is 0.0469 if there is not a difference in the proportion of voters who favor Candidate A prior to and after the debate.

12.64 (a) $H_0 : \pi_1 \geq \pi_2$ $\qquad$ $H_1 : \pi_1 < \pi_2$ $\qquad$ where 1 = last year, 2 = now

Decision rule: If $Z_{STAT} < -1.645$, reject H_0.

Test statistic: $Z_{STAT} = \dfrac{B - C}{\sqrt{B + C}} = \dfrac{5 - 20}{\sqrt{5 + 20}} = -3$

Decision: Since $Z_{STAT} = -3 < -1.645$, reject H_0. There is enough evidence to conclude that satisfaction was lower last year prior to introduction of Six Sigma management.

(b) p-value = 0.0014. The probability of obtaining a data set which gives rise to a test statistic smaller than -3 is 0.0014 if the satisfaction was not lower last year prior to introduction of Six Sigma management.

12.66 (a) For $df = 25$ and $\alpha = 0.01$, $\chi^2_{\alpha/2} = 10.520$ and $\chi^2_{1-\alpha/2} = 46.928$.

(b) For $df = 16$ and $\alpha = 0.05$, $\chi^2_{\alpha/2} = 6.908$ and $\chi^2_{1-\alpha/2} = 28.845$.

(c) For $df = 13$ and $\alpha = 0.10$, $\chi^2_{\alpha/2} = 5.892$ and $\chi^2_{1-\alpha/2} = 22.362$.

12.68 $\chi^2_{STAT} = \dfrac{(n-1) \cdot S^2}{\sigma^2} = \dfrac{24 \cdot 150^2}{100^2} = 54$

12.70 $df = n - 1 = 16 - 1 = 15$

12.72 (a) If $H_1 : \sigma \neq 12$, do not reject H_0 since the test statistic $\chi^2 = 10.417$ falls between the two critical bounds, $\chi^2_{\alpha/2} = 6.262$ and $\chi^2_{1-\alpha/2} = 27.488$.

(b) If $H_1 : \sigma < 12$, do not reject H_0 since the test statistic $\chi^2 = 10.417$ is greater than the critical bound 7.261.

12.74   (a) H_0: $\sigma \leq 1.2^{0}$ F. The standard deviation of the oven temperature has not increased above 1.2⁰F.

H_1: $\sigma > 1.2^{0}$ F. The standard deviation of the oven temperature has increased above 1.2⁰F.

Decision rule: $df = 29$. If $\chi^2_{STAT} > 42.557$, reject H_0.

Test statistic: $\chi^2_{STAT} = \dfrac{(n-1) \cdot S^2}{\sigma^2} = \dfrac{29 \cdot 2.1^2}{1.2^2} = 88.813$

Decision: Since the test statistic of $\chi^2_{STAT} = 88.813$ is greater than the critical boundary of 42.557, reject H_0. There is sufficient evidence to conclude that the standard deviation of the oven temperature has increased above 1.2⁰F.

(b)   You must assume that the data in the population are normally distributed to be able to use the chi-square test of a population variance or standard deviation.

(c)   p-value = 5.53 x 10^{-8} or 0.00000005. The probability that a sample is obtained whose standard deviation is equal to or larger than 2.1⁰F when the null hypothesis is true is 5.53 x 10^{-8}, a very small probability.

Note: The p-value was found using Excel.

12.76   (a) H_0: σ = \$12. The standard deviation of the monthly cost of calls within the local calling region is \$12.

H_1: $\sigma \neq$ \$12. The standard deviation of the monthly cost of calls within the local calling region differs from \$12.

Decision rule: $df = 14$. If $\chi^2_{STAT} < 6.571$ or $\chi^2_{STAT} > 23.685$, reject H_0.

Test statistic: $\chi^2_{STAT} = \dfrac{(n-1) \cdot S^2}{\sigma^2} = \dfrac{14 \cdot 9.25^2}{12^2} = 8.319$

Decision: Since the test statistic of $\chi^2_{STAT} = 8.319$ is between the critical boundaries of 6.571 and 23.685, do not reject H_0. There is insufficient evidence to conclude that the standard deviation of the monthly cost of calls within the local calling region differs from \$12.

(b)   You must assume that the data in the population are normally distributed to be able to use the chi-square test of a population variance or standard deviation.

(c)   p-value = 2(1 − 0.8721) = 0.2558. The probability of obtaining a test statistic equal to or more extreme than the result obtained from this sample data is 0.2558 if the standard deviation of the monthly cost of calls within the local calling region is \$12.

Note: Excel returns an upper-tail area of 0.8721 for χ^2_{STAT} = 8.319. But since the sample standard deviation is smaller than the hypothesized value, the amount of area in the lower tail is (1 − 0.8721). That value is doubled to accommodate the two-tail hypotheses.

12.78   (a) $W_L = 13$, $W_U = 53$
         (b) $W_L = 10$, $W_U = 56$
         (c) $W_L = 7$, $W_U = 59$
         (d) $W_L = 5$, $W_U = 61$

12.80   (a) $W_L = 13$
         (b) $W_L = 10$
         (c) $W_L = 7$
         (d) $W_L = 5$

12.82 $n' = 10$, $\alpha = 0.05$, $W_L = 8$, $W_U = 47$

12.84 $W = \sum_{i=1}^{n'} R_i^{(+)} = 67.5$

12.86 Since $W = 67.5 > W_U = 61$, reject H_0.

12.88 (a) H_0: $M_D = 0$ where Populations: $1 = $ TV $2 = $ Phone
            H_1: $M_D \neq 0$
            Minitab output:
            Wilcoxon Signed Rank Test: Difference

```
Test of median = 0.000000 versus median not = 0.000000

                    N for   Wilcoxon            Estimated
               N    Test    Statistic     P      Median
Difference    13     13          0.0   0.002     -9.000
```

Since the p-value $= 0.002$ is smaller than the 0.05 level of significance, reject H_0.

There is sufficient evidence of a difference in the median service rating between TV and phone services.

(b)   Using the paired-sample t-test in Problem 10.21, you reject the null hypothesis; you conclude that there is evidence of a difference in the mean service rating between TV and phone. Using the Wilcoxon signed rank test, you reject the null hypothesis; you conclude that there is enough evidence of a difference in the median service rating between TV and phone services.

12.90 (a) H_0: $M_D = 0$ where Populations: $1 = $ Global $2 = $ U.S.
            H_1: $M_D \neq 0$
            Minitab output:
            Wilcoxon Signed Rank Test: Difference

```
Test of median = 0.000000 versus median not = 0.000000

                    N for   Wilcoxon            Estimated
               N    Test    Statistic     P      Median
Difference    13     12         36.0   0.845     -1.000
```

Since the p-value $= 0.845$ is greater than the 0.05 level of significance, do not reject H_0.

There is insufficient evidence of a difference in the median rating between global and U.S. employees.

(b)   Using the paired-sample t-test in Problem 10.23, you do not reject the null hypothesis; you conclude that there is insufficient evidence of a difference in the mean rating between global and U.S. employees. Using the Wilcoxon signed rank test, you do not reject the null hypothesis; you conclude that there is insufficient evidence of a difference in the median rating between global and U.S. employees.

12.92 $d.f. = 5$, $\alpha = 0.1$, $\chi_U^2 = 9.2363$

12.94   Minitab output:

Friedman Test: Rating versus Brand, Expert

```
Friedman test for Rating by Brand blocked by Expert

S = 20.03   DF = 3   P = 0.000
S = 20.72   DF = 3   P = 0.000 (adjusted for ties)

                     Est      Sum of
Brand          N    Median    Ranks
A              9    25.000     25.0
B              9    26.750     34.5
C              9    24.000     20.0
D              9    22.250     10.5

Grand median   =    24.500
```

(a) $H_0 : M_A = M_B = M_C = M_D$ H_1: Not all medians are the equal.

Since the p-value is virtually zero, reject H_0 at 0.05 level of significance. There is evidence of a difference in the median summated ratings of the four brands of Colombian coffee.

(b)   In (a), you conclude that there is evidence of a difference in the median summated ratings of the four brands of Colombian coffee while in problem 11.23, you conclude that there is evidence of a difference in the mean summated ratings of the four brands of Colombian coffee.

12.96   Minitab output:

Friedman Test: Value versus Group blocked by Shopping Item

```
S = 23.79   DF = 3   P = 0.000
S = 24.69   DF = 3   P = 0.000 (adjusted for ties)

                            Sum of
Group          N  Est Median  Ranks
Publix        33    2.7887     92.0
Target        33    2.6262     76.5
Walmart       33    2.5088     56.5
Winn-Dixie    33    2.9712    105.0

Grand median = 2.7237
```

(a) $H_0 : M_A = M_B = M_C = M_D$ H_1: Not all medians are the equal.

Since the p-value is virtually zero, reject H_0 at 0.05 level of significance. There is evidence of a difference in the median prices for these items at the four supermarkets.

(b)   In (a), you conclude that there is evidence of a difference in the median prices for these items at the four supermarkets while in problem 11.25, you conclude that there is evidence of a difference between the mean price of these items at the four supermarkets.

12.98   Minitab output:

Friedman Test: Strength versus Days, Samples

```
Friedman test for Strength by Days blocked by Samples

S = 80.00   DF = 2   P = 0.000

                     Est      Sum of
Days          N    Median     Ranks
  2          40    3.0863     40.0
  7          40    3.5888     80.0
 28          40    4.5838     120.0

Grand median  =    3.7529
```

(a) $H_0 : M_2 = M_7 = M_{28}$ H_1 : Not all medians are equal.

        Since the p-value is virtually zero, reject H_0 at 0.05 level of significance. There is evidence of a difference in the median compressive strength after 2, 7 and 28 days.

(b)   In (a), you conclude that there is evidence of a difference in the median compressive strength after 2, 7 and 28 days, and in problem 11.28, you conclude that there is evidence of a difference in the mean compressive strength after 2, 7 and 28 days.

Chapter 16

16.66 (a) 2011 as the base year:

$$I_{2011} = \frac{P_{2011}}{P_{2011}}(100) = \frac{\$5}{\$5}(100) = 100$$

$$I_{2012} = \frac{P_{2012}}{P_{2011}}(100) = \frac{\$8}{\$5}(100) = 160$$

$$I_{2013} = \frac{P_{2013}}{P_{2011}}(100) = \frac{\$7}{\$5}(100) = 140$$

(b) 2012 as the base year:

$$I_{2011} = \frac{P_{2011}}{P_{2012}}(100) = \frac{\$5}{\$8}(100) = 62.5$$

$$I_{2012} = \frac{P_{2012}}{P_{2012}}(100) = \frac{\$8}{\$8}(100) = 100$$

$$I_{2013} = \frac{P_{2013}}{P_{2012}}(100) = \frac{\$7}{\$8}(100) = 87.5$$

16.68   (a),(b)

Year	DJIA	Price Index (base = 1979)	Price Index (base = 2000)
1979	838.7	100	7.77437894
1980	964.0	114.9397878	8.935854653
1981	875.0	104.3281269	8.110863923
1982	1046.5	124.7764397	9.700593252
1983	1258.6	150.0655777	11.66666667
1984	1211.6	144.4616669	11.2309974
1985	1546.7	184.4163587	14.33722655
1986	1896.0	226.0641469	17.57508343
1987	1938.8	231.1672827	17.97182054
1988	2168.6	258.5668296	20.10196515
1989	2753.2	328.2699416	25.5209492
1990	2633.7	314.0217003	24.41323693
1991	3168.8	377.822821	29.37337783
1992	3301.1	393.5972338	30.59974045
1993	3754.1	447.6093955	34.79885057
1994	3834.4	457.1837367	35.54319614
1995	5117.1	610.1228091	47.43325918
1996	6448.3	768.8446405	59.77289581
1997	7908.3	942.9235722	73.30645161
1998	9181.4	1094.718016	85.10752688
1999	11497.1	1370.823894	106.5730441
2000	10788.0	1286.27638	100
2001	10021.5	1194.884941	92.8948832
2002	8341.6	994.5868606	77.32295143
2003	10453.9	1246.44092	96.90304042
2004	10788.0	1286.27638	100
2005	10717.5	1277.870514	99.34649611
2006	12463.2	1486.014069	115.5283648
2007	13264.8	1581.590557	122.9588432
2008	8772.3	1045.934184	81.31488691
2009	10430.7	1243.673542	96.68789396
2010	11577.4	1380.398235	107.3173897
2011	12221.2	1457.15989	113.2851316
2012	13104.1	1562.429951	121.4692251

(c)   The price index using 2000 as the base year is more useful because it is closer to the present and the DJIA has grown more than 1500% over the period.

16.70 (a), (c)

Year	Price	Price Index (base = 1980)	Price Index (base = 1990)
1980	0.703	100	40.51873199
1981	0.792	112.6600284	45.64841499
1982	0.763	108.5348506	43.97694524
1983	0.726	103.2716927	41.8443804
1984	0.854	121.4793741	49.22190202
1985	0.697	99.14651494	40.17291066
1986	1.104	157.0412518	63.63112392
1987	0.943	134.1394026	54.35158501
1988	0.871	123.8975818	50.20172911
1989	0.797	113.371266	45.93659942
1990	1.735	246.799431	100
1991	0.912	129.7297297	52.5648415
1992	0.936	133.14367	53.9481268
1993	1.141	162.3044097	65.76368876
1994	1.604	228.1650071	92.44956772
1995	1.323	188.1934566	76.25360231
1996	1.103	156.8990043	63.57348703
1997	1.213	172.5462304	69.91354467
1998	1.452	206.5433855	83.68876081
1999	1.904	270.8392603	109.740634
2000	1.443	205.2631579	83.17002882
2001	1.414	201.1379801	81.49855908
2002	1.451	206.401138	83.63112392
2003	1.711	243.3854908	98.6167147
2004	1.472	209.3883357	84.84149856
2005	1.66	236.1308677	95.67723343
2006	2.162	307.5391181	124.610951
2007	1.647	234.2816501	94.92795389
2008	1.734	246.6571835	99.94236311
2009	1.961	278.9473684	113.0259366
2010	1.591	226.3157895	91.70028818
2011	1.531	217.7809388	88.24207493
2012	1.604	228.1650071	92.44956772

(b) The average price per pound of fresh tomatoes in 2012 in the U.S. is 128.17% higher than it was in 1980.

(d) The average price per pound of fresh tomatoes in 2012 in the U.S. is 92.44% of that in 1990 or 7.56% lower than it was in 1990.

(e)

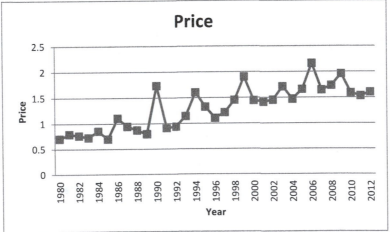

There is an upward trend in the cost of fresh tomatoes from 1980 to 2012 with a prominent cyclical component.